I0128374

DOES SOUTH ASIA EXIST? PROSPECTS FOR REGIONAL INTEGRATION

Edited by
Rafiq Dossani, Daniel C. Sneider, and
Vikram Sood

SHORENSTEIN
APARC
STANFORD

THE WALTER H. SHORENSTEIN
ASIA-PACIFIC RESEARCH CENTER

THE WALTER H. SHORENSTEIN ASIA-PACIFIC RESEARCH CENTER (Shorenstein APARC) is a unique Stanford University institution focused on the interdisciplinary study of contemporary Asia. Shorenstein APARC's mission is to produce and publish outstanding interdisciplinary, Asia-Pacific–focused research; to educate students, scholars, and corporate and governmental affiliates; to promote constructive interaction to influence U.S. policy toward the Asia-Pacific; and to guide Asian nations on key issues of societal transition, development, U.S.-Asia relations, and regional cooperation.

The Walter H. Shorenstein Asia-Pacific Research Center
Freeman Spogli Institute for International Studies
Stanford University
Encina Hall
Stanford, CA 94305-6055
tel. 650-723-9741
fax 650-723-6530
http://APARC.stanford.edu

Does South Asia Exist? Prospects for Regional Integration may be ordered from:
The Brookings Institution
c/o DFS, P.O. Box 50370, Baltimore, MD, USA
tel. 1-800-537-5487 or 410-516-6956
fax 410-516-6998
http://www.brookings.edu/press

Walter H. Shorenstein Asia-Pacific Research Center Books, 2010.
Copyright © 2010 by the Board of Trustees of the Leland Stanford Junior University.

All rights reserved. No part of this publication may be reproduced, stored in a retrieval system, or transmitted in any form or by any means, electronic, mechanical, photocopying, recording, or otherwise, without written permission of the publisher.

First printing, 2010.
13-digit ISBN 978-1-931368-17-9

DOES SOUTH ASIA EXIST? PROSPECTS FOR REGIONAL INTEGRATION

SHORENSTEIN
APARC
STANFORD

THE WALTER H. SHORENSTEIN
ASIA-PACIFIC RESEARCH CENTER

CONTENTS

PREFACE

Asian regionalism is a major topic of research for the Walter H. Shorenstein Asia-Pacific Research Center (Shorenstein APARC) at Stanford University. This volume is the third of a three-part series of books on Asian regionalism that the center began publishing in 2007. The first volume, *Cross Currents: Regionalism and Nationalism in Northeast Asia* (2007), looked at the tensions between increasing regional integration and rising nationalism in Northeast Asia. Its content was based on an international conference that was held at Stanford in May 2006.

The following year, in May 2007, my colleague Prof. Donald K. Emmerson led a conference at Shorenstein APARC that examined the interplay of security, democracy, and regionalism in Southeast Asia. That gathering was attended by scholars from Southeast Asia and across the region, and resulted in a second book, *Hard Choices: Security, Democracy, and Regionalism in South Asia* (2008), edited by Professor Emmerson.

For the final installment of our inquiry into Asian regionalism, we held a third conference, in June 2008, in cooperation with the Observer Research Foundation of India, which focused on the prospects for regionalism in South Asia. The papers from that gathering—which brought together scholars from across South Asia with experts from Russia, China, and the United States—have been significantly revised to compose the book you now hold in your hands.

This book and its companion volumes offer the provocative, detailed perspectives of some of the finest scholars working in Asian studies today. In publishing these books, we hope to bring this important material to a wider audience, and thereby to advance understanding of Asian regionalism and its impact on nations, both within Asia and beyond.

Gi-Wook Shin
Professor,
Director, Shorenstein APARC
Stanford University

Acknowledgments

The editors gratefully acknowledge the Walter H. Shorenstein Asia-Pacific Research Center, the Observer Research Foundation, Jet Airways, Mr. Kanwal Rekhi, insure1234.com, and G1G.com. All of these organizations generously funded the conference that ultimately led to this book.

Rafiq Dossani
Daniel C. Sneider
Vikram Sood

INTRODUCTION

DOES SOUTH ASIA EXIST?

Rafiq Dossani, Daniel C. Sneider, and Vikram Sood

The goal of collective regional action, or regionalism, is to enhance each member state's development and security.[1] South Asia has so far achieved neither outcome. A region that was, for the most part,[2] a single state prior to 1947 divided into multiple states that have moved apart politically, culturally, and economically. Such rifts are manifest in innumerable "sensitive lists"—of items that may not be traded, tariff walls, transport blockades, and intermittent armed conflict.

Today, interstate relations are tense at best. Failures in development and security cooperation have hurt the region, which contains two nuclear-armed states and has an extremely high incidence of cross-border human trafficking[3] and terrorism. South Asia's human development level is among the lowest in the world (on infant mortality, it ranks below sub-Saharan Africa). Regional trade is only 5 percent of total trade, compared with 26 percent in the Association of Southeast Asian Nations (ASEAN) and 22 percent in the Common Market for Eastern and Southern Africa (COMESA) countries. Although the South Asian Free Trade Area (SAFTA) was recently approved to promote regional trade, member nations' lists of items exempt from the agreement's conditions together constitute 53 percent of total current trade.

Given this lack of cooperation, it is almost as if South Asia does not exist as a region at all, or that it lives only in the memories of those who remember or study colonial times. Understanding the historical and institutional contexts of this failure is one goal of this book. The second goal is to understand the challenges ahead and to determine how to meet them. Not only does regional cooperation in South Asia promise great rewards, the contributors of this book argue, but it is a feasible goal in the near term.

This chapter summarizes the book's contents. In chapter 2, Ummu Salma Bava looks at how regional development and security interact around the world and what conditions—economic, political, and social—are needed to foster progress. In chapter 3, Muchkund Dubey discusses economic integration in South Asia—its history, underpinnings, and prospects. The authors of the book's second section, chapters 4–8, look at regional integration from a country-specific perspective. Focusing on the institution building needed for effective regionalism—and the challenges unique to each nation—Rehman Sobhan focuses on Bangladesh, Rajiv Kumar on India, Mahendra P. Lama on Bhutan and Nepal, Akmal Hussain on Pakistan, and Saman Kelegama on Sri Lanka.

They argue that regionalism holds great promise for development, as it is based on an already high degree of institutional commonality and maturity, prospects for significant market enlargement, and access to substantial cross-border public goods. Importantly, development and security issues are interrelated: South Asia has made little progress in developmental integration because member states have chosen not to confront the security issues up front. Consequently, the cooperative mechanisms they established were fundamentally faulty and destined to fail.

In chapters 9–11, the authors address, in detail, three major impediments to regional integration and suggest ways of overcoming them. Rafiq Dossani looks at supply-chain fragmentation, while Ainslee T. Embree addresses the history of democratization and suggests that immature democratic processes reduce the scope for crucial civil society influence on regional integration. Feroz Hassan Khan discusses the region's security challenges, showing that these arise from complex nation-state issues. As with development, the potential rewards of regional security arrangements are great. We might go so far as to say that the region's future rests with security policy and its effective implementation.

The complexity of the region's security issues reduces the scope for international influence. The book's final section looks at the attitudes of three global powers toward South Asia and its integration, with Xenia Dormandy focusing on the United States, Igor Torbakov on Russia, and Guihong Zhang on China.

Throughout the book, the authors propose conditions for regionalism's progress, showing that these conditions did not exist for several decades. As of 2010, however, they are in place, with India set to play a central role. Indeed, India has the capacity to make definitive decisions about the future of regionalism in South Asia. Nonetheless, perhaps as a consequence of regionalism's failure in the past, to which it contributed, India has tended to prefer bilateral engagements within the region as it has pursued its ambitious global agenda. India also downplays regionalism's significance, arguing that some member states, particularly Pakistan, are not ready for such coordination. While this stance does not negate the possibility of regional integration, it adversely affects its prospects.

Enhancing Development and Security

A state's security is defined here as the protection of a state's territorial integrity from threats originating within and outside the region. Development includes economic growth, the distribution of income, the management of cross-border public goods,[4] and the promotion of individual freedoms, thus defying easy definition;[5] however, we focus on economic growth and the management of cross-border public goods.

Do state actions influence regional development and security differently?[6] With important exceptions, development is a *positive* outcome—usually all the states in a region will be better off economically when one state invests in development. Security, on the other hand, can often be a *negative* outcome—member states' security can be reduced when one state enhances its own security, such as by acquiring nuclear weapons.[7]

South Asia illustrates these contrasts. Most individual countries' developmental initiatives benefited at least some regional members, as in the positive impact of India's 1991 economic reforms on Sri Lanka, Bhutan, and the Maldives (see chapter 9, in which Dossani discusses the IT industry's supply chain in South Asia). On the other hand, individual security initiatives, such as Sri Lanka's Western tilt in the late 1970s and nuclear tests by India (in 1974 and 1998) and Pakistan (in 1998) were seen to reduce the security of neighboring states. Hence, the way member states attempt regionalism will depend on whether the desired outcome is related to development, security, or both.

Collective actions to promote development are well tested and usually produce results.[8] Experiences within and outside South Asia suggest that the barriers to economic integration, such as asymmetric state power, can be managed (see Dubey, chapter 3). By promoting trust among states, economic collaboration also enhances security. But the reverse is not necessarily true. The effects of regional security efforts are unclear, with member states often holding differing views of what security means.[9] Experience shows that efforts in this area are vulnerable to false starts and failures and that collaborating on security may not in fact increase development.

Economic cooperation may occur without state coordination or even explicit goal setting. General economic reforms can promote regional integration by prompting the actions of individuals and firms. If bilateral development arrangements within a region are made, they will usually not harm other member states' development. By contrast, such arrangements may hurt some member states' security because they require policymaker coordination, thus consuming domestic political capital. These effects and interrelationships are shown in table 1.1.

These issues are difficult to resolve. Bava (chapter 2) explores the history and political implications of regionalism from an international perspective. Noting that regionalism is "identified by intentionality" and that intentionality determines how a region is to be defined, she argues that a necessary, though insufficient, condition for regionalism is agreement on the need for collective action.[10]

If intentionality is a necessary condition, effective implementation requires member states to overcome problems arising from institutional differences, asymmetric power, and domestic politics. For example, member states' institutional frameworks may differ (for instance, there may be a mix of autocracies and democracies), asymmetric gains might accrue due to the presence of a hegemonic state, or domestic politics in the member countries may be captured by interest groups with conflicting regional priorities (for instance, cross-border security versus the exploitation of transnational public goods).

Table 1.1 The Differential Impact of Coordinated and Uncoordinated Initiatives on Development and Security

Initiative	Development	Security
Uncoordinated state action	All states develop	Security reduced
Collective action	Well-tested pathways; bilateralism does not hurt regionalism	Uncertain pathways; bilateralism can hurt regionalism
Interrelationships and costs		
Interrelationship between developmental and security initiatives	Promotes security	Independent of development
Domestic political costs of developmental and security	Low	Uncertain: low to high

Source: Editors.

Bava's discussion of regional integration in Europe, Northeast Asia, and Southeast Asia shows that the collective action problem might be overcome if there is a powerful external force that encourages regionalism for its own interests, as the United States did in Europe, or if there is a common threat, like Communism in Southeast Asia.

Intentionality and Regionalism in South Asia

The intent to regionalize South Asia has been missing among key members. When Bangladesh's former president Ziaur Rahman first proposed a formal mechanism for regional cooperation, India and Pakistan responded coolly. Dubey (chapter 3) attributes the lack of political will to get regionalism off the ground to "the perpetually tense and often hostile political relations between India and Pakistan." Even during those periods when India-Pakistan relations improved, regional integration failed because it meant different things to the different sides; Bava's third sufficiency condition—the ability to overcome differences in domestic politics and priorities—was not met.

Indeed, the persistent unwillingness of regional leaders to acknowledge their shared interests in development and security, and to confront the complex issues that would promote those interests, raises the question of whether South Asia is, in fact, a region at all. While many scholars have asserted that South Asia is a "natural region" by virtue of its geography and integrated precolonial history and culture, others have argued that regions do not exist naturally. As Allen, Massey, and Cochrane note, "Regions are not . . . independent actors:

they exist and 'become' in social practice and discourse."[11] Slocum and Van Langenhove make a similar assertion:

> While, on the one hand, every area on Earth has the potential to be a "region," given suitable historical, economic, cultural and social conditions, regions will only exist as actors as the result of certain acts (e.g., the Maastricht Treaty). Such acts only make sense in a discursive social context, which means that other relevant actors must take up a certain storyline and thereby position the other actor(s) in a certain way.[12]

Perhaps South Asia never became a region because its leaders chose not to discuss the important questions.

Above, we identified the intraregional problems that any region must resolve before regionalism succeeds: intentionality, institutional differences, asymmetric power, and domestic politics. We also argued that external forces may affect outcomes. We turn now to South Asia's particular challenges.

Development and SAARC

The South Asian Association for Regional Cooperation (SAARC) was established in 1985. For its first decade it focused on confidence building (Dubey, chapter 3). Rasgotra points out that this was a conscious decision.[13] Aware of the subcontinent's recent history, its leaders avoided bilateral issues and questions of development and security and instead focused on an agenda item that all could agree on: poverty alleviation. Trade and capital flows were not discussed until 1995, when the South Asian Preferential Trade Arrangement (SAPTA) was put into effect.

In chapter 3, Dubey argues that while all the actors agreed to cooperate on poverty alleviation exclusively, this goal was actually low on the domestic political priority list of the two main actors, India and Pakistan. The discrepancy proved to be a key stumbling block to SAARC's progress. In Dubey's colorful phrasing, "most of the decisions made by SAARC are of the nature of public relations campaigns designed to impress domestic audiences and foreign powers. Thus the entire SAARC process is an exercise in competitive deception."

A developmental logic for regionalism ought to be established from the start; later, a regional body might be asked to confront security issues, something SAARC has yet to do at the time of this writing. Instead, SAARC began, as noted, with the goal of poverty alleviation, but it did not define what sort of regional cooperation, if any, would be required to achieve this. SAARC officials thus spent the better part of a decade analyzing the causes of poverty and evaluating solutions such as better nutrition, women's rights, and basic education. But almost no regional action took place. Indeed, how could it be otherwise? Lack of regional cooperation was not deemed to be a cause of poverty, and regional cooperation was not identified as a solution. The project was thus flawed in conception.

Yet a strong developmental logic for regionalism undoubtedly exists. Dubey shows that it lies in the set of opportunities arising from jointly managing common resources and market enlargement. He notes that institutional frameworks within South Asia have achieved a high degree of commonality (one of Bava's sufficiency conditions) due to a sustained, two-decades long period of sound macroeconomic management and market-friendly reforms across the region. A sensible road map that manages the issue of India's asymmetric power and achieves European-style integration also seems within reach—Indian policymakers, for instance, are aware of their country's asymmetric power, and have responded to it in bilateral arrangements with Sri Lanka.

In chapter 4, Sobhan looks at regionalism from the viewpoint of Bangladesh, South Asia's most consistent supporter of the idea. Developmentally, Bangladesh stands to gain from regionalism in two ways. First, the country's main obstacles to development—water, infrastructure and power connectivity, and transport—all require regional solutions. Second, to develop, Bangladesh needs to enlarge its market for traded goods, labor, and investment. Some of these problems, such as the need for market enlargement, could be addressed bilaterally with India. But as Sobhan notes, Bangladesh is in "a manifestly unequal relationship. This, indeed, was the perspective that informed the thinking of the late president Ziaur Rahman, who ruled Bangladesh from 1976 till his assassination in May 1981. Zia recognized that India was the dominant presence in Bangladesh's external relations but preferred to mediate this relationship within a broader regional entity such as a South Asia Association for Regional Cooperation (SAARC)." President Rahman was, in fact, among the first to promote SAARC.

Acknowledging that building trust at all levels is key to regionalism, Kumar examines India's role and responsibilities in chapter 5. He acknowledges the nation's major role in driving regional integration and states that it now has the means to effectively play this role. But, Kumar argues, regional cooperation will "generate benefits for *all* South Asian economies; therefore, any argument that India alone has to take this agenda forward is misplaced. Once over the tipping point, regional cooperation will place South Asia on a higher growth trajectory and generate externalities for inclusive and sustainable growth." Kumar also points to the importance of noneconomic gains, such as social cohesion and the promotion of cultural diversity, for smaller states in particular. As for economic gains, Kumar argues that the advantages of regionally integrated trade exceed the "relatively limited gains" from the outsourcing relationships that result from trade liberalization between developed and developing economies. This promises to be true even for the region's behemoth, India, which arguably needs its neighbors less than they need it. Kumar points to the success of the Indo–Sri Lanka Bilateral Free Trade Agreement (ILBFTA) to suggest that "a regional FTA would generate its own pressure to further integrate the domestic market within India and to regularize fiscal and other procedures across states."

Lama (chapter 6) presents the positions of Bhutan and Nepal, both of which have long-standing treaties with India[14] that recognize India's premier role in their foreign relations. India initiated these treaties due to Bhutan's and Nepal's geographical position; both are viewed as part of India's security frontier, protecting it against China.[15] Nevertheless, Bhutan and Nepal have both promoted regionalism because, unlike Sri Lanka, they must grapple with the problem of negotiating common resources such as hydropower and roads. Managing India's asymmetric power is therefore important for them. Yet India's superior bargaining power in bilateral trade arrangements is not the only reason Bhutan and Nepal are interested in regionalism. As monarchies, Lama notes, both countries have seen "regionalism as a way to resist the Indian brand of democracy." For Bhutan and Nepal, the failure of regionalism has led to a kind of "regionalization without regionalism," as discussed by Bava, characterized by commercial and illegal labor flows from Bhutan and Nepal to India and the rise of civil society groups with both regional and global links. Yet these are second-best outcomes. As for security, it is apparent that resolving security concerns through bilateral treaties has not helped improve the often troubled relations between India and its smaller neighbors.

Speaking of security, the political problems of India and Pakistan are widely seen as being at the heart of the failure of regionalism in South Asia. To overcome these problems, Hussain (chapter 7) argues in favor of relaxing trade barriers between the two countries; this, he says, will benefit the Pakistani middle class and lead to better political relations with India. In the short term, he suggests building trust through civil society, for example by holding a conference of South Asian parliamentarians on regional integration, building networks of institutes for regional cooperation, and easing travel restrictions.

Writing on Sri Lanka's view of regionalism, Kelegama (chapter 8) notes that Sri Lanka was the first South Asian nation to liberalize its economy. That was in the late 1970s, a time when India, Bangladesh, and Pakistan were mired in socialism. Yet Sri Lanka's enthusiasm for regionalism was for security rather than development. When interethnic strife between segments of the native Tamil and Sinhalese populations broke out in the early 1980s, Sri Lanka needed friends in the region. Over the ensuing decades, however, the failure of SAARC, along with the economic success of India, led Sri Lanka to conclude that "integration with South Asia eventually meant integration with India." Hence, it pursued a bilateral arrangement with India, one that has succeeded by focusing on noncompeting imports and investment and tourist inflows from India.

The foregoing examples demonstrate the importance of regionalism for development in South Asia. Regionalism can help achieve two developmental goals: (1) the management of common resources, such as water, and (2) market enlargement. Most of the smaller countries in South Asia pursuing such aims must deal directly with India, whose immense size leads to a power asymmetry in bilateral relations; regionalism helps to correct this imbalance. Security was also shown to be intertwined with development. The unwillingness of political leaders to confront security issues has led to failures in tackling common developmental problems.

Supporting Institutional Growth

Policymakers in the smaller countries of South Asia are deeply concerned that economic integration will lead to India's dominance over the region. In chapter 9, Dossani explores whether this fear is justified, using the software industry as a case study. According to his analysis, regional integration is more likely to result in the fragmentation of the supply chain than in India's economic dominance: India will end up playing a key role in the resulting supply chain as a hub for organizing and financing the work, while the other South Asian countries will offer programming and other lower-end services. Dossani concludes that India's vast scale offers the rest of South Asia an opportunity for considerably more work in this important field than they could do on their own. The software industry, in other words, could be "shared" by member countries.

Embree, in chapter 10, asks whether more widespread democracy might have made a difference to regionalism. Democratization[16] preceded independence by several decades, but while it was experienced across South Asia, the experience was not identical throughout. For example, he argues that the founding fathers of Pakistan "had much less experience in electoral politics than those that formed India." Focusing on the development of Pakistan's democracy, Embree points to an early rift whose repercussions can be felt today: the secular focus of Pakistan's founder, Muhammad Ali Jinnah, versus the religious ideals of Syed Abul A'ala Maududi, head of the influential organization Jama'at-i-Islami. "This fundamental clash over what constitutes a good society is one explanation for why Pakistan democratized differently than India," Embree writes.

For different reasons on both sides, shared democratic ideals have not warmed relations between India and Pakistan. For Pakistanis, the problem is that "Indian nationalists have at times claimed cultural and sometimes political hegemony over the whole of South Asia, a move resented by their neighbors." In India, negative feelings toward Pakistan—and regionalism in general—date back to the "immense physical suffering caused to millions of both Indians and Pakistanis by Partition. Added to this has been the sense in India that Pakistan represents the destruction of a united India encompassing the entire subcontinent, the rightful inheritance of the Indian people." Embree adds that "India's support for regionalism has been further dimmed by militant insurgent movements in its border regions" such as Kashmir, Punjab, and the northeast.

In chapter 11, Khan discusses the security challenges in Kashmir. Acknowledging that regionalism in South Asia is "stymied by interstate conflicts, internal challenges to domestic development, and global powers' security interests in the region," he concludes that:

India's recent rise heralds both promise and danger for the future stability of this fragile region. On the one hand, India's leaders can use their position to help muster the collective will to make the difficult political decisions needed to stabilize the region. On the other hand, they may assert that their past decisions are immutable and that the rest of South Asia should adjust to India. Both stances are observed, leaving the region's future uncertain.

The chapters by Dossani, Embree, and Khan argue that policymaking, democracy, and civil society in South Asia must mature further if they are to support security policy and the overall stability of the region.

Global Perspectives on the Region

The book's final section analyzes the interests of three global powers—the United States, China, and Russia—in South Asian regionalism. Dormandy, in chapter 12, considers U.S. interests, which she enumerates as (1) the curbing of terrorism and extremism, particularly in Pakistan and Afghanistan; (2) regional stability, given the nuclear status of India and Pakistan; (3) commercial engagement; (4) reducing narcotics production in Afghanistan; (5) collective action on energy and the environment; and (6) the propagation of democracy.

According to Dormandy, the United States does not believe that regional forums are always the best option for accomplishing its goals; thus, America's commitment to regionalism in South Asia is rather weak. SAARC's failure, of course, has contributed to the U.S. stance on South Asia, but it is also true that the United States has shown mixed support for multilateral and regional mechanisms worldwide. In many circumstances, ad hoc coalitions and bilateral actions appear to be the most promising means of achieving U.S. interests in the region.

Nevertheless, looking ahead, regional action may be the best approach in certain areas, such as energy security and the proliferation of democracy, while climate change requires global cooperation. Dormandy introduces the concept of "core groups" of interested nations that might come together to deal with "specific finite problems" such as cross-border narcotics flows. Bilateral agreements are probably best for efficient economic engagement, at least in the case of U.S. economic interests in South Asia.

Torbakov analyzes South Asian regionalism from the Russian perspective in chapter 13. He argues that "Russia's principal strategic concern is the post-Soviet lands"—in particular, Central Asia. Russia sees India as a potential balance to China's growing clout in Central Asia and as a valuable ally, in part because it shares Russia's concerns about a "unipolar" world in which the United States goes unchallenged. But there are also sources of potential discord between the two nations. First, "India's own increasingly multivector diplomacy leaves Russia as just one of several important strategic partners." Second, Russian democracy, unlike Indian democracy, is based "not so much on formal rules and institutions as on informal patronage networks." Russia also sees India as an important customer for its military (and now nuclear) hardware and is worried by U.S. advances in this arena.

Despite these concerns, Torbakov concludes that "India will likely remain Russia's main partner in South Asia." As a result, Russia is unlikely to be a strong supporter of South Asian regionalism.

Zhang (chapter 14) focuses on China, concluding that regionalism in South Asia would do little to further China's primary interests: the region's security and the development of western China. Zhang also notes that the "SAARC is not yet sufficiently mature to be a platform for dialogue between China and the South Asian countries."

In sum, the incredibly complex security issues in South Asia have resulted in irresolution, both among member states and global powers. If internal policymaking and outside forces will not help achieve regionalism, can civil society activism lead to state action? Will the evident spread of democracy in South Asia help? Several of this book's authors argue in favor of both as key drivers of regional integration.

Looking Back

How to divide the subcontinent was a thorny issue in 1947, when new states were carved out of British India, with its mix of principalities and directly governed territories and peoples ruled by exploitation of their cultural and historical divides. With few exceptions, the region was divided into its present shape by 1950.

But in 1971 the question of borders resurfaced, this time between the east and west wings of Pakistan. Following the western-based central government's inadequate handling of a devastating 1970 cyclone in the east, popular uprisings culminated in a nine-month war between the two wings of the nation-state. As Pakistan split, the founders of the new nation, Bangladesh, argued that despite sharing a religion (Islam) with Pakistan, East Pakistan's Bengalis constituted a separate nation due to their different culture and, in particular, different language. It was further argued that Bangladesh's relations with other states in South Asia would improve with its independence. In general, Bangladesh's founders turned out to be correct: Bangladesh's political and economic relations with India are better than Pakistan's relations with India both prior to Bangladesh's emergence and today.[17]

Given the success of Bangladesh, one might reasonably ask: Do South Asia's individual states lack the societal context for regionalism because they still contain too many significant nations that have yet to be fully integrated into the state framework? In cases where nations within the states persistently and militantly demand sovereignty or, at least, autonomy, the answer is yes. Pakistan's struggle to control violence in the North-West Frontier Province (NWFP), for example, keeps Pakistan from engaging more fully with its neighbors. And if subnations' ethnicities cross borders, the problem is even worse. Thus, when some Tamil groups in Sri Lanka in the 1980s demanded greater autonomy, Sri Lanka's relations with India deteriorated along with its ability to enter into regional arrangements. According to Kelegama, India pressured Sri Lanka to sign the Indo–Sri Lanka Political Accord as "a first step toward handling Tamil separatism." The long-running issue of Kashmir's status is another example of subnational struggles undermining India's engagement with its neighbors.

As these cases illustrate, regional integration will be difficult, perhaps impossible, if a member state's legitimacy is challenged by its own people or by another regional member. To begin with a counterexample, India's problems with Maoism in the tribal belt of central and northern India, though severe, are not a barrier to regional integration because no external party questions the Indian state's legitimacy to make policies on these people's behalf. However, if state A refuses to accept that state B is a legitimate spokesman for the entire area or all the peoples under its control, then the political context for regionalism is incomplete. Such is the case with Kashmir: The unwillingness of India and Pakistan to accept the legitimacy of the other side's claim to speak for Kashmir prevents the proper historical, economic, cultural, and social conditions for regional integration from coming together. If Kashmir turns out to be a key cause for the failure of South Asian regionalism, it speaks to the power of events at the margin—Kashmir's population is just about 1 percent of India's and 6 percent of Pakistan's—to derail progress on a far larger scale. Understanding why this could happen and what may be done about it is a key challenge of South Asian integration and, of course, one of the aims of this book.

Managing Common Resources

The main goals of regionalism in South Asia are managing common resources, enlarging markets, and improving security. As we have seen, these issues are interrelated. Regional cooperation also promises a better counterbalance to India's asymmetric power than bilateral action. Many of the institutional contexts for regionalism are in place; the primary obstacle to its implementation appears to be policymakers' unwillingness to accept the interrelationships among countries and to take a holistic view of regionalism—that is, one that tackles development and security together rather than separately. What accounts for this unwillingness? One explanation is that member states may prioritize domestic concerns over regional ones. Another is that the process may be elite driven. As Kumar notes in chapter 5, "the ruling elites in South Asia, including the armed forces in some cases, will have to understand that greater regional economic cooperation and integration does not impinge either on their spheres of influence or on national sovereignty and security. Regional cooperation will contribute to this goal, while noncooperation will likely hurt all the economies of the region." But are policymakers likely to behave differently in the future?

If so, we argue, the problems posed by state weaknesses, lack of public interest, elite-driven nationalism, and India's asymmetrical role in the region must be overcome. The different countries' key issues with regionalism are summarized in table 1.2.

Table 1.2 SAARC Member States' Key Issues for Regionalism

Collective action challenge ⇒ Country ⇓	Common resources	Market enlargement	Security	India's asymmetric power as a driver of regionalism
Bangladesh	Water, transport, environment	Trade, investment, and labor flows	None	High
Bhutan and Nepal	Hydropower, transport, environment	Trade, investment, and labor flows	None	High
India	Water (BD, P)	None	Nuclearization (P), migration (BD, BH, N), trafficking (N), Kashmir (P), China (BH, N)	NA
Pakistan	Water	None	Nuclearization, Kashmir	Medium
Sri Lanka	None	Trade and investment	Tamil insurgency	High

Source: Editors, based on contributors' conclusions.
Notes: The column headings are challenges that collective action could resolve. The rows provide details of problems under each category faced by the respective countries. Unless noted, the problem emanates from relations with India. Otherwise, the country from which the problem arises is indicated in parentheses (BD=Bangladesh, BH=Bhutan, I=India, N=Nepal, P=Pakistan, S=Sri Lanka).

For Bangladesh, as noted by Sobhan in chapter 4, regionalism should (1) resolve common resource problems relating to water, transport, and the environment; and (2) allow Bangladesh to benefit from India's markets for trade, investment, and labor. While security is not a concern for Bangladesh, India is concerned that illegal labor movements from Bangladesh will affect its own security. Although Bangladesh's problems need to be resolved with India,

Sobhan argues that Bangladesh prefers regionalism in order to ameliorate the problem of India's asymmetric power in bilateral discussions.

For Bhutan and Nepal, the problem of common resources—in particular hydropower, transport links, and the environment—looms large (see Lama, chapter 6). Like Bangladesh, they want access to India's markets for trade, investment, and labor. Also like Bangladesh, both countries are hampered by India's superior bargaining power in bilateral negotiations. However, the security issues are more significant than for Bangladesh and emanate from the Indian side. India is, as with Bangladesh, concerned about illegal labor migration from Bhutan and Nepal into India. In addition, human and drug trafficking, particularly from Nepal, are concerns. Further, as noted above, India views Bhutan and Nepal as part of India's security frontier with China. This has led it to sign bilateral security treaties with each of the two countries. China's growing importance has raised India's security concerns.

For India, resolving water disputes with Bangladesh and Pakistan is a developmental challenge. India's security concerns, in addition to those already noted, arise from Pakistan's nuclearization and the dispute over Kashmir. Pakistan is closest to India in its framework of challenges. Its developmental challenge is water, and its security challenges are India's nuclearization and Kashmir. Because Pakistan is the largest South Asian economy after India, the power gap between itself and India is the least asymmetric in the region.

Sri Lanka's main regional developmental concern is benefiting from India's economic growth (trade and investment flows). Its main security concern is stabilizing the northeast after the Tamil insurgency. Its attitude toward regionalism versus bilateralism is a consequence of India's size and power, thus mirroring that of the other small countries (Kelegama, chapter 8).

Ways Forward

What can Europe[18] teach us about regional integration? From their study of the European Union (EU), Bretherton and Vogler list the following conditions that individual states must meet in order to effectively undertake regional development:[19]

- A commitment to a set of overarching values and principles that is shared with other states in the region[20]
- The ability to identify policy priorities and to formulate coherent policies
- The ability to negotiate effectively with other actors in the international system
- The availability of, and capacity to utilize, policy instruments
- A domestic legitimacy of decision processes and priorities relating to external policy

Does the above list apply to South Asia? With the possible exception of the first item, we believe that it does. Whether all the countries of South Asia fulfill the remaining four conditions is a matter of debate, of course, because there have been times even in the recent past when this has not been the case. But this is typical of emerging economies. For example, even India, arguably the strongest and most stable state in South Asia, has failed to reach its targets in significant areas of human development for several decades now, including in rural poverty and urban health care.[21] Does this mean it does not fulfill the second condition? We don't believe so.

None of the states is so weak that it constantly fails to meet the last four conditions, and most of the time all the states fulfill them. Hence, with one exception, we shall not consider the capability to fulfill these conditions further, but take their fulfillment as a given.

That exception, in 2010, is Pakistan, particularly with regards to the last condition. Pakistan's shift to democratic rule in 2008 gave its civilian rulers the legitimacy to make decisions and set priorities relating to external policy, but in practice some of these decisions, as well as control over nuclear assets, are made jointly with the military.

One might be tempted to argue that states that experience great civic instability may be less willing to enter into regional arrangements—that is to say, even if rulers were willing to engage in regionalism, their preoccupation with internal issues might prevent them from seeking regional cooperation, except perhaps to solve internal issues, as Sri Lanka did with India in 1987 to help solve its Tamil problem (although the historical record on that score might dissuade such initiatives in the future).

Certainly, the willingness of Pakistan and Sri Lanka to cooperate regionally has varied in recent times due to internal problems. In Pakistan's case, civilian rule has alternated with military rule, and military leaders have been less inclined to participate in regional integration. In Sri Lanka's case, India's involvement in the 1980s in bolstering the Tamil cause through political, military, and financial support to certain groups in Sri Lanka, as noted earlier, led to a great distrust of India among Sri Lankans and an increased willingness to cooperate regionally.

Yet one can overstate the connection between civil instability and a reluctance to engage in regionalism, at least among the smaller states. Bangladesh, a politically fragile state, has nevertheless been a persistent proponent of regionalism. Nepal, a monarchy until the leftist-led democratic revolution, has also favored the strengthening of SAARC.

Further, state weakness may even bolster regionalism because weak leaders tend to participate in regional forums to shore up their domestic reputations. The ASEAN has seen this happen, as has the Arab League to an even greater degree. Members use the association to engage in the "competitive politics of regime survival."[22] Of course, such competition can weaken regional cooperation even as it strengthens a regional institution. As Barnett and Solingen argue, the members of the Arab League appear to be content with the existence of the league, but they do not want it to do anything "leading to collaboration and integration" since doing so might weaken "political leaders at home."[23]

Turning to the first condition, we identify two important values that should be shared among states in a region that would integrate: democracy and intentionality—the latter, as defined above, meaning interest in regional integration. Note that we include democracy despite the fact that it was not a necessity for Southeast Asian integration. Democracy's importance lies in its ability to allow expressions of popular will—for or against regional integration, for example—to be exercised relatively easily, as Europe has shown.

Although democracy is present in all the states of South Asia as of 2010, the region earlier experienced long periods of military rule (in Bangladesh and Pakistan) and monarchy (Bhutan and Nepal). But among the main states—Bangladesh, Nepal, India, Pakistan, and Sri Lanka[24]—the constant reversion to democracy stands out more remarkably than the episodes of autocracy.[25] That democracy has been unstable is true. The instability of democracy owes to perceptions of internal and external threats. For instance, Pakistan's military has often justified its coups by citing such threats and has usually been welcomed by the population at the beginning of military rule, thus providing it some legitimacy. However, the constant reversion to democracy suggests that most people in the region feel that democracy is the only legitimate form of government.[26] This sentiment has invariably forced autocrats into seeking election—sometimes successfully, as when General Ziaur Rahman created and led the Bangladesh National Party to victory in 1979,[27] but more often unsuccessfully, as when Indira Gandhi's Congress Party was defeated in the post-Emergency elections in India in 1977 and General Musharraf's party, the PML(Q), lost the elections in Pakistan in 2008.

Thus, democracy—remarkably—is the average South Asian's default preference. This preference fulfills the first key condition for successful regional integration—a commitment to shared values—and takes precedence to such an extent that other forms of governance are tolerated only temporarily. This is important because it allows us to argue that, while Southeast Asian regionalism was achieved despite the hurdle of widespread autocracy, South Asian regionalism (1) has failed despite its peoples' deep democratic impulses and (2) can succeed if other barriers are overcome, because these democratic impulses are not likely to obstruct regional integration.

The second value is interest in regional integration. South Asians are unlikely to show the same degree of interest in regionalism as Europeans did prior to the formation of the EU, but this lack of concern is at best a nonnegative force. Indeed, it extends all the way up to some members of parliament and may be explained as a natural outcome of extensive underdevelopment and poverty. The vastness of most of the South Asian states also deters people from thinking about regionalism: two of the three smaller states of South Asia—Pakistan and Bangladesh—would together dominate any other regional grouping. As Kumar notes in chapter 5, there is probably greater public interest in domestic market integration and social integration (within India, Pakistan, Bangladesh, and Sri Lanka) than in integrating across borders.

Not surprisingly, integration has been a harder sell to the South Asian public than it was to the European. Given the democratic impulses of South Asians, this lack of interest has effectively prevented the issue from ranking high on any politician's electoral agenda. This leaves us to consider whether the elite in power might promote regionalism for other reasons, such as improving security (the ASEAN's founding imperative) or encouraging development.

Prior to the advent of South Asia's nuclear age and China's economic great leap forward, India's leaders had little interest in security. When a formal mechanism of regional integration was first proposed by Bangladesh's Rahman in the late 1970s,[28] Sri Lanka welcomed it, but India did not[29]—India felt that the smaller nations of South Asia were about to gang up on it, specifically to pressure India to make political concessions on cross-border issues such as Kashmir, the Tamils, and the Farakka Barrage.

The elite in power may have changed in some ways over the past two decades—notably by embracing the rise of promarket forces—but essentially they are from the same class that has always ruled, and this has stymied progress on security. Whether these democratically elected elites are landowners (Pakistan), members of dominant caste groups (India), or scions of political dynasties (all), they have a strong sense of national identity and a correspondingly limited respect for other states' sovereignty. In other words, these leaders regard their country's sovereignty as a first principle even if it means impinging on the sovereignty of their neighbors. Since dynastic-democratic rule shows no signs of abating in the main South Asian countries, it may be difficult to resolve the sovereignty issue; under these circumstances the probability of South Asian regional integration appears to be dim. Thus, India and Pakistan have been unwilling to find common ground on Kashmir because the leaders on both sides imply that Kashmir is theirs. Similarly, Sri Lanka's struggles with its Tamil secessionist groups were made much more violent and ineffective because Indian politicians, primarily from Tamil Nadu, but with the covert acquiescence of national politicians, provided support to these groups.

But as of 2010, the main issue is Kashmir: as Kashmiris continue to struggle for greater autonomy, Pakistan supports the insurgency while India has made great efforts (both peaceful and military) to accommodate the Kashmiris' demands while keeping Kashmir within India. Arguably, until this problem is resolved, a key condition for regional integration—respect for one another's sovereignty—will not be met.

But other impulses may arise that would make regionalism a possibility. In most of the successful examples of regionalism, a major regional anchor played an important role in bringing countries together, at least in integration's early days. Thus, Germany's leadership was crucial to European regionalism, Indonesia's to the ASEAN, and the United States' to the North American Free

Trade Agreement (NAFTA). Likewise India will play a key part in determining SAARC's future.

Of the examples cited above, India's position is most similar to that of the United States' in North America, as the smaller states' land or littoral boundaries are mostly with India. While one can imagine the three or four smaller countries of South Asia forming their own group—thereby creating the world's fourth-largest grouping by population—this is unlikely to happen given these countries' internal weaknesses and the hostility such a move would provoke in India. A regional grouping consisting of at least Bangladesh, India, and Sri Lanka, but excluding Pakistan, is also possible, though Pakistan would most likely not accept it.

When the idea of South Asian regional cooperation was first proposed by Rahman in the late 1970s, India was in the midst of its most turbulent political period—the Emergency—which had started in 1975 and would not end until the Congress Party was reelected to power in 1980. At the time, India was unstable even relative to its neighbors. Further, it considered itself to be surrounded by forces inimical to its domestic and global interests, which were built around socialism and its close relationship with the Soviet Union. By contrast, Pakistan was experiencing a period of relative calm during these years, with President Muhammad Zia-ul-Haq—still the country's longest serving ruler—bringing his country close to the United States during the Afghan insurrection. Likewise, in Bangladesh, President Rahman moved his country closer to the United States and China during this period, while distancing his country from the Soviet Union. Sri Lanka's Junius Jayawardene, elected president in 1978 shortly after the electoral system was initiated, would go on to rule for the next twelve years, moving the country rightward in a sharp break from the socialist policies of his predecessors.

If the late 1970s were too challenging a period for India to embrace regional integration, the 1980s were no better. While India's economic condition finally started to improve in the 1980s, the decade was marked by great political instability, beginning with the Punjab agitation. After a brief period of stability in 1985 and 1986 during Rajiv Gandhi's post-election "honeymoon period" (SAARC was formed during this time), Gandhi's government was hit by the scandals of Bofors and other arms procurement projects and by the controversial 1987 Kashmir elections, whose impact took up the rest of the decade. Despite its internal turmoil, India kept up some regional efforts—mostly unsuccessful bilateral initiatives like the Rajiv-Benazir dialogue and the Indian Peace Keeping Force (IPKF) expedition in Sri Lanka (a successful exception was India's intervention in the Maldives in 1988). The IPKF episode, in particular, sharply diminished India's appetite for regional involvement. Political stability returned to India in 1991, but by then the country was mired in an economic crisis.

During the early to mid-1990s, India was preoccupied with internal economic reform and had little time for regional efforts. But once economic stability was restored, the country turned to regional integration, beginning with the ILBFTA in 1998. The SAFTA was inked in 2004 and ratified by member countries in 2006;[30] however, it has yet to be fully implemented. An India-Bangladesh Bilateral Free Trade Agreement was drafted in 2006 but has not progressed since then.[31]

Regardless of their particular status, these free trade agreements are all largely symbolic placeholders marking the beginning of a process of closer engagement rather than real trade liberalization. Nonetheless, regional trade has soared. Even the modest liberalizations under SAARC and the ILBFTA have led to large increases in trade. Optimists believe such increases augur well for truly free trade.

As of 2010, we are in an age when both India and Pakistan are declared nuclear powers, when the reality of China's growth demands a response from India, when terrorism is widespread in South Asia, and when India is becoming a growth engine for the world. The recent global downturn may alter some of these realities but most likely only at the margin. So how will South Asian regionalism fare in the face of these new opportunities and challenges?

No one outcome is inevitable. For instance, we earlier noted the possibility of a regional grouping that excludes Pakistan, with India persuading other participating countries that Pakistan is too troublesome a neighbor to include.

We posit the following two possibilities for regional integration in the future. Both center on India as the key first mover. The first scenario is that India, global ambitions firmly in sight, will decide that it needs the world more than it needs South Asia. This outcome would be largely the product of two strands of thought: (1) that India's development opportunities lie in trading and investing with the rest of the world, particularly the richer countries, and that it is important to match China's global influence in the medium term, and (2) that national security can best be achieved through global alignments like the one brokered with the United States in 2008. Heightened security might enable India to continue to assert the immutability of its stance on Kashmir and, with U.S. support, keep Pakistan at bay.[32]

The second scenario is that India will try to leverage its presence in South Asia by exploiting South Asia's assets—a large, developing market and the chance to build strategic depth to counter any external forces—while hoping that its greater engagement sets an example for the other countries of the region. For this to happen, India must gain the trust of the rest of South Asia, particularly Pakistan, on security. In the short term, India would likely negotiate greater autonomy for Kashmir with Pakistan and open its cross-border zones to economic integration. In the longer term, it would work to build a strong, holistic form of regional integration based on both development and security. Even assuming that the other nations, particularly Pakistan, played along, such a plan would cost India politically and economically. However, it is the job of good politicians to contain such costs, as was shown by Jawaharlal Nehru in the 1952 Delhi Agreement.[33]

As of 2010, India, bolstered by its strategic alliance with the United States, appears to have chosen policies that lead to the first scenario. That is to say, India has assumed that threats from China and Pakistan are long term rather than immediate, and that India's economic growth will lead to ample security when it is needed. As noted, the global downturn could prove this assumption wrong, as the string of terrorist attacks in India in 2008 already put into doubt how safe the country is from terrorism.

The title of this chapter asks the provocative question, Does South Asia exist? In response, we made three arguments. First, we argued that regions exist only when the right social, political, economic, cultural, and historical conditions are in place and that these conditions did not exist in South Asia until quite recently. Second, we argued that the time is ripe for the central country, India, to make definitive decisions about the future of regionalism in South Asia, and that these decisions must be made by policymakers rather than civil society or other stakeholders. As a growing country of global significance, India has foreign policy options that extend well beyond regionalism. It could, therefore, choose not to pursue regional integration at all. We argued that this would be a mistake, however, as the rewards of regionalism greatly outstrip the costs. It is crucial that India realizes its role and responsibility in making South Asian regional integration a success.

In our third and final argument, we showed that, for a variety of reasons, India has chosen to think global rather than regional. Specifically, India has downplayed the significance of regional integration, asserting that some member states, particularly Pakistan, are not ready for it. While this stance does not close the space for regional integration, it certainly dims its prospects. If India succeeds in its ambitions of achieving economic growth and global influence, an integrated South Asian region will likely not exist.

Notes

[1] *Security* is defined here in the conventional sense of meaning the protection of a state's territorial integrity from external threats.

[2] The Indian subcontinent included 568 principalities that were under indirect British rule. Nepal and Bhutan were independent kingdoms that had signed treaties of friendship with Great Britain. The extent of these countries' true political independence from Britain is a debated subject, as they were under the British sphere of influence and were integrated under British political economy. See R. English, "Himalayan State Formation and the Impact of British Rule in the Nineteenth Century, Convergences and Differences in Mountain Economies and Societies: A Comparison of the Andes and Himalayas," *Mountain Research and Development* 5, no. 1 (February 1985): 61–78. The Maldives was a British protectorate until 1965. Sri Lanka was a British colony that was ruled independent of British India. British influence over Afghanistan varied over the centuries, reaching its peak in the late nineteenth century.

[3] A United Nations representative described South Asia's human trafficking as the world's second worst, after Southeast Asia (Conference of UN Office on Drugs and Crime, http://burmadigest.info/2007/10/27/combating-human-trafficking-in-south-asia).

[4] Public goods includes public "bads," such as climate change.

[5] A. Sen, *Development as Freedom* (New York: Anchor Books, 1999), 13–15.

[6] We thank Thomas Fingar for discussions on this point.

[7] Externalities could cause exceptions. For instance, the security of all states may be enhanced if one state's actions reduce threats from a common, external hegemon. Likewise, development may not always be positive for all states. For example, a lower riparian's development may suffer if the upper riparian diverts the water for its own purposes, or foreign investors may switch destinations in response to regime change or reforms (especially in larger states), which then leads to reduced funding for smaller states. Perhaps the most-feared externality is that regions share endowments that may be more efficiently exploited by the industries of a large state and drive the industries of smaller states out of existence. The textile industry is the common example of such a case.

[8] Vested economic interests that will lose from regionalism always exist and will try to prevent regionalism.

[9] For example, in South Asia, Pakistan is more likely than India to argue that a settlement of the Kashmir problem is part of its security goals.

[10] Otherwise, regionalism may not result even though the region may be economically linked by the actions of individual firms. Bava illustrates this with the case of Northeast Asia, characterizing it as "regionalization without regionalism." See Bava (chapter 2) quoting S. Kim, "Northeast Asia in the Local-Regional-Global Nexus," in *The International Relations of Northeast Asia*, ed. S. Kim (Lanham, MD: Rowman & Littlefield, 2004).

[11] J. Allen, D. Massey, and A. Cochrane, *Rethinking the Region* (London: Routledge, 1998).

[12] N. Slocum and L. Van Langenhove, "The Meaning of Regional Integration: Introducing Positioning Theory in Regional Integration Studies," *European Integration* 26, no. 3 (September 2004): 227–52.

[13] M. Rasgotra, personal communication with authors, April 6, 2009.

[14] Bhutan's and Nepal's treaties with India date to 1949 and 1950, respectively.

[15] Bhutan (though not Nepal) has border disputes with China, which may have been a factor in its willingness to enter into a treaty with India.

[16] Embree's use of the term *democratization* means a movement away from authoritarian to elected rule. This is different from another common meaning, which is the increase in participation by underprivileged groups in democratic institutions. See A. Kohli, "Democracy and Development: Trends and Prospects," in *States, Markets and Just Growth: Development in the Twenty-first Century*, ed. A. Kohli, C. Moon, and G. Sorensen (Tokyo: United Nations University Press, 2003), 39–63. Democratization began in 1858 with Queen Victoria's pledge that all Indians would enjoy equal protection under the law. By the early twentieth century, Indians had already begun to vote in legislative elections.

[17] Pakistan's relations with India floundered for several decades preceding and succeeding Bangladesh's creation. It would be fallacious to argue that relations with India would have been better had Pakistan not been partitioned.

[18] European regionalism is the basis for most studies on regional integration, an imbalance that this volume (and the series to which it belongs) seeks to correct.

[19] C. Bretherton and J. Vogler, *The European Union as a Global Actor* (London: Routledge, 1999).

[20] An observer of Southeast Asia would surely conclude, as does a companion volume to this series, that its regional body, the ASEAN, is a success (perhaps a qualified success, but a much greater success than the South Asian equivalent, SAARC); yet, the

first point above is not generally true for the countries of Southeast Asia. For example, the commitment to democracy, which most would agree is an overarching value, is not shared across the region.

[21] On international negotiations, even India has had several failures, a notable example being its dealings with Enron in the 1990s and earlier arms-procurement-related issues in the 1980s. There have been notable successes also, one being the long-standing Indus Waters Treaty of 1960 as well as the Indo-U.S. Civilian Nuclear Energy Agreement of 2008.

[22] Barnett and Solingen, in *Crafting Cooperation: Regional International Institutions in Comparative Perspective*, ed. A. Acharya and A. Johnston (Cambridge: Cambridge Univ. Press, 2007), 180–220.

[23] Ibid.

[24] Afghanistan, though a frontline state for the United States as of 2010, is not as relevant for the future of regional cooperation. As discussed elsewhere in this chapter, it was admitted to SAARC in 2007.

[25] Sri Lanka has been a constant democracy; India had one reversion to autocracy, from 1975 to 1977.

[26] For an analysis of "democracy-reversion" in Pakistan, see H. Kennedy, "Constitutional and Political Change in Pakistan: The Military-Governance Paradigm," in *Prospects for Peace in South Asia, ed.* R. Dossani and H. Rowen (Stanford, CA: Stanford Univ. Press, 2005).

[27] The elections were criticized as not being free and fair (www.ti-bangladesh.org).

[28] http://banglapedia.search.com.bd/HT/R_0028.htm.

[29] Pakistan was also initially wary of the proposal, suspecting it of being a mechanism whereby India would dominate the smaller countries (Dubey, personal communication, March 19, 2009). According to Rasgotra (see note 13), who was a participant in the SAARC formation process, Prime Minister Indira Gandhi discussed and ultimately decided that a South Asian forum would be a good thing in that it might give India's smaller neighbors greater confidence in dealing with India.

[30] www.financialexpress.com/news/saarc-countries-ratify-safta/55611/.

[31] www.infodriveindia.com/Exim/Trade-Agreement/India-Bangladesh-Free-Trade-Agreement.aspx.

[32] Although this is a less likely scenario under U.S. president Barack Obama than under his predecessor, the United States may try and influence Pakistan to prevent it from engaging again with Kashmir-based insurgents. In return (and also in return for Pakistan's help in engaging with the Taliban), the Obama administration appears to be willing to be involved in finding a solution to the Kashmir problem.

[33] Those who assert that Kashmir is an integral part of India (the "integralists") or the opposite (the "separatists" and, possibly, "autonomists") tend, not surprisingly, to view each other's positions as untenable. A typical example of how entrenched views do not easily change is how, in the 2009 parliamentary elections, the high voter turnout in Jammu and Kashmir (60 percent) was interpreted. This may be seen either as evidence of the Kashmiris' greater interest in Indian statehood (the integralist view) or as a tactical move for better governance until their aims for autonomy or a separate state are met (the separatist/ autonomist view). A more scholarly basis is, for example, the opinion poll conducted by the University of Maryland's WorldPublicOpinion.org in 2007 (www.worldpublicopinion. org/pipa/articles/brasiapacificra/511.php?lb=bras&pnt=511&nid=&id=).

REGIONAL INTEGRATION: LESSONS FOR SOUTH ASIA FROM AROUND THE WORLD

Ummu Salma Bava

Nations everywhere are finding strength in numbers. Especially since the end of the Cold War, region-based trading, economic, and security blocs and associations have proliferated around the world. What theoretical frameworks explain this process? And what, if any, lessons can be drawn from the most successful such association—the European Union (EU)—for other regions of the world? This chapter briefly discusses the theoretical reasoning behind regional integration before focusing on the EU and the Association of Southeast Asian Nations (ASEAN) as examples of how regional integration processes evolve differently around the world, with diverse outcomes. The EU's achievements underscore what integration can accomplish and in the process challenge assumptions of state behavior with respect to borders and sovereignty. The EU has emerged as the benchmark against which to measure political and economic integration in other parts of the world. In this chapter, I explore the possible relevance of the EU and ASEAN to the South Asian Association for Regional Cooperation (SAARC) in South Asia, which as yet has failed to forge strong regional links despite being initiated more than twenty years ago. Using a comparative framework, I examine the challenges to regional integration in South Asia. In the first section, I briefly differentiate interchangeable terms and situate the theoretical framework and the factors that influence it. In section two, I present regional integration in Europe and Southeast Asia—and the case of the EU and ASEAN—as two distinct models of regional integration with different outcomes. In the last section, I examine the relevance of the preceding models to regional integration in South Asia and discuss the factors unique to South Asia.

Regional Integration: Definitions, Factors, and Theories

The terms *region, regionalism,* and *regional integration* are often used in a way that distorts their specific meanings. A *region* is a geographical, cultural, or social construct "created through politics."[1] By defining it as such, Katzenstein offers a social constructivist view and emphasizes the interplay of geography and politics; a region grows out of the spatial and political factors that define it. *Regionalism,* on the other hand, is identified by intentionality; it is a political process in which states actively pursue cooperative initiatives. According to Jayasuriya, "*regionalism* is a set of cognitive practices shaped by language and political discourse, which through the creation of concepts, metaphors, analogies, determine how the region is defined; these serve to define the actors who are included (and excluded) within the region and thereby enable the emergence of a regional entity and identity."[2]

Regionalization refers to economic integration, which, though influenced by state policies, is the uncoordinated consequence of private-sector activities.[3] Regionalization describes the geographic manifestation of international or global economic processes.[4]

Regional integration, as Haas has identified, is the shifting of certain national activities toward a new center.[5] It is an intentional collective action taken to accomplish certain common goals—whether they be political, economic, or related to national and regional security. In a Deutschian sense, a community is made where states identify common objectives and endorse similar political values. *Regionalism* refers to the political structures that evolve over time[6] to both reflect and shape the strategies of governments, business corporations, and a variety of nongovernmental organizations (NGOs) and social movements.[7] Nonetheless, views diverge on whether integration is only a process or an end.

Although regional integration can take place at the *market, functional,* or *institutional* level, the drivers and impact of each are very different. While *market integration* is more spontaneous and easier to achieve, *functional integration* is driven by an aim to expand market integration through specific economic measures. *Institutional integration,* however, involves more binding agreements among the governments concerned and also creates a new power center, thereby leading to multilevel governance. As in the case of the EU, as functional and institutional integration increases, decision-making power shifts from the national to the new power center, indicating a shift of sovereignty that can also be denoted as an "authority-legitimacy transfer." What needs to be emphasized here is that this process is achieved through noncoercive efforts.[8] In addition, it can display characteristics of both *loose* and *strong* integration. While loose integration is evident in intergovernmentalism and informal decision-making, strong integration is displayed by supranationalism and central decision-making through common institutions. Both strong and loose integration, however, lead to better cooperation and the formation of new identities.

The possibility for cooperation at the regional or international level is influenced by numerous factors. Geography is a critical shaper of interactions such as interstate trade and commerce. Proximity, against the backdrop of bad political relations, has the potential to escalate conflicts of interest and even lead to war. The geography, history, politics, and economy of the states in a particular region—and their relations to one another—all impinge on the process of integration. Other factors that facilitate interstate cooperation include a region's (1) collective historical experience, (2) homogeneity or diversity, (3) distribution of power, and (4) economic and military status relative to the rest of the world. External factors can also impel integration. For example, the actions of the prevailing global powers, external or regional crises, perceived common threats, and internal tariffs all act as drivers of cooperation at the regional level. It is precisely for this reason that there exists no one type of regional integration. On the contrary, forms of regional integration and cooperation are as diverse as the regions themselves. Ranging from the strong institutional framework of the EU to the loose one of ASEAN, there is SAARC, the North American Free Trade Agreement (NAFTA), the Mercado Común del Sur (MERCOSUR), and the South African Development Community (SADC), all of which display varied experiences in the construction of regionalism.

Depending on the theoretical paradigm employed to study regional integration, one finds different explanations for its occurrence. It is important to note, however, that most theories on regional integration use the EU as their model. This Eurocentric bias has long ignored the experience of regional integration around the world. In fact, examining cooperation under dissimilar conditions is critical to the understanding of how different factors enable or inhibit cooperation.

Meanwhile, debates over whether regional integration is a process or an end are increasingly focusing on product over process. From an international relations perspective, three different theoretical approaches—again developed in the context of the EU—offer insight into regional integration: (1) international power and security theories, (2) neofunctionalism and institutionalism, and (3) domestic politics and intergovernmentalism. Although all three identify international politics as anarchic, each interprets the potential for interstate cooperation differently.

From the perspective of international power and security theories, *neorealism* argues that the asymmetric gains from exchange tend to hinder international cooperation[9] and limit it to a narrow bandwidth. Such limited exchange is more likely among states that are political and military allies than among those that are potential or actual adversaries. The economic and security consequences of cooperation are thus intertwined, with one reinforcing the other. The *power transition* theory speaks of a hierarchic order presided over by the preponderant power.[10] Thus the dominant power establishes a set of status quo arrangements with the help of willing allies, either at the global or regional level—or both, depending on the size of the power (for example, the U.S. role in creating the European Community [EC] and the North Atlantic Treaty Organization [NATO]).

Along similar lines, the *hegemonic stability* theory[11] posits that the presence of a hegemonic state (that is capable of and committed to promoting economic liberalism) is a necessary condition for liberal international economic activity or trade (again, the U.S. role in creating the EC). The first theory mentioned, neorealism, identifies a perceived common threat and political interest in the endorsement of certain political values as critical factors enabling regional integration. The last two theories focus on the dominant state's role in facilitating regional integration as a basis for its own power in both regional and international politics.

From a *neofunctional* perspective, regional integration arises because complex interdependencies create conditions wherein states can no longer solve problems at the nation-state level.[12] This theory was very popular in the 1950s and '60s and was often used to examine and explain the nascent European Economic Community (EEC). It explains integration as a top-down process, ascribing its progress to the strong role of the elite. Thus, sectoral integration and cooperation in one field invariably lead to integration in others through a process of "spillover" (for example, the development of the European Coal and Steel Community [ECSC] into the EEC, with increased monetary integration finally leading to enhanced political cooperation as the EEC transformed into the EU). From an *institutional* perspective, international institutions are seen to promote cooperation by helping states overcome collective action problems. Here, the role of institutions is considered vital and the creation of new structures a necessity.

A third paradigm explains regional integration from the perspective of *domestic politics*. Accordingly, economic policies that lead to regional integration often reflect the preferences of the more powerful and better-organized interest groups in society.[13] Putnam argues that it is the politician who drives the process as he aims at interest maximization.[14] Others focus on economic interests as the driving force of regional integration, even offering a demand-and-supply argument for regional integration.[15]

If theory is a means to better understanding, the plethora of theories attempting to explain regional integration and cooperation underscore the lack of consensus on these complex phenomena. While no theory offers a comprehensive understanding of the process and its outcome, each provides clues to certain elements of regionalism. For example, several offer insight into the relation among the territory, identity, and functions of a state that has been "displaced" by the process of regional integration.[16]

Regional Integration in Europe: The European Union

The process of regional integration in Europe began even before World War II. By the war's end in 1945, dynamic changes in political, economic, and social conditions had transformed Europe from its strategic position as the geopolitical center of world politics to the object of others' foreign policy. A declining Europe caught in the web of Cold War politics could find a voice for itself only if it recast its nationalist interest in interstate contest into a focus on cooperation as the dominant driver of political action.

Regional integration, as it began in the 1950s in Europe, was heavily influenced by the interplay of ideas, visions, history, and geopolitics. It was an elite-driven process that drew upon the intellectual contribution of visionaries such as Jean Monnet, who adopted a gradualist approach to integration, and Robert Schuman. Both sought to write a new history for Europe that expanded notions of state sovereignty and borders, and proposed to "share or pool sovereignty." Thus, Europe—which had given the building block of the state to the world in 1648—was reinventing itself. It had little choice: nationalist states pitted against one another had caused two world wars in a span of twenty years. The vision enshrined in the 1957 Treaty of Rome was to lay "the foundations of an ever closer union among the peoples of Europe" with the aim "to ensure the economic and social progress of their countries by common action to eliminate the barriers which divide Europe."

One can say that the objective of cooperation in 1957 was to secure the economic and social well-being of the people of Europe and that the instrument used to achieve this goal was economic cooperation. This notion of economic cooperation beyond borders was politically driven and highlighted a new understanding of the link between security and economics. In other words, Western European countries sought to enhance their security not at the cost of one another but through consciously intertwining their economies. A critical factor that led to this economic cooperation was the political reconciliation of France and West Germany, which led to the rise of the so-called Franco-German engine of cooperation. Thus, economic cooperation became the driving force of Western European regionalism, beginning with the ECSC, which was formed in 1952 with six members: France, West Germany, Italy, Belgium, Netherlands, and Luxembourg. What began as a sectoral initiative merging coal and steel production had spillover effects that included the creation of a common market.[17]

Such integration was made possible by the preponderant role of the United States, which emerged as the guarantor of security in the Western European region. According to Wallace, "American commitment, American political and financial support, and American provision of security were all important to its establishment and sustainability."[18] The economic recovery of Europe launched under the Marshall Plan not only secured the U.S. presence in the region but also further enhanced economic, political, and security relations on both sides of the Atlantic.

In sum, Western Europe created a new identity driven by economic cooperation. Member states soon reaped the triple benefits of growth, security, and peace. Using the neofunctional theory as our base, we might say that this economic cooperation was instrumental in creating a new political community, or *Gemeinschaft*, as identified by Deutsch. Deutsch's emphasis was not on institutions but on the sociological explanation for integration. He believed that the "higher the level of socio-psychological community and thus of consensus in society, the greater the progress towards the integration of the segments into a larger purposive whole—'a community of attitudes and values.'"[19]

Significantly, and counter to Deutsch's emphasis, the process of regional integration in Europe has in fact been paralleled by increased institutionalization. Over the past fifty years, strong legislative structures have established new supranational authority. In a paradigm shift, Europe moved from the modern political template (the nation-state) to what we might term a postmodern political structure, especially in economic and trade matters. By pooling sovereignty, the EU's member states have pushed their internal borders to a new outside frontier. This has led to the creation of a new polity with multilevel governance. In addition, the EU has over time sought to distinguish itself from the United States as a "soft" power (especially in its emphasis on negotiation and diplomacy as a means to conflict resolution). The EU has also arisen as a normative power,[20] be it in matters of climate control or through the International Criminal Court. These activities endorse particular values that Europe is seen to export to other parts of the world. Thus, the EU is more than an expression of modified interstate politics; it is the focus for processes that bring together new varieties of identity and need.[21]

While the EU has achieved growing brand identification as an economic heavyweight in international trade, its influence is not as strong in political matters. This is because member states are still possessive of their national interests, especially with respect to foreign policy. This differential between economic cooperation and political independence is expressed in several ways. Increasingly, it is in the area of economic activity that the EU speaks with a unanimous voice because, in this, the member states have created a system of shared rule. On matters pertaining to larger political issues and common foreign and security policy (CFSP), however, decision-making is still done within an intergovernmental framework. In other words, the veto voice of member states is intact, and this has hindered the articulation of a common position on foreign policy. In turn, this hinders the EU's political visibility and effectiveness as an influential political actor on the world stage. The recent Irish "no vote" on the Lisbon Treaty underscores member states' reluctance to transfer control—especially on foreign policy—to Brussels.

Since 1957 the goalposts of European integration have widened, which reinforces the point that the goal is not a given. Rather, the region has tried to manage integration within the changing economic and political requirements of the day. The Cold War came to an end in 1990, as Europe's common market gave way to a single market made up of twelve countries. When German unification became inevitable, the EEC was also transformed into an economic and monetary union with a single currency. This new economic identity was further enhanced to encompass a growing political presence after the end of the Cold War. With the launching of the EU in 1992, member states tried to construct a new political and security identity for Europe, as well as to constitute a new European social identity.[22] European integration has not only created a large market for business. It has set benchmarks across the EU-27 member states on hundreds of economic, political, and social issues; given them a strong currency; and expanded the benefits of economic growth and political solidarity through democracy and a focus on human rights. What is striking is not only the pooling of sovereignty but the merger of public resources to address common concerns through new loci of authority that parallel existing institutions in each member state.

In sum, Europe's focus on economics has not only yielded results but kept divisive politics at bay. Its integration has successfully transformed the weakened post–World War II states into a hegemon in economics and trade (though not in international politics). The biggest success has been that its members have witnessed their own Europeanization in the process of their integration. The new community, the *Gemeinschaft*, promises to construct a new identity in international politics as well.

Regional Integration in Asia

Compared with Europe's strong, institutional-based regional integration, integration processes in other parts of the world are loose. One reason for this outlook, however, is the prevalent use of the EU as a benchmark against which to measure the outcome of similar processes in other regions of the world. Given that the political, economic, and social factors contributing to regional integration are located in unique regional geopolitics, the EU is not a norm as much as a specific case. As such, it is an inadequate basis for measurement.

Defining East Asia

A geographical overview of East Asia immediately elucidates the difficulty of considering it a single entity. From the standpoint of politics, powerful actors have created competing zones of influence over their smaller neighbors. Taken together, we can identify two distinct geopolitical areas: Northeast Asia and Southeast Asia.

Northeast Asia: Limits on Regional Integration

Three actors are critical to Northeast Asia: China, Japan, and South Korea. While they are among the world's most powerful economies, they have made limited progress toward identifying and exploring possibilities of common interest. Undoubtedly, the region's raw memory of a conflict-marred past may obstruct cooperation. The current balance of power in the region has also exacerbated old dynamics, given the tension between China and Japan for primacy in the region, the North Korean nuclear imbroglio, and the role of the United States as a critical external actor.

The prospect of regional integration in a war-torn Europe was facilitated by two crucial factors: (1) the beginning of the Cold War, which provided a common threat perception, in particular to the former enemies France and West Germany, and (2) the proactive role of the United States. Both factors enabled community building and gave members economic and security benefits. In Northeast Asia, meanwhile, common goals have gone unidentified. After 1945

Japan looked to the United States for its economic and security needs. As part of the growing U.S. network of security alliances, Japan found its interests reciprocated across the Pacific Ocean. While in Europe the United States actively pushed for cooperation among West European countries, in Northeast Asia it directly engaged Japan and South Korea within its larger Cold War strategy. Thus, two distinct patterns of U.S. engagement—with strikingly different results—can be perceived in Europe and in Northeast Asia.

Because of its global economic prowess, Northeast Asia can be characterized by "regionalization without regionalism."[23] With no sign of reconciliation between Japan and China, the region's push-pull dynamics show little promise of changing. China's economic rise has a big impact on the global and regional economy, and China's huge capacity for imports and exports has also transformed the regional dynamics. In sum, the residue of Cold War politics and a concomitant balance of power is holding a region captive and preventing it from unleashing its huge potential for intraregional trade.

In sum, Northeast Asian regionalism is hampered by the pursuit of individual state power, be it at the political or economic level. For example, Japan is seeking to thoroughly revise its foreign policy approach, which dates back to the Cold War. It has sent its self-defense force abroad for participation in United Nations peacekeeping operations (UNPKO) and also sent troops to Iraq under the U.S.-led military operation called the "coalition of the willing." As Japan revisits the notion of transforming its self-defense forces into a real military by revising Article 9 of its constitution, many analysts warn of revived tension. From a Chinese and South Korean perspective, such a move would reinforce a historical view of Japan as the region's aggressor. Old wounds were further exacerbated by former Japanese prime minister Junichiro Koizumi's repeated visits to the country's war shrines, which drew sharp protests from both China and South Korea.

China, meanwhile, has increased its military budgets to modernize its defense forces. In other words, war as a policy option—no longer expounded within the EU—remains an active instrument in Northeast Asia. Japan and China seek to change the balance of power in the region, even as North Korea tips the applecart by going nuclear and enhancing its missile program. By contrast, it is impossible to think that the two longtime rivals France and Germany would attack each other again given the institutional engagement and cooperation they have achieved within the EU. The pooling of sovereignty in the EU has created a different kind of relation among its member states as each realizes the high cost of noncooperation—a factor that does not seem to get enough attention in Northeast Asia. Further, China's growing economic visibility and its presence in every regional forum underscores the notion that it does not endorse the idea of shared leadership.

As stated, the United States is a key actor in the geopolitics of Northeast Asia. The long-standing U.S. strategic engagement and influence here that has maintained the balance of power in the region—what might be termed an "engaged balance"—is gradually being countered by China.[24] A resurgent China with extremely strong economic performance unprecedented in growth models seeks to change the balance of power in the region by moving beyond the notion of the "Middle Kingdom."[25]

Viewing geopolitics through the prism of nationalism reinforces a nation's status both regionally and globally. Thus, national identity is repeatedly reinforced and the idea of shifting to an emphasis on commonality among neighbors recedes. A divided Korea—one of the last outposts of the Cold War—is a constant reminder of this fact. True, the increase in trade among China, Japan, and South Korea has given rise to international contacts and networks. And each is seen as a leader in the larger context of Asia: consider, for example, Japan's role as a powerbroker in Southeast Asia through the Asian Development Bank (ADB). But while economic relations are not a zero-sum game, they do not necessarily lead to cooperation. Creating a win-win integration process requires a shift from the pursuit of national ambitions to cooperative gains for all countries.

What facilitates the construction of a region is cooperation, and constructing political trust is critical to cooperation. A loose network spans the large region, the Asia-Pacific Economic Cooperation (APEC). The objective of APEC is "to enhance economic growth and prosperity for the region and to strengthen the Asia-Pacific community."[26] However, promoting economic growth without synergizing policies or even using the APEC platform to facilitate greater political interaction has maintained the status quo.

Southeast Asia

Southeast Asia is home to an extremely diverse population living in different political and economic systems. Yet, in contrast to Northeast Asia, its countries are on a trajectory toward increasing cooperation and regional integration. Steps toward regional integration were first made in response to a perceived common security threat. Thus, political perception led to economic cooperation. ASEAN was established in 1967 with five countries—Indonesia, Malaysia, Philippines, Singapore, and Thailand—and subsequently expanded to include Brunei Darussalam, Vietnam, Lao PDR, Myanmar, and Cambodia.

The creation of ASEAN was facilitated by consensus, a point emphasized by Walt,[27] who writes that it was promoted to "demonstrate solidarity against communist expansion in Vietnam and insurgency" within the overall region. The adoption of the Treaty of Amity and Cooperation (TAC) at the First ASEAN Summit in Bali in 1976 can be viewed as one of the key steps toward building regional confidence. The treaty legally binds all ASEAN signatories to peaceful coexistence and respect for the principles of sovereignty, territorial integrity, noninterference in internal affairs, and nonuse of force. In other words, the TAC expounds the "ASEAN way" enshrined in the Bangkok Declaration.

Similar to what the Treaty of Rome envisaged for Europe in 1957, ASEAN represents the will of its member nations "to bind themselves together in friendship and cooperation and, through joint efforts and sacrifices, secure for their peoples and for posterity the blessings of peace, freedom, and prosperity." While both treaties emphasize prosperity and peace for their peoples, the difference lies in the political and economic means adopted by the EC/EU and ASEAN in securing these goals.

The enforcement of commonly accepted rules ensures the predictability of interstate relations and their outcomes. But a shift in the balance of power, where the interests of one are maximized at the expense of the others, jeopardizes the predictability of outcomes. This is what ASEAN sought to do—to establish rules of engagement whereby no state could make another more vulnerable. By fostering political stability it has led to economic cooperation (an interesting reversal of the European experience). In addition, on the security front, member states launched the ASEAN Regional Forum (ARF) in 1994 to bring together ASEAN member states, observers, and the consultative and dialogue partners of ASEAN.

Unlike in Europe, however, institutionalization has been weak in Southeast Asia. With little role for civil society, the state remains the primary actor in the region. In addition, there has been no transfer of sovereignty to a new institution within ASEAN. Developments in Southeast Asia have been marked by a preference for intergovernmentalism over supranationality.

The ASEAN integration process lags far behind its European counterpart for two reasons. While Europe has moved beyond the notion of absolute sovereignty at least in economic and trade matters, countries in Northeast and Southeast Asia show a marked fixation on the pursuit of national interest. Interstate contest is not conducive to integration. As a result, East Asians have endorsed a "gradual, incremental approach to cooperation over legalistic and fast-track modalities of institution-building."[28] Unlike in Europe, where the pooling of sovereignty has created a new level of governance, Southeast Asia has been reticent to adopt that particular aspect of regional integration. Simon has gone a step further, calling the ARF and the Council for Security Cooperation in the Asia Pacific (CSCAP) "talk shops." The ARF, as Katzenstein explains, "has sidestepped the most pressing security issues in Asia: conflicts on the Korean Peninsula, across the Taiwan Strait, and in the South China Sea."[29] But, as previously stated, using the EU as a benchmark supposes that other regions in the world have similar histories and problems for which regional integration is the solution. Such an approach fails to understand that differences in geography, history, politics, economics, and society lead to different outcomes.

Southeast Asia's success in the 1960s and '70s in repulsing Communist expansion in the region came as states jumped on the U.S. bandwagon. However, the main challenge to ASEAN today is China's rise. China not only has emerged as a major actor in the region but has also become a part of every regional organization and is critical to the strategic geopolitical framework of the region. For Southeast Asia, China is a decisive factor in the changing strategic calculus. The increasing economic and political asymmetry between China and the other countries in the region has also created a new political impulse. ASEAN is now engaging India with a view perhaps to balance Chinese presence and influence. Another signal of the new political intent is the ASEAN charter, signed in November 2007 and ratified by all ten countries a year later. Aiming for an EU-style of economic community building by 2015, the ASEAN charter provides for a legal and institutional framework with periodic meetings of the heads of state. The ASEAN secretary-general, Dr. Surin Pitsuwan, has stated that with the charter coming into force, "ASEAN will be a rules-based, people-oriented and more integrated entity."

Although ASEAN has adopted certain aspects of the EU framework, the process of regional integration in Southeast Asia has been very different from that in Europe. This is in part because the region's varied political structures restrict consensus building. Despite this and other challenges, however, the lesson to be drawn from Southeast Asia is that states can cooperate to create a common public good that will benefit a large pool of people beyond national boundaries.

Pan-Asian Integration

As Ellen Frost has noted, "Asia is an especially porous region than can be defined in different ways for different purposes. Its boundaries have always been subject to interpretation and imagination."[30] While its economic dynamism provides global stability, its geopolitical conflicts generate global uncertainty.[31] Asia today is undergoing a rapid transformation in terms of its politics, economics, and security. With the two major global economic drivers situated here, the political dynamics of the region are also beginning to change. In light of this, we may ask whether the East Asia Summit—whose sixteen participants included China, Japan, and India (but not the United States)—is an effort to create a pan-Asian regional identity. East Asia is in transition, driven by both internal and external political, economic, and security impulses. Is Asia trying to redefine itself in the post–Cold War context?

Efforts at creating a new regional identity and platform that project East Asia at the regional and global level have drawn mixed responses. One can ask whether the presence of large actors such as China, Japan, and India will lead to a contest for leadership, or if the creation of such a community would balance power in the region. Is it possible to envision collective leadership emerging from this part of the world, poised at the forefront of the global economic agenda? With the presence of the two regional giants, Japan and China, and the footprint of a South Asian giant, India, Asia now has both new regional and global actors. Will economic and political developments in East and South Asia lead to consensus or contest? ASEAN's effort to be the driving force of the East Asian Summit and thereby reduce the influence of China corroborates the idea that regional leadership is being contested.

If East Asia is a region in flux, it reflects a changing world order whose power structure is far from clear. Critical to understanding the changing dynamics in East Asia is the U.S. role in the region—and its future. Whether the United States will be an insider, a stabilizer of geopolitics in flux, or an outside hegemon has yet to be determined. That the United States is not part of the East Asia Summit signals a rising Asia's attempt to construct a new platform without the dominant global military power.

As previously noted, the rise of China has transformed the East Asian equation. Without a coequal power from within the region (other than Japan, with whom relations are tense at best), China may freely claim leadership—much to the discomfort of the Southeast Asian countries. As China's neighbors seek to hedge their bets, they are looking to India. The United States, a regional enabler in Western Europe, has only divided Asia. U.S. bilateral relationships in the region gave rise to a "hub and spokes" model, making regional integration a remote prospect throughout the Cold War period.[32] It will be interesting to see how the United States now engages the region in a bilateral and multilateral framework given the rise of China and its growing economic and political influence in the region.

Table 2.1 Regional Integration in Europe and East Asia

	European Union (EU)	East Asia
Integration type	Functional and institutional	Market integration dominant
Decision-making	Intergovernmentalism, supranationalism	Informal
Rules	Binding agreements	Flexible, consensus
Actors	National politicians, EU bureaucrats	Companies and national politicians
Government role	Leader	Facilitator
Members	Democracies	Mixed political group
Trade	Intraregional	World market, intraregional trade growing
Investment	Dense links	Production network growing
Monetary integration	Tight (introduction of new currency, the Euro)	Still weak
Identity	*New identity*: In trade—one voice (WTO) In foreign policy—still evolving	*Old identity*: No unified position on trade and foreign policy

Source: Modified from W. Pascha, "Economic Integration in East Asia and Europe—A Comparison," Duisburg Working Papers on East Asian Economic Studies #68 (2004): 1–22.
Note: WTO = World Trade Organization.

A Model of Regional Integration for South Asia

The examples provided reveal several possible modes of regional integration. On the one hand, the EU endorses common political values and exports these to the rest of the world; meanwhile, ASEAN is characterized by states with different political ideologies and little space for consensus. The public good created in both cases—however different—emphasizes the point that integration is a process unique to each region, without a common end.

This point takes on greater meaning in the case of South Asia, which was interconnected within a large administrative framework (the British Raj) prior to 1947. Since, old fault lines and new borders have defined political entities pursuing nationalist interests inimical to one another and thus fracturing any semblance of regional unity.

South Asia has eight countries (Afghanistan, Bangladesh, Bhutan, India, Maldives, Nepal, Pakistan, and Sri Lanka) linked together in the regional framework of SAARC. Although South Asia is characterized by a long integrated history, conflict is not unfamiliar. Political instability in Nepal and Pakistan, the presence of two nuclear states (India and Pakistan), the growing Indian economy and its significance to the world, high population densities, unabated poverty, sweeping cultural affinities, and divisive political ideologies are some of the challenges and opportunities that this region embodies.

How can regionalism be a catalyst for change in South Asia? Launched in 1985, SAARC has been slow to build regional consensus. Evident in the challenges enumerated above, the costs of noncooperation are high. Regional integration and cooperation promise to transform the region—and the biggest beneficiaries of the process would be the people. The current focus of all states is on enhancing state security in the region. Given the huge socioeconomic development challenges, any approach that seeks to enhance human security will be a win-win for all, if the politics of the region can transcend the existing status quo.

The politics of division are prevalent in South Asia, where cross-border cooperation has become hostage to political divisions and ambitions. What geography unites, politics divides, and so promoting regionalism in South Asia requires leadership and vision. The real challenge is to create a dialogue among states in which they envision the creation of a regional rather than a fragmented public good. It is in this context that we might ask whether regional integration can be offered as a new development paradigm for the region.

The challenge for South Asia has been the absence of any rallying point for cohesion, be it an external security threat or economic concern. Instead, the perceived threats are among the states themselves, a condition that has repulsed cooperation. In the coming decades it is imperative that South Asia go beyond the security dilemma of the individual state to define security in a more comprehensive manner—to encompass the well-being of all. Vital to building regional integration is a redefinition of interstate relations. True, the prevailing security dilemmas of individual states need to be addressed, but the future of South Asia depends on states moving beyond the dyadic conflict mode to address security challenges to the *entire* region.

The South Asian case bears some resemblance to MERCOSUR in South America, in that the presence of one dominant actor (India and Brazil, respectively) creates asymmetric power relations throughout the region. In the absence of an equal other, India is seen as a bully against which the small states rally. India should capitalize on this asymmetry to leverage a new political identity that is based on power of vision, not size. Geographically, India is the region's pivotal state. It is also the anchor of democracy. As such, it should reach out to its neighbors and engage them on the basis of nonreciprocity of action to construct a greater unity. Removing barriers that are inimical to trade and managing economic reforms will be critical to the transformation of South Asia. India, the dominant actor and trade partner in the region, should facilitate this process. Although pathbreaking in its advocacy of a new foreign policy vision, the Gujral Doctrine has met heavy resistance within the Indian establishment. Thus, resistance to change in regional dynamics often can be found within the state itself, where vested interests would like to see conflict continue or perhaps even escalate.

Links among the people of the region could be increased, as could civil society dialogue. On the political level, the SAARC need not be the only medium of regional cooperation. Exploring other avenues of regional and subregional cooperation would bring tremendous economic benefits to the concerned states and also facilitate new dialogues. For example, establishing the equivalent of the ASEAN TAC would go a long way toward region building. As globalization undermines individual state power, the South Asian nations will have to move toward cooperation if they are to harness their economic power and ensure regional security now and in the future.

Conclusion

By and large, integration processes are endorsed as processes of peaceful change. According to Haas, "the main reason for studying . . . regional integration . . . is normative: the units and actions provide a living laboratory for observing the peaceful creation of possible new types of human communities at a very high level of organization and of the processes that may lead to such conditions."[33]

As such, one cannot forget that numerous factors influence regional integration. The EU has managed to create a win-win situation for its members through a formal institutional structure. East Asia has developed a network style of open regionalism. The trajectories of history and politics shaping South Asia and the impact of globalization will lead to a different process of regional integration. Europe is writing a postmodern chapter of its history, while the countries of Asia continue to define themselves as modern nation-states. Therein lies a major difference in the experience and outcome of regional integration.

Notes

[1] Peter Katzenstein, "Regionalism and Asia," *New Political Economy* 5, no. 3 (2000): 353–70.

[2] Kanishka Jayasuriya, "Singapore: The Politics of Regional Definition," *The Pacific Review* 7, no. 4 (1994): 411–20.

[3] Shaun Breslin and Richard Higgot, "Studying Regions: Assessing the New, Learning from the Old," *New Political Economy* 5, no. 3 (November 2000): 333–53.

[4] Katzenstein, "Regionalism and Asia."

[5] Ernst B. Haas, *The Uniting of Europe* (Stanford, CA: Stanford Univ. Press, 1958).

[6] Leon Lindberg, "Political Integration as a Multidimensional Phenomenon Requiring Multivariate Measurement," in *Regional Integration: Theory and Research*, ed. Leon Lindberg and Stuart Scheingold (Cambridge, MA: Harvard Univ. Press, 1971), 46.

[7] Katzenstein, "Regionalism and Asia."

[8] Ernst B. Haas, "The Study of Regional Integration," in Lindberg and Scheingold, *Regional Integration*.

[9] Kenneth Waltz, *Theory of International Politics* (New York: McGraw-Hill, 1979); Richard Grieco, "Anarchy and the Limits of Cooperation: A Realist Critique of the Newest Liberal Institutionalism," *International Organization* 42, no. 3 (1988): 485–507.

[10] A. F. K. Organski, *World Politics* (New York: Alfred A. Knopf, 1958); A. F. K. Organski and Jacek Kugler, "The Cost of Major Wars: The Phoenix Factor," *American Political Science Review* 71 (1977): 1347–66; and Organski and Kugler, *The War Ledger* (Chicago: Univ. of Chicago Press, 1980).

[11] Stephen Krasner, "State Power and the Structure of International Trade," *World Politics* 28, no. 3 (1976): 317–47; Robert Gilpin, *The Political Economy of International Relations* (Princeton, NJ: Princeton Univ. Press, 1987).

[12] Haas, *The Uniting of Europe*; David Mitrany, *The Functional Theory of Politics* (London: Martin Robertson, 1975).

[13] See Helen Milner, *Resisting Protectionism: Global Industries and the Politics of International Trade* (Princeton, NJ: Princeton Univ. Press, 1988); Helen Milner, *Interests, Institutions and Information: Domestic Politics and International Relations* (Princeton, NJ: Princeton Univ. Press, 1997); Ronald Rogowski, *Commerce and Coalitions: How Trade Affects Domestic Political Alignments* (Princeton, NJ: Princeton Univ. Press, 1989); Andrew Moravcsik, "Taking Preferences Seriously: A Liberal Theory of International Politics," *International Organization* 51, no. 4 (1997): 513–53.

[14] Robert D. Putnam, "Diplomacy and Domestic Politics: The Logic of Two-level Games," *International Organization* 42 (1988): 427–60.

[15] Walter Mattli, *The Logic of Regional Integration: Europe and Beyond* (Cambridge: Cambridge Univ. Press, 1999).

[16] Brigid Laffan, "The European Union: A Distinct Model of Internationalization," *Journal of European Public Policy* 5, no. 2 (1998): 235–53.

[17] William Wallace, *Regional Integration: The West European Experience* (Washington, D.C.: Brookings Institution Press, 1994).

[18] Wallace, *Regional Integration*, 2.

[19] Dimitris Chryssochoou, *Theorizing European Integration* (London and New York: Routledge, 2009), 27.

[20] Ian Manners, "Normative Power Europe: A Contradiction in Terms?" *Journal of Common Market Studies* 40, no. 2 (2002): 235–58; Ian Manners, "Normative Power

Europe Reconsidered: Beyond the Crossroads," *Journal of European Public Policy* 13 (2006): 2, 182.

[21] Brigid Laffan, Rory O' Donnell, and Michael Smith, *Europe's Experimental Union: Rethinking Integration* (London: Routledge, 1999), 39.

[22] David Dunkerley, *Changing Europe: Identities, Nations and Citizens* (London: Routledge, 2002).

[23] S. Kim, "Northeast Asia in the Local-Regional-Global Nexus," in *The International Relations of Northeast Asi, ed.* Samuel S. Kim (Lanham, MD: Rowman & Littlefield, 2004), 13.

[24] Kenneth Pyle, "Japan's Change of Course," papers from the Workshop on Japan and East Asian Integration, 2006, Stimson Center. www.stimson.org/southeastasia/?SN =SE20060425983.

[25] Ludwig Kühnhardt, "Northeast Asia: Obstacles to Regional Integration. The Interests of the European Union," Discussion Paper C105, Centre for European Studies, Bonn (2005): 11.

[26] www.apecsec.org.sg/apec/about_apec.html.

[27] Stephen Walt, "Testing Theories of Alliance Formation: The Case of Southwest Asia," *International Organization* 42, no. 2 (1988): 313–15.

[28] Amitav Acharya, "Regional Institutions and Asian Security Order: Norms, Power, and Prospects for Peaceful Change," in *Asian Security Order: Instrumental and Normative Features* ed. M. Alagappa (Stanford, CA: Stanford Univ. Press, 2003), 15.

[29] Peter Katzenstein and Allen Carlson, eds., *Rethinking Security in East Asia: Identity, Power and Efficiency* (Stanford, CA: Stanford Univ. Press, 2004), 115.

[30] Ellen Frost, *Asia's New Regionalism* (Boulder, CO: Lynne Reinner, 2008), 35.

[31] Kühnhardt, "Northeast Asia," 1.

[32] Christopher J. Hemmer and Peter Katzenstein, "Why Is There No NATO in Asia? Collective Identity, Regionalism, and the Origins of Multilateralism," *International Organization* 56, no. 3 (2002): 575–607.

[33] Haas, "The Study of Regional Integration," 4.

REGIONAL ECONOMIC INTEGRATION IN SOUTH ASIA: THE DEVELOPMENT OF INSTITUTIONS AND THE ROLE OF POLITICS

Muchkund Dubey

The logic for regional integration in South Asia is compelling. It derives from the area's huge contiguous landmass, common cultural heritage, common ethnicities broadly defined, common physical and institutional infrastructure, and significant externalities. Besides, South Asia is a relatively large market with rising per capita incomes. There is also a convergence of macroeconomic policies toward liberalization and the free play of market forces. Moreover, both the governments and the people of the South Asian countries are fully aware of the huge opportunity costs of noncooperation in the economic field. In spite of this, South Asia is a late starter in the movement of regional integration and has until now made little progress in this direction.

If political differences among the member states are set aside, then South Asia constitutes an ideal grouping for economic integration. It is a very large geographically contiguous region crisscrossed by mighty common rivers, and with a rich wealth of natural resources, a variety of climatic conditions, and with common history, heritage, language, literature, and religions. The Indian subcontinent, in which the bulk of the South Asian region falls, has inherited common institutions and a legal system and common physical infrastructure from the colonial period, including roads, railways, and inland waterways. These became disrupted and disconnected at certain places because of neglect, disuse, and deliberate destruction during periods of conflict. Most can be restored without involving exorbitant costs.

South Asia has a market of 1.4 billion consumers with rising incomes, primarily due to relatively faster rates of growth of the region's economies during the past fifteen years. Indeed, South Asia is, as of 2009, the fastest growing region in the world. Between 1997 and 2002, the average gross domestic product (GDP) growth rate (in real terms) for South Asia was 4.9 percent, compared to 4.2 percent for emerging and developing economies, 2.1 percent for the original members of the Association of Southeast Asian Nations (ASEAN-5), and 2.7 percent for the European Union (EU). The corresponding average growth rates for the years 2003–2007 were 8.3 percent, 7.3 percent, 5.9 percent, and 2.5 percent, respectively.[1] India's annual GDP growth rate increased from 5.5

percent between 1991 and 2000 to 6.8 percent between 2001 and 2005. The annual GDP of Bangladesh increased from 4.8 percent to 5.4 percent during the same period, while Pakistan's annual GDP increased from 3.9 percent to 4.8 percent.[2] India's GDP growth rate between 1981–1982 and 1990–1991 was an average of 5.6 percent per annum. It increased to 6.1 percent per annum during the period 1992–1993 and 2002–2003.[3] Estimated GDP growth in 2006 was 8 percent for Afghanistan, 6.6 percent for Bangladesh, 8.8 percent for Bhutan, 9.2 percent for India, 18 percent for the Maldives, 6.6 percent for Pakistan, and 7.5 percent for Sri Lanka. Only the estimate for Nepal was low, at 1.9 percent.[4] These are portents of the ability of these countries to sustain—if not to further increase—their current rates of growth.

The fundamentals of these countries' economies appear to be sound, in spite of ongoing political strife and the global recession. Most of these countries are incurring only modest deficits in their current account. They have stable exchange rates, sustainable ratios of external debt to GDP, and comfortable foreign exchange reserves. They have also kept their rates of inflation reasonably well under control.

One of the most significant developments conducive to achieving economic integration in the region has been the convergence of these nations' macroeconomic policies. All the countries of the region have embarked on the path of the liberalization of their economies, starting with Sri Lanka in the late 1970s, followed by Bangladesh and Pakistan from the late 1980s, and by India in the early 1990s. As a result, the average most-favored-nation (MFN) customs duty came down to 20.2 percent in India (March 2004), 17.3 percent in Pakistan (2003), 16.3 percent in Bangladesh (2004–2005), and 11.3 percent in Sri Lanka (2004).[5]

In the budget for the 2007–2008 financial year, the import duties on nonagricultural products in India were reduced to 10 percent, bringing the trade-weighted average tariff down to 9 percent, compared with 87 percent in 1991.[6] In response to a verdict by the World Trade Organization (WTO) Dispute Settlement Mechanism, the government of India eliminated all quantitative restrictions (QRs), including those on agricultural products, between 2000 and 2001. At the same time, negotiations were held for raising some of the unusually low agricultural tariffs to higher levels. In some cases they were elevated to 100 percent.[7] In April 2007, the average tariffs on agricultural products were 40.8 percent.[8]

In addition to substantially reducing their peak and average tariffs, South Asian countries have implemented many measures for removing other restrictions and regulations that were earlier characteristic features of their economies. These include simplification and rationalization of their earlier system of dual or multiple exchange rates. Most South Asian countries are now allowing market forces to determine the exchange rates for their currencies. They have also introduced convertibility on current accounts, and some have gone quite far in making their currencies convertible on capital accounts as well.

For example, to facilitate increased flow of foreign direct investment (FDI), India introduced procedural simplifications, increased caps on equity participation, and brought more sectors under automatic approval. To facilitate portfolio investment, it allowed foreign institutional investment and derivative trading by foreign players. It also lifted the ban on forward trading and allowed the carry-forward system in the stock market, interest rates swaps, and currency forward trading. Other South Asian countries, particularly Pakistan, Bangladesh, and Sri Lanka, have gone even further in the direction of capital account convertibility. For example, in Pakistan, apart from allowing 100 percent foreign equity, there are no bars on repatriation of capital, profits, or royalties. In addition, individuals, firms, and companies are allowed to freely undertake all international transactions through the interbank market.[9]

As a result of the trade liberalization measures adopted by the South Asian countries, exports now contribute significantly to their GDP growth, and the trade openness of their economies has increased. The trade-GDP ratio of these countries increased from 18.37 percent in 1991 to 30.41 percent in 2005.[10] Nevertheless, the share of intraregional trade to total trade has remained low, hovering around 5 percent. This figure seems insignificant when compared to the trend in other regions. For example, intraregional trade accounted for 67 percent of total trade of the EU, 62 percent of the members of the North American Free Trade Agreement (NAFTA), and 26 percent of the ASEAN countries.[11]

However, there are some silver linings in South Asia. First, there is a trend of an increase in intraregional trade, from 3.2 percent of total trade in 1981 to 4.9 percent in 1998.[12] Second, a considerable amount of informal trade is taking place among the countries of the region, which is not reflected in the official figures for intraregional trade. Estimates of informal trade indicate that it is almost as large as formal trade.[13] Third, for some countries of the region, the importance of other regional countries as a source of imports or a destination for exports has increased significantly. For example, Nepal's exports to South Asian Association for Regional Cooperation (SAARC) countries, as a percentage of its total exports, increased from 20.58 percent in 1996 to 54.40 percent in 2005. The commensurate increase for Sri Lanka during this period was from 2.67 percent to 8.82 percent. Nepal's imports from SAARC countries as a percentage of its total imports increased from 33.89 percent to 47.26 percent during the same period, and those of Sri Lanka rose from 13.65 percent to 18.32 percent.[14]

There has also been a dramatic increase in recent years in India's exports to SAARC countries, mainly because the trade liberalization measures that these countries have adopted have allowed India to exercise its natural competitive advantage. For example, between 1988 and 1995, India's exports to Bangladesh increased by 565 percent, to Sri Lanka by 425 percent, to the Maldives by 400 percent, and to Pakistan by about 380 percent (in spite of trade being confined to a limited number of goods permitted by the Pakistani government). Exports to Nepal regained and exceeded the level reached in 1989. India's exports to Nepal declined sharply between 1990 and 1994 because of the partial freeze in economic relations in 1989 due to a political misunderstanding. Exports to Bhutan increased twelvefold between 1991 and 1995.[15] This trend has by and large continued since then. Between 2003 and 2006, India's exports to Bangladesh increased by over 23 percent, by 89 percent to Sri Lanka, by 197 percent to Pakistan, by 74 percent to Nepal, by 94 percent to the Maldives, and by 53 percent to Bhutan.[16] These figures, however, do not reflect any significant increase in India's exports to SAARC countries as a proportion of its total exports. This is mainly due to even more dramatic increases in India's exports to Southeast Asian and East Asian countries.

South Asian countries are incurring huge opportunity costs by not cooperating with one another. Using an augmented gravity model, a Research and Information System for Developing Countries (RIS) analysis found that nearly 74 percent of potential intraregional trade remained to be realized in 2006. The potential that year was estimated at nearly $40 billion, compared with the $10.5 billion of formal trade that actually took place. This potential would be much higher if the impact of liberalization of trade in services and of augmentation in intraregional investment flows were also factored into the model.[17]

It has been argued on an intuitive basis that cooperation between India and Nepal on the taming of common rivers will result in savings by India of billions of dollars, as it will enable the country to control the flooding and silting of its fertile lands, both of which occur on a large scale every year. It will also generate additional income, by creating additional capacity for irrigation and electricity generation. Economic integration with India will enable Pakistan to attract higher inflows of FDI by enlarging its market. Moreover, by being able to import goods and services from India at relatively cheaper costs, Pakistan will significantly enhance the competitiveness of its exports—not to mention its economy as a whole—both to the region and to the rest of the world.

Steps toward Regional Integration

South Asia is a late starter in the movement for regional integration. It remained untouched by the first wave of regionalism that swept parts of Africa and Latin America in the early 1960s.[18] The initiative for regional cooperation in South Asia was taken by President Ziaur Rahman of Bangladesh in 1980 and it assumed an institutionalized form only in 1985, with the creation of SAARC.

For nearly ten years after the association was established, cooperation under SAARC did not extend to the hardcore economic areas of trade, manufacturing, money, and finance. Trade was brought into SAARC's ambit only in 1991, with the signing of the agreement on the South Asian Preferential Trade Arrangement (SAPTA). But SAPTA was operationalized only four years later, in 1995, when the first round of negotiations concluded and the concessions exchanged under it were duly notified. After 1995, two more rounds of negotiations were completed and a fourth round was in progress when the process was interrupted by a virtual hiatus of more than two years in regional cooperation under SAARC, following the 1999 military coup in Pakistan.

The tariff concessions exchanged during the three rounds of negotiations under SAPTA hardly made any impact on intraregional trade transactions. Apart from proving laborious and time-consuming, the commodity-by-commodity negotiations under SAPTA suffered from several other deficiencies. The tariff cuts were not deep, the trade coverage was inadequate, and some of the most important sectors of trade were left out of negotiations. Some of the tariff concessions were offered on products not even traded between member countries. Finally, no beginning was made toward the removal of nontariff barriers.

The idea of creating a South Asian Free Trade Area (SAFTA) was first mooted in the SAARC summit held in Delhi in 1995, when the heads of government declared their intention to establish a free trade area by 2005. At the Ninth SAARC Summit, held in Malé in 1997, they decided to move up the date for establishing SAFTA, to 2001. At the same time, they established a Group of Eminent Persons (GEP) to articulate a vision for South Asian cooperation over the next twenty years and to draw up a road map to realize that vision.

In its report submitted in 1998,[19] the GEP projected a vision of South Asia moving toward a free trade area by the year 2010, a customs union by 2015, and an economic union by 2020. It spelled out the concrete measures that had to be taken at each stage to realize the vision. The GEP made two other important contributions. First, it pointed out that there was no way the region could make an automatic transition from SAPTA to SAFTA. To move toward a free trade area, it was necessary for the member countries to have a separate treaty establishing such an area. The GEP laid down the timeline for starting the negotiations and for operationalizing the free trade area. It underscored that—unlike SAPTA, which was legally justified on the basis of the flexible preferential arrangement among developing countries specified in the WTO's "enabling clause"—SAFTA would have to be justified under the more rigorous provisions of Article XXIV of the General Agreement on Trade and Tariffs (GATT 1994). The SAFTA treaty in particular would have to comply with the two essential provisions under Article XXIV, that is, adhering to a time frame and a schedule for the establishment of a free trade agreement (FTA), and covering "substantially all the trade."

Second, the GEP pointed out that the experience of regionalism in other parts of the developing world demonstrated that the principal reason for the failure of regional groupings among developing countries was their inability to provide for and implement adequate measures to enable their less developed members to benefit equitably from economic integration. The GEP, therefore, recommended a set of special measures in favor of the least-developed countries (LDCs) that are members of SAARC. Apart from such traditional measures in favor of LDCs—including allowing them a longer time frame to reach the stage of free trade, giving them flexibility to decide the sequencing of the removal of trade restrictions, and enabling them to resort to stronger safeguard measures in the event of a surge in imports and consequent disruption of domestic industry—the GEP suggested the creation of a reasonably large fund to develop the infrastructure, human resources, and export production capacity of the LDCs. It was felt that without the removal of supply-side constraints, which required sizeable investments, the LDCs were unlikely to derive equitable benefits from economic integration under SAFTA.

The GEP report was not discussed in its entirety at the Tenth SAARC Summit, held in Colombo, Sri Lanka in 1998. There was, therefore, no endorsement of the vision articulated in the report, let alone of the time frames suggested for reaching the milestones en route to the final destination of an economic union. However, some of the recommendations of the report were picked up at random and endorsed in general terms. For example, the desirability of adopting special measures for the LDCs was endorsed in principle. Another major step taken at the Tenth Summit was the establishment of an expert group to prepare a draft treaty for SAFTA by 2001.

In a related development, at their meeting on the eve of that summit, the Council of Ministers asked the secretary-general of SAARC to prepare a draft statement on the future vision of SAARC, and transmit it to the member states by January 1999, so that the respective ministers could consider it at their informal meetings alongside the United Nations (UN) General Assembly session in New York. Unfortunately, this proposal was not pursued, nor was there any follow-up on the other recommendations of the GEP report, partly because Indo-Pakistan relations deteriorated shortly after the tenth summit and brought the entire SAARC process to a halt. Only in 2002 did it become possible to hold the next SAARC summit, in Kathmandu. That gathering did not result in any major decisions but tried to get the process of cooperation under SAARC back on track.

The atmosphere of drift and despondency on the issue of establishing a free trade area in South Asia was transformed by the sudden and unexpected but very welcome decision at the Twelfth SAARC Summit in Islamabad in 2004 to sign a framework agreement for SAFTA. The agreement formally came into force on January 1, 2005, after the member states ratified it. It was not operationalized until July 2006, when the liberalization program under it came into force. Thus, the beginning of regional integration in South Asia through a free trade area was made some six years after the GEP report laid down the schedule. At the time that SAFTA was operationalized, Pakistan announced that it would not adhere to the commitments it had made under SAFTA, so far as its trade with India was concerned.

One of the major deficiencies of the SAFTA framework agreement was that it left unnegotiated many issues critical to the operationalization of the free trade area.[20] These included the establishment of rules of origin and of sensitive lists of products, the compensation to the LDCs for the loss of revenue due to the elimination of customs duties, and the scope and modalities for extending technical assistance to the LDCs. These negotiations were duly completed during the two-year interval stipulated in the agreement. As a result, the SAFTA agreement now has an annex[21] containing one of the most liberal rules of origin provided for in any free trade regime. The mechanism for compensating the LDC members for loss in revenue constitutes another annex.[22] Yet another annex[23] contains the sensitive lists. By way of extending technical assistance to the LDCs, all that has been agreed on in Annex II[24] is to identify the areas in which such assistance could be given. The non-LDC member countries made no firm commitment in this issue; their obligation is only on a best-endeavor basis.

In the liberalization program, the LDC members have been provided with a number of special dispensations. They have been given longer periods to reduce their tariff barriers and to reach the free trade mark of 0 to 5 percent tariff levels. They have also been given greater flexibility in establishing their sensitive lists and in applying the antidumping and countervailing measures. Another significant development has been that three member countries—Bangladesh, India, and Nepal—have established separate smaller lists of sensitive products for the LDCs. Among these, only the Indian list for the LDCs is significantly smaller than its list for the non-LDCs (763 for the LDCs as compared to 884 for non-LDCs). India has since further reduced its sensitive list for the LDCs.

In spite of these positive features, SAFTA remains a deeply flawed agreement, and this by political choice:

- The goal of free trade—that is, reducing tariffs to the 0 to 5 percent level—is going to be realized over a very long period of time, between 2013 to 2016. By then, the whole process may be irrelevant because tariffs may already have been reduced to even lower levels as a result of multilateral trade negotiations under WTO and under bilateral FTAs between SAARC member countries.
- There is no commitment to phase out the sensitive lists within a timebound framework. The agreement merely stipulates that the lists be reviewed at least once every four years "with a view to reducing the number of items." India's sensitive list under SAFTA is more than three times as large as the one it offered in the latest round of negotiations for an FTA with ASEAN.
- There is no commitment to eliminate nontariff and para-tariff barriers within a set time frame.
- There is no specific provision in the agreement to adopt measures of deeper integration.
- There is no specific provision or road map for moving beyond free trade. The agreement is likewise silent on the goal of establishing a customs union or economic union in South Asia, as recommended by the GEP.
- Finally, Pakistan's decision not to extend its obligations under the agreement to its trade with India excludes potentially the largest segment

of regional trade from the SAFTA process. This makes regional economic integration, *ab initio*, a nonstarter in South Asia.

If we look at SAARC's twenty-five-year history, it would appear that the member countries have not even accepted the goal of regional economic integration in South Asia, let alone adopted measures to reach that goal. The principal reason behind this is a lack of trust among the countries, with the possible exception of relations between India and Sri Lanka, due to political differences. In the absence of trust, the member countries have simply refused to play even positive-sum games, lest the other party benefit. There is a tendency on the part of member countries to make things deliberately difficult for neighbors in order to strike undefined and undefinable future bargains in the context of the disputes that remain to be resolved. But by far the biggest stumbling block has been the perpetually tense and often hostile political relations between India and Pakistan. These two countries together share 90 percent of the GDP of the region, 84.9 percent of its population, and 86 percent of its total exports. These broad aggregative figures show that without the integration of the economies of India and Pakistan, all the talks, negotiations, and actions intended to achieve economic integration in South Asia comprise a game played on the periphery in order to hide the reality at the center. This game, by its very nature, is futile and largely unproductive.

Various calculations have been made of the possible gains in trade if the normal trade between India and Pakistan were fully liberalized. The most common estimate is that the trade between the two countries has the potential to reach $10 billion annually within the next three to five years. That would be within the present static framework. If, however, one takes into account the influence of dynamic factors unleashed by economic integration—such as enlargement of the market, increased inflow of foreign investment, growth in the competitiveness of Pakistan's exports, and restructuring of industries in both countries—then the potential trade transactions between the two countries could very well reach the level of $40 billion to $50 billion annually within ten years.

Due to the lack of genuine commitment to regional integration, most of the decisions made by SAARC are of the nature of public relations campaigns designed to impress domestic audiences and foreign powers. Thus the entire SAARC process is an exercise in competitive deception.[25] The institutions are created, and decisions, recommendations, declarations, and even legal instruments are signed with the implicit understanding and intention not to allow the institutions to function effectively and not to abide by the obligations incorporated in the agreed-upon documents.

The second reason why SAARC has not succeeded is that member countries, particularly India and Pakistan, have allowed progress, in both their bilateral relations and under the SAARC framework, to be held hostage to their largely exaggerated and misplaced security concerns. In fact, the South Asian countries have become security states more comprehensively and pathologically than most other states in the world. They remain obsessed with state security while the rest of the world is relatively relaxed about it and increasingly turning to human security. Because of this obsession, South Asian states put up formidable obstacles to the movement of people and ideas, without which there can be no mutual trust; and without trust there can be no cooperation.

The third reason for the failure of regionalism in South Asia has been the reluctance of the larger countries, particularly India, to discharge the responsibilities that devolve upon them by virtue of being the stronger economies of the region. Experts on regional integration have assigned a key role to hegemonic or dominant powers, to provide both the leadership that will carry forward the process of economic integration in a region, and the financial resources that will ensure an equitable distribution of the gains from such integration. For example, the role of France and Germany is frequently cited as a factor in the EU's success. By contrast, the first wave of regional integration among developing countries collapsed mainly because economically stronger member states did not comply with provisions in the relevant FTAs for the adoption of special measures in favor of the less-developed member countries. India has adopted an unusually timid approach in this regard. It has taken India two decades, since the suggestion was first mooted, to extend duty-free and quota-free access to its market for manufactured products from the LDCs of the SAARC region. This measure came into effect only on December 31, 2007. Along with other economically strong South Asian countries, India also took no interest in the GEP's proposal to create a large fund to assist in the development of LDC member countries of SAARC. The negotiations on a Comprehensive Economic Partnership Agreement (CEPA) with Sri Lanka began almost three years ago, but the agreement is yet to be finalized and signed. And these are only a few examples.

In order to translate into reality the vision of South Asian economic integration, it is essential that the basic constraints to such integration, all of which are of a political nature, be removed. Pakistan should make a decision to deal with India across the entire spectrum of economic relations in a full-fledged manner, mainly driven by market forces. Doing so would enable both the countries to come out of the current state-security syndrome and give primacy to human security. Finally, India, and to a large extent Pakistan, should agree to bear the main burden of South Asian integration. This might seem a negative-sum game in the short run, but it would turn out to be a hugely successful positive-sum game in the medium and long run. If these assumptions come true, then things will start falling in place. There will not only be a rapid movement toward economic integration in South Asia but these countries together would also be able to link more effectively to the rest of Asia and the global economy.

Implications of New Regionalism and the Rise of Asia

The advent of new regionalism has coincided with the current phase of globalization, which began in the mid-1980s. The new regionalism is competition-driven. Competitive gains are sought by enlarging markets and pooling larger resources for investment in science and technology. Under the second wave of regionalism, important mega-groupings have been formed, bringing together countries both big and small, both developed and developing, and not necessarily contiguous. Countries outside the mega-groupings have, for fear of being isolated and discriminated against, revived their old groupings and established new groupings for economic integration.[26] South Asian countries also have to embrace economic integration in order to avoid isolation and discrimination.

The economic power balance in the world has shifted toward Asia, largely because several of the Asian economies have displayed unprecedented dynamism. As a result, there is a de facto linking of the economies of Asia at a very fast pace, essentially driven by the market. There is a veritable competition among Asian economies to mingle with one another. For instance, Indian companies are going to China, South Korea, Japan, and Thailand and establishing themselves there, and companies from these countries are establishing themselves in India. This activity is obviously generating new trade and contributing to the changes taking place in the entire geography of world trade. In the past five to ten years, the rates of growth of India's trade with China and the ASEAN countries have been phenomenally high. The share of Asia in India's trade increased from 20.65 percent in 2000 to 28.31 percent in 2004.[27]

In more recent years, India's trade with China has grown almost 30 percent per year. The total trade has grown from a mere $400 million about ten years ago to close to $40 billion today. The rate of growth of India's trade with the ASEAN countries has been nearly 27 percent per annum during this period.[28]

The market-driven integration among the major economies of Asia is being sought to be strengthened and institutionalized by FTAs that these countries have concluded or are in the process of concluding with one another. For example, India has FTAs already in place or under negotiation or consideration with practically all the countries in Asia, as does China. Major Asian countries such as India and China are not only trying to link with each other through bilateral FTAs but are also negotiating FTAs with the only existing regional economic integration grouping in Asia, ASEAN. Thus, for the first time in the postwar years, a pan-Asian structure of economic linkages is emerging. For years there have been pancontinental structures, both political and economic, in Europe, Latin America and Africa, but they have been conspicuously absent in Asia. The Indian prime minister Jawaharlal Nehru made a valiant attempt to create such a structure in Asia at the Asian Relations Conference held in Delhi in March 1947, but not much came of it. Today, mainly driven by market forces, a pan-Asian economic structure is on the horizon. The East Asian Summit

Conferences, which have been held annually since the end of 2005, constitute the furthest point reached in this direction.

India is playing an active role in this emerging scenario. It has concluded FTAs with Singapore and Thailand and a CEPA with Singapore, which provides, among other items, for the liberalization of investment flows and trade in services. As of 2009, negotiations for an FTA between India and ASEAN are at an advanced stage and likely to be concluded soon. Study groups or task forces have been set up to explore the possibility of India entering into free trade or economic cooperation agreements with Malaysia, Japan, Korea, and China.

South Asian economic integration should have an important place in this wider movement of new regionalism in Asia. This is mainly because the South Asian countries can link with the Pan-Asian movement more effectively and meaningfully if they do it together. Without economic integration among themselves, South Asian countries will be linking with dynamic economies of Asia and with the emerging pan-Asian movement with their hands tied behind their back. This underscores the importance of achieving economic integration in South Asia as a springboard for linking with the emerging Asian economic community. Moreover, if India alone and not the whole of South Asia moves toward East Asia, the East Asian countries will benefit from access to the growing Indian market. The South Asian countries, which have a better claim on the Indian market, will be left behind.

The South Asian countries are in an advantageous position for seeking linkages with the wider Asian and global economies. In spite of the frequent turmoil, the current world economic downturn, and domestic political upheaval, the South Asian countries have emerged as dynamic economies after a prolonged period of sluggish growth. Now even the outside world has developed stakes in the success of South Asia's economic endeavors. Moreover, in South Asia itself, we have the example of the Indo–Sri Lanka Bilateral Free Trade Agreement (ILBFTA) of 1998, which has contributed significantly to expanding trade between the two countries and moving capital from India to Sri Lanka. As of 2009, the two countries were on the verge of signing a CEPA, which will also cover trade in services and investment. If this can happen between India and Sri Lanka, there is no reason why it cannot happen across all of South Asia.

Economic integration in South Asia—or anywhere, for that matter—cannot be achieved by liberalizing trade in goods alone. Besides, there are strong reasons to believe that South Asia is poised for genuine comprehensive economic integration. This is because, due to historical reasons and geographical proximity, there is a great deal of *de facto* linking of the economies of the South Asian countries.[29] There is already a large-scale clandestine regional movement of goods and services, including labor and capital. New linkages are also emerging in the cultural, social, and human rights fields. All these developments warrant an ambitious approach toward regional integration in South Asia.

Road Map for Regional Economic Integration

Moving toward an Economic Union

The South Asian countries should without any further delay accept at the highest political level the objective of a South Asian economic union. This has already been achieved in Europe and to a large extent in North America. In Asia, the ASEAN countries in 2003 agreed to establish the ASEAN Economic Community by the year 2020, consisting of a single market in which goods, services, capital, and skilled labor would move freely. Subsequently, this deadline was moved up to 2015. In Africa also, the goal of an African economic union, with an accompanying charter, has already been adopted, though progress in realizing this goal has been slow. The South Asian heads of government should take a decision to achieve an economic union within the time frame suggested by the GEP, that is, by 2020. This deadline can be met.

Measures within SAFTA

Reducing and Phasing Out Sensitive Lists

The sensitive lists provided in Annex I to the SAFTA agreement are not conducive to achieving regional integration in South Asia. First, the decision to adopt a percentage of total tariff lines—in this case 20 percent—as a benchmark is misplaced. Second, several countries (Bangladesh, Nepal, and Pakistan) have exceeded even this benchmark. The benchmark should be a percentage of the total trade and not of tariff lines. In order to comply with Article XXIV of the GATT 1994, at least 80 percent of total trade should have been covered under the liberalization program, but this requirement will not be met, since nearly 53 percent of current intra-SAARC imports are currently restricted under the sensitive lists. This is worse than in bilateral FTAs. Less than 14 percent of Sri Lanka's exports are covered by the Indian sensitive list under the ILBFTA, but nearly 42 percent of Sri Lanka's exports are covered in the Indian sensitive list under the SAFTA agreement.[30] Moreover, the phasing out of the sensitive lists should be included in the schedule for achieving free trade, as required under Article XXIV. As far as the LDC members are concerned, it is not enough for the non-LDC members to have smaller sensitive lists for the LDCs. These lists must be established in consultation with the LDCs to ensure that their main export products are not included in the lists. The LDCs have a very narrow range of exportable goods, and therefore the inclusion of even a small percentage of these goods in the sensitive lists can render the free trade area of little consequence to them. In 2008 India reduced its sensitive list for the LDCs to 500. This is a laudable initiative. The list should be further reviewed to ensure that goods of export interest to Bangladesh—the main beneficiary of India's liberalization under SAFTA—are entirely excluded from the list.

Nontariff and Para-tariff Barriers

There can be no economic integration without the removal of all nontariff and para-tariff barriers, except those that are compatible with the WTO. In spite of the progress made by individual member countries in the identification and notification of nontariff and para-tariff measures, and the response to these measures received from other member countries, there is unlikely to be much progress in removing these barriers. This is mainly because of politics and lack of trust. Member countries do not even accept that they maintain any nontariff or para-tariff barriers. Therefore, the scrutiny and the final identification of these barriers should be left to a neutral expert group whose recommendations should be binding on the member countries concerned. The SAARC members should also agree on a time frame for finally identifying these barriers on an objective basis. The time limit should be one year, as provided in the GEP report; for eliminating the barriers, the time limit should be three years.

Special Measures for the Least-Developed Countries

The areas identified for technical assistance in Annex II of the SAFTA agreement are of little consequence because the member countries have not committed to provide such assistance. In fact, technical assistance contributes only marginally to removing supply-side constraints. What is really needed are investment funds to help LDCs achieve higher levels of development, and particularly to enhance their export production capacity. In the EU, a conscious effort has been made to bring the economically weaker countries up to or as near as possible to the development level of the stronger ones. To achieve this goal, a development fund has been created, out of which resources are made available to the economically weaker members to help them to catch up. The resources in this fund are not token amounts. For example, the total resources made available to Ireland after it joined the EU as a new member amounted to over 3 percent of its gross national product (GNP). The resources made available to Poland after its accession to EU amounted to €90 billion over a five-year period, of which €27 billion was paid out during the first year.

The GEP has made a similar recommendation for bringing up the level of development of the least-developed member countries of South Asia. It has proposed the creation of a large fund (the amount mentioned informally was $5 billion) to be contributed by the non-LDC members, according to an agreed criterion of capacity to pay. Going by any such criterion, it was obvious that India would be required to provide almost 70 percent of the resources for this fund, with Pakistan coming next. This is inescapable to ensure the success of the FTA in South Asia. A contribution on this scale will indeed be a burden on India in the short term, but it is likely to redound to its benefit in the medium and long term.

A scheme like the South Asian Development Fund (SADF), now renamed the SAARC Development Fund (SDF), is unlikely to contribute significantly to achieving regional integration in South Asia. The SADF has been in existence for eleven years and still languishes at a $6.5 million funding level. Recently India and Pakistan have announced contributions to the fund of $100 million and $70 million, respectively, but based on past experience, there is no guarantee that these amounts will really be paid up and utilized. India's contribution of $100 million, for instance, has been on the table since the Twelfth SAARC Summit in 2004.

Trade Facilitation

The mere elimination of barriers to trade is not enough to ensure free movement of goods. It is difficult to operationalize an FTA unless it is accompanied by a set of measures for trade facilitation. Apart from removing tariff and nontariff barriers, it is essential to remove institutional and physical barriers to the movement of goods across borders and through the territory of member countries.

Years before SAFTA came into being, mechanisms for removing physical, legal, and institutional barriers to trade were set up under SAARC. But these mechanisms just scratch the surface. Even when ideas have been put forward and recommendations have been made, the member countries have been unable to implement them for want of political will. And it is very unlikely that progress will be made in the near future unless the political resistance to necessary measures is overcome. The villain of the piece in this area, as in several others, has been the obsessive security concerns of the member states.

Trade facilitation is covered in the SAFTA agreement in Article 3 among the principles governing SAFTA, and in Article 8 under the title "Additional Measures." Seven out of the thirteen additional measures relate to trade facilitation. These include harmonization of standards; reciprocal recognition of tests, accreditation, and certification of products; simplification and harmonization of customs clearance procedures; harmonization of national customs classification; simplification and harmonization of import licensing and registration procedures; simplification of banking procedures for import financing; and transit facilities for efficient intra-SAARC trade. The agreement, however, does not provide any mechanism for pursuing any of these ideas, nor does it lay down any deadlines by which these measures must be taken.

The pre-SAFTA mechanisms in this area consist of the SAARC Group on Customs Cooperation established in 1996 (which has so far held five meetings) and the SAARC Standing Group on Standards, Quality Control and Measurement, set up in 1998. Under the latter, a SAARC Standards Coordination Board has been established as a precursor to the South Asian Regional Standards Organizations. The main reason why progress has been confined to the proliferation of institutional arrangements and their meetings is that countries rush through harmonization and mutual recognition of standards only when they decide to integrate their economies. Since such a decision is yet to be taken in South Asia, there is very little progress in the areas of standards, quality control, and measurement.

Once the political commitment to integration is made, it will become important to build appropriate provisions for trade facilitation (which have already been identified) into the SAFTA treaty.

Transport

By far the most important trade facilitation measure is the availability of efficient and adequate transport facilities for the movement of goods. SAARC member countries have long recognized the importance of transport for facilitating regional trade; a mechanism for cooperation in this field has been in existence for close to two decades. In the declaration adopted at the Twelfth SAARC Summit in Islamabad in 2004, it was stated that "for accelerated and balanced growth it is essential to strengthen transportation, transit, and communication links across the region."

In spite of all this, transport connectivity across the region leaves much to be desired. One of the major constraints to cooperation in this area is the refusal of some member countries to allow transit facilities through their territory for goods and persons from other countries, either to other parts of the same country or to other countries, whether within or outside the region. Bangladesh continues to deny transit facilities through its territories for the movement of Indian goods or persons to other parts of India. The opportunity costs for India that result from this denial are horrendous. For example, today it takes forty-five days to transport a container from Delhi to Dhaka; if through railway traffic were permitted by Bangladesh, it would take two to three days. The southern border of the Indian state of Tripura is only 75 kilometers (km) from the Chittagong port in Bangladesh, but since Indian goods are denied access to the Chittagong port, goods from Agartala must cover a distance of 1,645 km to reach Kolkata. If transit were allowed through the Bangladesh territory, the distance for reaching the Kolkata port from Agartala would be reduced to 350 km. If shipment of Assam tea were allowed through the Chittagong airport, which is the traditional route, it would be possible to cut the journey time by 60 percent. For a landlocked country like Afghanistan, a new member of SAARC, cooperation under the association has little meaning if it is not granted transit facilities for its goods through Pakistan in order to reach other SAARC countries. Similarly, Bhutan and Nepal can make large savings in transporting their goods to destinations outside the region if India would extend transit facilities so that their goods could reach ports in Bangladesh.

Thus, one of the most important political decisions to be taken by the SAARC countries to achieve South Asian economic integration is simultaneous agreement to provide transit facilities through their territories for other member countries' goods.

Measures of Deeper Integration

Measures of deeper integration confer immense benefits on countries participating in regional integration, over and above those that accrue from the enlargement of the market and other static and dynamic benefits that flow from an FTA. These measures include the liberalization of trade in services, freer flow of investment, joint development of infrastructure (particularly transport and energy), cooperation in the financial and monetary fields, cooperation in upgrading skills and technologies in specific sectors, harmonization or coordination of macroeconomic policies, development of common policies on issues under negotiation in international forums, and the adoption of common strategies for negotiations in these forums. In the treaty that established the Mercado Común del Sur (MERCOSUR)—the regional trade grouping that includes Argentina, Brazil, Paraguay, and Uruguay—there is a specific provision for formulating common positions on international economic issues and negotiating these issues on behalf of the group.

There is no provision for deeper integration built into the SAFTA agreement aside from a brief mention of some of the measures for such integration in Article 8, under the title "Additional Measures." These measures include removal of barriers to intra-SAARC investment, macroeconomic consultations, rules for fair competition, and development of communications and transport. However, as in the case of trade facilitation measures, with respect to these deeper integration measures also, the agreement provides no mechanism for follow-up, no procedure for negotiation, and no deadline for implementation. Besides, Article 8 is couched in such general terms that it implies no commitment on the part of the member states to pursue any of the measures it contains.

The declaration adopted at the Twelfth SAARC Summit refers to some of the measures of deeper integration, particularly to South Asian energy cooperation; strengthening transportation, transit, and communications links across the region; and the possibility of setting up a South Asian Development Bank. But the very fact that these measures have been kept out of the SAFTA agreement, and mentioned only in a declaratory form, implies that the member countries do not want to undertake any commitments in these areas.

Deeper integration measures are among the essential preconditions for a preferential trading arrangement to work. South Asia cannot move toward a customs or economic union without implementing measures of deeper integration, particularly in the financial, fiscal, and monetary fields.

Measures of deeper integration are of particular significance to the LDC members of a regional grouping. They are the most effective and direct means of enabling these countries to derive equitable benefits from an FTA. The LDCs are likely to benefit most from coordinated development of infrastructure; larger inflows of FDI because of the enlargement of the market; cooperation in the fields of science and technology; cooperation in upgrading skills, developing human resources, and enhancing the general competitiveness of the economy;

and cooperation in developing the service sectors in the region and in liberalizing trade in services and investment flows. Some measures can be specifically designed and adjusted to suit their conditions and interests.[31]

Trade in Services

Most of the new-generation FTAs include services within their scope. That services are *not* included in the SAFTA agreement is a major lacuna because of the salience acquired by services both in the GDP of the SAARC member countries and in their informal trade transactions. An RIS/Institute of Policy Studies of Sri Lanka (IPS) study for the South Asia Center for Policy Studies (SACEPS) suggests that South Asia as a whole has strong comparative advantage vis-à-vis the rest of the world in commercial services, especially in the export of semiskilled and unskilled labor. This has been demonstrated by the latest data on remittance to their home countries from South Asian nationals working abroad. South Asia has emerged as the second-largest remittance recipient (20 percent) after Latin America. The RIS/IPS study has identified six service areas as having high potential for cooperation among SAARC member countries:

- Telecommunications and information technology (IT)
- Aviation
- Agriculture research, standards, and testing
- Surface transport
- Tourism
- Medical services

To these should be added labor and educational services. In spite of the state regulations to prevent free movement of labor across the region, labor is already moving from one country to another on a sizable scale, mainly in a clandestine manner. Attempts to restrict such movement have led to immense human suffering and, in several cases, the violation of human rights. Labor movements across the region have also assumed the character of trafficking in women and children, in gross violation of their human rights, and in narcotics. There is therefore a very strong case, on humanitarian grounds, to regularize the illegal movement of labor and to prevent human trafficking. Measures to this end should have been included in the SAFTA agreement itself. Moreover, labor market integration is bound to be a central component of the proposed South Asian economic union. It is essential to facilitate labor movement across the region for genuine economic purposes and to regulate such movement for noneconomic purposes.

Some social services, particularly education and health, offer considerable scope for cooperation among SAARC countries. These services are already being provided on a fairly substantial scale by some member countries, particularly India, to other member countries, through Mode-2 of service provision under the General Agreement on Trade in Services (GATS)—that is, the movement of consumers seeking services. The problem with such movement of services is that much of it takes place in a clandestine manner that disadvantages and inconveniences the service seekers. This calls for harmonization of educational and related standards, transparent rules and regulations and procedures for seeking such services under Mode-2, and provisions for making things easier for the service seekers. There is also a need for the coordinated development of such services in the region, particularly for assistance to the LDC members in developing such services. The private sector, of course, has an important role to play in this arena by establishing institutions that will provide such services in other member countries, either on their own or jointly with local service providers.

An important development has been that the need to integrate trade in services with the SAFTA process was recognized at the political level as soon as the agreement was signed. The declaration adopted at the Thirteenth SAARC Summit, in Dhaka in 2005, called for a study to find out how services could be integrated with SAFTA. In its meeting in April 2006, the SAARC Ministerial Council agreed to include services in SAFTA and formed a committee to examine the issue. The Fourteenth SAARC Summit Declaration also emphasized the importance of integrating trade in services in SAFTA. As a result of these decisions, country studies on trade in services were carried out and later amalgamated into a regional study. A decision was taken to prepare a draft SAARC framework agreement on trade in services, and RIS was ask to undertake this task and submit a draft report.

Even after the draft is prepared, facilitating and regularizing trade in services in the SAARC region will likely encounter hurdles of a political nature. Problems will arise on the issue of movement of labor, which has security and other adverse economic implications, and on the question of the right to establish the movement of services under Mode-3 of the GATS. In any event, the framework agreement should lay down the time frame for initiating and completing negotiations in selected sectors as well as a schedule for the horizontal exchange of concessions.

Trade-Investment Linkages

Forging strong trade-investment links in the South Asian region is essential both to reinforce and to take full advantage of the process of economic integration in the region. It is not possible to take full advantage of the enlargement of the market brought about by trade liberalization without freer movement of capital. This is particularly true for LDCs and smaller economies of the region. Their chronic imbalance of trade with their larger neighbors can be best compensated by moving capital from the larger countries to the smaller ones. Therefore, the removal of constraints to movement of capital in the region is necessary to stimulate trade-creating investment in the smaller countries, and for efficiency-seeking restructuring of selected industrial sectors in the region as a whole. It is only through such restructuring that economies of scale can be attained and advantages of specialization can be reaped to the fullest extent.

The limited experience of free trade in South Asia—that is, bilateral free trade between India and Sri Lanka and between India and Nepal—has shown that free trade has served as an incentive for Indian companies to invest in these countries. A large part of Nepal's manufacturing capacity was created under the stimulus of free trade. This experience has been repeated to some extent recently in Sri Lanka.[32]

In the era of globalization, investment flows have played a crucial role in accelerating development. South Asia unfortunately has had a very minor share of this flow. The intraregional FDI flow has been even less significant due to the various barriers put up by member countries. The foreign investment flow from India, for example, to countries outside South Asia has been on a much larger scale than that to other South Asian countries.[33] It is therefore important that the SAFTA agreement include provisions for facilitating a larger flow of investment within the region and for taking advantage of the enlarged market brought about by free trade to attract investment from outside the region. Unfortunately, the agreement does not cover liberalization of investment in the region. It only makes a reference to it in Article 8, under the title "Additional Measures."

The GEP report had recommended the creation of a Common Investment Area under SAARC. It argued that such an area would enable the smaller countries, in particular, to take advantage of the higher credit ratings of the bigger countries and thereby to attract capital from the international market. The GEP suggested that, for establishing the Common Investment Area, it would be necessary to design a mutually beneficial, coordinated, and harmonized incentive policy; to lay down common guidelines and rules for the establishment, operation, control, and accountability of foreign investors; and to harmonize member states' policies on the transfer of funds and on the exclusion of sensitive sectors. The GEP also suggested that the member countries should remove restrictions on investment in their respective stock markets and eventually move toward setting up a common stock exchange.

Well before the adoption of the SAFTA agreement, initiatives were taken under SAARC to facilitate investment flow within the region. It was agreed that in order to do so the South Asian countries would take measures to remove administrative and regulatory constraints on the flow of investment among them, to exchange information on possibilities of investment, and to promote investment from the other regional countries. It was also suggested that to facilitate intra-SAARC movement of capital, these countries should offer the same treatment they give in bilateral investment agreements with countries outside the region to investors from within the region.

A draft investment agreement incorporating some of these and other ideas for permitting freer flow of intraregional investment was circulated by India as early as 1997. This draft is still in limbo, despite glimpses of progress from time to time. At one point, it appeared that the absence of an arbitration tribunal to settle intrastate disputes on matters relating to foreign investment stood in the way of the draft's finalization. This seeming constraint was removed and the agreement for the establishment of a SAARC Arbitration Council entered into force on July 2, 2007. The Sub-Group on Investment and Arbitration, which was scheduled to meet at the end of November 2007, was expected to give final touches to the text of the draft Agreement on Promotion and Protection of Investment in the region.

It is possible that this draft may be finalized and even adopted at some future SAARC summit, but it will carry little assurance that investment capital will start moving freely across the borders in the region or that South Asian countries can establish a Common Investment Area, as suggested by the GEP. This is again because of political constraints on progress. Political obstacles to the flow of capital—particularly among India, Bangladesh, and Pakistan—still remain. Pakistan's acceptance of Indian investment, and vice-versa, would be a giant step toward the normalization of economic relations between the two countries. But successive Pakistani governments have rejected Indian investment and denied India MFN treatment in trade relations in order to keep the Kashmir issue alive in Pakistan. Thus, the acceptance of Indian investment, in as much as it is an extension of MFN treatment, is essentially a political decision by Pakistan as to whether it wants to normalize its economic relations with India.

To some extent, the same is true of Bangladesh. Otherwise, Bangladesh would not have stayed in limbo and virtually rejected a proposal by the Tata Group to invest an initial $3 billion to establish power, steel, and fertilizer mills in the country. Whatever the explanations given in public for indecision on or rejection of the offer, the real reason is that those in power in Bangladesh do not wish to be seen as coming too close to India in the economic field. This behavior is typical of the big-neighbor–smaller-neighbor syndrome. For its part, India, on the grounds of security, had restricted the flow of investment from Bangladesh and Pakistan. The restriction on Bangladesh has recently been withdrawn but those on investment flows from Pakistan persist. Maintenance of this restriction is only a formality, as investment flow between India and Pakistan is dependent on the normalization of economic relations between the two countries. Even after normalization, Indian capital is more likely to move to Pakistan than the other way round.

Another crucial factor impeding the flow of investment in the region is the business community's perception of the political atmosphere and the related security threat to investors in some SAARC countries. Such a perception cannot be wished away by the mere assertion that there is no security threat to foreign investors in the countries concerned. Nor can it be resolved by a suitable formulation on this point, agreed upon in the forum of SAARC, particularly in the proposed SAARC investment agreement. What is needed is a conscious effort by all the agents concerned—and particularly the host governments, political parties, media, and the local business community—to improve the political climate for investment in these countries.

The South Asian Development Fund

The SADF is the name of one of the games that has been played under the aegis of SAARC to create the appearance of cooperation in the financial field. It was never intended to be a window for investment financing, though claims to this effect have been made from time to time. The scheme was launched essentially to provide funding for pre-investment research and studies. Subsequently, various windows under it were opened even though the funding more or less remained at the $5 million dollar level initially announced. A very small part of even this meager amount has been spent. The GEP report noted the anomaly of the meager funding of this scheme. It recommended, among others, to expand the resource base of the SADF to reach a level of at least $500 million. It also recommended that contributions to the fund should continue to come predominantly from regional countries and should be on the basis of assessment according to some criteria of capacity to pay. Contributions from outside will be welcomed only if they are in addition to the assessed contributions and not substitutes for it. The GEP also suggested that instead of setting up separate windows of the fund to accommodate contributions from different outside sources, these sources should be obliged to make their contributions directly to the SADF, which should be solely responsible for prioritizing projects to be implemented and monitoring progress in implementation. The SADF has now been converted into the SDF, but none of the GEP's suggestions were accepted in effecting this change. Contributions to the fund remain voluntary.

India has announced a contribution of $100 million for projects in the social field, particularly for poverty alleviation. Pakistan has pledged $70 million. Other member countries have announced smaller contributions. But it remains uncertain whether any member country will submit projects to be financed through the SDF. The obstacles to submitting such projects are political in nature. It is difficult for the Government of Pakistan and even for Bangladesh to convince their citizens that they are mitigating hunger and alleviating poverty in their countries with Indian assistance. Therefore, for any progress in this area to occur, the political climate will have to change drastically. An interim solution, for what it is worth, could be to establish an independent group of experts. Proposals for projects to be financed under the fund could be submitted to this group, which would select projects for financing on objective grounds. Member governments have generally found this second-track idea to be unacceptable. Consequently, the original contribution of the same amount made by India at the Twelfth SAARC Summit, for the same purpose, has remained unutilized.

South Asian Development Bank

The GEP had advanced the idea of setting up a South Asian Development Bank to which contributions could come from both regional and international financial institutions, as well as from member governments. Funds could also be raised from the regional and international capital markets. The South Asian governments have not as yet found it worthwhile even to consider this eminently reasonable, workable, and useful proposal.

Monetary Cooperation

Ideas for monetary cooperation have been discussed under the aegis of SAARC, both intergovernmentally and at the level of experts and intellectuals in seminars and conferences. At least two seminars of experts on the subject have been held so far, in which concrete suggestions have been made for monetary cooperation in the region. One of the ideas that has gained currency from time to time is the adoption of a common currency by South Asian countries. When this idea was also advanced in 2004 by Shri Atal Bihari Vajpayee, then prime minister of India, it attracted a great deal of public attention. The suggestion for a common currency for South Asia is laudable as a long-term objective, but the South Asian countries have a long way to go by way of harmonizing their economic policies (particularly exchange rates, interest rates, fiscal deficits, and price control measures) before reaching such a goal.

The first condition, of course, is that substantially all the trade within the region must be free and that intraregional trade exchanges should reach a particular percentage of the global trade of the member countries. In a study, the IPS of Sri Lanka has suggested that the level of intraregional trade should exceed 50 percent of the global trade of the regional countries before they can embark upon an effective program for monetary cooperation. For this to happen, it will be necessary not only to bring tariffs to 0 to 5 percent, as stipulated in the SAFTA agreement, but also to implement most of the suggestions advanced in this chapter, almost all of which require the exercise of political will by the member governments.

Listed below are some measures for monetary cooperation that can be implemented in the short and medium term and that are feasible even without complete market integration:

- Establishment of a regional consultative machinery to hold regular consultations on key economic policy parameters;
- Creation of a reserve fund to provide a cushion to member countries facing economic crises (the present is the most opportune time to create such a fund because almost all the countries of the region have been able to accumulate sizeable reserves of foreign exchange); and
- Creation of a parallel currency, and not a common currency, to replace the national currencies, to be used for limited transactions like payments

under a clearing system, contributions to a regional fund or program, or as a unit of account for settling deficits in transactions under regional payment arrangements. The currency could also be used to fund the provision of regional public goods in the areas of transport and communication, energy, information technology, biotechnology, food security, and tourism.[34]

Cooperation in the Field of Infrastructure

Adequate and efficiently functioning infrastructure in the member countries, and its integration across the region, is a precondition for regional economic integration. The joint development and integration of infrastructure is therefore one of the most important measures for deeper integration in South Asia. Most South Asian countries have inherited common infrastructure such as railways, roads, inland water transport, ports, and energy grids. After the end of the colonial period, much of this infrastructure was disrupted and fragmented. Gaps also appeared because of sheer neglect. Moreover, for want of adequate investment, the infrastructure was not updated for a long time at the national level. Missing links can be restored without incurring heavy costs, but larger investments will be necessary to update the outmoded infrastructure and to build new ones. There is an urgent need in the region to take up joint projects for building a network of world-class motorways and railways, developing and upgrading ports, building cold storage and warehousing facilities, constructing dams, and improving the efficiency of the existing network of canals and water courses in the region.[35]

Undertaking such projects has been held hostage to political considerations. On the one hand, unless political differences within the region are resolved and member governments exercise the required political will, it is unlikely that there will be any meaningful progress. On the other hand, once political decisions are taken, such projects are unlikely to be kept starved of funds. For example, once Bangladesh decides to allow transit facilities for goods from India to move through Bangladesh to other parts of India, there will be no dearth of Indian or even foreign investors putting in money to upgrade the transport and related infrastructure in Bangladesh. This will significantly accelerate development in Bangladesh and also bring in additional earnings by way of freight charges on Indian goods. The most important areas for cooperation in the field of infrastructure are transport, discussed earlier in this chapter, and energy.

Cooperation in the Field of Energy

In the South Asian region, some countries suffer from a chronic energy deficit, which is likely to grow as development progresses, while other countries, by virtue of their vast energy potential, have important export interests. This is a situation of conspicuous complementarity that needs to be harnessed in a coordinated and planned manner. Scholars and regional institutions have carried out a number of studies on the region's energy resources and cooperation in this field. These studies have shown that cooperative development of the region's diverse energy resources can significantly raise the level of member countries' energy security and accelerate the growth of their economies. As the experience of cooperation between India and Bhutan in this field has demonstrated, coordinated development of energy resources and their trading has the potential to transform the economic future of the countries involved.

Cross-border energy trading can increase the reliability of power supply, achieve economies in the operation of power plants, and act as an effective confidence-building measure, setting the stage for other forms of cooperation. One of the most important conclusions common to the various studies undertaken on the subject is that there is a need for a common distribution system in the region, based on a single regional energy grid connecting the national grids. This point was highlighted in the Twelfth SAARC Summit Declaration, which called for a study on South Asian energy cooperation, including the concept of an Energy Ring, to be undertaken by the Working Group on Energy.

Another important area of coordinated action recommended in various studies is the laying of pipelines across the region to transport natural gas from both West Asia and Central Asia in the west, and Myanmar in the east, to the energy-deficit countries of the region, mainly India and Pakistan.

In the current global energy scenario, petroleum is becoming an increasingly scarce resource. Given its significance for sustaining and fueling development and the fact that it is still the single most important source of energy in the world, access to petroleum-bearing assets and to oil and gas supply is increasingly becoming a part of the political strategies of different countries. The South Asian countries must get involved in this strategic game. But the chances of their emerging as winners depends on their ability to collectively harness their own regional energy potential. The latter endeavor has its own politics. There is a popular resistance to sharing resources with neighboring countries that even the well-meaning governments of the region are finding it difficult to overcome. This resentment arises from long-standing mistrust. Often, governments themselves, lured by the temptation of domestic political gain, have fueled such mistrust. At times, important projects have stalled because of outside political interference. In the process, there has been very little progress in this area. In any case, the long-term vision—of shared destiny in the context of the burgeoning global energy crisis—is missing.

Vertical Integration and Horizontal Specialization in Select Industrial Sectors

South Asian countries still derive most of their foreign exchange earnings from production in a few sectors. Chief among them is the textiles and garments sector. Some other sectors in this category are leather goods, rubber goods, timber products, and products of small-scale manufacturing. Exports from these sectors are, in the era of liberalization, facing the challenge of the imports of similar foreign goods as well as of the phasing out of the Multi-Fiber Agreement (MFA) according to the WTO Agreement on Textiles and Clothing. The South Asian countries can minimize their losses and maximize their advantages by means of vertical integration and horizontal specialization in these sectors. This can be brought about by careful identification, through research and study, of the lines of production in which vertical integration can take place, and those in which horizontal specialization can be fully exploited. Accordingly, the GEP has suggested studies on vertical integration in select sectors, but these suggestions do not appear in the SAFTA agreement. As in other areas, progress in this area is predicated on the exercise of the necessary political will by the governments concerned to embrace such integration and specialization, which in turn calls for mutual trust and cooperation.

Macroeconomic Policy Coordination

Macroeconomic policies adopted by the SAARC member countries, particularly the more developed ones, can have far-reaching implications for the economic development of the other countries of the region. The LDC member countries are particularly vulnerable in this respect. The greater the degree of regional economic integration, the greater the impact of one member government's macropolicies on the economy of another. A slight variation in one country's exchange rate could nullify the trade advantages of other countries derived from the SAFTA. Some fiscal levies can have the same effect. Government control and regulations of prices and other forms of state intervention in the market by one country can adversely affect the competitiveness and trade prospects of other countries. Interest rate variations can influence the flow of investment to particular countries in preference to other countries of the region. They can also affect the level of external indebtedness of member countries to the extent that debts are owed to the country effecting the interest rate change.

At the present stage of economic integration and in the absence of political harmony, the South Asian countries can hardly think of attempting a harmonization of their macroeconomic policies. But there is no doubt that a fair degree of such harmonization is an essential precondition for moving toward the goal of an economic union.

The GEP has noted that even if there is limited scope for the harmonization of economic policies at this stage, there is a strong case for consultation and coordination among member countries in this area. The group stated that "through greater mutual transparency and regular consultations, member countries can at least achieve a measure of coordination in the formulation and implementation of these policies so that the interests of the other member countries are taken into account." It recommended that "the scope of present consultations at the level of finance and planning ministers under the three-tier mechanism should be widened to facilitate the coordination of the macro-economic policies of the member states." If South Asia is to move toward the goal of an economic union, the procedure for macroeconomic policy coordination must be institutionalized and integrated into the SAFTA agreement.

Common Positions and Negotiating Strategies on Emerging Global Economic Issues

The GEP has underscored the need for South Asian countries to evolve common positions on emerging global economic issues and to respond to them jointly. The GEP also identified a number of areas where it was particularly important for South Asian countries to forge common positions and negotiating strategies. These included issues mostly negotiated within the forums of the WTO, the World Bank, and the International Monetary Fund (IMF), as well as issues pertaining to globalization.

The GEP stressed the need for South Asian countries to develop common policies and take joint actions "to retain the ownership and to develop their capacity to protect their rich bio-diversity." It also suggested the formulation of a joint strategy to meet the challenges of the phasing out of the MFA and the meltdown of the economies of Southeast Asian countries at that time. A number of independent experts have also critically reviewed the efforts of the South Asian countries to evolve common positions on global economic issues and identified the areas in which common positions should be adopted.[36]

As a mechanism for evolving a common position, the GEP suggested the establishment of a standing committee of high-level experts to constantly review economic issues of global concern and to suggest common positions on them. A SAARC-wide business-level expert group should also be set up with a similar mandate. Inputs provided by these two bodies should be made available for annual consultations on this subject at the ministerial level.

Consultations among SAARC member countries on global economic issues, both at the ministerial and official level, are currently ad hoc. On some occasions, consultations are held and common positions are formulated. On other occasions, adoption of common positions and strategies is done by default. In this era of seismic changes and in the context of pressure to impose new regimes and regulations on developing nations—which in turn have drastically curtailed the space for macroeconomic policymaking—it is extremely important that the present ad hoc mechanism for South Asian countries to consult and formulate common positions and strategies be institutionalized and integrated into the SAFTA agreement.

Conclusion

Objectively speaking, South Asia is an ideal grouping for economic integration. In spite of this, movement toward institutionalized regional cooperation started only in the mid-1980s and has progressed slowly since then. A major development along the way was the signing of a framework agreement for the SAFTA at the Twelfth SAARC summit in Islamabad in January 2004. Though

SAFTA was operationalized two years later, in July 2006, it remains a deeply flawed agreement. In fact, the SAARC member countries have not publicly or formally subscribed to the goal of regional economic integration. The principal reasons behind this failure are the lack of trust due to political differences, the largely exaggerated and misplaced security concerns of the member governments, and the reluctance of the larger regional members, particularly India, to discharge the responsibilities that devolve upon them by virtue of being economically stronger. Recent developments, particularly the phenomena of new regionalism triggered by globalization, the resurgence of Asian economies, and the market-driven integration of these economies, have reinforced the logic of regional integration in South Asia. Without economic integration, South Asia is in danger of being isolated and discriminated against in the world market. Without economic integration, South Asian countries will be linking with the dynamic economies of Asia and the pan-Asian movement with their hands tied behind their backs.

To translate the vision of South Asian economic integration into reality, it is essential that the basic constraints, most of which are of a political nature, be removed. The South Asian countries should accept, at the highest political level and without any further delay, the objective of a South Asian economic union. To make SAFTA an effective instrument for economic integration, the lists of sensitive products should be drastically shortened, particularly for the LDC members, and phased out within a time-bound framework. All nontariff and para-tariff barriers to mutual trade should be identified within a period of one year and eliminated within three years. A large fund (at least $5 billion) should be created in favor of the LDC members, in order to remove the supply-side constraints to their gaining equitable benefits from regional integration. Going beyond SAFTA, member countries should adopt measures of deeper integration, such as trade facilitation (including the seamless movement of goods across borders); joint development of infrastructure, particularly transport and energy; liberalization of trade in services; free flow of investment; cooperation in the financial and monetary fields; cooperation in upgrading skills and technologies in specific areas; harmonization or coordination of macroeconomic policies; and formulation of common policies and negotiating strategies on issues under negotiation in international economic forums.

Notes

[1] International Monetary Fund (IMF), *World Economic Outlook Database* (Washington, D.C.: 2008); and Asian Development Bank, *Asian Development Outlook*, 2002 and 2008.

[2] Ramesh Chandra and Rajiv Kumar, "South Asian Integration: Prospects and Lessons from East Asia," ICRIER Working Paper No. 202, New Delhi, 2008, table 3.

[3] Amita Batra, "South Asian Free Trade Area: Opportunities and Challenges," U.S.AID (Washington, D.C.: 2005), table 3.1.

[4] Estimates based on IMF, *World Economic Outlook* (April 2007).

[5] Batra, "South Asian Free Trade Area," 17 (table 1.4).

[6] Chandra and Kumar, "South Asian Integration," 5.

[7] Batra, "South Asian Free Trade Area," table 1.3.

[8] Report by the WTO Secretariat, *Trade Policy Review of India* (April 18, 2007), viii.

[9] From a speech by Dr. Shamshad Akhar, governor of the State Bank of Pakistan, at the J.P. Morgan-Pakistani Corporate Access Forum, Dubai, March 5, 2008.

[10] Chandra and Kumar, "South Asian Integration," table 10.

[11] Batra, "South Asian Free Trade Area," 13.

[12] Ibid., 13 (tables 1–2).

[13] Nisha Taneja, "Informal Trade in South Asia: How to Channelize to a Formal Trade?" Briefing paper, CUTS, Jaipur, India, 2005.

[14] Research and Information System for Developing Countries (RIS), "South Asian Economic Integration: SAFTA and Beyond," paper prepared for South Asia Centre for Policy Studies (September 2006), 8 (table 2.1).

[15] These figures are compiled from official data on trade issued by the Government of India.

[16] Compiled on the basis of data in IMF, *Direction of Trade Statistics* (2007).

[17] RIS, "South Asia Development and Cooperation Report" (New Delhi: Oxford Univ. Press, 2008): 63.

[18] Muchkund Dubey, "New Regionalism and Countries of the South," paper presented at an RIS seminar, New Delhi, 1998.

[19] SAARC, *Vision Beyond the Year 2000: Report of the SAARC Group of Eminent Persons* (Kathmandu: South Asia Centre for Policy Studies, SAARC Secretariat, 1998).

[20] Dubey, "SAFTA: A Perspective," *The Hindu*, January 10, 2004.

[21] The Agreement on South Asian Free Trade Area (SAFTA), www.saarc-sec.org/data/agenda/economic/safta/SAFTA percent20AGREEMENT.pdf, Annex IV, SAFTA Rules of Origin.

[22] Ibid., Annex III, Mechanism for Compensation of Revenue Loss for LDC Member States.

[23] Ibid., Annex I, Sensitive Lists.

[24] Ibid., Annex II, Areas Identified for Technical Assistance to Least Developed Countries States.

[25] Dubey, "SAARC and South Asian Economic Integration," *Economic and Political Weekly*, Mumbai (April 7, 2007): 1238–40.

[26] Dubey, "New Regionalism and Countries of the South."

[27] Batra, "South Asian Free Trade Area," 62 (table 3.9).

[28] Compiled from IMF data.

[29] Rehman Sobhan, "Regional Cooperation in South Asia: A Quest for Identity," the first Dinesh Singh Memorial Lecture, New Delhi (April 1997).

[30] Dushni Weerakoon, Colombo: Institute of Policy Studies (IPS), 2007.

[31] Dubey, "The Twelfth SAARC Summit: Deeper Integration in South Asia," *South Asian Survey* 12, no. 1 (2005).

[32] See RIS, "South Asian Economic Integration," box 4.4 and 4.5.

[33] Ibid., box 4.4.

[34] RIS, *South Asia Development Cooperation Report*, 2004.

[35] Akmal Hussain, "The Challenges and Drivers of Regionalism in South Asia: The India Pakistan Peace Process," conference on "Strengthening Integration in South Asia," South Asia Centre for Policy Studies (SACEPS), Colombo Sri Lanka, May 30–31, 2008.

[36] See Dubey, "Coping with Globalisation," in *South Asia 2010: Challenges and Opportunities*, ed. K. K. Bhargava and Sridhar Khatri (New Delhi: Konark Publishers Private Ltd., 2001); and Dubey, "South Asia and the WTO," in *South Asia in the WTO*, ed. Saman Kalegama (New Delhi: SAGE Publications, 2007).

Building the Institutions for Regional Integration: Country-specific Issues and Attitudes

Bangladeshi Perspectives on South Asian Regional Integration

Rehman Sobhan

Within South Asia perspectives on the need for a regional community will vary. India may feel it can do without a regional community and can afford to deal bilaterally with each of its neighbors. Bangladesh, on the other hand, needs South Asia and reckons it has much to gain through the construction of a broader South Asian community. In the absence of such a community it would have to deal with its largest and most important neighbor, India, bilaterally within a manifestly unequal relationship. This, indeed, was the perspective that informed the thinking of the late president Ziaur Rahman (Zia), who ruled Bangladesh from 1976 till his assassination in May 1981. Zia recognized that India was the dominant presence in Bangladesh's external relations but preferred to mediate this relationship within a broader regional entity such as the South Asian Association for Regional Cooperation (SAARC). Zia took the initiative in promoting the idea of SAARC but did not live to see its birth as a regional organization, in Dhaka, in 1985.

In practice, SAARC has remained an Indo-centric organization because the region cannot escape from the reality of India's size, economic strength, and centrality. India shares land and maritime borders with every SAARC member except Afghanistan. The only other SAARC country to share an intraregional border is Pakistan, with Afghanistan.

Whatever may have been the strategic perspective of President Zia, this could not transcend the reality of India's imminent presence in Bangladesh's life. In the years since SAARC was established, Bangladesh's relations with India dominated its relations with SAARC. It could not be otherwise, since Bangladesh was surrounded on all sides by India, shared fifty-seven rivers in the role of a lower riparian, shared a transport infrastructure, depended on India as its principal source of imports, and came to depend on India as an outlet for its surplus labor. Over and above these dominant links, Bangladesh shares cultural, linguistic and religious ties with the immediate neighboring states of India, as it does with some other South Asian countries.

It is argued in this chapter that the Indo-centric nature of Bangladesh's relations with South Asia have not prejudiced Bangladesh's compulsion to build a South Asian community. In virtually every area of importance that defines Bangladesh's relations with India, it remains advantageous for Bangladesh to

85

address these issues from a regional perspective. This argument will be spelled out by looking at four areas that serve to define Bangladesh's relations with India, but which can be more satisfactorily addressed within a broader regional perspective. The four issues are water, trade, connectivity, and labor markets. These issues are discussed below and lead us into the concluding section, which examines the salience of political influences in building a broader South Asian community.

Sharing the Himalayan Waters

Bangladesh's India-locked geography is most closely forged through its riverine links. As long as Bangladesh was part of the single nation-state of India, water was perceived as a shared resource. With the Partition of India in 1947 these same waters, in particular the Ganges, emerged as a major source of contestation. The Farakka barrage—constructed unilaterally by India across the border from Bangladesh, in West Bengal, to divert the flow of the Ganges—became a perennial source of tension from 1975 and 1996 between the two countries since it contributed to severe ecological damage in Bangladesh. The Farakka issue was finally resolved in December 1996, when a treaty was signed to share the Ganges waters. The treaty was negotiated between an Awami League government, which had been reelected to power six months earlier, with a coalition government in India, led by I. K. Gujral, which had a strong commitment to both good bilateral relations with its neighbors as well as the strengthening of SAARC. However, a shared approach to the utilization of the waters of fifty-six other rivers still remains to be addressed among the coriparians. One of these rivers, the Teesta, is already in contention as both India and Bangladesh have built structures on their respective parts of the river to utilize its shared waters. A recently concluded Indo-Bangladesh Summit has held out promise that an agreement to share the waters of the Teesta may be concluded.

Most of these shared waters originate in the Himalayas, where Nepal is a coriparian with India and Bangladesh. Any long-term solution to the problem of sharing these waters obviously lies in a joint approach to the development of the Himalayan rivers, the Ganges, Brahmaputra, and Meghna. Such an approach would be essential to construct storage dams in the upper reaches of these rivers in Nepal for the use of the Ganges waters and in northeast India for utilizing the Brahmaputra/Meghna waters. Such a program would enable these countries to once and for all liberate their people from the historic curse of floods. It would give them an abundant source of irrigation water in the dry winter season, which is the period of contestation over shared rivers, and it would have the potential to generate around 80,000 MW of hydropower for the development of the energy-starved economies of South Asia. Such a shared initiative, which would need to also include Bhutan, a coriparian with India, would be able to transform the eastern region of South Asia, making eastern/ northeast India, Nepal, Bhutan, and Bangladesh into not just a global bread basket but also a major industrial hub in the region.

Such a perspective on water sharing is central to the concerns of Bangladesh, which has sought to use regional cooperation as a means of transforming what remain (to quote the distinguished Indian scholar George Verghese) "rivers of sorrow into waters of hope." Bangladesh's perspective on the use of the Himalayan waters, which is also largely shared by Nepal, has not been encouraged by the relevant policy constituencies in India, which prefer to address such issues bilaterally with India's coriparians Bangladesh, Bhutan, and Nepal. What sets Bangladesh apart from its coriparians is the unfortunate reality that it is the lower riparian in relation to all its shared rivers. This makes Bangladesh dependent on the upper riparians for addressing its most important water-related problems, indicated below:

- Bangladesh is the principal victim of floods originating in the upper reaches of the Ganges and the Brahmaputra.
- Bangladesh needs to augment the flow of these waters in the dry season to promote winter irrigation, which is now essential to its food security.
- Bangladesh needs to use these waters to contain the process of saline intrusion damaging the ecology of its deltaic region.
- Bangladesh is threatened with an acute shortage of power as its gas reserves run out and will need to draw on the hydroelectric power potential of the Himalayan rivers.

Given the need to involve several countries as stakeholders in the utilization of the Himalayan rivers, SAARC would have been an appropriate forum to deal with the issue of the joint development of the Himalayan waters. But so far the issue of water has never been placed on the SAARC agenda. As a result, a more practical vehicle to utilize these waters has surfaced in the shape of a prospective subregional entity, the South Asian Growth Quadrangle (SAGQ), encompassing Bangladesh, Bhutan, India, and Nepal. Unfortunately, the SAGQ has not moved ahead due to rather lukewarm patronage from the Government of India (GOI). It has been left to multilateral agencies such as the Asian Development Bank (ADB) and the World Bank, along with various civil society initiatives in the region, to promote agendas for subregional cooperation. So far no program in the SAGQ has fructified, least of all in the area of water.

The Search for Market Access

Promoting Trade

Bangladesh's other principal interest in SAARC has been to use it as a vehicle for obtaining access to the large and growing Indian market. India was, for the past decade, Bangladesh's principal source of imports, accounting for $3.4 billion in imports in 2007–2008, which is around 15.7 percent of its global imports. However, in 2008–2009 imports from India declined slightly to $2.8 billion, and

China overtook India as Bangladesh's principal import source, accounting for 15.2 percent of imports compared to around 12.6 percent from India. Because of Bangladesh's shared borders with India, perhaps another $3 billion of Indian imports enter Bangladesh illicitly, so that India effectively remains Bangladesh's largest source of import. All business investment decisions in Bangladesh are made on the assumption that it will have to compete with Indian imports, whether official or unofficial. This applies to both agricultural and industrial products. In return, Bangladesh has made little headway in the Indian market mostly due to the structural constraints on its export capacity but also due to India's more restrictive trade regime.

This growing trade gap with India should normally have provoked a strong protectionist response from the Bangladeshi business community. This may have been the initial reaction in the 1970s and 1980s. But with the liberalization of trade in the 1990s Bangladesh's business community has moved forward to seek reciprocity from India through providing it with duty-free access to the Indian market. This quest for access was initially pursued bilaterally by the Bangladesh government, without much result. The South Asia Free Trade Area (SAFTA) agreement, signed in 2004, has served as a more useful vehicle for realizing this access. However, the operationalization of SAFTA has moved ahead rather sluggishly. Each country has retained a long list of "sensitive" products with a view to protecting particular economic sectors against exemption of duties under SAFTA. A variety of nontariff barriers (NTBs) have also served to frustrate trade. SAFTA has provided some advantage to Bangladesh in accessing the Indian market, so that Bangladesh's exports to India have more then tripled over the past five years to reach $260 million in 2006–2007. But this still leaves a bilateral deficit of around $1.7 billion with India.

Initially Bangladesh sought to fast-track its access to the Indian market through negotiations to conclude a bilateral free trade agreement (FTA) on the lines of the highly productive FTA concluded earlier between India and Sri Lanka. However, at the Fourteenth SAARC Summit in New Delhi in March 2007, the prime minister of India offered unilateral duty-free access to India's market to all least-developed countries (LDCs) in the region. Since India already has FTAs with two LDCs, Nepal and Bhutan, and the other LDC, Maldives, has virtually no commodities to export to India, this concession was principally directed to Bangladesh.

This duty-free concession to Bangladesh by India has, to some extent, been vitiated by the retention of the long sensitive list that had limited the impact of SAFTA and which continues to restrict a number of items of export interest to Bangladesh from entry to the Indian market. This has led to bilateral discussions between the ministries of commerce in which Bangladesh has requested India to modify its sensitive list. Bangladesh has identified one hundred items on India's sensitive list that can be competitively exported from Bangladesh, now under consideration by India. As a gesture of goodwill India has agreed to permit Bangladesh to export 8 million pieces of readymade garments (RMGs), which are Bangladesh's principal global export, but which were retained on India's sensitive list. Eight million RMGs would generate exports from Bangladesh worth about $35–40 million, which is a rather modest sum, considering Bangladesh's global RMG exports of around $7 billion, but the concession by India holds promise for the future. Unfortunately, this gesture by India has not been taken further by a positive response to Bangladesh's request for vacating the one hundred items from its sensitive list.

In practice, Bangladesh wants complete duty-free access under SAFTA, not just to India, but also to other SAARC countries. Up to 1971, Pakistan was an important trading partner of Bangladesh within the common market provided by their shared nationhood. Jute goods, tea and leather, hides and skins commanded a sizeable export market for Bangladesh in Pakistan. In turn, Bangladesh was Pakistan's largest market for manufactured goods. This trade came to a standstill after the emergence of Bangladesh. Pakistan has cut itself off from Bangladesh's jute manufacturing exports by developing a rather uneconomic jute industry under heavy protection. Imports of tea have been diverted to Sri Lanka and Kenya. Bangladesh substituted virtually all its imports from Pakistan. These lost markets are being slowly reopened for both Pakistan and Bangladesh under SAFTA, but the volume of trade remains modest. Bangladesh can also export its RMGs very competitively to Nepal, Bhutan, and now Afghanistan. Once there is a more open horizon for accessing all these markets across South Asia through SAFTA, Bangladesh can aspire to attract sizeable foreign direct investment (FDI) to use the country as a potential export platform to reach the much larger market of India and also the rest of South Asia.

The Opening of the Capital Market

LDCs such as Bangladesh have limited capacity to take advantage of market access to the more developed countries such as India due to the narrow structural base of their economies. Bangladesh will need significant capital inflows to develop its infrastructure, as well as enhance and diversify its export capacity to make use of the opportunities provided by SAFTA. Bangladesh will, accordingly, need to make itself more receptive to FDI through opening up its capital market, to both expand and diversify its export base. Currently Bangladesh's exports remain heavily concentrated in the RMG sector, which today accounts for 75 percent of its global exports. Here a principal source of FDI for Bangladesh is India itself, whose prospective investors could be attracted by the opportunity of targeting the Indian market once it is opened up to Bangladesh through SAFTA.

Until recently, Indian investors showed little interest in investing in Bangladesh. However, with the signing of SAFTA two years ago, several such investment opportunities have surfaced for Bangladesh. India's leading conglomerate, Tata, came forward with an offer to invest around $3 billion in Bangladesh to set up a urea fertilizer plant, a steel mill, and a power plant. The steel mill and fertilizer plant could have served as potential sources of export to India for part of their output. Yet another investment proposal came from the Mittal Group, another major Indian conglomerate, which is linked to the world's largest steel producer. The Mittal Group sought to invest $2.5 billion in a steel plant in Bangladesh, again with export capacity to India. The significant point of these investments was the value addition to Bangladesh's natural gas, which was a critical input in the viability of the two proposals.

This approach of adding value to Bangladesh's principal natural resource, gas, to optimize its value—whether for export or domestic use—was initially conceived by the Bangladesh Planning Commission, as early as 1972. The goal was to reduce Bangladesh's large trade deficit with India by expanding and structurally diversifying its export base, which was then exclusively dependent on jute. Around 1974, agreements were negotiated between the Government of Bangladesh (GOB) and the GOI to set up plants in Bangladesh to produce urea fertilizer and sponge iron, both using Bangladesh's natural gas. The output of these projects was to be dedicated for exports to India. The sponge iron plant would import iron ore from India and export it back to India as sponge iron. Bangladesh would also import limestone from India and use its natural gas as inputs for a large cement plant in Sylhet, with part of its output exportable to northeast India. These projects were conceived as joint ventures to be implemented by public-sector corporations in the two countries. Feasibility studies were completed for all three projects but their implementation was frustrated by the assassination of Sheikh Mujibur Rahman in August 1975, and a resultant change of regime that led to a hiatus in relations between India and Bangladesh.

The paramount position of politics in defining the scope for economic relations between India and Bangladesh is evident in the fact that it has taken thirty years for these projects to be revived, this time as FDI in the private sector. A modern cement plant, based on limestone imported from Megalaya, has recently been commissioned in Sylhet through investment by a French multinational, Lafarge Cement. Tata and Mittal have targeted steel and fertilizer in their proposals. All three FDI projects were in the private sector but their advancement remained captive to politics. Even the Lafarge project took over five years to be operationalized because of long delays by the GOI in giving clearance for the extraction and export of limestone from Megalaya to the plant located just across the border in Chattak, Sylhet.

The BNP-led government, which held power in Bangladesh between 2001 and 2006, stalled on taking decisions on both the Tata and Mittal projects. The GOB apprehended that its approval of such large projects involving Indian investment, just prior to a national election in Bangladesh, would be prejudicial to its electoral stance against the supposedly India-friendly Awami League. The public reason given by the GOB for not moving ahead with two investment projects of a magnitude that could have transformed Bangladesh's far-from-exciting image as an FDI destination, was that Bangladesh could not guarantee enough gas supplies to the two projects to ensure their long-term sustainability. This argument had some intrinsic merit but could not hold water since the prospect of serving such large, assured markets for gas, offered by Tata and Mittal, would have encouraged significant FDI in further gas exploration and development, which had been stagnant for the previous two decades in Bangladesh.

Now that an Awami League–led political alliance has been elected to office with an overwhelming majority in parliament and a mandate to improve relations with its neighbors, such investment proposals may yield a more positive response. However, the current global investment climate is not yet propitious for the initiation of such major proposals. We shall have to see whether the improved state of Indo-Bangladesh relations will, in the days ahead, revive these or other sizeable investment proposals from India.

Reconnecting with South Asia

A further area where Bangladesh stands to gain through using SAARC is in the area of transport integration. Bangladesh is positioned between Southeast Asia and South Asia and between northeast India and the rest of India. Its crucial geographical location has the potential of transforming Bangladesh into the Singapore of the land routes in Asia. Once Bangladesh completed the construction of the Bangabandhu Bridge across the Jamuna River in 1997, scope was provided for uninterrupted movement between the Yunnan Province of China and Thailand, across Myanmar and Bangladesh, into India, Pakistan, Afghanistan, Central Asia, and eventually to Europe. Bangladesh could thus have emerged as a major beneficiary in the integration of South Asia's fractured transport network.

A recently concluded Regional Multimodal Transport Study, commissioned by the SAARC Secretariat, has spelled out the scope and actions needed to reconnect South Asia's transport network. Bangladesh, India, and Pakistan have crucial roles to play in this process of reconnecting South Asia. Bangladesh's reluctance to provide India with transit rights to connect northeast India with the rest of India remains a crucial factor in mending these broken links since these routes remain important arteries of the United Nations–sponsored Asian Highway and Railway network. India has responded to Bangladesh's denial of transit rights by limiting transit for Nepal and Bhutan across its land area to Bangladesh and denying both these countries the right to export to third countries through the Bangladeshi ports of Chittagong and Mongla. India also denies Bangladesh and Pakistan opportunities to transport their traded goods across India by road or rail. As a result, a container of raw cotton, destined to travel from Punjab in Pakistan to a textile mill in Bangladesh, which would normally take 6–7 days to reach Bangladesh by container wagon or truck moving across India, now takes 4–6 weeks through sea transport from Karachi to Chittagong, with a transshipment in Singapore. India, in turn, is denied access to move its cargo across Pakistan to Afghanistan and Central Asia, which now have to be reached through shipments from Mumbai via the port of Bandar Abbas in Iran.

Bangladesh's inhibitions in denying India transit are particularly mystifying because up to 1965, Pakistan permitted the river routes of then–East Pakistan to be used as a major artery for movement of goods and people between Calcutta and northeast India. This route was, in fact, a major source of business for inland water transport companies in East Pakistan and was an important revenue source for the provincial government, who invested considerable foreign aid in keeping the rivers perennially navigable. This river route across East Pakistan was closed down after the Indo-Pakistan war in 1965, as was the rail link between Kolkata and Goalando ghat, on the banks of the Jamuna in Bangladesh, a major source of passenger traffic between the two countries. The river route was partially revived after the emergence of an independent Bangladesh in 1971 but was barely used due to the silting up of the rivers and the restrictions imposed by Bangladesh on the use of the route by Indian vessels. The rail link was revived in 2006 after a hiatus of 43 years. A further option for Bangladesh is to provide scope for the landlocked regions of northeast India to use Chittaong Port, which is 100 km from the Tripura border, as their point of connection with the global economy rather than to move these goods over 1,700 km to Kolkata and the Haldia port in West Bengal.

The obstacle to providing India with transit facilities over the river and land routes appears to originate in Bangladeshi security concerns. The precise nature of these concerns is never made clear and is rarely discussed either within Bangladesh or between the two countries. Since India attaches considerable importance to reviving transit links with its northeast region, Bangladesh's reluctance to concede this has remained a source of some interstate rancor. India has, for diplomatic reasons, not pushed this issue, merely arguing that both transit facilities across Bangladesh and access for its northeastern states to Chittagong Port would be economically of great benefit to Bangladesh.

India has meanwhile developed serviceable if time-consuming road and rail connections across the land link between Bangladesh and Nepal, which have served it well since 1947. India has now moved to ease the landlocked status of the northeast states by opening a link with Sittwe Port in Myanmar through the Kaladan River, which connects the two countries. It has also moved to develop the Asian Highway route connecting Thailand and Myanmar with mainland India by bypassing Bangladesh and has invested in upgrading Myanmar's road network connecting it to northeast India. All these investments are much less cost-effective than providing access to the northeast states to Chittagong port or moving goods and people across Bangladesh by road and rail transport across the Bangabandhu Bridge. But India has made it clear that it will not keep its transport links with the northeast or the Association of Southeast Asian Nations (ASEAN) region hostage to Bangladesh's political sensitivities.

Bangladesh therefore has much to lose by its political indecision and much to gain by encouraging the use of its transport network to connect northeast

India with the rest of India as well as the global economy. However, it is possibly politically more expedient for Bangladesh to promote these linkages through the SAARC process, rather than bilaterally, through moves to integrate South Asia's transport system with the Asian Highway and Railway network. Bangladesh provides a highly attractive option for both Nepal and Bhutan, who remain exclusively dependant on India's ports, to trade with the global community. To ensure connectivity for Nepal to Bangladesh's ports, India needs to open up rail links between Raxaul on the Indo-Nepal border and Rohanpur in northwest Bangladesh so that cargo from Nepal can be moved by rail to Chittagong or Mongla ports. It also needs to provide ready and uninterrupted access across India for road transport between Nepal and Bhutan with Bangladesh. Ideally, container trucks and wagons from these two countries should be able to move to ports in Chittagong or Mongla in Bangladesh as smoothly as transport moves from Vienna to Hamburg or Zurich to Genoa.

At the same time, Bangladesh would have an interest in opening up transport links with Pakistan through road and rail routes across India. Within such an integrated and seamless transport network, Bangladesh would be able to upgrade its rail system and develop Chittagong Port or even invest in a new sea port, to establish itself as a regional hub which provides global access both to northeast India as well as Nepal and Bhutan. Eventually, even Yunnan Province in China, which is keen to use the Bay of Bengal rather than the more distant ports on the Pacific coast or the Gulf of Tonkin as its access to the world, would also have a stake in Bangladesh's regional hub port. Such a development would transform the port area of Bangladesh into a major regional trading metropolis and would open up a new growth zone connecting the landlocked, investment-starved areas of northeast India with eastern Bangladesh.

Northeast India's significant natural wealth can be most effectively developed through investments, whether in these states or in Bangladesh, if its products are offered unrestricted access to the Bangladeshi and global markets. Few investors in India find it worthwhile to invest in the northeast because of its landlocked status and remoteness from markets in mainland India. This accounts, in some measure, for the region's underdevelopment and its ongoing political instability. It follows that within a more integrated trade and transport system that connects the northeast with its natural hinterland, Bangladesh could emerge as the primary trading partner of the northeast both as a supplier of goods as well as a market outlet for its natural resources and value-added investments. By reconnecting the northeast both with Bangladesh and also, through the Asia Highway and Railway system, with Myanmar and points east, a whole new world of opportunity could open up for the region, which could put it on the road to a more prosperous and peaceful future.

All these possibilities of reaping the economic benefits of improved connectivity in the SAARC region have been given a fresh impetus in the wake of the recently concluded summit in New Delhi, held in January 2010, between the Bangladeshi prime minister, Sheikh Hasina, and the Indian prime minister,

Manmohan Singh, whose party has also been recently reelected to office with an enhanced majority in parliament. The summit declaration offered the northeast Indian states access to Chittagong Port and West Bengal access to Mongla Port in southwest Bangladesh. In turn India indicated its willingness to provide unrestricted transit to Nepal and Bhutan not just for their bilateral trade with Bangladesh but also use of its ports for third-country trade. These agreements will need, in due course, to be operationalized but have already opened up a new set of opportunities for improving connectivity, not just between India and Bangladesh but across South Asia. The summit declaration, particularly on connectivity, generated a hostile political response from the BNP-led political opposition. But the strong position of the ruling alliance in the parliament indicates that it is willing to move ahead in such areas, without surrendering to pressure from the political opposition.

Integrating South Asia's Labor Market

South Asia was once an integrated labor market where workers moved freely across the landscape of Imperial India. The partition of India and the emergence of new national borders transformed market-determined labor flows into illegal immigration. Bangladeshis have spent the last half-century trying to reintegrate the region's labor markets and look to SAARC to institutionalize rather than frustrate their efforts. As it stands, the regional labor market remains segmented. Nepal and Bhutan already have unrestricted access to India's labor market, while the Maldives, with a population of half a million, depends heavily on South Asian countries for meeting its labor needs. Bangladeshis, for example, account for around 10 percent of the Maldivian labor force. However, the Nepalese in Bhutan have become an endangered minority while migrants from what is now Bangladesh, who have been moving into northeast India over the past century, have become a source of severe political division in some northeastern states. In Nepal, yesterday's migrants from Bihar into the Terai region in southern Nepal have become today's contestants for political power in Nepal. Labor movements among most countries of South Asia are, these days, severely restricted. As a result, labor flows across the region are mostly taking place on an unofficial basis. This trend has no longer restricted itself to provoking domestic political conflicts but has aroused internal security concerns and contributed to interstate tensions.

Bangladesh, given its historical experience and domestic economic circumstances, remains a major stakeholder in the integration of labor markets within South Asia. Since their liberation Bangladeshis have become even more outwardly mobile than their predecessors. Today some 6 million Bangladeshi migrants are working abroad; they remitted around $10 billion to their families in 2008–2009. These remittances are the largest source of net foreign exchange earnings for Bangladesh and are more than four times the annual foreign aid and FDI inflows into Bangladesh.

A sizeable number of Bangladeshis have also moved abroad unofficially, spanning out all over the world, from the jungles of Bolivia to the northernmost parts of Finland. Their remittances amount to several billion dollars, serving in some measure to finance Bangladesh's large unofficial trade deficit with India. While such nonformal migrant Bangladeshis are to be found across the world, a sizeable number have moved within South Asia. It is estimated that over a million Bangladeshis are, today, working in Pakistan. This is acknowledged in no official records of migration or statistics on migrant remittance. It may be noted that when Bangladesh was part of Pakistan not more than 300,000 Bangladeshis were known to have moved for work to West Pakistan. The present generation of Bangladeshis works in the domestic service sector and also provides crucial labor inputs in a number of industries in Pakistan.

A much larger number of Bangladeshis have moved informally into India. Estimates vary widely, depending on the source. These Bangladeshis not only work and reside in the northeastern states of India, where the demographics of some states have undergone noticeable change, but now work in West Bengal and further afield in northern and western India. These migrants have integrated themselves into the labor market, where they fill important gaps, and have become part of the local community. Much of metropolitan India is a melting pot of ethnic groups where a Bangladeshi is no more or less an alien than a migrant from Kolkata, northeast India, or even Bihar.

Though many such Bangladeshi migrants are accommodated by the host labor market in various parts of India, they always remain vulnerable to politically motivated agitations that seek to link them to acts of terrorism or to claims that they are denying locals access to jobs or public benefits. It is therefore more sensible to legitimize such labor movements across South Asia's borders within the framework of an SAARC policy initiative. All SAARC countries join hands in WTO negotiations to argue for incorporating labor movements as part of the opening up of trade in services. What they demand at the global level should logically be practiced within the region. Of all people, L. K. Advani, whose party, the BJP, has been in the vanguard of political agitation for repatriating illicit Bengali migrants, has proposed to legitimize the presence of these migrants through a system of labor permits. Such permits have been in vogue for many years in the oil-exporting countries of the Middle East, who have depended on migrant labor to sustain their economic transformation. Bangladesh would like to see this issue of legalizing some form of labor movement across SAARC borders serve as a prelude to integrating the region's labor market, as has taken place in the European Union (EU).

Conclusion: The Need for Political Statesmanship

Bangladesh would stand to gain from more open access to the commodity, labor, and capital markets of its larger neighbors in South Asia. As a lower riparian its food security and capacity to deal with the hazards of climate change would also depend greatly on an integrated move toward the development of the shared Himalayan waters. The development of an SAARC Food Security Reserve or Food Bank would serve to mitigate weather-related food shortages for Bangladesh and other vulnerable countries in South Asia. Bangladesh also has much to gain from a reintegration of the transport and energy infrastructure across the region. However, in attempting to move South Asia in this direction Bangladesh's political leaders will have to divest themselves of the pathologies that affect weaker countries living in the shadow of a larger neighbor.

Bangladesh cannot aspire to let its less skilled migrants have ready entry to the labor markets of neighbors and then complain if Indian doctors and nurses or Pakistani textile managers are imported to serve its expanding private hospitals and textile mills. Nor can Bangladesh aspire to develop Chittagong as a hub port while denying India opportunities to move its goods and people across Bangladesh to northeast India. In all such cases, legitimate security concerns must be recognized, as must the vulnerabilities of weaker economies interacting with economically more developed neighbors. There are well-established precedents, drawn from the experience of the EU, ASEAN, and Latin America, to deal with such concerns. But at the end of the day, Bangladesh, to the extent that it has more to gain than lose from an integrated South Asia, will have to come to terms with its future relations with its larger neighbor, India.

Bangladesh's inhibitions, which in varying degrees are shared by all the other SAARC countries, relate to the apprehension that a more integrated South Asia would expose it to domination by India, which is already emerging as a global power. Businessmen fear that India's more mature and increasingly globalized conglomerates will swamp their markets and buy up their enterprises. The security establishment fears that a more harmonious SAARC, where India is seen as a benign partner and not a hegemonic power, would lead to a progressive depreciation in its influence within the domestic polity. In Bangladesh, as in Pakistan, Nepal, and Sri Lanka, particular political parties have made good use of these apprehensions to play the anti-Indian card as an instrument of electoral gain in domestic politics. A similar trend has emerged in recent years in Indian politics, where anti-Pakistan and to a lesser extent anti-Bangladesh rhetoric has been used as an area of opportunity by some parties, whether on issues of terrorism or illicit migrants.

These exercises in political opportunism have spilled over from bilateral relations into the regional arena and served as a constraint on the advancement of SAARC. Pakistan refuses to operationalize SAFTA because of the unresolved Kashmir issue, while Bangladesh refused to sign on to transport integration because of constituencies that have made a livelihood out of opposing transit to India. Today, the changed domestic political equations in Bangladesh have opened up windows of opportunity in the area of connectivity. In India there is a backlash that has not just impacted bilateral relations but has served to distance its leadership from SAARC and encouraged it to invest its energies globally or within a broader Asian community. These positions in India may also be revisited if the changing pattern of Indo-Bangladeshi relations can reignite the commitment of India's leadership to greater cooperation in at least some areas across the South Asian region.

Notwithstanding those constituencies inimical to promoting greater integration in South Asia, most Bangladeshis are now voting with their feet and purses for constructing a broader regional community. Many of the present generation of Bangladeshis have recognized that 55,000 square miles of land area is too narrow a space to contain their aspirations. Millions of people are moving across the borders of this region, in many if not most cases, without reference to the preferences of governments to trade, work, and to seek health care, education, recreation, and even spiritual solace. Invocation by the GOB of public opinion as a constricting factor in frustrating advances in regional integration fly in the face of a fast-changing reality.

South Asia is now being integrated more rapidly through the marketplace and at the initiative of its citizens than through the official role of SAARC. In spite of the revealed preference of its citizens, the respective governments still remain captive to the inhibitions that have historically held back the integration of South Asia. In such circumstances, the emergence of a South Asian community would be greatly accelerated if its governments, in particular the GOI, were to commit themselves to invest their political and diplomatic resources in advancing the process of integration. This would require an element of statesmanship on all sides and particularly in India, where leaders must be willing to override bureaucratic obstacles, advanced in the name of security concerns, to open up transit routes and markets to India's neighbors, including Pakistan. India would need to invest its resources in enhancing the economic capacities of its weaker neighbors to benefit from the integration process. In supporting such initiatives India would need to move beyond the bilateralism that has been favored by its bureaucracies to seek solutions within a broader South Asian community.

Such an approach demands greater maturity from Bangladesh's political leaders in relations with their South Asian neighbors. There is some indication that the incumbent political leadership is demonstrating this maturity as it redefines its relations with India. However, domestic political consensus must be built to support such initiatives for closer Indo-Bangladesh relations, rather than to use the relationship as a weapon for political confrontation. This would empower the political leadership in Bangladesh to use their democratic mandate to face up to the various constituencies that have so far served as roadblocks to promoting greater integration with its neighbors. They must continue to take necessary political risks and invest their electoral mandate in connecting Bangladesh's transport and energy infrastructure within a regional system. They must be bold enough to encourage the flow of trade and investment across the region and permit Bangladesh's citizens to build their own autonomous links with the broader South Asian community. Such a vision for the future once appeared to be a distant dream. In Bangladesh, at least, it now appears closer to realization than one had once thought possible. After a long time, Bangladesh's political leadership is demonstrating an awareness that the future is impinging on its present much more rapidly than it did in the past. Its main challenge may therefore be to seize the moment and lead the way into the future rather than to be led there.

IS A SUCCESSFUL SAARC
AN IMPERATIVE FOR INDIA?

Rajiv Kumar

The changing realities in South Asia necessitate a fresh look at the prospects of and challenges to economic integration in the region. To that end, this chapter focuses on three arguments: First, there has been and continues to be strong support for economic integration in South Asia.[1] Quantitative estimates of the benefits of regional cooperation in South Asia fail to fully capture the gains that would be generated because they are almost always based on static assumptions and do not take into account the likely gains from the intraindustry trade that always emerges among economies at similar economic levels. Second, now is the time to provide the needed impetus to push the development process in the region over the "tipping point." Third, as an integrated economic space stretching from Kabul, Afghanistan, to Chittagong, Bangladesh,[2] India has a vested interest in providing this impetus; it also has the means to do so. Regional cooperation in South Asia will, however, generate benefits for *all* South Asian economies; therefore, any argument that India alone has to take this agenda forward is misplaced. Once over the tipping point, regional cooperation will place South Asia on a higher growth trajectory and generate externalities for inclusive and sustainable growth. And higher growth will not benefit South Asia alone—with its large population, expanding middle class, and skilled workforce, the region could well become a major engine for global growth in coming years. That said, noneconomic gains from successful regional cooperation will be as important as economic gains, if not more so. These noneconomic gains will contribute enormously to the attractiveness of the region as an investment destination and have a positive impact on regional political stability, social cohesion, and subnational cultures—all of which will enrich South Asia.

The first section below sketches out the historical background of South Asia and describes why its level of economic integration has remained so low. In the second section, the changing global and regional realities that are now strengthening the area's prospects for regional cooperation are discussed. The third section explains why India, the dominant economy in South Asia, should support cooperation and economic integration in the region. The last section brings together the main arguments of the chapter, points to a possible way forward, and details the likely hurdles to regional cooperation in South Asia.

South Asia: A Persistent Low Level of Economic Integration

Though it is home to about 1.5 billion people, or 23 percent of the world's population,[3] South Asia accounts for barely 2.5 percent of the world's gross domestic product (GDP) and 2 percent of world trade. It thus remains a small player in the global markets. The region is relatively underdeveloped and seeks better integration with the global labor market. It is also perhaps the only region in the world that has seen the continuous fragmentation of a once-integrated economic space.

Table 5.1 South Asia's Share in the World Economy, 2008 (%)

Indicator	2008
Population	23.1
Surface area	3.8
Gross domestic product (GDP)	2.5
Trade	2.0
Inward foreign direct investment (FDI) flows	2.9
Inward FDI stock	1.1
Total reserves minus gold	5.4

Source: World Development Indicators Database (WDI) 2009, Asia Regional Integration Center (ARIC)–Integration Indicators Database, United Nations Conference on Trade and Development (UNCTAD)–FDI Database.

The eight countries that constitute South Asia have diverse economic features. India's GDP and population are by far the largest in the region, with Pakistan's GDP and population running a distant second. India's dominance in nearly all aspects of South Asia is a special feature of the region, one that works both for and against greater economic cooperation. In 2008 India accounted for nearly 80.6 percent of the region's GDP, 40.3 percent of its trade, and 84.5 percent of the incoming foreign direct investment (FDI).[4]

India is the only South Asian country that shares borders with all the other countries of the region; its geography thus reinforces its central position in South Asia. However, in terms of economic well-being, as measured by the human development index, India lags behind Sri Lanka and the Maldives[5] and is only just ahead of Pakistan and Bhutan. According to recent estimates, nearly 75 percent of India's population lives on less than fifty cents per day.[6] India needs a stable, peaceful, and prosperous neighborhood to achieve sustained and inclusive growth across all its regions and communities and to successfully tackle poverty.

Table 5.2 Share of Member Countries in the South Asian Economy, 2008

Indicator	Afghanistan	Bangladesh	Bhutan	India	Maldives	Nepal	Pakistan	Sri Lanka
				% Share in the SAARC				
Population	1.71	10.03	0.04	74.05	0.02	1.81	11.09	1.26
Land area	13.64	2.72	0.98	62.18	0.01	2.99	16.12	1.35
GDP, PPP	N/A	5.08	0.08	80.60	0.04	0.76	10.44	2.19
Trade in goods	0.92	5.78	N/A	78.37	0.24	0.62	10.49	3.58
Export of services	N/A	1.72	N/A	91.56	0.63	0.64	3.67	1.78
FDI inflows	0.61	2.21	0.06	84.50	0.03	0.002	11.06	1.53

Source: Calculations based on data from World Development Indicators Database (WDI) 2009, Asia Regional Integration Center (ARIC) Integration Indicators Database, Balance of Payments (BOP) statistics, International Monetary Fund (IMF), United Nations Conference on Trade and Development (UNCTAD)–FDI Database.

Note: GDP = gross domestic product; PPP = purchasing power parity; FDI = foreign direct investment.

Proposed by Bangladeshi president Ziaur Rahman in the late 1970s, the South Asian Association for Regional Cooperation (SAARC)[7] was established in 1985 in an attempt to reverse the tide of conflict in the post-independence era. Young national leaders such as Benazir Bhutto and Rajiv Gandhi were vocal supporters of the group. Yet SAARC has proved to be a premature and top-down attempt at promoting regional cooperation, since realities on the ground—particularly trade and investment flows and political will—have not been in place to support it. By the late 1980s, the SAARC had lost its champions and become somewhat directionless. This loss of political support at the top, combined with member countries' mistrust of one another and constant preoccupation with domestic crises, has resulted in meager progress toward regional integration. Indeed, today the region ranks as one of the world's most troubled and unstable neighborhoods. Six of the eight SAARC members are grappling with racial, communal, extremist, or regional strife. With two nuclear-armed countries and ongoing subregional conflicts, it would be fair for an outsider to characterize South Asia as ripe for a major global conflagration.[8]

In 2008 the total value of merchandise trade reported by the South Asian countries (excluding Bhutan) was $651.46 billion, of which only $30.63 billion was destined for the SAARC member states.[9] In other words, intraregional trade in South Asia accounted for approximately only 4.7 percent of the region's total trade. This figure had been more or less stagnant for the previous fifteen years, ranging from 3 to 5 percent, though according to some reports, unofficial border trade equals or exceeds official trade in several SAARC countries.

Figure 5.1 Intraregional Trade as Share of Total SAARC Trade, 1991–2008

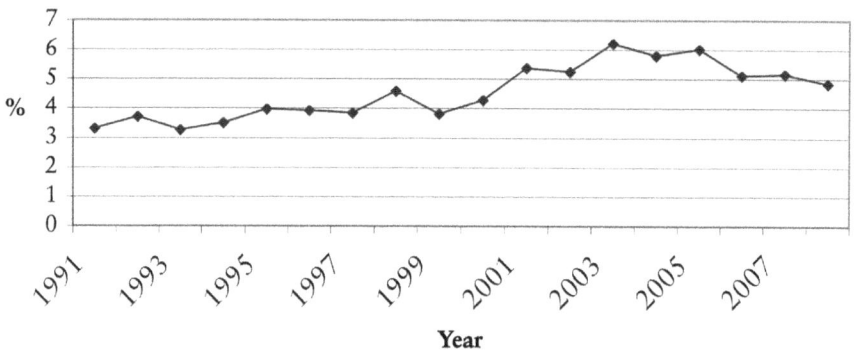

Source: Asia Regional Integration Center–Integration Indicators Database.

Given the prospect of trade diversion and unequal sharing of benefits and the relatively high levels of protection in the region, several empirical studies have shown that trade gains from the South Asian Free Trade Area (SAFTA) might be expected to be minimal.[10] However, some researchers have found that regional economic cooperation, especially if it leads to greater investment flows, could yield significant net benefits.[11] The substantial informal or border trade also contributes to the low level of intraregional trade in South Asia.[12] However, even if one takes into account trade estimates,[13] intraregional trade would still be less than a tenth of the region's total trade, the reasons being:

- *Too small and too few economies* with similar revealed comparative advantage and low levels of trade complementarity.[14]
- *Fear of India.* This is perhaps more pronounced in the bureaucracies than in industry or civil society.
- *Weak port and transport infrastructure.* One estimate shows that if South Asia's infrastructure capacity were increased to even half of East Asia's, then intraregional trade could increase by 60 percent.[15]
- *High tariffs.* South Asia is one of the most heavily protected regions in the world;[16] moreover, a wide range of nontariff barriers (NTBs) are also used to protect national interests, and these are even more difficult to identify and remove than tariffs.[17]
- *Difficult business environment.* South Asia ranks as the second-least-business-friendly region in the world, after sub-Saharan Africa. None of the South Asian countries ranks among the top fifty countries in the world for ease of trading across borders.[18] In contrast, China ranks forty-second.
- *Restrictive rules of origin and destination* even under bilateral free trade agreements (FTAs), which restrict imports. The coexistence of high tariff barriers and tight rules of origin raises the risk of trade diversion.[19]
- *Lack of commitment to regional free trade.* While a decision was taken at the Fourteenth SAARC Summit in New Delhi to bring services under the scope of the SAFTA, members still have prohibitively long "sensitive" lists of protected items. Going even further, Pakistan still insists that its trade with India be determined by a "positive" list of tradable commodities.[20]
- *Services are not included in the SAFTA* although they account for more than half the GDP in most South Asian economies.

It is important to emphasize that all the quantitative estimates, whether they are based on gravity or augmented gravity models or on computational general equilibrium (CGE) models using the Global Trade Analysis Project (GTAP) database, are understandably undertaken in a static framework; therefore, they fail to capture the likely gains in a dynamic setting. None of the static estimates, for example, had predicted that trade between Sri Lanka and India would nearly quadruple in the aftermath of their bilateral FTA, despite a number of trade-restrictive features that remain in place. Moreover, trade liberalization between economies that are at a similar stage of development generates a large volume of intraindustry trade—trade that cannot be captured in static models. These gains emerge from a discovery of relative comparative advantages among firms in a situation where supply chains often overlap.[21] This is quite distinct from trade liberalization between developed and developing economies, which typically results in outsourcing from the former to the latter with relatively limited gains.[22]

Changing Realities in South Asia

That SAARC succeeded in pushing through the SAFTA agreement in 2006—albeit a watered-down version—indicates that there may still be sufficient political will among participating countries to keep the forum alive. Global and regional conditions have changed somewhat dramatically since SAARC's founding twenty-five years ago. During this period, all South Asian economies have been pursuing unilateral economic liberalization, and all of them (except Nepal) have seen higher economic growth since the beginning of this century as a result (see table 5.3).

Table 5.3 Growth Rates of Gross Domestic Product (GDP) and GDP per capita in South Asia

Country	Average growth in GDP (%)		Average growth in GDP per capita (%)*	
	In the 1990s	2003–2008	In the 1990s	2003–2008
Afghanistan	N/A	10.6	N/A	6.8
Bangladesh	4.5	6.2	2.7	4.4
Bhutan	5.3	9.3	5.2	8.1
India	4.2	8.4	3.5	6.8
Maldives	11.3	7.4	4.3	5.3
Nepal	4.5	3.9	3.3	2.5
Pakistan	4.5	5.6	1.5	3.6
Sri Lanka	7.4	6.3	3.9	5.4

Source: Calculations based on data from World Economic Outlook (WEO), International Monetary Fund (IMF), October 2009.
Note: * Calculations for this indicator based on GDP per capita, constant prices (national currency).

So, if unilateral economic liberalization has led to growth, what does greater economic cooperation have to offer South Asia? First, South Asian countries will experience pure economic gains through the more efficient use of capital and labor resulting from the freer cross-border movement of goods and services. Once cross-border production networks expand in South Asia, as they have done in Southeast Asia, these gains will be even greater: as the networks grow, so will intraindustry trade, the most dynamic aspect of intraregional trade. But for this to happen, the regional business environment and connectivity must be improved. South Asian governments should make such improvements a high priority.

Second, greater regional integration will lead to nontraditional gains such as the increased flow of FDI, as regional markets become more accessible to outside investors. Third, when the South Asian countries negotiate as a unified group in multilateral forums, they will reap strategic benefits including greater market access, lower transaction costs, and higher investment flows both to and from these regional economies. Finally, regional integration will bring substantial developmental and environmental efficiency gains. Working together, the South Asian countries can take an integrated approach toward the provision of regional public goods such as water, infrastructure, and natural resources like ecosystems and related biodiversity. Countries working alone cannot address these issues as effectively.

While the economic and nontraditional gains that arise from intraindustry trade and investment flows have been widely discussed, the political and security benefits of regional cooperation in South Asia also deserve consideration, for they are often the main driving force behind the emergence of regional blocs.[23] For example, it was the fear of China's dominance that initially drove the Southeast Asian economies to form the Association of Southeast Asian Nations (ASEAN), and the European Union (EU) was formed in part as a response to the emergence of the United States and the USSR as world powers. Likewise the terrorist threat to India and Pakistan has prompted these governments to improve their relationship and engage in political dialogue to ensure political stability and social harmony. The "composite dialogue" process, established in 2007, reflects a real advance from the countries' positions in the past, when no forward movement was possible without addressing the so-called core issue of Kashmir. Greater regional and bilateral cooperation among emerging economies can also be seen as a response to the slow progress of multilateral trade agreements and the increasing tendency of developed economies to pursue regionalism.[24]

The other main driver of economic integration in South Asia is the need for greater energy security. All these countries are dependent on energy imports, specifically on oil and gas from Central and West Asia. If they worked together, the SAARC economies could be a unified energy market, connected to oil and gas fields by overland pipelines. Boosting energy trade in the region could also act as a confidence-building measure and a way to ensure long-term economic interdependence.[25] Given Afghanistan's membership in SAARC, the region can expect further gains through alliances with Central Asian countries—alliances that will bring immediate and significant benefits to Afghanistan as well. This is a golden opportunity, and if South Asia does not achieve regional economic integration soon, it may lose out on its share of Central Asia's massive energy resources. Other regions, such as Europe and China, have already advanced plans for extracting these resources by laying the required pipelines and finalizing the necessary agreements.

Some say that India would achieve much greater gains by "signing an FTA with itself," as it were, than by integrating with the other South Asian economies. This is a valid argument: numerous border restrictions and other procedural features still impede the flow of goods and factors of production across state borders within India. While there has been some progress in reducing these impediments, the Indian domestic market is still not fully integrated. So should India focus first on removing these domestic restrictions and then tackle the cross-border issues with its neighbors? In my view, progress on these two fronts may take place simultaneously, as the two issues are handled by completely different parts of the government. Moreover, the success of the Indo–Sri Lanka Bilateral Free Trade Agreement (ILBFTA) suggests that a regional FTA would generate its own pressure to further integrate the domestic market within India and to regularize fiscal and other procedures across states.[26]

Regional cooperation is likely to produce substantial noneconomic gains as well. First and foremost, it will likely reduce South Asia's political instability and tension, making South Asia a more attractive place for FDI and remittances from nonresidents, lowering defense budgets, and creating a more favorable climate for overall development. And as argued at length below, the border regions are especially likely to benefit, with decreased militancy and terrorist activity and increased social and cultural interaction.

India's Changing Attitude toward Regional Cooperation

Four factors have helped to change India's perspective on SAARC. First, India has come to see regional cooperation as less of a threat. For years, the Indian security and foreign policy establishment viewed SAARC as a mechanism to help its smaller neighbors compete against it more effectively, thus denying India its rightful place in the regional and global polity and undermining India's national interests. While vestiges of this mind-set can still be found in the South Block, which houses both the Ministry of External Affairs and the Ministry of Defense, this perception has changed since the 1990s. India's neighbors have come to realize that forming a coalition that excludes India would be neither feasible nor successful. Moreover, major powers from outside the region seem to have finally accepted India's relatively dominant position in South Asia (especially following its robust economic growth since 1991) and have backed off from using their bilateral or regional relationships with India's neighbors to try and "redress the asymmetry" within the region. Both these political developments have given India greater confidence in the SAARC process.

The second factor behind India's improved attitude toward SAARC is its realization that collective regional initiatives are the best means of securing territorial integrity in its peripheral regions and of fighting poverty in its border states. India's lagging regions are primarily on its borders with other South Asian countries; conditions in the seven provinces of the northeastern region are especially poor, with significant militant activity further threatening stability. These can be opened up only through successful cooperation with the neighboring countries. (For example, the challenges posed by the northeastern states' landlocked status can be addressed by negotiating transport through Bangladesh.) India's realization of this point has recently led the government to allow multilateral organizations to play a part in infrastructure development and transport connectivity in its border regions.

The third factor that has helped to change India's changing perception of regional cooperation has been its own economic performance since its 1991 reforms. Especially since 2000, India has taken off economically and won worldwide recognition as a global player. This has given the country, particularly its political and industrial leaders and bureaucrats, confidence that the world will engage with India regardless of its relationships with its neighbors. This has made India less defensive about its neighbors' policies and more open toward them, though in some policy and industry circles there is a feeling (albeit a weak one) that India can afford to neglect its neighborhood as its future prospects don't really depend on regional developments.

The fourth major reason for India's changing perception of SAARC is directly related to China's growing influence in the region. As of 2009 all the South Asian economies except Bhutan and Nepal had larger bilateral trade volumes with China than with India, despite the fact that China does not have preferential FTAs with any of these countries aside from Pakistan. China pursued a strategic political-cum-economic relationship with Pakistan and in 2006 the two countries finally signed an FTA laying out a multidimensional economic partnership on energy, communication, and agriculture; technical cooperation; joint investment ventures; and so on.[27] China is finalizing FTAs with other South Asian economies as well and has already proposed one with India.

The growing Chinese economic presence in South Asia is a matter of concern to Delhi, as well it should be. Other South Asian countries are apt to follow the lead of Myanmar, which has extensive and growing relations with China, unless India shores up its bilateral and regional relations with its neighbors. Indo-China trade has burgeoned from virtually nothing at all to more than $43 billion in 2009.[28] This is itself seen as a major competitive threat to India's manufacturing sector, which is now seeking new markets to increase its export demand. Moreover, China is making strategic investments in infrastructure projects in South Asia, such as in the Gwadar port in Pakistan, as part of its "string of pearls" strategy of extending its influence and access to ports and airfields around the Bay of Bengal and Arabian Sea. China has also achieved greater penetration of global markets by making itself a hub for export-oriented production networks in Southeast Asia.

Table 5.4 Total Trade with South Asia: India versus China

	2000		2008		CAGR	
	India	China	India	China	India	China
	US$ million				%	
Afghanistan	53.0	25.3	368.3	155.4	27.4	25.5
Bangladesh	940.2	918.4	3,543.8	4,685.0	18.0	22.6
Bhutan	N/A	N/A	N/A	N/A	N/A	N/A
India	N/A	2,911.2	N/A	51,857.7	N/A	43.3
Maldives	20.5	1.4	100.7	32.7	22.0	48.8
Nepal	381.9	204.2	2,179.4	380.5	24.3	8.1
Pakistan	228.4	1,162.5	2,388.6	6,998.5	34.1	25.2
Sri Lanka	649.7	458.3	3,737.5	1,683.8	24.4	17.7

Source: Calculated from the data given in the Asia Regional Integration Center (ARIC) Integration Indicators Database.
Note: CAGR=compound annual growth rate.

India has responded to China's growing power by getting involved in the Bay of Bengal Initiative for Multisectoral Technical and Economic Cooperation (BIMSTEC), spearheading the Swarnabhoomi initiative, establishing a bilateral FTA with Thailand, and finalizing the Indo-ASEAN FTA. India has also initiated a "look East" policy that purports not only to give greater attention to India's northeastern region but to expand India's influence in Southeast Asia and East Asia.[29] But despite these positive developments, India has not fully committed to the SAARC for two reasons. First, it believes that Pakistan's government is holding up the group's progress, and second, it believes its neighbors are making unreasonable demands on it. India has thus concluded that its national interests are better served by supporting other regional programs, such as the BIMSTEC, the Indian Ocean Rim Initiative, and the Swarnabhoomi initiative, and devoting more attention to bilateral FTAs. There is perhaps some merit to this approach: India is now accepted as a global player, as is reflected by its membership in the World Trade Organization's (WTO's) "new quad" and the Outreach 5 group of important developing economies. Accordingly, some might argue that India is right to ignore its neighborhood, rife as it is with dissent, conflict, and instability. But I believe this view is incorrect and that India ought to actively work to make SAARC successful for the following reasons:

- *Make de facto de jure.* India already has extensive interaction with its neighbors in the form of informal border trade. By activating SAFTA and including trade in services within the agreement, India will merely formalize this de facto situation, with no impact on the Indian industry or service sectors. This also applies to the flow of human resources into India from neighboring countries, which cannot be controlled by any border fencing or other measures.

- *Increased FDI.* Although FDI inflows to the region have increased in recent years, they continue to be well below their potential.[30] A more peaceful, stable, and regionally integrated South Asia will attract greater volumes of FDI.
- *Dynamic trade gains.* Contrary to predictions based on quantitative models, Indo–Sri Lanka trade has more than tripled since both nations entered into the ILBFTA in 2000.[31] Bilateral investment has grown as well. However, a bit paradoxically, the highest growth in Sri Lanka's imports from India has been in products covered by the sensitive list.[32]
- *Returns to scale.* Regional integration will provide a larger market and scope for intraindustry trade. And by exploiting economies of scale and scope, industry in India and South Asia as a whole will be able to lower costs and become more globally competitive.
- *Increased efficiency in the provision of public goods and services.* The South Asian subcontinent is an integrated geoecological system. Thus, some public goods and services—such as energy, water management and conservation, prevention against pandemics, and promotion of tourism—can be most efficiently provided on a regional basis. It is in India's interests to take a cooperative approach to the delivery of regional public goods and services.
- *Connectivity with the rest of Asia.* South Asia lies between Central Asia and Southeast Asia, both of which are increasingly engaged in regional cooperation and infrastructure development with China's strong encouragement. If South Asia were integrated, resources from Central and West Asia could be moved to East and Southeast Asia by overland pipelines, thus improving trans-Asian connectivity and bringing greater energy security to the region. South Asian economies, including India's, would also benefit significantly from the greater flow of trade, commerce, and investment such pipelines would bring.
- *Increased cross-border interaction.* Cross-border cooperation would help to transform India's peripheral and lagging regions into hubs of economic activity. It would also strengthen India's multireligious, multiethnic, and pluralistic society by giving minority groups that might feel isolated within India the opportunity to connect with their counterparts across the border.

Supporting SAARC will thus facilitate India's ongoing modernization as well as contribute to the cultural diversity that is a hallmark of the South Asian subcontinent.

Conclusion: The Way Forward

At this point, the path toward South Asian integration is not a clear or direct one. Several hurdles and vested interests will have to be overcome. First, the confidence-building and trade-expanding measures that are already in place or in the pipeline should be pursued with greater vigor. These include a further strengthening of the SAARC Secretariat by bringing in more professional expertise and increasing the pay for secretariat positions so as to attract better candidates. The ongoing work in identifying and eliminating the plethora of nontariff measures that are not transparent and vitiate the trade environment should also be completed as soon as possible.

Second, the ruling elites in South Asia, including the armed forces in some cases, will have to understand that greater regional economic cooperation and integration do not impinge either on their spheres of influence or on national sovereignty and security. Today, the credibility of the ruling elites in all South Asian countries depends on their ability to foster rapid and sustainable growth that benefits all sectors of society. Regional cooperation will contribute to this goal, while noncooperation will likely hurt all the economies of the region.

Third, the business lobbies in all the SAARC member countries—particularly those involved in industry—will have to be convinced that regional cooperation and the opening of markets will give them a larger space to thrive. South Asian industrialists have long shown a persistent preference for producing national brands and trading in finished products over producing and trading in semifinished products or, especially, primary resources. This is perhaps one of the reasons why both India and China have a major trade surplus with the South Asian economies, which is not the case with China and its Southeast Asian neighbors. South Asian policymakers and industry leaders must break out of this mind-set and accept that all exports are worthwhile and important, as long as they generate much-needed employment and have value on the international market.

Fourth, SAARC countries must reconsider their stance toward security and locate the real source of the threat. Though security is a major concern across the region, it is likely that external security threats, such as those reportedly posed by neighboring countries, have been exaggerated to protect vested interests, while internal security threats—such as poverty, government corruption, and inequitable growth—have been downplayed. SAARC countries, particularly India, should realize that regional cooperation could actually increase internal security and ameliorate some of these problems. Yet a decade after signing an FTA with Sri Lanka, India has yet to reciprocate Sri Lanka's "visa on arrival" facility for Indian tourists. It should be evident that attempts to enhance security by fencing borders or by further tightening visa regimes (by insisting on "police reporting requirements" and so on) do not really work.

Fifth, SAARC countries must work not only to stem any further rise in ultranationalistic positions but to create a better understanding of neighboring cultures and societies. To some extent awareness is already being raised through the spread of films, television series, and cricket, but this not enough. SAARC countries should initiate a large student exchange program for improving cross-cultural understanding among the younger generation; these types of programs produced excellent results in Europe after World War II and are now bearing fruit in East Asia.

In the rapidly changing global environment, regional integration in South Asia has assumed a new strategic significance, and the potential political, economic, and strategic benefits from SAARC for all the country partners are larger than ever before. The economic and noneconomic payoffs for India are particularly substantial. Indeed, India's status in the world economic order in the twenty-first century will be greatly enhanced if it can ensure a stable and secure South Asian region. It is thus incumbent on India, as the largest economy of the region, to generate an environment of trust among its SAARC partners, which in turn would increase their commitment to regional integration. Stretching from Kabul in the west to Chittagong and indeed to Yangon in the east and to Colombo and Malé in the south, South Asia was an integrated economic, cultural, and environmental space until its independence from colonial rule. Its move toward increasing fragmentation needs to be reversed if the region's countries are to fully realize their potential and achieve rapid, sustainable, and inclusive economic growth.

Notes

[1] See also Dubey, chapter 3 in this volume.

[2] I have argued elsewhere that the objective for regional cooperation in South Asia should be to integrate the economic space from Kabul to Yangon, Myanmar, as this was the integrated economy prior to the independence of Afghanistan and Myanmar after World War II.

[3] See World Development Indicators Database (WDI) 2009. Data on Afghanistan, which joined in 2006, is not available. Historically, this region has been referred to as the Indian subcontinent, which results in some level of apprehension in the smaller countries about their ability to retain their individual identities in the post-SAARC context. This is now changing to a more common use of "South Asia" for describing the region.

[4] See World Development Indicators Database 2009, Asia Regional Integration Center (ARIC) Integration Indicators Database, United Nations Conference on Trade and Development (UNCTAD) FDI database.

[5] In 2004 the United Nations (UN) General Assembly decided to graduate the Maldives out of the least-developed country (LDC) group, but revised the decision following the devastation caused by the tsunami a few days later. The Maldives will be graduated out of the LDC group in 2011. See UNCTAD (United Nations Conference on Trade and Development), *World Investment Report 2006—FDI from Developing and Transition Economies: Implications for Development* (Geneva: UNCTAD, 2006), 47.

[6] See National Commission for Enterprises in the Unorganized Sector, *Report on Conditions of Work and Promotion of Livelihoods in the Unorganized Sector* (Government of India, August 2007).

[7] Established by the seven countries of Bangladesh, Bhutan, India, Maldives, Nepal, Pakistan, and Sri Lanka; Afghanistan became the eighth member in 2005.

[8] South Asia has been often characterized as the second-most-likely spot, after the Middle East, where the world could see a nuclear conflagration. Steve Cohen and several U.S. security experts have written along these lines.

[9] Based on data on exports from Afghanistan, Bangladesh, India, Maldives, Nepal, Pakistan, and Sri Lanka from the Asia Regional Integration Center (ARIC) Integration Indicators Database.

[10] Bandara and Yu use a general equilibrium model to show that gains under the SAFTA are skewed, with only India gaining substantially. See Jayatilleke S. Bandara and Wusheng Yu, "How Desirable is the South Asian Free Trade Area? A Quantitative Economic Assessment," *World Economy* 26 (2003): 1293–322. Pitigala and Baysan, Panagariya, and Pitigala argue, however, that given the level of protection in South Asia vis-à-vis the rest of the world, the risk of trade diversion is rather high. See Nihal Pitigala, "What Does Regional Trade in South Asia Reveal about Future Trade Integration?: Some Empirical Evidence," Policy Research Working Paper 3497, World Bank, Washington, D.C., 2005; Tercan Baysan, Arvind Panagariya, and Nihal Pitigala, "Preferential Trading in South Asia," Policy Research Working Paper 3813, World Bank, Washington, D.C., 2006.

[11] S. W. Hirantha finds evidence of significant trade creation under the South Asian Preferential Trade Arrangement (SAPTA), using the gravity model analysis, and no evidence of a trade diversion effect with the rest of the world. See Hirantha, "From SAPTA to SAFTA: Gravity Analysis of South Asian Free Trade," mimeo, University of Jayewardenepura, Sri Lanka, 2004.

[12] For instance, Taneja shows that India's unofficial trade (exports plus imports) with Bhutan, Nepal, Pakistan, and Sri Lanka was estimated to be more than its official trade with them in the 1990s. Taneja provides a good overview of the causes, pattern, and extent of informal trade among the SAARC countries. See Nisha Taneja, "Informal Trade in the SAARC Region," Working Paper no. 47, Indian Council for Research on International Economic Relations, New Delhi, 1999.

[13] See chapter 3, Dubey, in this volume.

[14] See A. R. Kemal, "SAFTA and Economic Cooperation," 2005, www. southasianmedia.net/conference/Regional_Conference/safta.htm.

[15] See John S. Wilson and Tsunehiro Ostuki, "Trade Facilitation and Regional Integration in South Asia: Accelerating the Gains to Trade with Capacity Building," South Asia Region, World Bank, Washington, D.C., 2005.

[16] In particular, India is considered to be the least open among the group in terms of its trade-weighted average applied tariff, with a rate of 30.1 percent, followed by Bangladesh with 21.3 percent, Pakistan with 17.4 percent, and Nepal with 15.5 percent; Sri Lanka is the most open with an average applied tariff of 6.2 percent. See UNCTAD, *Developing Countries in International Trade 2005: Trade and Development Index* (Geneva: UNCTAD, 2005), table A2.

[17] The SAARC members specify the port of entry sometimes for all imports and often for selective products. While this approach has been ostensibly implemented to curb illegal imports, it also seems to be driven by inadequate administrative capacity

and as a protective measure, as it raises transport and transaction costs of formal trade and promotes informal border trade.

[18] *Doing Business 2008*, a copublication of the World Bank and the International Finance Corporation, www.doingbusiness.org/EconomyRanking.

[19] Baysan, Panagariya, and Pitigala contend that a persuasive case for the SAFTA can be made if the countries in the region lower their overall tariff down to 5 percent or below, as well as ease the restrictive rules of origin and sectoral exceptions. See Baysan, Panagariya, and Pitigala, "Preferential Trading in South Asia."

[20] Almost 53 percent of the total import trade among the SAFTA members has been subject to the sensitive lists of the member countries. For example, India and Sri Lanka have restricted up to 38 percent and 52 percent, respectively, of their total imports by value from the SAFTA members under the sensitive list category. See Dushni Weerakoon and Jayanthi Thennakoon, "SAFTA Myth of Free Trade," *Economic and Political Weekly* (September 16, 2006): 3920–23.

[21] See also Dossani, Sneider, and Sood, chapter 1 in this volume.

[22] This remains a potential area for empirical research; to the best of our knowledge there is no such work for South Asia.

[23] See Jo Ann Crawford and Roberto V. Fiorentino, "The Changing Landscape of Regional Trade Agreements," WTO Discussion Paper 8, World Trade Organization, Geneva, 2005.

[24] A total of 211 regional trade agreements for goods and services are in force today. While 124 regional trade agreements for goods were notified in the General Agreement on Trade and Tariffs (GATT) (some no longer in force) during 1948–1994, more than 130 agreements covering trade in goods and services have been notified since 1995 under the WTO (as of September 15, 2006). See WTO, *International Trade Statistics 2006* (Geneva: World Trade Organization, 2006), www.wto.org/english/tratop_e/region_e/summary_e.xls.

[25] See S. G. Pandian, "Energy Trade as a Confidence-Building Measure between India and Pakistan: A Study of the Indo-Iran trans-Pakistan Pipeline Project," *Contemporary South Asia* 14, no. 3 (2005): 307–20.

[26] Sri Lankan exporters complain about the differential effective rates of import tariffs that they face when supplying their goods to different states in India. Moreover, states are prone to charge state-specific entry taxes even on imports, which is not legal but cannot always be monitored and prevented. There is also a possibility that a landlocked Indian state could press for easier access across the border for imports from a neighboring country. This adds to the internal pressure to reform the domestic regime and make it consistent across the nation.

[27] The two countries signed an FTA in November 2006 that is expected to increase their bilateral trade from $4.3 billion in 2005 to $15 billion in the next five years. See "China, Pakistan sign free trade agreement," *People's Daily Online* (English), November 25, 2006, http://english.people.com.cn/200611/24/eng20061124_324918.html.

[28] Embassy of India (Beijing), *Economic and Commercial Report*, 2009.

[29] Please see Emmott Bill, *Rivals, India, China and Japan* (Oxford: Oxford Univ. Press, 2008).

[30] UNCTAD, *World Investment Report 2006*.

[31] The gravity model analysis of Batra (2004) found that India's bilateral trade with Sri Lanka and Nepal has gone far beyond the level of trade predicted on the basis

of natural factors (distance, landlockedness, population, and income) based on the 2000 database. See Amita Batra, "India's Global Trade Potential: The Gravity Model Approach," ICRIER Working Paper 151, New Delhi, 2004.

[32] How much of this trade expansion represents trade diversion or trade creation is still an open question. See Baysan, Panagariya, and Pitigala, "Preferential Trading in South Asia."

BHUTAN, NEPAL, AND SAARC: HARNESSING OLD RESOURCES WITH NEW INSTRUMENTS

Mahendra P. Lama

Bhutan and Nepal are among the five least-developed countries (LDCs) in the eight-member regional grouping of the South Asian Association for Regional Cooperation (SAARC).[1] Together they account for 1.67 percent of the population of South Asia, 3.97 percent of its landmass, 1.04 percent of its gross domestic product (GDP), 0.82 percent of its exports, and 0.13 percent of its foreign direct investment (FDI). Though both countries have been actively participating in SAARC since its inception, their position in this regional body is characterized by a number of special features.

- *Both countries are landlocked and are largely hilly and mountainous.*[2] Their only access to sea routes is through India. Nepal, for instance, depends on the Kolkata and Chennai ports (see table 6.1).
- *Both have treaties with India that recognize India's asymmetric power in the region.* The India-Nepal Treaty of Peace and Friendship of 1950,[3] for example, established the framework for unique ties between the two countries. It provided a basis for the preservation and protection of mutual security interests[4] and, recognizing the importance of keeping borders open, contained far-reaching provisions for reciprocity in the movement of people and their socioeconomic interactions.[5] Letters of amendment subsequently exchanged between the two nations on this treaty further restricted Nepal's ability to invite other countries to undertake development projects.[6] Nepal has since raised concerns about these amendments and even mentioned abrogating the treaty. In addition, Nepal has signed three other agreements with India: on trade (1960), transit (1960), and unauthorized trade (1978, with subsequent amendments).
- Similarly, the India-Bhutan Treaty of Friendship of 1949[7] stipulated that India would have a role in regulating Bhutan's foreign policy.[8] Significant amendments in 2007[9] drastically reduced India's role and emphasized Bhutan's national interest.[10] However, key provisions on free trade[11] and arms imports by Bhutan,[12] as well as guarantees that equal legal treatment be accorded to each other's citizens,[13] remained intact.

- *Both have rich hydropower potential.* That potential, however, remains largely untapped, especially in Nepal (see table 6.2).
- *Both act as buffer states between India and China.*[14] Bhutan and Nepal share long and porous land borders with India and China. The Nepal-India border is 1,751 km long, the Nepal-China border 1,414 km, the Bhutan-India border 699 km, and the Bhutan-China border 470 km.[15] Bhutan and China continue to have border disputes, as documented in the Bhutan-China agreement of 1998.[16] The two countries have held eighteen rounds of meetings since April 1984 to reach a settlement, but China's "package deal" has not been acceptable to Bhutan[17] and the issue remains unresolved.
- *Both are accustomed to monarchic rule.* Nepal's 248-year-old monarchy came to an end in 2008. A popularly elected constituent assembly is in the process of designing and drafting a new constitution. Bhutan's monarchy continues, but major reforms have been instituted recently, including the establishment of an elected parliament under a new constitution. King Jigme Khesar Namgyel Wangchuck was coronated in 2008.[18]
- *Both are considered to be security frontiers by India.* As India's first prime minister, Jawaharlal Nehru, noted in 1950: "Apart from our sympathetic interest in Nepal, we are also interested in the security of our own country. From time immemorial, the Himalayas have provided us with a magnificent frontier. Of course, they are no longer impassable as they used to be, but are still fairly effective. We cannot allow that barrier to be penetrated because it is also the principal barrier to India. Therefore, much as we appreciate the importance of Nepal, we cannot allow anything to go wrong in Nepal or permit that barrier to be crossed or weakened because that would also be a risk to our security."[19]

A New Paradigm for Regionalism

Bhutan and Nepal are key participants in the "new regionalism" emerging in South Asia. What is new regionalism? Most visibly, it is a worldwide movement to strengthen civil society and to develop regional solutions to local, national, and global problems. In South Asia, regional economic, social, and cultural networks are at a more advanced stage of development than region-based political institutions. Accordingly, these networks are beginning to drive policymakers' agendas. For instance, the number of nongovernmental organizations (NGOs) working in Nepal jumped from 566 in 1991 to more than 8,000 in 2001, with the most significant growth taking place in the central development region—that is, in and around Kathmandu, where policy decisions are made. Most of these NGOs are directly or indirectly supported by international NGOs, and thus have strong regional and global links. The areas of operation of these NGOs have also undergone a major transformation.

Table 6.1 Main Trade and Transit Points along the Nepal-India Border

	Agreed-upon routes for mutual trade		Transit points to Kolkata Port
1.	Pashupatinagar–Sukhia Pokhari	1.	Sukhia Pokhari (Darjeeling district)
2.	Kakarbhitta–Naxalbari	2.	Naxalbari (Panitanki) (Darjeeling district)
3.	Bhadrapur–Galgalia	3.	Galgalia
4.	Biratnagar–Jogbani	4.	Jogbani (Bihar)
5.	Setobandha–Bhimnagar	5.	Bhimnagar
6.	Rajbiraj–Kunauli	6.	Jayanagar
7.	Siraha, Janakpur–Jayanagar	7.	Bhitamore
8.	Jaleswar–Bhitamore(Sursand)	8.	Raxaul (Bihar)
9.	Malangawa–Sonabarsa	9.	Nautanwa (Sonuali)
10.	Gaur–Bairgania	10.	Barhni
11.	Birgunj–Raxaul	11	Jarwa (Bihar)
12.	Bhairahawa–Nautanwa	12.	Nepalgunj Road (Uttar Pradesh)
13.	Taulihawe–Khunwa	13.	Tikonia
14.	Krishnanagar–Barhni	14.	Gauriphanta
15.	Koilabas–Jarwa	15.	Banbasa (Uttarakhand)
16.	Nepalgunj–Nepalgunj Road		
17.	Rajapur–Katerniyaghat		
18.	Prithivipur–Sati (Kailali)–Tikonia		
19.	Dhangadhi–Gauriphanta		
20.	Mahendranagar–Banbasa		
21.	Mahakali–Jhulaghat (Pithoragarh)		
22.	Darchula–Dharchula		

Source: Department of Customs, HMG–Nepal.

Table 6.2 Hydroelectric Potential and Installed Capacity in South Asia

Country	Hydroelectric potential (MW) (a)	Total installed hydelpower capacity (MW) (b)	Percentage harnessed of the total (b) as % of (a) (c)
Afghanistan	745	216	28.99
Bangladesh	555	218	39.27
Bhutan	30,000	1,500	5.00
India	75,400	36,878	48.9
Nepal*	45,610	627	1.37
Pakistan	40,000	6,500	16.25
Sri Lanka	2,000	1,247	62.35
Total	194,310	47,186	24.28

Sources: Water and Energy Commission Secretariat, Energy Synopsis Report 1994/95 (Kathmandu, 1996). Various national documents published by the electricity authorities of these countries during 2006–2008. Also see Energy Sector Management Assistance Programme, Potential and Prospects for Regional Energy Trade in South Asia, Formal Report 334/08, World Bank, Washington, D.C., August 2008.
Note: * In the case of Nepal, out of the theoretical potentiality of 83,290 MW, the technically feasible quantity is estimated at 45,610 MW.

New regionalism enlarges the scope of what we might term "old regionalism" by incorporating new understandings. These are revealed in five current definitions of a region as:

1. A geographical unit, delimited by more or less natural physical barriers and marked by ecological characteristics
2. A social system, implying translocal relations of varying natures among human groups
3. An organizational framework that promotes cultural, economic, political, and military cooperation
4. A policy environment that fosters—and is shaped by—strong civil society through the definition and communication of shared values
5. A global player with a distinct identity, capability, legitimacy, and decision-making structure[20]

Unlike the top-down approach traditionally adopted,[21] new regionalism is mainly triggered from below by (1) private markets and businesses and (2) civil society.[22] In the context of South Asia, a growing set of civil society actors has begun to challenge the state's monopoly in determining issues of public interest. These actors, which include NGOs, religious organizations, environmental groups, human rights organizations, regional economic cooperatives, local communities, multinational corporations (MNCs), diasporas, and migrants/refugees,[23] have entered into dynamic and flexible forms of regional cooperation and collaboration, ranging from informal coalitions to global conferences.[24] Such cooperation has led to the revitalization of civil society at the national, regional, and global level. The NGOs have a particularly vital role in both the management and resolution of some conflict situations. In other cases, they have acted as major agents in preventive diplomacy.[25]

Some of the nonstate actors advancing regionalism in Nepal do so for ethical reasons, as witnessed in the recent cooperation among organizations and activists working to prevent the trafficking of girls and women in South Asia. As one of the countries most affected by this practice, Nepal has one of the strongest anti-human-trafficking organizations in the region, Maiti Nepal. It has been networking with other groups in the region to prevent illegal trafficking by pressuring regional governments to make adequate legal provisions for fighting this menace. Ultimately it was this networking of civil society activists that led SAARC leaders to sign the Convention on Preventing and Combating Trafficking in Women and Children for Prostitution at the Eleventh SAARC Summit, held in Kathmandu in 2002.[26]

Bhutan and Nepal: Their Roles in SAARC

Bhutan and Nepal have been active members in SAARC since its inception in 1985. Like India's other small neighbors, both countries see the regional association as an important alternative to exclusively bilateral dealings with India. Their need for multilateral dialogue became more pressing after Sikkim, a protectorate of India, was merged into India as its twenty-second constituent state in 1975. Earlier, Bhutan had perceived a major threat from China after the takeover of Tibet in the 1950s. Meanwhile, despite its historically friendly relations with India, Nepal has tried to maintain equal political distance from both India and China.

As absolute monarchies, Bhutan and Nepal also saw regionalism as a way to resist the Indian brand of democracy. For Nepal this was particularly true from the time King Mahendra dissolved the first democratically elected government in 1960 until the reestablishment of democracy in 2008. Meanwhile, it remains an issue for Bhutan's monarchy. Pakistan and Bangladesh had similar motivations in joining SAARC as both these countries were, at various times, under military regimes. For its part, India was initially reluctant to join SAARC, fearing that its smaller neighbors would gang up against it in a regional forum. Thus, India insisted that two clauses[27] be included in the SAARC charter: first, that "decisions at all levels in SAARC are taken on the basis of unanimity" and, second, that "bilateral and contentious issues shall be excluded from the deliberations."

Finally, both Bhutan and Nepal joined SAARC in the hope that it would open economic opportunities.[28] Both of them hoped to expand their markets in the areas of trade, foreign investment, biodiversity harnessing, hydropower resources, industrial activities, and services such as tourism. In all these areas they have been dependent on India. Their need for multilateral economic relations is clearly expressed by recent government moves to open their diplomatic missions abroad, refrain from interfering in both internal and international affairs, and provide access to a variety of bilateral and multilateral agencies in the national development process. It was Bhutan that hosted the crucial foreign ministers meeting in 1985 where the SAARC charter was drafted; this paved the way for the formal launching of SAARC as a regional association in Dhaka later that year. Similarly, it was Nepal's enthusiasm for the group that led to the establishment of a permanent Secretariat of SAARC in Kathmandu.

Subsequently, both countries have hosted numerous SAARC activities, including meetings of ministers and foreign secretaries, seminars, workshops, conferences, trade fairs and exhibitions, sports and games, and training sessions, and have actively participated in a variety of SAARC programs (see table 6.3). For instance, the SAARC Tuberculosis Centre, established in Kathmandu in 1992, has played an important role in the prevention and control of tuberculosis in the SAARC region and has recently expanded its work to address the spread of HIV/AIDS, as reflected by its new name, SAARC Tuberculosis & HIV/AIDS Centre, or STAC. The center's most important program is its Partnership Programme in TB and HIV/AIDS. The STAC here plays an advocacy role, unlike other SAARC centers located in member countries. It is estimated that between 2010 and 2105, up to 25 percent of TB cases in South Asia will arise from HIV. This has prompted STAC to redouble its efforts, initiated in 2000, to educate students (schools/colleges), the media, pharmacists and druggists, medical colleges, the private sector, industry workers, and human resources agencies about these diseases. This center also coordinates the efforts of the national TB and HIV/AIDS programs of SAARC member countries.[29]

Similarly, in relative terms, Bhutan and Nepal has each contributed more than any other SAARC country to the South Asian Preferential Trade Arrangement (SAPTA) and South Asian Free Trade Area (SAFTA). Nepal's exports and imports within the region constitute more than 65 percent of its total global trade, whereas India's constitute only 3 percent, Pakistan's 6 percent, Sri Lanka's 17 percent, and Bangladesh's 9 percent. Bhutan's exports and imports within the region have been more than 80 percent of its total global trade. Both these countries also have bilateral trade treaties with India, which allow Nepalese and Bhutanese goods into the Indian market duty-free. India has vowed to extend the same access to all the South Asian LDCs.

Table 6.3 Major SAARC Activities

I. SAARC Integrated Program of Action (SIPA)
- Agricultural and rural development
- Communications and transport
- Social development
- Environmental conditions, meteorology, and forestry
- Science and technology
- Human resources development and energy

II. SAARC Agreements, Conventions, and Legal Issues
- Agreement on establishing the SAARC Food Security Reserve
- Regional Convention on Suppression of Terrorism
- Regional Convention on Narcotic Drugs and Psychotropic Substances
- SAARC Convention on Preventing and Combating the Trafficking of Women and Children for Prostitution
- SAARC Convention on Regional Arrangements for the Promotion of Child Welfare in South Asia
- Coordination of positions on multilateral legal issues
- Agreement for establishment of a South Asian University

III. SAARC Programs
- Poverty eradication
- Agreement on SAARC Preferential
- SAARC Preferential Trading Arrangement (SAPTA) and transition from SAPTA to South Asian Free Trade Area (SAFTA)
- The Social Charter
- SAARC Development Fund (SDF)
- Regional connectivity program

IV. SAARC Regional Centers
- Agricultural Information Centre (SAIC) (Dhaka, 1988)
- Tuberculosis Centre (STC) (Kathmandu, 1992)
- Documentation Center (SDC) (New Delhi, 1994)
- Meteorological Research Centre (SMRC) (Dhaka, 1995)
- Human Resources Development Centre (Islamabad, 1999)
- Energy Centre (Islamabad, 2005)
- Disaster Management Centre (New Delhi, 2006)

V. Other Major Activities
- People-to-people contact program
- Agreements with international organizations
- Recognition of apex professional regional bodies

Nepal headed the first Independent South Asian Commission on Poverty Alleviation (ISACPA), which, after conducting an in-depth study of the issue, reported its findings and recommendations at the Seventh SAARC Summit in 1992.[30] In addition to setting the rather formidable goal of eradicating poverty in South Asia by 2002, the commission provided a radical conceptual framework for poverty alleviation through social mobilization and empowerment. In particular, it called for the following:

- An annual growth rate of 9.1 percent
- Doubling of per capita income from $300 to $600
- Lowering of incremental capital-output ratio from 4:1 to 3:1
- An increase in the marginal savings rate from the then-current level to 27 percent or more

The commission also discussed microlevel interventions and lessons from the tedious delivery systems of the state mechanism.

At the summit, Nepal was appointed cochair of another ISACPA, which was asked to review the report of the erstwhile commission, to suggest further strategies for reducing the incidence of poverty in the region, to implement those strategies, and to monitor their effectiveness. The second ISACPA submitted its report, *Our Future, Our Responsibility: A Road Map towards a Poverty-Free South Asia*, in 2004.[31]

It was Bhutan that proposed the idea of the South Asian Development Fund (SADF) mooted at the Sixth SAARC Summit (in Colombo in 1991). The basic objective of the SADF was to provide finances for industrial development, poverty alleviation, environmental protection, balance-of-payments support, and promotion of economic projects in the region. The SADF was established in 1996 with the merger of the two earlier funds: the SAARC Fund for Regional Projects (SFRP) and the SAARC Regional Fund (SRF).[32]

The SADF had three objectives: (1) identification and development of projects, (2) institutional and human resources development, and (3) social and infrastructural development. To meet the first objective, the SADF funded feasibility studies for sixteen approved projects, of which twelve were completed by 2008. At its sixth meeting, in Malé, Maldives, the SADF governing board drew up a proposal, to be considered by the member states, to substantially increase its core capital base. Its current core capital base stands at $5.8 million.

In 1994 the Kathmandu-based Institute of Sustainable Development was entrusted with redesigning regional transport networks. It produced its *Report on Transport Linkages and Transit Facilities in the SAARC Region*, which was given to the Committee on Economic Cooperation (CEC) to review. The CEC asked member states to examine the report and send their comments, but as of 2009, no action has been taken on the issue (see Dubey, chapter 3 of this volume, for a further discussion of regional transport).

Yet despite their avid participation in the organization, SAARC has not been popular in either Nepal or Bhutan.[33] This lack of interest arises from a number of factors:

- The slow or delayed implementation of projects announced by SAARC
- The fact that poor regional transport connectivity continues to compound the physical isolation of both countries
- Both countries' small size and ongoing dependence on India, furthered by India's preference for engaging them in bilateral terms
- Poor institutional capabilities and internal political weaknesses
- The perception that SAARC is held hostage by India-Pakistan relations
- The belief that SAARC is susceptible to governmental machinations and lacks accountability (see Dubey, chapter 3)

Bhutan, Nepal, and the Promise of Regionalism

There is huge scope for Bhutan and Nepal to harness the opportunities created by the slowly deepening regionalism in South Asia and the vicinity. As of 2010 both countries have undergone substantive political changes and have made strides toward economic reform. A variety of development agencies and commercial players, including MNCs, are also at work in each, and cross-border investment flows are active. Both countries seem to realize the necessity of harnessing their natural resources and playing a greater geopolitical role by taking advantage of the burgeoning economies of India and China. Accordingly, Bhutan and Nepal should now be supplying the region with energy and more vigorously integrating with the peripheries of neighboring countries, such as the northern and eastern states of India and the southwestern provinces of China. In other words, Bhutan and Nepal should steadily expand their outlook and outreach as they move from being bilateral players to regional ones.

Bhutan and Nepal could use nontraditional instruments, such as the harnessing of natural resources including hydropower and customs-union-style liberal trading arrangements, to physically connect India with China. This initiative could transform the two countries into transit countries and promote extensive trans-Himalayan tourism ventures. As such, these two landlocked countries could leverage their core competencies and comparative advantages and thereby play a regional role in the management of crucial cross-border ventures. For instance, Bhutan and Nepal could be entrepots for trade and tourism among South Asian countries as well as China and the Southeast Asian countries. This could be realized by substantially expanding transport connectivity within and across their borders.

Energy Cooperation

Given its history, topographic and demographic features, natural resource endowments, and sociocultural ethos, South Asia is a natural unit of cooperation and integration. Creation of a South Asian energy market and cooperative development of its diverse energy sources would help increase the level of energy security in the region and thus contribute to stronger long-term economic growth. Competition among producers, both public and private, would also help to ensure the economic and efficient delivery of services to consumers in the region. At the same time, the power system networks of Bangladesh, Bhutan, India, Nepal, Pakistan, and even Sri Lanka could be interconnected to achieve greater regional efficiency and economy.[34]

Regional cooperation in the energy sector presents an array of enticing options. Cross-border energy trading is one of them: Bhutan's success story could be extended to Nepal, Bangladesh, and even Pakistan. Gas deposits in Bangladesh and hydropower potential in Bhutan, Nepal, and northeast India could supply the burgeoning South Asian market. The seasonality of both the generation of and demand for power in South Asia is particularly conducive to cross-border power trading, though in some cases, the imprudent use of power during a typical day and season has led to major losses. For instance, in Bangladesh at least 1,200 megawatts (MW) of electricity remain unutilized during the off-peak hours, so power plants remain essentially shut for these hours—they produce power only when they are requisitioned to produce. If the proper infrastructure were in place, this capacity could be traded with neighboring countries.[35]

Both Bhutan and Nepal have tremendous hydropower potential, but only a tiny percentage of this potential has been harnessed (see table 6.2). Indian cooperation in harnessing water resources has been widely accepted in Bhutan, resulting in projects that have yielded great benefits, but there have been obstacles in Nepal. India and Nepal started out cooperating well in the construction of projects such as the Gandak (15 MW), Kosi (18 MW), Trisuli (21 MW), and Devighat (14 MW) during the 1960s and 1970s.[36] However, little has been done since then—the Karnali, Rapti, and Pancheswar projects have been discussed for nearly four decades without any concrete progress. As a resource-rich country, Nepal has suffered on two vital counts. First, the power shortage in the country has seriously affected its economic, commercial, and social activities. Today Nepal faces one of the worst power crises in the world, with load shedding in the Kathmandu Valley running into twelve to fifteen hours, and its rural electrification efforts are in shambles. Second, Nepal has missed out on the huge amount of resources—not to mention political clout—it could have earned through exporting surplus power to its neighbors.

Differences between India and Nepal in three vital areas jeopardize the prospects of the projects that have already been agreed on, as well as any future collaboration in the energy sector. First, due to both historical reasons and present-day contexts, Nepal lacks confidence in India. Historically, Nepal feels that it did not get a good deal in the Kosi and Gandak projects,[37] a feeling that is exploited by interest groups. For its part, India has never seriously addressed these concerns. The situation is made more complex by domestic power politics: with nationalism on the rise, many influential Nepalese are actively trying to limit India and its influence. Second, India has been single-mindedly advocating a bilateral approach to projects with its neighbors, while Nepal has been emphasizing a multilateral approach. Through multilateralism, Nepal feels that it can avoid delays and huge cost overruns as well as address its low confidence in India's design expertise. It substantiates the latter aspect by pointing at Kosi and Gandak, which were found to be badly designed.

And third, India and Nepal have had difficulty agreeing on how the benefits of these projects should be shared; this is a particularly thorny issue that is being avoided more often than addressed. The two sides have even failed to decide whether they should discuss water-resource issues in isolation or in relation to broader issues such as energy and environmental security, trade and transit, and exchange and payments arrangements. Nepal's effort to bring these issues to the multilateral forum has added further complexity to the situation.

The 1996 signing of the Mahakali Treaty—which outlined an integrated development of the Mahakali river including the Sarda barrage, the Tanakpur barrage, and the Pancheswar project (a major high dam project)—seemed to signal a new beginning of relations between Nepal and India.[38] But a detailed project report, supposedly in progress for more than a decade, has yet to be delivered. Interestingly, the agreement is the first to encourage the private sector's role in such projects. It envisions two powerhouses, one on either side of the river, with a capacity of 3,240 MW each. The bulk of Nepal's share of the 3,240 MW would be sold to the Indian market at a mutually agreed-upon price. A separate trading arrangement through the Power Trade Agreement signed between Nepal and India will pave the way to this end.

The seasonal capacity surpluses in Nepal closely match the shortages in India. Hydropower plants in Nepal produce the most power in the wet months of May–September, precisely the months that India is hottest and thus requires the most electricity. India's northern, southern, and western regions have the greatest need for power imports. (The eastern region, which is less developed, does not require as much.) The northern region has particularly large energy needs, since it contains the nation's capital, Delhi, and some of the most populous states— Uttar Pradesh, Punjab, and Haryana—which all have significant industrial sectors. For instance, Delhi, Haryana, and western Uttar Pradesh alone have a load of around 9,000 MW, an amount that the Ministry of Power expects to rise to 23,000 MW by 2012. But by 2012, all of India's major power markets (that is, the north, south, and west) are expected to experience energy shortfalls, and the likely surpluses emanating from the eastern and northeastern regions are unlikely to close the gaps. Hence, importing power from neighboring countries appears to be the only viable option (see table 6.4).

Table 6.4 India's Projected Power Supply and Demand, 2012 (MW)

Region	Demand in 2001	Projected demand, 2012	Planned* capacity addition by 2012	Surplus or shortfall
North	21,000	49,000	14,000	(-)14,000
South	20,400	42,000	10,000	(-)12,000
West	24,900	46,000	16,000	(-)5,100
East and northeast	8,750	19,000	23,000	(+)12,750
Total	75,050	156,000	63,000	(-)17,950

Source: USAID, *The Four Borders Project: Reliability Improvement and Power Transfer in South Asia: A Pre-feasibility Study*, prepared for the USAID-SARI/E Program by Nexant, November 2001, 2–11.
Note: * By India's central government.

At the same time, the Water Resource Strategy Formulation (WRSF) studies conducted in Nepal predict that Nepal's exportable surplus will grow to 7,500 MW by 2027, a figure that could be much higher (19,314 MW) if upper-limit growth rates are considered[39] (table 6.5). Total power requirements have been assessed under moderate and revised high-growth scenarios (an annual GDP growth rate of 6.5 percent versus an annual GDP growth rate of 6.5 percent, rising to 7 percent and then to 8 percent). Domestic power demand under both scenarios has been assessed on the basis of the Master Plan Report, which makes predictions up to 2020. From 2020 to 2027, the average growth rate from 2012 to 2020 has been taken, which stands at 8.65 percent under the moderate case and 11.3 percent under the revised high-growth case.[40]

Thirty-four projects in Nepal are slated for expansion of generation capacity (table 6.6), and India can in fact absorb all this power. These projects are at different stages of planning and implementation.

Regional Initiatives

A number of organizations both within and outside the region have been working to increase cooperation in the energy sector in South Asia. These include technical and professional public-sector organizations, including Petrobangla; the power grid and power trading corporations of India; and the electricity authorities of India, Nepal, Sri Lanka, and Pakistan. International agencies such as the World Bank, the United Nations Economic and Social Commission for Asia and the Pacific (ESCAP), the Asian Development Bank (ADB), the United States Agency for International Development (USAID, SARI-E initiatives), and the United Nations Development Programme (UNDP) have also been fairly active in promoting these "pipelines and powergrids for peace."[41] SAARC has set up a technical committee exclusively on energy-sector cooperation under its Integrated Programme of Action and has now established the SAARC Energy Centre in Islamabad.

Table 6.5 Nepal: Demand Projections versus Exportable Surplus (MW)

FY	Total requirements		Exportable surplus	
	Moderate	Revised high	Moderate	Revised high
2002	660.0	660.0	189.2	189.2
2003	768.4	799.5	256.5	270.2
2004	894.7	968.6	330.9	363.9
2005	1,041.6	1,173.4	420.1	478.8
2006	1,212.8	1,421.5	531.6	612.2
2007	1,412.0	1,722.0	665.4	839.9
2008	1,561.6	2,022.5	744.8	1,055.7
2009	1,727.0	2,375.5	838.0	1,321.2
2010	1,909.9	2,790.1	935.9	1,632.0
2011	2,112.2	3,277.1	1,044.2	2,003.5
2012	2,336.0	3,849.0	1,163.9	2,446.9
2013	2,611.7	4,434.6	1,323.6	2,880.8
2014	2,920.1	5,109.3	1,502.4	3,385.2
2015	3,264.7	5,886.6	1,701.3	3,971.1
2016	3,650.1	6,782.2	1,965.8	4,651.4
2017	4,081.0	7,814.0	2,265.8	5,440.9
2018	4,447.8	8,908.9	2,490.8	6,262.6
2019	4,847.7	10,157.2	2,737.2	7,202.9
2020	5,283.4	11,580.4	3,006.4	8,278.4
2021	5,758.4	13,203.0	3,284.3	9,527.8
2022	6,276.0	15,053.0	3,587.8	10,962.5
2023	7,092.8	16,830.3	4,172.0	12,277.6
2024	8,016.0	18,817.5	4,842.4	13,750.3
2025	9,059.3	21,039.4	5,611.0	15,399.4
2026	10,238.4	23,523.5	6,491.7	17,246.2
2027	11,571.0	26,301.0	7,500.0	19,314.3

Source: Water Resources Strategy Formulation (WRSF), *Hydropower, Water Resources Strategy Formulation Report* (Kathmandu: WRSF, December 2000).

Table 6.6 Nepal: Potential Power Projects

Project	Type	Installed capacity (MW)	Average energy (GWh)
Kulekhani-3	Sto	42	49
Thulo Dhunga	ROR	25	180
Khimti-2	PROR	27	158
Chameliya	PROR	30	195
Middle Marsyangdi	PROR	61	393
Upper Modi	ROR	14	90
Kabeli-A	PROR	30	164
Tamur-Mewa	ROR	101	489
Budhi Ganga	PROR	20	106
Rahughat	PROR	27	165
Dudh Koshi-1	Sto	300	1,735
Likhu-4	PROR	44	271
Upper Arun	PROR	335	2,734
Andhi Khola	Sto	176	547
Upper Karnali-A	PROR	300	2,133
Lower Arun	PROR	308	2,371
Arun-3	PROR	402	3,030
Kali Gandaki-2	Sto	660	3,071
Burhi Gandaki	Sto	600	2,602
Upper Trishuli-2	ROR	300	1,804
Mai Loop-2	Sto	60	245
Tamakoshi-2	ROR	207	1,025
Lower Bhotekoshi-1	ROR	96	678
Bheri Babai	PROR	83	723
Bhotekoshi-5	ROR	46	322
Tila River-2	ROR	203	934
Naumure	Sto	245	845
Upper Marsyangdi-3	ROR	121	723
Tamakoshi-3	Sto	330	1,466
Chisapani	Sto	10,800	20,830
West Seti	Sto	750	3,330
Pancheshwer	Sto	3,240	5,341
Rolwaling	PROR	120	630
Melamchi	ROR	25	119

Source: WRSF, *Water Resources Strategy Formulation Report*, 2000.
Notes: Sto = storage; ROR = run of the river; GWh = Gigawatt hour.

Regional institutes and universities have also played a very active role in advocating cooperation on both water and energy issues in the region, and many of them have conducted studies on the issue. Among the research organizations that have been active are the South Asia Network of Economic Research Institutes (SANEI), the Coalition for Action on South Asian Cooperation (CASAC), the South Asia Center of Policy Studies (SACEPS), the Bangladesh Unnayan Parishad (Dhaka), the Centre for Policy Dialogue (Dhaka), the Institute for Integrated Development Studies (Kathmandu), the Centre for Policy Research (New Delhi), and the Energy and Resource Institute (New Delhi). Universities that have conducted studies include Jawaharlal Nehru University (New Delhi), Bangladesh University of Engineering and Technology (Dhaka), Quad-i-Azam University (Islamabad), Lahore University of Management Sciences, Tribhuvan University (Kathmandu), and Colombo University (Sri Lanka). The ADB, World Bank, and UNDP have also sponsored studies.[42]

The private-sector role in energy cooperation in the region is steadily emerging—signaling a shift away from the situation in the 1980s, when the private sector was excluded. This change is mainly due to reforms that have been initiated in the energy sector across South Asia since the 1990s.[43] Most of the South Asian countries have focused on the following strategies in power-sector reforms:

- Shifting regulatory functions from the government to an independent regulatory commission
- Unbundling the various activities from a vertically integrated unit to distinct and separate units based on functions
- Corporatization of various units, namely, vesting the units in a company incorporated under the Companies Act of 1956
- Tariff reform
- Encouraging private-sector participation wherever it is considered advantageous by the state

Options and Models

An energy exchange project in South Asia can take any number of forms. The historical precedent already exists: most of the region participated in an integrated energy market and system until 1947. But to reestablish such a system, a good model for trading or exchanging electric power and other types of energy must be chosen. Successful examples of regional gas and power trading mechanisms abound, but one feature that most of them share is competitive energy trade legislation.

The prospect of energy trading has opened up new vistas of cooperation. Cross-border energy trading could lead to (1) efficient use of natural resources; (2) increased reliability of power supply; (3) economy in operation and mutual support during contingencies; (4) large-scale transformation in the sectors, contributing to economic growth; (5) participation of multiple stakeholders, including nonstate actors with substantial influence; and (6) substantial market integration in energy-related goods and services.[44]

Linking and coordinating the power systems of contiguous countries also provides immense technical and economic benefits. These interconnections allow each electrical utility to save on power plant investment and operating costs, to provide more reliable electricity to its customers, and to reduce environmental damage. Reducing losses in the power system is often more cost-effective than constructing more generation capacity.

An international comparison is instructive. The Southern African Power Pool (SAPP), created in 1995, encompasses the Southern African Development Community (SADC) countries of South Africa, Lesotho, Mozambique, Namibia, Malawi, Zimbabwe, and Zambia, among others. The SAPP trades in energy with a view to providing a reliable and economical power supply. The SAPP member countries have a diverse mix of hydro- and thermal-generation plants serving a population of more than two hundred million people. A coordination center located in Harare, Zimbabwe, carries out a number of functions including monitoring the SAPP's operations, collecting data, undertaking planning studies and training activities, and disseminating information to its members. The pool is working satisfactorily with immense gains to all the participating countries. There are, of course, other examples of such regional power pools successfully operating elsewhere in the world (see table 6.7).

A considerable network of interconnections among the South Asian countries already exists. India's Power Grid Corporation has worked out the additional interconnections required, their feasibility, and the cost and benefits to the participating countries in the South Asia Growth Quadrangle (SAGQ) region consisting of Bangladesh, Bhutan, the northeastern region of India, and Nepal. All these interconnecting channels will support the Indian effort to get the whole region onto one power grid by the end the Eleventh Five-year Plan in 2012.

We can cite the following three mechanisms for power trading in the broader scope of regional cooperation in South Asia: bilateral, pool-based, and wheeling. Cross-border power trade on a bilateral basis already takes place widely between India and Bhutan and to a lesser extent between India and Nepal.

Table 6.7 Regional Power Pools around the World

Regional arrangement	Member countries
Union for the Coordination of Transmission of Electricity (UTCE)	Spain, Portugal, France, Belgium, Italy, Netherlands, Luxemburg, Austria, Germany, Switzerland—now extended to Poland, Czech Republic, Slovak Republic, Hungary, Slovenia, and Croatia
Nord Pool	Norway, Sweden, Finland, and Denmark
North American Electric Reliability Council (NERC)	United States and Canada
Southern African Power Pool (SAPP)	South Africa, Lesotho, Mozambique, Namibia, Malawi, Zimbabwe, and Zambia
The Commission of Regional Power Integration (CIER)	Jordan, Bahrain, Tunisia, Algeria, Saudi Arabia, Syria, Libya, Egypt, Morocco, Mauritania, Yemen, Iraq, Lebanon, Palestine, Dubai, and Qatar
South America, power trading	Argentina, Paraguay, and Uruguay; Central America

India-Bhutan Power Trading

Bhutan exports its surplus power (1,200 to 1,400 MW) to eastern, northern, and western India, all areas with large power deficits. During 2007–2008, Bhutan exported more than five billion units of energy from the Chukha (336 MW), Kurichu (60 MW), and Tala (1,020 MW) projects. All three of these power projects were built in the past two decades with technical and financial (both loan and grant) assistance from India. Bhutan hopes to generate another 10,000 MW of power by 2020, and has been working closely with India on developing hydroelectric projects and transmission interconnections to meet this objective.[45] The revenue generated by these projects, along with others in the pipeline, could transform Bhutan into a middle-income country in the next fifteen years.

The completion of a 400-kilovolt (kv), 1,200 km double circuit line in 2006, through a joint venture called Powerlinks Transmission Limited between Tata Power and the Power Grid Corporation of India, has enabled Bhutan to export an unprecedented amount of energy. This line is likely to be upgraded from a 3,000 MW transfer capacity to 4,500 MW for the evacuation of power from other large plants, including the 1,095 MW Punatsangchu hydroelectric project being built in Bhutan. Very recently Bhutan and India have agreed to a final list of ten hydropower projects with a total capacity of 11,576 MW to be constructed in Bhutan by 2020. Of the ten, six projects with a total power output of 9,340

MW will be carried out between the two countries on the "intergovernmental model" of 40 percent grant and 60 percent loan. The remaining four, with 2,236 MW, will be constructed on a joint venture model, whereby public-sector companies from both countries will carry out the work.[46]

India-Nepal Power Trading

India and Nepal have been exchanging power for three decades (see table 6.8). The two governments have an agreement that allows for the exchange of power up to 50 MW when the border towns need it. The Bihar State Electricity Board, Uttar Pradesh Power Corporation (formerly known as Uttar Pradesh State Electricity Board), and the newly created state of Uttarakhand provide the interconnections. The power exchange at present takes place on a goodwill basis.

Power exchange is done through two 132 KV and fourteen 33 KV transmission interconnections, primarily on a radial mode.[47] There is another 132 KV interconnection in the far western region committed under the Mahakali Treaty, which is intended to import power to Nepal from India. There are practical difficulties in operating the two systems in a synchronous mode. For a more meaningful exchange of power in the future, the Nepalese and Indian systems should be synchronized. Doing so would require that several studies on load flow, voltage regulation, and system stability be carried out to ensure the smooth operation of the combined system.

To increase the quantum of exchange of power to 150 MW, three additional 132 KV transmission links (with 25 and 45 km lengths on each side of the border)—namely, Butwal-Anandnagar, Birgunj-Motihari, and Dhalkebar-Sitamarhi—have been agreed upon (as of 2009). Each side is to build, operate, and maintain its own side of the lines.[48]

The West Seti Project: A New Direction for Nepal

The planned 750 MW West Seti power project in western Nepal represents a third type of bilateral power exchange that is likely to take place in the region. In such arrangements, a private independent power producer (IPP) develops the power plant, and in this case all the power generated by it will be exported to India through the Power Trading Corporation of India. The West Seti project suggests that the paradigm of power exchange is changing—a direct outcome of a new hydropower development policy that has opened power development to private producers.[49] Moreover, it does not require grid synchronization, as the entire output will be transmitted to the Indian grid without connection to the Nepal Electricity Authority (NEA) system and as such will work as an integral part of the Indian system. The power tariff deal is being negotiated for twenty-five years, for which the levelized tariff would be computed at a cost of not more than seven cents. If this agreement is implemented on schedule, Nepal is likely to receive the total payment of Rs. 56.8 billion ($1.25 billion) by 2031.[50]

Table 6.8 Exchange of Power between India and Nepal

	1993	1995	1997	1999	2001	2003	2004	2007
Bulk energy sale to India (GWh)	46.1	39.5	100.2	64.2	126.0	192.2	138.9	78.25
Bulk energy purchase from India (GWh)	82.2	113.8	154.0	232.4	226.5	149.8	185.6	328.2
Revenue from bulk sale to India (NRs million)	75.5	97.6	249.3	198.1	396.0	808.9	661.1	N/A

Source: NEA, *A Year in Review, 2003/04* (Kathmandu, August 2004); Rakesh Kumar, "Sub-Regionalism Approach to Regional Integration—Energy," paper presented at the "International Conference on Sub-regionalism Approach to Regional Integration in South Asia: Prospects and Opportunities," December 19–20, 2008, Sikkim University, Sikkim.

Note: GWh = gigawatt hour; US$1 = NRs. 71; N/A = not available.

The pool-based approach (also known as agent-based integrated simulation) can support the development of competitive long-run market equilibrium in regional power trading arrangements. This approach involves a set of agents, each representing one of the generating firms, working closely with a monitoring, advisory, and channelizing regional body. These agents develop their own strategies to exploit the capacity and other constraints of their plants and the market. They also evolve their own market-clearing and settlement mechanisms. A key feature of this model is its grassroots representation of the market, with each generating (public and private) firm represented at the individual plant level.

A regional power trading corporation (RPTC) could help launch this type of market mechanism in the SAARC region. It could be called the SAARC-RPTC and could provide market feedback to individual power producers (agents) as well as power consumers. The SAARC-RPTC could maintain and disseminate information on plant structures and sales prices, avoidable costs of production, sales volumes, rates of utilization, profits, target utilization and market conditions, consumer behavior, construction projects, and future investments in the sector.[51]

In essence, such a mechanism would pool the surplus power generated by the individual plants in participating countries and transport it as needed based on the coordinated exchange of demand and consumption information. Because information asymmetry could prompt market failure in such a model, a major task of the SAARC-RPTC would be to gather and analyze data on generation, demand, transmission, and payment well in advance to ensure smooth operations. The goal should be to evolve an effective bidding system for individual plant generators (depending on plant capacity, fuel use, and so on) across the entire spectrum of activities.

Before establishing an organization such as the SAARC-RPTC, it is important to assess the nature, direction, and extent of power exchanges across South Asia. Such an assessment would include intercountry exchanges and the nature of power trading within each country, including the geographical locations of load centers. It would then compare data for South Asia as a whole against that of other regions worldwide.

Geographically, India is at the center of the region and shares common borders with almost all SAARC members (only Pakistan and Afghanistan share a non-Indian border). However, even considering the transport costs, there are two very distinct advantages for countries such as Bangladesh, Pakistan, and Sri Lanka to import power from Bhutan and Nepal: lower tariffs and supply reliability. Meanwhile, Bhutan and Nepal would do well to diversify their markets beyond India. As of 2009, for example, India is the only buyer of Bhutan's power; meanwhile, a number of hydroplants are under construction in northeast India, which may drastically diminish the area's demand for Bhutanese power. As Bhutan and Nepal seek to sell their power beyond India, they could utilize the expansive transmission lines running through most states on India's periphery, including those in the northeast region, Tamil Nadu to the southeast, Jammu and Kashmir and Punjab to the north, and Gujarat to the west. Using India as a transit corridor for power transfer could boost both power-trading activities and the process of regional cooperation and integration. India, meanwhile, could ensure full use of its transmission lines and generate substantial revenue from wheeling charges.[52]

As of now, however, power trading across South Asia is weak at best. Whatever "trade" takes place as of today is bilateral or is an apportioning of surplus power to temporarily needy areas. No power purchase agreement (PPA) has been signed between India and either Bhutan or Nepal, and there are still no long-term standards governing power purchase rates. In most cases, tariffs have been determined based on political considerations, diplomatic goodwill, and convenience.

Such ad hoc arrangements (based on negotiations and goodwill) worked in the past, mainly because the quantum of power purchase was limited. But in years to come regional power needs will become substantial. Power trading will rely on bulk supply and will require a standardized framework for contractual agreements and operating procedures.

Connecting Regional Trade to Investment

India, Bhutan, and Nepal should urgently consider joining forces to form a customs union. This could pave the way for closer regional cooperation and integration and serve three major purposes. First, it would transform the countries' present trading arrangements (practiced over the past fifty years)—which provide unilateral, free access to India—into a robust and progressive regime that addresses many critical issues, including balance-of-trade deficits. In fact, India and Nepal considered moving to a common market (a step ahead of a customs union) back in 1960, as mentioned in the 1960 Trade Treaty between these countries.[53] Today's circumstances promise even more benefits from economic cooperation. A trilateral customs union could minimize the distortions and disturbances created by the rules-of-origin criteria that bind these nations' trade relations, whether through bilateral or SAFTA agreements. The move would encourage specialization and shift labor and investment from less to more efficient uses. It would accomplish these and other aims by stimulating competition and enabling firms to reap economies of scale. Second, it would boost trade in the service sectors—for example, education, tourism, communications, health, and insurance—a vital addition to current patterns of economic exchange. Third, it would expedite the establishment of an economic union in South Asia and facilitate more comprehensive free trade arrangements.[54]

For both Bhutan and Nepal, interregional trade is a significant income source. While Nepal's diversified export policies of the 1960s, 1970s, and 1980s led it to find outside buyers, mainly for carpets and readymade garments (RMGs), the bulk of its trade is again in South Asia. Regional trade-investment exchanges are of critical importance to Nepal and Bhutan because of their (1) poor industrial base, (2) narrow export base, and (3) endemic structural weakness. Of these, the narrow export base is frequently pointed to as the main reason that these countries suffer a balance-of-trade deficit with their more industrialized neighbors (India in particular). Whether through regional trade treaties or FDI policies, the vital connection between trade and investment needs to be addressed to break poor countries' cycles of debt.

Like other regional groupings around the world, to effectively tap the income potential of *all* South Asia—and not only its most powerful countries—SAARC and its individual members must establish policies that link trade facilitation and investment measures. It is shared investment that ultimately integrates and sustains a region. Successful regional groupings such as the European Union and the Association of Southeast Asian Nations (ASEAN), for example, have (1) established regional investment agreements, (2) harmonized FDI policies, (3) linked regional trade to regional investment, (4) strengthened the private-sector role in development, and (5) promoted intraregional investment (such as in transport, energy, and industry). For instance, the ASEAN Industrial Cooperation Scheme (AICO) was launched in 1996 to:

- Encourage intra-ASEAN regional industrial cooperation
- Simplify and harmonize investment procedures
- Make the ASEAN more enticing to foreign investors
- Promote intra-ASEAN trade in line with the Common Effective Preferential Tariff (CEPT) scheme/ASEAN Free Trade Area (AFTA)

This arrangement allows companies to enjoy the benefits of a free trade environment (that is, preferential tariff rates of 0–5 percent) immediately upon approval, without having to wait until the free trade provisions are put in place. Projects under the AICO will benefit from low import tariffs for raw materials and machinery and be subject to the same tax structure as domestic items. Participating companies can also claim local content accreditation.

Nepal is exporting more manufactured items and fewer primary materials to India, a shift that is in part due to the process of trade-investment integration. Over the past decade or so, consumer goods such as toothpaste have constituted between 5 and 23 percent of Nepal's total exports to India. Most such items are products of joint India-Nepal ventures, including DaburNepal, Nepal-Liver, and Colgate-Palmolive. Ventures like these need to be both diversified and consolidated. For example, India's investment in Bhutan's hydropower resources (mostly by way of grant or loan)—and the way this has been integrated into electricity trading between the two nations—is a model to follow. As previously stated, the trade-investment connection can be further explored in the service sectors.

It is important to note that the effects of trade liberalization measures such as the SAFTA vary according to individual countries' industrialization levels. For example, countries with advanced industry infrastructure have gained more from preferential trading arrangements than less developed countries, whose share in total intraregional trade has not undergone any significant change. This has led to discontent, with the result that the less developed impose restrictions on industrial product imports from other member countries.[55]

Nepal and Bhutan in the World Trade Organization (WTO): Next Steps

Now that Nepal has joined the WTO—and Bhutan is in the application process—the two nations face both new opportunities and challenges. Meeting these head-on requires adequate preparation and an intensive restructuring of existing institutions. To complicate matters further, current national-level policies often do not take into account the intricate matrices of each country's diverse geographical, sociocultural, and economic dimensions. Bhutan and Nepal have to take these matrices into consideration[56] as they begin to deal with multilateral trading regimes. Since the WTO guidelines are rather new and many of them are yet to be put into practice in Bhutan and Nepal, the need for establishing adequate capacity is critical. Policymakers in both nations are coming to terms with the growing need for the private sector, NGOs, and civil society at large to play a role in evolving and framing negotiations at both the domestic and international levels.

At the same time, sensitizing international organizations such as the WTO to the unique needs of stakeholder nations is an important task that may best be undertaken at the regional level. The process of amending the norms of international trading is complicated and intricate.[57] India, with a growing presence in the global market and a higher capability, should help set up a WTO Center of Excellence in Bhutan and Nepal to address these issues in a comprehensive, careful, and sustained manner. Given that similar problems are faced by other countries in the region, the center could be replicated in other nations at a later stage. The center's goal would be to support government ministries in particular and policymakers in general in the preparation of trade policies based on sound and comprehensive research.[58] Another aim would be to create a database of relevant information to be disseminated and used to support policymakers in negotiations. Research would cover both region- and sector-specific issues, and the proposed center of excellence would provide inputs to the government on a continuous basis.[59]

Trade-related infrastructure (including that necessary for banking, insurance, transport, customs, communication, and phytosanitary measures) should be constantly upgraded in a targeted manner. Given the impact of the SAFTA and the reopening of markets in China's unharnessed western region, Nepal and Bhutan should focus on establishing high-quality trading and commercial facilities along their borders with India.

Initiatives have already been taken. For instance, India is linking to the Bhutanese border town of Phuntsoling via railway, and is already connected by rail to Nepal. The Indian Ministry of Commerce has identified thirteen integrated checkpoints and land custom stations (LCSs) for upgrade, which include four LCSs on the Indo-Nepal border. As of 2010, however, there has been no progress made. The development of these LCSs should be put on a fast track. A study undertaken by the Indian state consultancy RITES projected that, if developed, these trading points would act as a development catalyst. Nepal has established three dry ports on the Nepalese side for the transport of goods directly to and from the Kolkata Port. They are located in Biratnagar, Sirshiya (east of Birgung), and Bhairahawa. The dry port at Sirshiya is connected by rail, via Raxaul, to the Kolkata Port. The Nepal Multi-Modal Transit and Trade Facilitation Project (NMTTFP) would also augment facilities at road-based freight terminals at Biratnagar and Bhairawa.

Nepalese goods traded outside the region, both imports and exports, also pass through the Kolkata Port. Most of these (about 70 percent of the nation's total trade) are routed through the Raxaul-Birgunj border crossing (there are twenty points for trade with India, and fifteen transit points for trade with other countries). The decision of the Indian railways to convert from meter to broad gauge, including the Muzaffarpur-Raxaul section, promises new possibilities for Nepal. For example, a direct railway link between Nepal and the gateway port of Kolkata would be invaluable.

A fully automated system of customs data (ASYCUDA), to be used at major checkpoints, and an advanced cargo information system (ACIS) are being operationalized. The NMTTFP will further facilitate these efforts. A progress report prepared by the Ministry of Industry, Commerce and Supplies in March 2003 recommended steps to:

- Improve Nepal's transit operations
- Implement trade facilitation measures
- Modernize transport policy and legislation
- Prepare for the express transit of containerized cargo by rail
- Establish a technical team
- Promote the benefits of multimode transport along the Nepal/Kolkata corridor
- Upgrade immigration points along the Indo-Nepal border (for the entry and exit of nationals at Banbasa, Dhangadhi, Nepalganj, Bhairahawa [Sunauli], Birganj, and Kakarbhita)

These steps, most of which are as yet unfulfilled, would have a marked impact on Indo-Nepal relations. By ensuring that trade be systematic and transparent, they would drastically reduce informal and illegal trade by making the agents and institutions engaged in it redundant and ineffective.

Strengthening Connections to China

China has been consciously trying to develop its western periphery, using extensive border trade as a means to realize the goal of local economic integration. It is estimated that border trade in the 120 towns and ports on China's perimeter constitute nearly half of China's total foreign trade of $1.7 trillion. The practice of such trade has been largely supported and regulated by a comprehensive policy document known as the "Provisions of Administration on Border Trade of Small Amount and Foreign Economic and Technical Cooperation of Border Regions," promulgated by the Ministry of Foreign Trade and Economic Cooperation and China's Customs General Administration in 1996.[60] Along the Indo-Chinese border, examples include (1) the Lipulekh Pass trade route in the central Himalayas, which connects Dharchula-Pithoragrah and Uttaranchal in India with Taklakot in the Purang County of the Tibet Autonomous Region (TAR) and (2) the Shipkila Pass, which connects Namgya in the Kinnaur District of Himachal Pradesh with Jiuba in the TAR's Zada County. Both are highly seasonal and difficult trade routes through rugged terrain.

Though many in India consider the reopening of the Nathu la pass in Sikkim a symbolic gesture, China sees it, at least in the long run, as an entry point to South Asia's 1.3 billion potential customers. This is arguably the shortest route (it is roughly 590 km from Lhasa, Tibet, to Gangtok, Sikkim) to the ever-bourgeoning middle class on the Indian mainland and in Bangladesh, Bhutan, and Nepal. The 2006 completion of the 1,142 km railway line from Golmud City in Qinghai Province to Lhasa and the refurbished Sichuan-Tibet Highway could ultimately transform trading between Mainland China and Tibet and the neighboring countries.[61] In the medium term they will at least reduce the need for the circuitous and inefficient sea passage between regional markets. This may go a long way toward triggering development in China's otherwise backward western region and even dispelling discontent among its residents, including in Tibet. For India, besides Lhasa, these new transport routes promise better access to business centers on China's western, eastern, and southeastern sea coasts.

China's style of furthering trade is in marked contrast to that of India. For instance, there have been several visits paid by trade, development, and investment officials—and private-sector representatives—from Yunnan Province to India's northeastern and eastern states, including West Bengal. With a single-item agenda of establishing trade and investment links with the vast untapped market of eastern India, these delegates give an impression that they have been given a "free hand" by their federal government to negotiate the larger process of the so-called Kunming initiative. As such, they are actively promoting the reopening of Stilwell Road (named after Gen. Joseph Warren Stilwell, 1883–1946, Chief of Staff to Allied Forces in China-Burma-India). Built by the U.S. forces during World War II, this double-track all-weather road connects Assam (61 km) in India with Kunming (632 km) in China via Myanmar (1,033 km) and has remained unused for the past six decades. Supporters are advocating for its refurbishment and use throughout the region, including in Bangladesh and Myanmar.[62]

Such visits are certainly a sign of the decentralizing strategy China has followed since 1979. The Central Committee of the Communist Party of China has allowed Guangdong and Fujian provinces to adopt "special policies and flexible measures," in particular with regard to investment and trade in the area's special economic zones (SEZs). Meanwhile, Yunnan is involved in other economic zones at the provincial level, such as the Greater Mekong Subregion (GMS).

Provincial governments are no longer confined to an administrative role and have increasingly adopted economic functions. Preferential policies have made the provinces in the coastal regions important economic actors with locally tailored policies. The inland provinces, too, are moving in the same direction. "The inability of the centre to dictate regional economic policies and the strong economic role of provinces is reflected in a new type of regional planning which focuses on smaller trans-provincial economic regions growing out of economic interchange between sub-provincial regions with specific economic advantages."[63] In 1995 the state transferred one of its key powers—the grain (food-security) policy—to the provinces,[64] a move that promised to change China politically and economically.

Yet the pull of China's center remains strong, and the promotion of trade and investment in the western provinces is not without political underpinnings. The western region, which covers two-thirds of the nation's territory, with a population making up nearly 23 percent of the national total, comprises nine provinces and autonomous regions: Gansu, Guizhou, Ningxia, Qinghai, Shaanxi, Sichuan, Tibet, Xinjiang, and Yunnan in addition to the Chongqing Municipality. The area is culturally diverse and politically volatile. It also has plenty of land and natural resources, including oil and gas. It is hoped that since eastern China's 14,000-km-long coastlines reaped fortunes for the mainland over the past two decades, it is western China's turn, with its 3,500-km frontier, to become a golden area of growth.

Premier Zhu Rongji's "Report on National Economic and Social Development during the Tenth Five Year Plan" identified eight important tasks to be achieved during the Tenth Five-year Plan period (2001–2005). These tasks included developing the western region and furthering reform and the open-door policy. The Chinese government launched its "develop the west" campaign in 2000. Under this a number of preferential policies, including capital input, trade liberalization, and initiatives in science education and human resources were offered to the western region. In a break from past practice, the Chinese government also liberalized labor policies, allowing professionals working in western China to retain their old workplace registration even as they held their new one.

Nepal-China Border Trade

The first formal border-trade engagement between Nepal and China commenced after the construction of the Kathmandu-Kodari highway, one of the first major Chinese projects in Nepal. The 114-km road connects Lhasa to Kathmandu. The agreement was signed in 1961 and the road was inaugurated in 1967.[65] The road enabled Chinese goods to reach Kathmandu in the shortest possible time and was of tremendous military advantage to China as it provided a straight route to the Indian Gangetic plain. Meanwhile, another seven important transit trade posts were refurbished, including those at Rasuwa (Rasuwagadhi), Mustang (Nhechung), Olangchungola (Taplejung), Kimathanka (Sankhuwasabha), Lamabagar (Dolakha), Larke (Sirdhibas), Mugu (Mugu), and Yarinaka (Yari, Humla). Though the original agreement was for only a 30-km-radius trade-free zone (TFZ) around the epicenter of the Tatopani Custom Office, trade through this route is even more robust than planned.[66]

The Kathmandu-Kodari Highway was expected to be a conduit for only a very small percentage of total Nepal-China trade. This implied that at least 95 percent of Nepal's trade with China would be conducted by sea (via the Kolkata Port) or air. This was the impression held for decades until the Nepalese government made it mandatory for those conducting Nepal-Tibet trade to use proper banking channels in 2000–2001. In the very first year after that stipulation, the letters of credit opened by Nepalese banks for trade with Lhasa and Khasa (both on the Chinese side) amounted to Rs. 1.32 billion ($18 million). The total trade jumped from Rs. 2.2 billion in 1998–1999 to Rs. 5.4 billion in 2000–2001. Since then it has steadily increased to Rs. 6.8 billion. This shows that the Kathmandu-Kodari Highway was widely used by traders illegally disseminating Chinese goods to other parts of the region.

Nepal's exports to the TAR have also been increasing in recent years, from NRs. 203 million in 1991–1992 to NRs. 1.8 billion in 2004–2005. Nepal's exports to China via Tatopani remain confined to traditional items such as rice, white flour, vegetable ghee, noodles, copper vessels, incense sticks, sugar, chocolates, biscuits, copper wire, leather, solar sets, medical supplies, and other edibles.[67]

On the other hand, Nepal's imports from China via Tatopani have undergone significant changes in both volume and content. They increased from NRs. 464 million in 1991–1992 to NRs. 5,997 million in 2005–2006—a thirteenfold increase over fourteen years. At the same time, Chinese goods imported through the Kolkata Port increased sharply from a mere Rs. 693 million in 1991–1992 to Rs. 6.63 billion in 2005–2006. It is interesting to note that Nepal's trade deficit with China shot up from Rs. 953 million in 1991–1992 to over Rs. 11 billion in 2005–2006 without Nepal raising the issue in a public forum. The area's rising demand for Chinese goods and products are strongly supported by quick and efficient supply. Most Chinese goods that come to Nepal find their ways into the Indian market via Dhulabari, Pashupatinagar, Kakarbhitta, Raxaul, Gorakhpur, Nepalganj, Sunaoli, Tanakpur, and Birgunj. Most of these are smuggled or, to use a euphemism, "informally traded." The Nepalese government has recently started initiatives to formalize and regulate the traffic of these goods.

The agreement signed by Nepal and China on March 19, 2006, is expected to have a long-term impact on Nepal's economy and trade patterns. As per this agreement, China will provide Nepali products duty-free access to the Chinese market. This raises the following questions for Indian policymakers:

- Are the Nepalese markets really in a position to absorb such a consistently high volume of Chinese imports as they have imported over the past years? If not, where are these imports headed?
- Are the Chinese trying to make Nepal an entrepot, a transit route by which to enter the huge Indian market (even as they have used the Karakoram highway to enter Pakistan and Myanmar routes to access Bangladesh)?
- Are the Chinese adopting the same modus operandi as in the Indo-China region of Southeast Asia?

Sino-Indian trade, which had steadily increased from $270 million in 1990 to over $40 billion in 2007–2008, could in fact be much higher given the steady increase in imports of Chinese goods into India through its borders with Bangladesh, Bhutan, Myanmar, Nepal, and Pakistan. This would increase even more following the opening of five to ten more passes in the mountain border areas for trade with Nepal.

While Indian policymakers may have reason for concern, Nepal and to a certain extent Bhutan have an opportunity to leverage their geographical position between the vast markets of India and China. Through these nations, they have access to other South Asian countries, states in southwest China, China's major cities—and even Central Asia. China already has highways linking Tibet and the Xinjiang regions. Meanwhile, the Qinghai-Tibet railway line from Golmund in Qinghai Province connects the rest of China with several Central Asian republics, including Mongolia.

The fear that South Asian markets will be flooded by a one-way flow of cheap Chinese goods is an obvious one. What is proposed here is balancing this one-way flow by steadily increasing the export of South Asian goods to the huge western China market and formally declaring the buffer countries (such as Nepal) as transit countries and using them as entrepots (already a reality in the arena of informal trading). The Nepalese government[68] has in fact proposed construction of seven highways connecting the country's northern border with its southern border and an electric railway line between Birgunj in the south and Tatopani in the north via Kathmandu. This could further connect the Birgunj (Nepal)-Raxaul (India) border in the south and Tatopani (Nepal)-Zhangmu (China) border in the north. Such moves could in fact convert the historical constraint of Nepal's landlocked position into a major geoeconomic advantage and could consolidate the economic integration process of South Asia as a whole. In the case of Nepal, emerging as a transit route between South Asia and China—with links to Central Asia—would also serve the Himalayan republic by transforming its internal transport and trade patterns. Villagers in remote districts (particularly in Nepal's north and west) would gain access to internal and cross-border markets, while the movement of tourists at both the domestic and regional level would be promoted.

Nepal and Bhutan as Key Players in Promoting Regional Tourism

Historically, trade was conducted along tourist routes, in particular those used for pilgrimage. As John Clarke notes, "[O]ften trade and pilgrimage were combined. For example, pilgrims from Mongolia visiting the shrines of Lhasa would bring goods to sell in the capital to finance their trip. At the same time Mongolian traders going to Lhasa with Chinese silver, silk and ponies would, as a matter of course, visit the holy places once they arrived."[69] The exchange of tourists between Nepal and Tibet through the land route of the Kathmandu-Kodari highway can be cited as an important example. A large number of tourists (30,000) from China, Nepal, and other parts of the world already use this route for tourism purposes. This route is likely to be used even more for tourism after the Kathmandu-Lhasa bus service is started and the likely railway link between Lhasa and border of Nepal is established. The wayside hotels and other tourist amenities developed along this route could generate further income for the Nepalese and the Chinese as they have in Nepal's Solokhumbu region (home to Mount Everest and the associated adventure tourism).

South Asia is emerging as a tourist attraction for both regional and international travelers. In response, Bhutan has recently liberalized its tourism policies to accommodate greater private-sector participation, reflected in the marked increase of tourists from 5,599 in 2002 to 21,094 in 2007.[70] Improved regional connectivity would expand possibilities of trade, tourism, and other areas of potential growth. The issue has been continually discussed at regional meetings, such as the Twelfth SAARC Summit, held in 2004 in Islamabad, where it was again decided to strengthen transport, transit, and communication links across the region. It was in pursuance of this decision that SAARC, with financial and technical support from the ADB, initiated the SAARC Regional Multimodal Transport Study (SRMTS). The study suggested ten regional road corridors, five regional rail corridors, two regional inland waterway corridors, ten maritime gateways, and sixteen aviation gateways. Further assessment of these corridors and gateways revealed their physical and nonphysical barriers, and specific measures have been suggested to address them. In all these plans, Bhutan and Nepal figure prominently.[71]

Interestingly, even trade can be a tourist attraction. Tourists are making a beeline to watch how trade actually takes place between India and China at Sherathang in Sikkim and Renqinggang in the TAR. In the past few years, the Nathu la Pass has itself become a major tourist spot with hundreds of people visiting the border and enjoying the "pleasure" of shaking hands with Chinese soldiers. Globally known as the roof of the world, Tibet has recently focused on ecotourism. In 2008, 2.25 million tourists visited Tibet—up from 0.928 million in 2003—with a recorded revenue of 2.259 billion yuan ($376.5 million) in 2008 as against 1 billion yuan ($125 million) in 2003.[72] There are over a hundred major tourist attractions within the TAR, which has also seen a surge in domestic tourism.

Ecotourism in Bhutan and Nepal can be well integrated with pilgrimage routes to places such as the Kailash-Mansarovar Lake in Tibet. This holy lake attracts a large number of pilgrims from India and other countries. The Indian pilgrims generally take an arduous route, but the journey could be much easier and shorter from either Bhutan or Nepal.

In this context, a fascinating venture would be the cross-border Buddhist circuit, which has now been identified as a priority area in the tourism development policy of several South Asian governments, including that of India. Sikkim (India) and Bhutan could be the hubs connecting all the major Buddhist destinations in India and its neighboring countries—Bodh Gaya in

Bihar, Rumtek in Sikkim, and Tawang in Arunachal Pradesh, India; Lumbini in Nepal; Taktsang in Bhutan; and Jokhang and Potala in Lhasa. Most of the Himalayan regions would also be direct beneficiaries. For those who can afford it, travel would be expedited by proposed airlinks between the Bagdogra airport in Darjeeling and the Sikkim airport with the airports of Kathmandu, Thimphu, and other Indian cities. The Druk Airways of Bhutan is already operating flights to Bagdogra and Bangkok. The Nathu la trade route, if opened to tourist traffic, could integrate the tourism industry of the Himalayan states in the northeast with neighboring countries such as China, Bangladesh, Bhutan, Myanmar, and Nepal. Such moves toward integration could transform the region by tapping its vast tourism potential—with development opportunities galore.

Forging Ahead: India's Role

A fast-developing India is changing many of its traditional policies and strategies. Unlike in the past, India has started to think of its borders and frontiers in more comprehensive terms not limited to the old security-centric view. This is of vital necessity as a rising India grapples with issues and opportunities related to markets, the sharing of natural resources, investment opportunities, trade in services, access to energy markets, and tourism. It must move fast or be overtaken, even as China rapidly develops infrastructure along its borders, both with India and other neighbors. Such infrastructure includes the proposed railway lines to the China-Nepal border at Tatopani, north of Kathmandu, and the Indo-China border at Nathu la in Sikkim. In part prompted by China's moves, India has decided to connect all its border areas, particularly in the hills and mountain areas, with highways, railway links, and greenfield airports.

While this will help India more easily access its own border districts, it will also help neighboring countries (including Bhutan and Nepal) access Indian markets and through them the markets of other countries in South Asia and beyond.

We have argued that for a variety of reasons both internal and external, regional integration has and continues to be of vital importance to policymakers in Bhutan and Nepal. As of 2010, the likelihood of regional integration has increased due to India's increased willingness to work with Bhutan and Nepal on trade-investment linkages with regional implications. To this has been added an increased capacity to implement projects, whether through state, private, or NGO initiatives. Much, however, remains to be done. As other chapters in this volume indicate, substantial responsibility rests with India to further the interests of its neighbors alongside its own.

Notes

[1] SAARC, a regional cooperation grouping, was formally initiated in 1985 with Bangladesh, Bhutan, India, Maldives, Nepal, Pakistan, and Sri Lanka as its members. Afghanistan was included as a new member at the Fourteenth SAARC Summit held in

New Delhi in April 2007. Afghanistan, Bangladesh, Bhutan, Maldives, and Nepal are listed as the region's LDCs.

[2] Gajendra Mani Pradhan, *Transit of Land-locked Countries and Nepal* (Jaipur: Nirala Publications, 1990).

[3] For the full text of the treaty see Avtar Singh Bhasin, *Nepal-India; Nepal-China Relations—Documents 1947–June 2005*, Vol. 1 (New Delhi: Geetika Publishers, 2005).

[4] For the full text of the treaty and the letters exchanged therein see Bhasin, *Nepal-India; Nepal-China Relations*, Vol. 1. Article II of the Treaty states that "the two Governments hereby undertake to inform each other of any serious friction or misunderstanding with any neighbouring state likely to cause any breach in the friendly relations subsisting between the two Governments." Article V states that "the Government of Nepal shall be free to import, from or through the territory of India, arms, ammunition or warlike material and equipment necessary for the security of Nepal. The procedure for giving effect to this arrangement shall be worked out by the two Governments acting in consultation."

[5] Article VI of the treaty states that "each Government undertakes, in token of the neighbourly friendship between India and Nepal, to give to the nationals of the other, in its territory, national treatment with regard to participation in industrial and economic development of such territory and to the grant of concessions and contracts relating to such development." And Article VII further states that "The Governments of India and Nepal agree to grant, on a reciprocal basis, to the nationals of one country in the territories of the other the same privileges in the matter of residence, ownership of property, participation in trade and commerce, movement and other privileges of a similar nature."

[6] One such letter states that "if the Government of Nepal should decide to seek foreign assistance in regard to the development of the natural resources of, or of any industrial project in Nepal, the Government of Nepal shall give first preference to the Government or the nationals of India, as the case may be, provided that the terms offered by the Government of India or Indian nationals, as the case may be, are not less favourable to Nepal than the terms offered by any other foreign Government or by other foreign nationals." "Nothing in the foregoing provision shall apply to assistance that the Government of Nepal may seek from the United Nations Organization or any of its specialized agencies" (Letter, para 4).

[7] For the full text of the Treaty of Perpetual Peace and Friendship between the Government of India and the Government of Bhutan, signed in Darjeeling on August 8, 1949, see http://meaindia.nic.in/treatiesagreement/1949/chap26.htm.

[8] Article II of the India-Bhutan Treaty 1949 states that "The Government of India undertakes to exercise no interference in the internal administration of Bhutan. On its part, the Government of Bhutan agrees to be guided by the advice of the Government of India in its external relations."

[9] For the full text of the India-Bhutan Friendship Treaty signed in New Delhi on February 8, 2007, see http://meaindia.nic.in/pressrelease/2007/03/treaty.pdf.

[10] Article II of the India-Bhutan Friendship Treaty 2007 states that "in keeping with the abiding ties of close friendship and cooperation between Bhutan and India, the Government of the Kingdom of Bhutan and the Government of the Republic of India shall cooperate closely with each other on issues relating to their national interests. Neither Government shall allow the use of its territory for activities harmful to the national security and interest of the other."

[11] Article V (1949 Treaty) states that "there shall, as heretofore, be free trade and commerce between the territories of the Government of India and of the Government of Bhutan; and the Government of India agrees to grant the Government of Bhutan every

facility for the carriage, by land and water, of its produce throughout the territory of the Government of India, including the right to use such forest roads as may be specified by mutual agreement from time to time."

Article III (2007 Treaty) states that "there shall, as heretofore, be free trade and commerce between the territories of the Government of Bhutan and the Government of India. Both the Governments shall provide full cooperation and assistance to each other in the matter of trade and commerce."

[12] Article VI (1949 Treaty) states that "the Government of India agrees that the Government of Bhutan shall be free to import with the assistance and approval of the Government of India, from or through India into Bhutan, whatever arms, ammunition, machinery, warlike material or stores may be required or desired for the strength and welfare of Bhutan, and that this arrangement shall hold good for all time as long as the Government of India is satisfied that the intentions of the Government of Bhutan are friendly and that there is no danger to India from such importations. The Government of Bhutan, on the other hand, agrees that there shall be no export of such arms, ammunition, etc., across the frontier of Bhutan either by the Government of Bhutan or by private individuals."

Article 4 (2007 Treaty) states that "the Government of India agrees that the Government of Bhutan shall be free to import, from or through India into Bhutan, whatever arms, ammunition, machinery, warlike material or stores as may be required or desired for the strength and welfare of Bhutan, and that this arrangement shall hold good for all time as long as the Government of India is satisfied that the intentions of the Government of Bhutan are friendly and that there is no danger to India from such importations."

[13] Article VII (1949 Treaty) states that "the Government of India and the Government of Bhutan agree that Bhutanese subjects residing in Indian territories shall have equal justice with Indian subjects, and that Indian subjects residing in Bhutan shall have equal justice with the subjects of the Government of Bhutan."

Article V (2007 Treaty) states that "the Government of Bhutan and the Government of India agree that Bhutanese subjects residing in Indian territories shall have equal justice with Indian subjects, and that Indian subjects residing in Bhutan shall have equal justice with the subjects of the Government of Bhutan."

[14] Mahendra P. Lama, "Nepal and Bhutan: Comprehensive and Cooperative Security in South Asia," in *Comprehensive and Cooperative Security in South Asia*, ed. Dipankar Banerjee (Delhi: Institute for Peace and Conflict Studies, 1998).

[15] Dilli Prasad Bhattarai, "Nepal at the First and Second Cross Roads: Opportunities for a Win/Win in the New Development Context," in *Nepal as Transit State: Emerging Possibilities*, ed. Nischal Nath Pandey (Kathmandu: Institute of Foreign Affairs, 2006).

[16] Article II and Article III of the Bhutan-China Agreement on Maintenance of Peace and Tranquility along the Sino-Bhutanese Border Areas signed on December 8, 1998, in Beijing states the following points (www.bhutannewsonline.com/treaties.html):

> Both sides are of the view that during the ten rounds of talks that have been held so far, they have reached consensus on the guiding principles on the settlement of the boundary issues and narrowed their differences on the boundary issues in the spirit of mutual accommodation, mutual trust and cooperation and through friendly consultations. The mutual understanding and traditional friendship between the two countries have been deepened. Both sides stand ready to adhere to the above-mentioned spirit and make joint efforts for an early and fair solution of the boundary issues between the two countries. (Article II)

Both sides agreed that prior to the ultimate solution of the boundary issues, peace and tranquility along the border should be maintained and the status quo of the boundary prior to March 1959 should be upheld, and not to resort to unilateral action to alter the status quo of the border. (Article III)

[17] Statement by Foreign Minster Ugyen Tshering at the National Assembly of Bhutan, *Kuensel*, December 31, 2008.

[18] After the result of the historic Constituent Assembly election of April 2008 in Nepal, the institution of monarchy was demolished.

[19] Jawaharlal Nehru, *India's Foreign Policy: Selected Speeches, September 1946–April 1961* (New Delhi: Publications Division, Government of India, 1971), 436.

[20] Bjorn Hettne, "Globalisation and the New Regionalism: The Second Great Transformation," in *Globalism and the New Regionalism*, ed. Bjorn Hettne, Andres Inotai, and Osvaldo Sunkel (London: UNU/WIDER Study, Macmillan, 1999), 7–11.

[21] Bjorn Hettne, "The New Regionalism: Implications for Development of Peace," in *Comparing Regionalism: Implications for Global Development and International Security*, ed. Bjorn Hettne and Andras Inotai (Helsinki: UNU/WIDER Study, 1994).

[22] Michael Schultz, Fredrick Söderbaum, and Joakim Öjendal, "Key Issues in the New Regionalism: Comparisons, from Asia, Africa, and the Middle East," in Hettne and Inotai, *Comparing Regionalism*, 254–55.

[23] R. Latham, "Thinking about Security after the Cold War," *International Studies Notes* 20, no. 3 (1995): 13.

[24] Timothy M. Shaw and Sandra J. Maclean, "The Emergence of Regional Civil Society: Contributions to a New Human Security Agenda," in *The New Agenda for Peace Research*, ed. Ho-Won Jeong (England: Ashgate, 1999), 290.

[25] E. Voutira and Shaun A. W. Brown, *Conflict Resolution: A Review of Some Non-Governmental Practices* (Oxford: Refugees Studies Programme, University of Oxford, 1995).

[26] SAARC (South Asian Association for Regional Cooperation), *Declaration of the Eleventh SAARC Summit*, SAARC/SUMMIT.11/12, Kathmandu, January 4–6, 2002.

[27] Article X (General Provisions) in the *Charter of the South Asian Association for Regional Cooperation*, SAARC Secretariat, Kathmandu, 1985.

[28] Tshering Phuntsho, "SAARC: Perspective from Bhutan," in *New Life within SAARC*, ed. Dev Raj Dahal and Nischal Nath Pandey (Kathmandu: Institute of Foreign Affairs—Friedrich Ebert Stiftung, 2005).

[29] Mahendra P. Lama, *SAARC Programmes and Activities: Assessment, Monitoring and Evaluation (1985-2008)* (SACEPS, Kathmandu, and ADB, Manila, 2008).

[30] SAARC Secretariat, *Meeting the Challenge: Report of the Independent South Asian Commission on Poverty Alleviation* (Kathmandu: SAARC Secretariat, 1992).

[31] SAARC Secretariat, *Report of the Independent South Asian Commission on Poverty Alleviation, Our Future Our Responsibility: A Road Map towards a Poverty Free South Asia* (Kathmandu: SAARC Secretariat, 2004).

[32] SAARC Secretariat, *South Asian Association for Regional Cooperation: A Profile* (Kathmandu: SAARC Secretariat, 1998).

[33] Mahendra P. Lama, "SAARC: Shallow Regionalism, Political Abstinence and Economic Imperatives," *BIISS Journal* 21, no. 1 (January 2000); Mahendra P. Lama, "Strengthening the SAARC Activities," in *Peace and Cooperative Security in South Asia*, ed. V. T. Patil and N. K. Jha (New Delhi: PR Books, 2000).

[34] Mahendra P. Lama, "Energy Cooperation in South Asia: Integrating the Stakeholders for Robust Regionalism," *SAFMA South Asia Journal*, Lahore (June 2005).

[35] Mahendra P. Lama, "Geopolitics of Power Trading in South Asia: Opportunities and Challenges," *Strategic Analysis* 31, no. 2 (March 2007).

[36] Mahendra P. Lama, "Indian and Chinese Aid to Nepal: Comparison of Certain Critical Parameters," *Man and Development,* Chandigarh (March 1999).

[37] Estimates of the benefits shared by India and Nepal, in terms of irrigated area, conflict. According to Nepalese figures, 0.0298 million acres in Nepal benefit, versus 2.21 million acres in India. On the other hand KPA sources claim that Nepal is irrigating 0.06 million acres and India 2.4 million acres. In the case of flood protection, Nepal's share consists of 0.15 million acres whereas India's share is 0.55 million acres (KPA figures). Power generation is said to be shared equally, though Kataiya has mostly been working at less than 50 percent capacity due to siltation. Trying to allay the fears of Nepal, the Kosi and Gandak projects were unwisely left to the Bihar government, but India had not developed adequate technology to make the project durable. Unpublished official documents prepared by the Economic Co-operation Wing of the Indian Embassy, Kathmandu, p. 2.

[38] "Treaty between His Majesty's Government of Nepal and the Government of India concerning the Integrated Development of the Mahakali River including Sarada Barrage, Tanakpur Barrage and Pancheshwar Project," New Delhi, February 12, 1996; Bhasin, *Nepal-India; Nepal-China Relations,* Vol. 2, 1624–32.

[39] The basis of the studies was the load forecast prepared for the Power System Master Plan. The high-growth load forecast was revised slightly, with the starting figures of moderate growth used from the year 2002. Export requirements were calculated and included in the demand.

[40] WRSF (Water Resources Strategy Formulation), *Hydropower, Water Resources Strategy Formulation Report* (Kathmandu: WRSF, December 2000).

[41] Mahendra P. Lama and Rasul Bakhsh Rais, "Pipelines and Powergrids for Peace," Occasional Paper, International Centre for Peace Initiatives (ICPI), Mumbai, and Kings College, London, 2001.

[42] Also see Mahendra P. Lama, "Economic Reforms and Cross Border Power Trade in South Asia," *South Asian Survey, New Delhi* (January–June 2000).

[43] These reforms are reflected in various national policies including the *National Energy Policy 1995* of Bangladesh; *Electricity Act 2003* of India; *Nepal Electricity Authority Act 1992* and the *Hydropower Development Policy 2001* of Nepal; *Power Sector Strategic Plan 1992, Private Power Policy Framework 1994, Hydel Power Policy Framework 1995, Policy for New Private Independent Power Projects 1998,* and *Policy for Power Generation Projects 2002* of Pakistan, and *Electricity Reforms Act 2002* of Sri Lanka.

[44] Mahendra P. Lama, Q. K. Ahmad, and Mohan Man Sainju, "Reforms in Power Sector and Cross Border Power Trade in South Asia" in *Economic Development in South Asia,* ed. Mohsin Khan (New Delhi: Tata McGRaw-Hill, 2005).

[45] *Selected Economic Indicators,* Royal Monetary Authority of Bhutan, September 2000; Rakesh Kumar, "Sub-Regionalism Approach to Regional Integration—Energy," paper presented at the International Conference on Sub-regionalism Approach to Regional Integration in South Asia: Prospects and Opportunities, Sikkim University, Sikkim, December, 19–20, 2008.

[46] This was decided during the visit of the Economic Affairs Minister Lyonpo Khandu Wangchuk to India in early 2009.

Sunkosh reservoir: 4,000 MW (intergovt.)

Kuri Gangri: 1,800 MW (intergovt.)

Chamkarchu: 1,670 MW (joint venture)

Punatsangchu 1: 1,200 MW (intergovt.) tendered out
Punatsangchu 2: 1,000 MW (intergovt.)
Wangchu reservoir: 900 MW (joint venture)
Mangdechu: 720 MW (intergovt.)
Amochu reservoir: 620 MW (intergovt.)
Kholong Chu: 486 MW (joint venture)
Bunakha reservoir: 180 MW (joint venture)
Total: 11,576 MW

(*Kuensel*, Thimphu, March 26, 2009). Also see speech of Manmohan Singh, prime minister of India, at the National Assembly of Bhutan, May 17, 2008, Thimphu, http://meaindia.nic.in/speech/2008/17ss01.html.

[47] Power exchanges between Nepal and India currently take place in an isolated manner. The Indian system served by Nepal's supply is connected to the Nepalese system and disconnected from the Indian system. Similarly the Nepalese system served by India's supply is connected to the Indian system and disconnected from the Nepalese system. This is called a radial mode of supply. This mode can only continue while the quantum of power exchange is limited. For a high transfer of power, the two systems would have to work in a synchronous mode.

[48] NEA (Nepal Electricity Authority), *A Year in Review, 2000/01* (Kathmandu: NEA, August 2001).

[49] The government earns revenue through royalty and export tax and gives several incentives and concessions to private developers. Once private developers agree to the terms and conditions laid down in the regulations, they receive a license to develop the project and subsequently take on the role of marketing the power.

[50] Lama, "Energy Cooperation in South Asia."

[51] Mahendra P. Lama, *Energy Cooperation in South Asia: Issues, Challenges and Potential*, conference on South-South Solidarity, New Delhi, November 1999. Also see Lama, Ahmad, and Sainju, "Reforms in Power Sector and Cross Border Power Trade in South Asia."

[52] CPD-CASAC (Centre for Policy Dialogue/Coalition for Action on South Asian Cooperation), "Energy Cooperation in South Asia: Opportunities, Strategies and Modalities," regional synthesis prepared by Mahendra P. Lama, Dhaka, 2004.

[53] "Being animated by the desire to strengthen economic cooperation between the two countries, and convinced of the benefits likely to accrue from the development of their economies towards the goal of common market," *Treaty of Trade and Transit*, Kathmandu, September 11, 1960, Bhasin, *Nepal-India; Nepal-China Relations*, Volume III, 1949–52.

[54] Mahendra P. Lama, "External Sector Reforms in Nepal: Implications and Policy Options for Regional Integration," in *Economic Reform and Trade Performance in South Asia*, ed. Omar Haider Chowdhury and Willem van der Geest (Dhaka: The Univ. Press Ltd., 2005). Also see Mahendra P. Lama, "India and Nepal: The Intricacies of Free Trade," in *India-Nepal Relations: The Challenges Ahead* (New Delhi: Observer Research Foundation, Rupa & Co., 2004).

[55] Mahendra P. Lama, "Investment in South Asia: Trends and Issues," *South Asian Economic Journal*, Colombo (March 2000).

[56] Bhutan has applied for membership in the WTO and is likely to get it soon. Benjamin Shepard and Ronald Hayduk, *From Act up to the WTO: Urban Protest and Community Building in the Era of Globalisation* (London: Verso, 2003).

[57] Ratnakar Adhikari, "Nepal and WTO: How Prepared We Are," *Spotlight* 20, no. 39 (April 13–19, 2001); Mahendra P. Lama, "Nepal and World Trade Organisation: Challenges and Opportunities," in *WTO and Implications for South Asia*, ed. K. C. Reddy and T. Nirmala Devi (New Delhi: Serial Publications), 2006.

[58] Aaditya Mattoo and Robert M. Stern, *India and the WTO* (Oxford: The World Bank, 2003; CUTS (Consumer Unity & Trust Society), *Putting our Fears on the Table: Analysis of the Proposals on Investment and Competition Agreements at the WTO* (Jaipur: CUTS, 2003).

[59] See Trade Promotion Centre, *WTO Provisions on Least-Developed Countries* (Kathmandu: Trade Promotion Centre, March 1999); UNCTAD, *The Least Developed Countries 2000 Report* (Geneva, 2000).

[60] This was actually promulgated in 1984 as the "Provisional Regulations for the Management of 'Small Volume' Border Trade." The 1996 version of this promulgation took shape after a series of amendments.

[61] For details see Mahendra P. Lama, *Sikkim-Tibet Trade via Nathu la: A Policy Study on Prospects, Opportunities and Requisite Preparedness*, prepared by Nathu la Trade Study Group for the Government of Sikkim, August 2005.

[62] Mahendra P. Lama, "India and China in Border Trade," *Hindustan Times*, New Delhi, April 27, 2005.

[63] Hans Hendrischke, "Provinces in Competitions: Region, Identity and Cultural Construction," in *The Political Economy of China's Provinces*, ed. Hans Hendrischke and Feng Chongyi (London: Routledge, 1999), 6–7.

[64] Kenneth C. W. Keng, "China's Economic Prospects in the New Century," in *Dilemmas of Reform in Jiang Zemin's China*, ed. Andrew J. Nathan, Zhaohui Hong, and Steven R. Smith (London: Lynne Rienner, 1999), 189.

[65] "Agreement for the Construction of the Road" in *Documents on Nepal's Relations with India and China, 1949–66*, ed. A. S. Bhasin (New Delhi: Academic, 1970).

[66] Mahendra P. Lama, "The Dragon's Local Turn: Hu's South Asia Visit fits in with China's South Asia Plans," *DNA (Daily News and Analysis)*, Bombay, November 20, 2006.

[67] Mahendra P. Lama, "The Forward Policy and Southasia," *Himal Southasian*, Kathmandu, September 2006. Also Research and Information Division of Federation of Nepalese Chambers of Commerce and Industry, *Nepal and the World; A Statistical Profile 2006*, http/www.fncci/org/text/all.

[68] Shankar P. Sharma, "Inaugural Speech," in Pandey, *Nepal as Transit State.*

[69] John Clarke, *Tibet: Caught in Time* (Reading: Garnet Publications, 1997), 39.

[70] Phuntosho Gyeltshen, "Tourism in Bhutan," a paper presented in the international conference on *Sub-regionalism Approach to Regional Integration in South Asia: Prospects and Opportunities*, Sikkim University, Sikkim, December 19–20, 2008.

[71] ADB, *SAARC Regional Multimodal Transport Study* (Manila: ADB, 2007). Also see Uma Subramanian and John Arnold, *Forging Subregional Links in Transportation and Logistics in South Asia* (Washington, D.C.: World Bank, 2001).

[72] http://english.cri.cn/6909/2009/04/22/1461s477471.htm.

The Challenges and Drivers of Regionalism in South Asia: The India-Pakistan Peace Process

Akmal Hussain[1]

This is a moment of reckoning for South Asia. The region's economic dynamism and innovation are catapulting it into a position of global leadership even as the world economy's center of gravity shifts from the West to Asia. Yet, at the same time, South Asia's very existence is being threatened: by the specter of nuclear holocaust, by religious extremism and an increasingly fragmented society, by the persistent poverty of the masses amid the growing affluence of the elite, and by the breaking down of basic ecological life-support systems. The challenges are great, but so are the opportunities. Regional cooperation offers a vital channel for addressing both.

In this chapter, I outline the economic opportunities now available to South Asia, whose rich cultural traditions, I argue, have much to contribute to the world. I then discuss the need for a new policy paradigm to address the multiple challenges of conflict, poverty, and environmental degradation, a paradigm that utilizes modern sensibilities even as it remains rooted in traditional South Asian values of human solidarity, harmony with nature, and social responsibility. I then look at the implications of the India-Pakistan peace process for regional economic development and security. In the final section, I discuss constraints to the peace process and several short- and medium-term initiatives to achieve peace and regional cooperation.

Can South Asia Lead the World?[2]

South Asia will likely play a key role in the global economy in the twenty-first century. It could also contribute its rich talent and core values drawn from its cultural heritage, to meet the global challenges of poverty, armed conflict, and environmental degradation. However, first its member nations must resolve the political and economic issues that divide them.

If South Asia is to realize its potential as an integrated region, there is no time to act like the present. For the first time in three-hundred-and-fifty years, the global economy's center of gravity is shifting from Europe and North America to Asia. If present trends of gross domestic product (GDP) growth continue, in two decades China will be the largest economy in the world, followed by the United States, then India. However, economic integration could enable South Asia to become the second-largest economy after China. Given the geographic proximity and economic complementarities of South Asia and China, Asia could soon consolidate into the greatest economic powerhouse in human history.

Yet the world cannot be sustained by economic growth alone. Human life is threatened by environmental crises and conflicts arising from the overuse of public goods, endemic poverty, and the danger of violent extremism and interstate conflicts. South Asian societies have often succeeded, throughout their long history, in achieving unity in diversity.[3] In bringing this approach to bear on contemporary challenges, it is hoped that the people of the region can introduce not only new institutions but higher ideals to guide the mechanisms of the global market. Together, South Asia and China could put the world on a new trajectory of sustainable development and human security in the twenty-first century and thereby contribute to enriching human civilization.

Changing the Policy Paradigm

As South Asia acquires a leadership role in the global economy, its nation-states must shift their policy stance from conflict to cooperation. As of now, the production of new weapons is the emblem of state power. I suggest that if global economic growth is to be sustainable—indeed, if life is to survive on earth—a new dynamic must guide the interactions of human beings with one another and with the world around them. South Asia, with its living folk traditions of pursuing human needs within the framework of human solidarity and harmony with nature, may be uniquely equipped to face this challenge.

The Global Ecological Crisis

In perhaps the largest scientific collaboration in world history, many of the world's leading environmental scientists joined together to form the Intergovernmental Panel on Climate Change (IPCC). The IPCC's 2007 assessment report[4] echoes the similarly comprehensive work of the Millennium Ecosystem Assessment. Both present evidence of an impending ecological crisis and show that over the past fifty years, humans have caused "substantial and largely irreversible loss in the diversity of life on Earth," including the forced extinction of 25 percent of the earth's species. Meanwhile, "60% of the ecosystem services that were examined in the study are being degraded . . . including fresh water . . . air and the regulation of regional and local climate."[5]

The IPCC's assessment of global warming and associated climate change indicates that the planet's life-support systems are being destabilized by human intervention.[6] It can be argued that this is due to the levels and forms of production, consumption, waste disposal, and types of technologies used over the past three centuries within the dynamic and sustained economic growth process that was specific to capitalism.

The IPCC report projects, with a high degree of confidence, that increased global average temperatures will result in major changes in "ecosystem structure and function," leading to "negative consequences for biodiversity and ecosystem goods and services, such as water and food supply."[7] It is projected that global warming could decrease crop yields in South Asia by 30 percent by 2050, which would further the food crisis and sharply increase poverty. Meanwhile, approximately 20–30 percent of the world's plant and animal species are at risk of extinction;[8] any further reduction in biodiversity would make the world's ecosystems more fragile and thus more susceptible to exogenous shocks.

Current production and consumption processes inject toxic gases and materials into the air, land, and water systems. Since the earth's ecology has a maximum load capacity, it is clear that the present consumer culture, economic growth patterns, and underlying institutional structures cannot be sustained indefinitely without undermining the planet. A new relationship between humans, commodities, and nature needs to be forged. The question is, what role can South Asia play?

A New Sensibility

The post-2007 slowdown in Western economic growth has quelled the usually unrestrained praise of market forces. As of 2010, the predominant view is that market forces, though a necessary feature of the global economy, require regulation. Yet, as we have seen in recent decades, regulation faces vociferous opposition from those who argue against it in good times, and as the recent downturn attests, succeed in doing so. The growth of Asian firms, some of which are based on a different set of social norms than those of the West, exemplify a paradigm based on market forces but tempered by norms of social responsibility within and between collaborative networks. In other words, they model a sustainable alternative to unrestrained free markets. As Mahatma Gandhi said: "There is enough in the world for everybody's need but not for everybody's greed."

Perhaps South Asia can contribute its historical experience to the contemporary world by weaving its cultural and ethical values into a twenty-first-century sensibility that can regulate competitive forces at the micro level within a new institutional framework of cooperation at the macro level.

Human Security, Development, and the Peace Process

For all its rich traditions, South Asia, as of 2010, is suspended between hope of a better life and fear of cataclysmic destruction. On the one hand, the region's tremendous human innovations and natural resource potential, not to mention its rich cultural diversity, promise to flourish within the unifying framework of the region's shared history and civilization. On the other hand, South Asia is not only the poorest region in the world, but its people live under the threat of nuclear destruction. The very fabric of South Asia's society and state structures

153

are being torn asunder by armed extremist groups who use fear and violence to achieve their political goals, and to fuel interstate tensions.

It can therefore be argued that interstate peace in the region—not enhanced military capability—is the key to national security, indeed human survival. In this chapter, I will propose that peace between India and Pakistan is necessary, not only for sustaining economic growth but also for building pluralistic democracies, thereby sustaining the integrity of both states and societies in the region.

Militarization and National Integrity

India and Pakistan, the most powerful states in South Asia, have pursued national security through the building of military capability for mass annihilation of each other's citizens. Therefore, it is not surprising that South Asia is the poorest and yet the most militarized region in the world:[9] it contains almost half the world's poor and yet has the capability (even in a limited nuclear exchange) to immediately kill over a hundred million people, with many hundreds of millions more dying from radiation-related illnesses.[10]

The arms race between India and Pakistan—both countries account for 93 percent of South Asia's total military expenditure—is responsible for this cruel irony. India ranks 142nd in terms of per capita income but 1st in the world in terms of arms imports; Pakistan is not far behind, ranking 119th in per capita income and 10th in arms imports.[11] These military expenditures, on a scale that is unprecedented in the developing world, are being undertaken in the name of national security, even as the majority of South Asians continue to live below the international poverty line ($2 a day),[12] 46 percent of children are malnourished,[13] and 35 percent of the population suffers from health deprivation (measured in terms of people who lack access to safe water and are undernourished).[14] The trade-off between military expenditure and the provision of basic services is worth considering; for example, a modern submarine with associated support systems costs $300 million—enough to provide safe drinking water to sixty million people. These figures challenge the logic of increased military expenditure as a means to national security.

The deadly nuclear dimension added to the India-Pakistan arms race in 1998 is assumed to reinforce national security through "deterrence." Yet three defining features of the India-Pakistan situation imply a high probability of an accidental or deliberate nuclear war, thereby making this presumed deterrence unstable: (1) the flying time of nuclear missiles between India and Pakistan is less than five minutes, (2) the unresolved Kashmir dispute fuels tensions between the two countries and makes them susceptible to disinformation about each other's intentions, and (3) intrastate social conflicts in each country feed off—and spur—interstate tensions.

India-Pakistan relations are strained to the point that a chance terrorist attack could induce military mobilization and a conventional armed conflict that could quickly escalate to a nuclear war. Consider the current situation:

- Armed militant groups continue to conduct what they view as a war of liberation in Kashmir. Pakistan's government claims that such groups are not under its control, while India continues to accuse it of "cross-border terrorism."
- When a high-profile terrorist attack occurs in India, Pakistan is immediately held responsible—as it was following the December 2001 attack on the Indian Parliament and the more recent barbaric bombings in Bombay (July 2006 and November 2008); in the former case, India actually mobilized its military forces in a warlike deployment on the India-Pakistan border.
- In the case of an Indian incursion into Pakistani territory following a chance terrorist attack: if the territorial gains of Indian forces reach an unspecified critical level, Pakistan has already made clear that it will use nuclear weapons to defend itself; at the same time, the declared Indian nuclear doctrine involves an all-out nuclear attack on Pakistan. As then–Indian defense minister George Fernandes clarified in December 2002, such an all-out nuclear retaliation would occur even if Pakistan drops a nuclear bomb on Indian forces operating within Pakistani territory.[15]

These elements could spark a military confrontation between the two states at any time. Moreover, there is grave danger that, given the fact that most of Pakistan's major cities are within less than 100 kilometers of the border with India, loss of one or more of these cities following a conventional assault could spark a nuclear response. That this prospect is terribly real was illustrated on at least three occasions:

- *India's Operation Brass Tacks in 1986.* This military exercise, which was seen by Pakistan as a prelude to an Indian invasion, prompted then–Pakistani foreign minister Sahibzada Yaqub Khan to convey the explicit threat of nuclear war to his old collegemate, Indian foreign minister I. K. Gujral, during a meeting in Delhi.
- *The Kargil conflict in 1999.* The quickly escalated mobilization of military force along the border made the danger of an all-out war so grave that then-Pakistani prime minister Nawaz Sharif rushed to Washington to get U.S. president Bill Clinton's support to avoid it. Bruce Reidel,[16] who was present during the Sharif-Clinton meeting, claims that the United States had information that Pakistan was preparing its nuclear arsenal for possible use. Reidel claims that Clinton actually asked Sharif "if he knew how advanced the threat of nuclear war really was?"[17]
- *After the attack by armed militants on the Indian Parliament in 2001,* India mobilized its military forces along the border with Pakistan; tensions rose and Pakistan threatened "unconventional" military retaliation if war broke out.[18]

These and other incidents of India-Pakistan tension suggest that any war between the two countries would not be localized or conventional. With the stakes of catastrophic destruction as high as they are in the region, any nonzero probability of nuclear war ought to be unacceptable. Yet the defining features of the nuclear environment in South Asia make the probability of an intentional or accidental nuclear war higher than in any other region of the world.

Even as their governments are preoccupied with achieving "national security" through a paradigm of military conflict, the citizens of these adversarial states share a common concern for human security: from the threat of war, religious extremism, economic deprivation, social injustice, and environmental degradation. Bridging the gap between the preoccupations of the state and those of civil society is necessary to maintain the social contract that underlies the writ of the state and sustains national integrity. At the same time, establishing a framework for lasting peace is essential for regional stability in South Asia. The question is: What are the obstacles to peace, and what can be done to overcome them?

The India-Pakistan Peace Process: Obstacles and Drivers

Let us first look at the political economies of India and Pakistan as backdrop to the peace process. India's economic strength lies in the fact that, having established a heavy industrial base in the 1950s under Jawaharlal Nehru, it reconfigured its policy framework in the 1990s to play a greater role in the globalized economy, launching it on a high-growth trajectory. With a large domestic market, an infrastructure for technological change, international competitiveness in select cutting-edge sectors (such as software and electronics), and large capital inflows, India has sustained impressive GDP growth over the past two decades. Yet, growth has been predominantly based in the home market; India's exports as a percentage of world exports stood at less than 1 percent in 2008. Continued GDP growth in the future will require India's accelerated export growth and the establishment of: (1) markets for manufactured exports in South Asia and abroad and (2) an infrastructure for the supply of oil, gas, and electricity. It is in this context of sustaining GDP growth that the three strategic imperatives for India become apparent: (1) achieving a regionally integrated economy through an early implementation of the Islamabad South Asian Association for Regional Cooperation (SAARC) Summit Declaration on the South Asian Free Trade Area (SAFTA) (January 2004); (2) securing oil and gas pipelines and rail and road transportation routes between Central Asia and India via Pakistan; and (3) overcoming political disputes with Pakistan and other South Asian neighbors to establish a political framework of lasting peace and a regional economic union.

Peace and economic cooperation with Pakistan is necessary for India to not only secure its strategic economic interests but also to maintain its secular democratic polity. India's current high-growth open economy is inseparable from a liberal, democratic political structure. The existing social forces of Hindu nationalism—intolerant of minorities—threaten to undermine India's secular democratic structure as much as its economic endeavors. Continued tension between India and Pakistan will only fuel extremist religious forces in both countries, to the detriment of their economy and polity. The tension between India and Pakistan and the rise of violent extremist forces are is exacerbated by the fact that both the Indian government and influential U.S. scholars and politicians believe that some extremist groups have received support from elements of the state apparatus in Pakistan.[19] Similarly, the Pakistani establishment now believes that the separatist nationalist movement in Balochistan, as well as some extremist Taliban groups, is receiving support from India.[20]

Pakistan's economy, by contrast, is facing a crisis as it is unable to sustain high GDP growth due to an aid-dependent economic structure, inadequate export capability, and recurrent balance-of-payments crises. Persistent high levels of poverty and continued tension with India fuel the forces of religious extremism. Armed militant groups have now emerged as rivals to the state, threatening its structure and territorial control as well as the very fabric of society. Peace with India would encourage much-needed foreign and domestic investment, which could play an important role in accelerating and sustaining GDP growth and poverty reduction in Pakistan.

It is clear that, through peace, both India and Pakistan can reap economic benefits for their people and secure their respective democratic structures against the forces of religious extremism. The national security of both countries is threatened not by the neighbor across the border but by internal forces of intolerance, violence, and poverty. A new framework of lasting peace would reduce the danger of cataclysmic destruction from nuclear war and also provide economic and political stability; thus, national security would enhance security of life and livelihood.

Trade and investment have historically been both the cause and consequence of institutional change; this is true for Pakistan, India, and indeed all South Asia. Thus, implementation of the Islamabad SAARC Declaration[21] with respect to the SAFTA at the Sixteenth SAARC Summit, held in April 2010 in Bhutan, might prove a strategic step toward regional economic integration and peace, and thus serve to strength the institutional structures of democracy in the region. Some of the main issues before the leaders at the summit were allowing free trade in services; setting up an enforcement mechanism to implement the provision of the SAFTA agreement that tariff barriers for intra-SAARC trade be reduced to the 5 percent level by 2010; and establishing an institutional framework to indentify and remove nontariff barriers, which prevent 60 percent of the potential intra-SAARC trade.

In connection with the SAFTA, Pakistan should establish free trade and mutual investment strategies with India and other South Asian countries, while easing travel restrictions on their citizens. Such steps would (1) set up a powerful economic stimulus, (2) give voice to stakeholders of peace and the demilitarization of the polity in Pakistan, (3) strengthen civil society influence, and (4) help build a tolerant and pluralistic democratic culture. Let us briefly examine the dimensions of institutional change that would result from an India-Pakistan peace settlement.

Economic Cooperation

An economic opening with India would accelerate Pakistan's GDP growth via increased investment by Indian entrepreneurs. Moreover, imports of relatively cheaper capital and intermediate goods from India could reduce capital-output ratios in Pakistan and thereby generate higher GDP growth for given levels of investment. Imports of food products during seasonal shortages could reduce food inflation and improve the distribution of real income in Pakistan. Easing of travel restrictions would boost Pakistan's tourism, services, and retail sectors and would increase employment elasticities by stimulating employment-intensive GDP growth (since the tourism sector is labor intensive); this would in turn accelerate the growth of employment and improve income distribution. Thus, free trade relations with India would enable Pakistan to achieve better and more equitable GDP growth.

Free Trade and a Culture of Democracy

As free trade and investment bring substantial economic dividends to the middle and lower-middle classes, a large constituency will be created in Pakistan that no longer identifies with a "national security state" that is presumed to be "threatened by India" and that therefore requires the military to dominate national policy. Shifting from the ideology of a national security state to a democratic one will make it possible to acknowledge that the security and welfare of citizens are primarily achieved through peace and development, and will go far toward strengthening civil society influence within the polity.

Important constraints on the building of a democratic polity—and indeed the principal threats to state structures in South Asia—are internal conflicts such as those sparked by religious extremism; ethnic, communal, and caste differences; and other subnational fractures. Containing these conflicts requires the building of institutions for a pluralistic society. In such a society, not only can diverse identities coexist, but multiple identities can be maintained by each individual.[22] Thus, for example, Muslims and Hindus should be able to live in peace; at the same time, a particular individual may be at once a Muslim, a Balochi, a Karachite, a Pakistani, a South Asian, and a Commonwealth citizen.

The cultural diversity of South Asia is nurtured by shared wellsprings of human civilization. Thus, national integrity is strengthened not by the denial of multiple identities but by the creation of a democratic polity in which they can flourish. Essential to the building of pluralistic democracies in India and Pakistan is the opening up of new economic and cultural spaces within which people of the two countries can encounter the "other" and experience the diversity and richness of the self. Yet, in the past, state-sponsored interest groups have sustained interstate conflict by demonizing the other; this involves a narrowing of the mind and a constriction of the identity, placing the self and the other into a mutually exclusive dichotomy. Yet, through human relationship the other is experienced as a vital catalyst to the growth of the self; engaging erstwhile "enemies" in such a dynamic could enrich identity and help strengthen pluralistic democracy in Pakistan and India.[23]

The Dialectic of Cooperation and Confrontation

Obstacles to regional peace can be understood in terms of a dialectic between the strategic political imperatives for peace on the one hand and the military establishment's tendency for path dependence on the other. I will briefly discuss this dialectic in order to explain the stop-go nature of the peace process and the opportunities now available for triggering medium-term change.

Strategic Imperatives for the Peace Process

The decision in July 2001 by Gen. Pervez Musharraf's administration to engage India in a peace process was predicated on three imperatives:

1. Reducing tensions with India in order to focus on economic growth, which was seen by the new military regime as a means to political legitimacy
2. Closing the front with India (at least temporarily) in order to avoid a two-front situation after 2001, when Pakistan joined the West in the war against terrorism in Afghanistan
3. Responding to popular demand for peace with India

These strategic military and political imperatives induced General Musharraf to engage with India on the basis of a new policy formulated around several key innovations. First, Pakistan moved away from its previous demand that a plebiscite in Kashmir be a precondition for normalizing economic relations with India. This was replaced by a new focus on a composite dialogue within which cross-border economic relations were to be discussed alongside the resolution of outstanding political and territorial disputes, including that over Kashmir. The different dynamics of the two tracks were acknowledged, including the probability that trade relations would yield results sooner than the Kashmir dispute, given its intractable nature. It was initially thought that success in economic relations and the resultant peace dividend would not only create advocates for lasting peace in both countries, but would also help build confidence in jointly resolving the political dispute-resolution process. Third, there was a significant move away from talking about the plebescite in Kashmir as the "unfinished business of partition" and therefore essentially a bilateral dispute. Instead, General Musharraf proposed that Pakistan and India set aside their traditionally rigid positions and seek to find a resolution acceptable to India, Pakistan, *and* the people of Kashmir.

159

At the same time, the Indian government shifted its position from insisting that Kashmir was an entirely internal issue to allowing it as a viable subject of bilateral discussion on economic cooperation.

Constraints to Peace

General Musharraf's stated policy initially produced encouraging results, with a substantial increase in trade volumes between India and Pakistan and confidence-building measures, such as increased visa permits for a larger number of cross-border travelers. However, structural restrictions to trade and indeed investment could only be overcome if Pakistan granted most favored nation (MFN) status to India whereby trade, instead of being restricted to a few officially negotiated items, could be open for the free flow of goods and capital, as among World Trade Organization (WTO) members. Instead, constraints on trade persisted even as Pakistan, under the SAARC umbrella, signed the Islamabad Declaration making the SAFTA a national objective.

It was at this point that special interests kicked in to effectively stall the process: influential members of Pakistan's establishment saw a rapid improvement in economic relations and a permanent peace with India as a threat to the raison d'etre of the large military establishment. This same military was getting the lion's share of the budget on the basis of the "Indian threat" and the ideology of a national security state; fears that the Pakistani economy would be swamped by cheap Indian goods began to circulate, as did the notion that the very identity of the state would be threatened by the normalization of relations with India.

These considerations put the brakes on the peace process as then–prime minister Shaukat Aziz pointedly declared that improvement in economic relations was contingent on progress in resolving the Kashmir dispute. The policy of delinking the economic and political tracks was thus reversed, and progress in economic relations was once again made hostage to the intractable Kashmir dispute. The setback was furthered as President Musharraf's political position weakened and his reliance on the support of his military constituency increased amid the gathering storm of a judicial crisis. The peace process was effectively put on hold as Musharraf faced a double threat to his government from the democratic opposition on the one hand and the intensified attacks of militant extremists on the other.

The democratic government in Pakistan, which emerged after the February 2008 elections, restarted dialogue on the same terms as before the military held up progress. Foreign Minister Shah Mahmood Qureshi called for a "comprehensive settlement" with India and President Asif Ali Zardari declared the government's intentions to accelerate the peace process and focus on economic cooperation.[24] The imperatives of building a dynamic economy and a democratic polity are clearly apparent to the leadership of Pakistan's fragile democracy. The terrible Mumbai massacre in 2008 by Pakistan-based militants again disrupted the peace process. After a hiatus of several months, the peace dialogue restarted in February 2010, with a formal meeting of the foreign secretaries of the two countries in New Delhi.

Path Dependence and Short-Term Ways of Accelerating the Peace Process

The concept of path dependence has been conceived by Douglass North as the tendency of individuals and groups to resist institutional change where such a change threatens their interests; such individuals and groups are willing to invest their energy, resources, and time to resist institutional change.[25] Therefore, as North points out, path dependence is guided by "the constraints on the choice set in the present that are derived from historical experiences of the past."[26] The 2008 terrorist attack in Mumbai and the later attack against the Sri Lankan cricket team in Lahore indicate the urgent importance of addressing the issue of terrorism if economic activity, let alone cooperation, is to be sustained.

The problem of path dependence in this context is located in the mind-sets of Pakistan and India's respective bureaucracies, shaped as they are by years of mutual demonization. These mind-sets were reinforced by the India-Pakistan wars in 1965 and 1971, the more limited Kargil conflict in 1999, and the protracted insurgency in India-occupied Kashmir. Recurrent military confrontations and the perception of each other as adversaries in a zero-sum game has bred attitudes of mutual mistrust and suspicion among the military establishments, the bureaucracies, and to some extent, the political leadership of the two countries. While the attitudes—or at least the words—of the political leadership in Pakistan and India have changed significantly over the past decade as a result of popular pressure to pursue peace, the "trust deficit" in the military and bureaucratic establishments remains unchanged.

The problem of path dependence, in this context, is illustrated by an observation made by Prime Minister Manmohan Singh when addressing scholars at the South Asia Center for Policy Studies in New Delhi in 2004:[27] "the gains from peace are immense, yet old attitudes of strife, mistrust, and suspicion could lead us to a sub-optimal solution"; he went on to say that he was, however, willing to make a "new beginning" and that any ideas for peace would have his "fullest support" and he hoped that of his government.[28]

Thus, constraints to peace are primarily located in the bureaucratic and military establishments of the two countries. Such establishments are locked in old attitudes, not only because of persistent modes of thought elsewhere considered obsolete, but also because their present economic power and political influence rest on "national security"—or, in other words, on maintaining the status quo. The possibility of overcoming old attitudes for the sake of securing peace is available to democratic governments; all that is required is that the power structures of the bureaucracy and military translate the will of their people into political action.

Clearly, free trade between Pakistan and India would be an important medium-term objective that could sustain and substantially accelerate the long-term political process of institutionalizing a lasting peace between the two countries. It can be argued that the best short-term initiatives involve strengthening and deepening both democracy and the institutional structure of civil society. Achieving free trade, for instance, would essentially be an act of persuasion whereby special interests would be compelled to bow to the popular consensus created among civil society organizations, think tanks, and a responsive parliament. This is not outside the realm of the imagination—even the military establishment might be persuaded by the promise of greater corporate gains. Given the wide range of private-sector corporations floated by the military (ranging from banks to breakfast cereals),[29] stimulation of Pakistan's GDP growth following trade and investment with India would also enhance the growth and profits of these corporations.

Four specific short-term initiatives could be taken toward achieving economic cooperation between India and Pakistan:

- *Convening a conference of South Asian parliamentarians on the topic of regional economic cooperation.*[30] The issue of free trade and in particular the implementation of the SAFTA agreement ought to be the main item on the agenda. The participants of the conference could also include representatives from regional think tanks, experts who have worked on regional cooperation, representatives of civil society advocacy organizations for peace and economic cooperation, civil servants involved in the peace process, lawyers, the media, and representatives from the faculties of the Command and Staff College and the National Defense University.
- *Establishing a network of South Asian institutes for regional cooperation.* These would be devoted to policy research and advocacy for peace and economic cooperation. Organized workshops would generate policy recommendations on economic cooperation in South Asia and, specifically, the dynamics of the peace process.
- *Developing an advocacy program for South Asian parliaments and governments.* Such a program would establish an institutional base for bringing together representatives of civil society organizations in Pakistan and India, as well as representatives from regional think tanks. The objective would be to undertake a short-term advocacy program with respective parliaments and governments to create the institutional basis in civil society that would allow the SAFTA agreement to be completed and implemented. SAFTA should be followed up with another agreement for achieving an economic union for South Asia in the coming decade.
- *Easing of travel restrictions to promote regional tourism in South Asia.* Easing travel restrictions on South Asians traveling to SAARC member countries would enable greater economic, cultural, and social interaction among the citizens of India and Pakistan in particular and South Asia in general. The resulting increase in tourism would be a powerful stimulus

to the economies of the region; in fact, tourism could become one of the largest industries in Pakistan and some of the smaller South Asian countries. Moreover, as restaurants, hotels, and other tourism-related industries respond to the growing demand for services, the secondary effects of tourism would increase incomes across populations.

Medium-Term Drivers of Peace and Economic Cooperation

Meanwhile, several medium-term initiatives could be undertaken by the private sector and civil society, with support from SAARC, to overcome path dependence. These include the establishment of a regional health foundation with the aim to make the benefits of regional peace and cooperation palpable to people through improved health care. The objective of the foundation would be to establish high-quality model hospitals, together with satellite clinics and outreach programs for preventive health care, in select backward districts in each country of South Asia.[31] In addition, a South Asia Education Foundation (SAEF) could be created on the basis of contributions by SAARC member countries, individual philanthropists, and, more substantially, multilateral donor agencies. The purpose of the SAEF would be to create a network of high schools at an international standard across South Asia, with at least one such high school built in every administrative district. These schools could be models for both private-sector and government-run schools to follow.

Such a school network might play a particularly important role in Pakistan, where it would counteract the growing influence of madrassas run by militant religious groups, who are expanding their influence particularly in the rural areas and small towns of the North-West Frontier Province (NWFP) and Punjab. One factor that attracts youths to such madrassas is that, in most cases, they get free lodging and boarding, with parents required to pay only nominal fees. The SAEF schools, which would provide a broad-based liberal education, should utilize a tiered fee system whereby students from affluent families pay higher fees to partially subsidize poor families. An endowment fund for scholarships could provide free education to students from poor families, and schools could provide residential facilities for out-of-town students and free lunches to day students.

With the goal of promoting energy cooperation to meet growing regional demand, high-voltage connections must be established among national grids across the region. India, Pakistan, and Bangladesh should also cooperate closely to build a gas pipeline for transporting gas from Iran, Qatar, Turkmenistan, and even Myanmar. The precondition to a competitive power market is to allow generators to produce electricity and distributors to sell it in the market. In this context, the joint development, trading, and sharing of energy should be pursued. Apart from electricity production and distribution through large hydroelectric projects, joint efforts to develop innovative new technologies (such as solar and wind energy) and single turbines, powered by canal flows in the extensive canal networks in both the Indus basin and the Ganges and Brahmaputra valleys. The electricity produced through these innovative technologies, combined with the electricity generation from hydroelectric power projects in South Asia, could be linked up with district, national, and regional grids.

Joint-venture projects promote shared regional investment and tap shared resources. Such projects might include private-sector investment in a high-quality network of roads and railways to connect South Asia. These modern roads and rail lines would join all major commercial centers, towns, and cities of the SAARC countries with one another and with the economies of Central, West, and East Asia. Regional and global investment in new ports along the western and eastern seaboard of South Asia should accompany the upgrading of existing ports to the highest international standards. Regional investment should also be put into refurbishing and building airports, which together with cold-storage warehouses would stimulate not only tourism but also the export of perishable commodities such as milk, meat, fish, fruits, and vegetables.

The huge potential for energy and irrigation in the mountain ranges of South Asia remains untapped. Dams should be designed and located strictly in accordance with existing international treaties, such as the Indus Basin Treaty. Regional projects for improving the irrigation efficiency of canal networks and waterways would go far to increase agricultural potential throughout South Asia.

One of the most important aspects of regional cooperation should be environmental protection. For example there should be institutionalized cooperation, in the face of growing water scarcity, to conserve water and improve delivery and application efficiencies of irrigation.[32] Related efforts could include the construction of medium- and small-sized dams to increase water availability in the off-season; the establishment of water distribution—on an equitable basis—across countries and provinces; the lining of canals and water courses; and improved on-farm water management. Joint efforts to reduce emissions of greenhouse gases within South Asia should accompany joint diplomatic efforts to achieve the same objective on a global scale.

In addition, SAARC countries should cooperate to develop heat-resistant varieties of grain and conduct biotechnology research to achieve a new green revolution in South Asia—even as the old green revolution comes to an end. Joint efforts toward the reforestation of water sheds and the treatment of industrial and urban effluent waste would help reduce soil erosion, devastating flash floods, and the toxicity of rivers. Sharing of biosaline research and technical know-how would help mitigate the desertification of soils—for example, by using plants such as halogenic phradophytes to control salinity. Member countries would also do well to share know-how on ecologically sound industrial technologies and cost-effective and safe methods of effluent disposal. Sharing of information on river water flow will go far to aid accurate flood forecasting. Engaging in joint development of Himalayan resources, including the prevention of deforestation and soil erosion on the mountain slopes is another worthy project with implications both regional and global. For these and other projects it would be invaluable to collect, systematize, and evaluate the traditional knowledge systems of South Asian communities, with a focus on innovative techniques of earning a livelihood in harmony with nature.

One of SAARC's primary goals—and one that requires concerted regional effort—is to accelerate poverty reduction across South Asia. To improve the material conditions of the people of South Asia requires not only a faster economic growth rate but also a restructuring of growth so as to make it pro-poor.[33] This requires providing the institutional bases and economic incentives for increased investment in those sectors that generate relatively more employment, productivity, and incomes.[34] In this context three sets of measures can be undertaken at the national as well as regional levels. First, joint-venture projects need to be undertaken to rapidly accelerate the increase in yield per acre of small farms in agriculture and small-scale industry, which have relatively higher employment elasticities and can more effectively increase the productivity and incomes of the poor. These subsectors include production and regional exports of high-value-added agricultural products, such as milk, vegetables, fruits, flowers, and fish. Second, regional networks of private-sector support institutions can provide small-scale industries located in regional growth nodes with specialized facilities—such as heat treatment, forging, quality-control systems, and provision of marketing facilities in both national and regional economies. Third, a SAARC fund for vocational training should be set up to help establish a network of high-quality vocational training institutes for the poor. Improved training in marketable skills would enable a shift of the labor force from low- to higher-skill sectors and thereby increase productivity and income-earning capability. It would, at the same time, generate higher returns on investment by increasing factor productivity.

Conclusion

In this chapter, I have argued that South Asia has an opportunity to address the critical challenges of poverty, armed conflict, and environmental degradation through regional cooperation. In doing so, member countries will foster a new form of equitable and sustainable economic growth. The process would involve new initiatives for restructuring the growth process to make it pro-poor. Efforts at the regional, national, and local levels could be made to develop new institutions and technologies in the areas of water-resource management, energy production, heat-resistant seed varieties, soil depletion, and greenhouse gas emissions. Most importantly, the process of sustainable development would be underpinned by South Asia's rich cultural traditions, including the value placed on human solidarity and harmony with nature.

For most South Asians, a choice between life and comprehensive destruction looms larger than before; both Pakistan and India are party to this dilemma and share responsibility for its solution. While sustainable development seems to be the answer, it requires a shift in mind-set. Suffering an adversarial relationship with one's neighbor can no longer be the emblem of patriotism.

Instead, cooperation and regional unity through plurality promise to guide the region—and the world—into a new dawn.

Notes

[1] An earlier version of this chapter was among the South Asia Center for Policy Studies (SACEPS) proposals for deepening regional integration, submitted to the SAARC heads of state scheduled to meet in Colombo for the SAARC Summit in August 2008. The same version was also circulated among the participants of the SACEPS/Institute of Policy Studies (IPS) Conference on Strengthening Economic and Social Integration of South Asia, Colombo, May 30–31, 2008. Another, longer version of this paper has just been published as chapter 1 in Sadiq Ahmed, Saman Kelegama, and Ejaz Ghani, eds., *Promoting Economic Cooperation in South Asia* (New Delhi: The World Bank and SAGE Publications 2010).

[2] This section is based on a more elaborate paper presented by the author before the parliamentarians from South Asian countries at the South Asian Free Media Association (SAFMA) Conference on Evolving a South Asian Fraternity, Bhurban, May 16, 2005.

[3] See Najam Hussain Syed, *Recurrent Patterns in Punjabi Poetry* (Lahore: Majlis Shah Hussain, 1968), 9–22; Jawaharlal Nehru, *The Discovery of India* (London: Penguin Books, 2004), "Section: The Indian Philosophical Approach"; R. Fernando, ed., *The Unanimous Tradition: Essays on the Essential Unity of All Religions* (Colombo: The Sri Lanka Institute of Traditional Studies, 1991), especially chapter 1 by Whitall N. Perry, "The Revival of Interest in Tradition," and chapter 2 by Frithjof Schuon, "The Perennial Philosophy."

[4] IPCC, *Climate Change: Impacts, Adaptation and Vulnerability*, Working Group-II Contribution to the Fourth Assessment Report of the Inter-Governmental Panel on Climate Change (IPCC), Cambridge Univ. Press, NY, 2007.

[5] See Millennium Ecosystem Assessment, *Ecosystems and Human-Well-Being, Current State and Trends*, Millennium Ecosystem Assessment Report (Volumes 1–4), Island Press, Washington, D.C., 2005.

[6] IPCC, *Climate Change: Impacts, Adaptation and Vulnerability.*

[7] Ibid.,11.

[8] Ibid.

[9] See Mahbub ul Haq, *Human Development in South Asia* (Karachi: Oxford Univ. Press, 1997).

[10] *Newsweek*, June 8, 1998: 17.

[11] See Haq, *Human Development in South Asia.*

[12] In terms of the international poverty line of $2 a day per person, the percentage of the population living below the poverty line is 80 percent in India, 65 percent in Pakistan, just over 80 percent in Nepal, and 50 percent in Sri Lanka. See Mahbub ul Haq Human Development Center, *Human Development in South Asia* (Karachi: Oxford Univ. Press, 2006), figure 3.1, p. 51.

[13] Ibid., table 4.4, p. 70.

[14] Ibid., table 4.2, p. 68.

[15] *Global Security Newswire*, December 30, 2002.

[16] Bruce Reidel was at that time the special assistant for Near Eastern and South Asia affairs at the National Security Council.

[17] See Bruce Reidel, "American Diplomacy and the 1999 Kargil Summit at Blair House," Center for the Advanced Study of India, Univ. of Pennsylvania, 2002.

[18] President Musharraf was reported to have said that Pakistan was not afraid to use unconventional weapons if attacked according to the daily, *The Hindu*; see *Global Security Newswire*, January 7, 2003.

[19] For example, during the March 2010 hearings of the U.S. House Subcommittee on the Middle East and South Asia, Panel Chairman Gary Ackerman is reported to have said, "There is in fact no reason to doubt that Pakistan's military is likely paying compensation to the families of the terrorists killed in the Mumbai Attack." Even a Pakistani American scholar, Shuja Nawaz, acknowledged that the Lashkar-e-Taiba was a "Frankenstein's monster" that assumed a broader regional role. (The Indian government accused the Lashkar-e-Taiba of launching the 2008 Mumbai attack.) See *Daily Dawn*, Lahore (March 13, 2010).

[20] For example, on March 12, after the terrorist attack against military personnel in the crowded R.A. bazaar of Lahore Cantonment, Pakistan's interior minister, Rehman Malik, stated that Pakistan had "solid evidence of [Indian] involvement in the Balochistan unrest." See *Daily Dawn*, Lahore (March 13, 2010). On the same day, the commissioner of Lahore claimed on Pakistan's private television networks that an Indian hand was behind the terrorist attacks in Lahore Cantonment that day.

[21] Islamabad SAARC Declaration, January 2004.

[22] For a discussion of multiple identities, see Amartya Sen, *Identity and Violence: The Illusion of Destiny* (London: Allen Lane, 2006), 3–5.

[23] This subsection is drawn from Akmal Hussain, *Human Security, Economic Development and the Peace Process*, chapter, "Non-Traditional and Human Security in South Asia," 233–34, collection of papers presented at an international seminar jointly organized by the Institute of Regional Studies and National Commission for Human Development, Islamabad, October 31–November 1, 2006.

[24] In an interview on the CNN-IBN program "Devil's Advocate," Asif Ali Zardari said that good relations with India would not be held hostage to the Kashmir dispute. He said the two countries would wait for future generations to resolve the issue and should focus on trade ties for now (reported in the *Daily Times*, Sunday, March 2, 2008).

[25] Douglass C. North, *Understanding the Process of Economic Change* (New Jersey: Princeton Univ. Press, 2005), 51.

[26] Ibid., 52.

[27] The author attended this event, which took place on August 30, 2004, at the prime minister's residence.

[28] This discussion was first reported in Akmal Hussain, "Taking the Peace Process Forward," *Daily Times*, Lahore, September 23, 2004. Significantly, Prime Minister Manmohan Singh subsequently repeated his remark about making a "new beginning" in the United Nations.

[29] For evidence on the corporate interests of the military see Ayesha Siddiqa, *Military Inc., Inside Pakistan's Military Economy* (Karachi: Oxford Univ. Press, 2009).

[30] A few years ago, SAFMA organized a highly successful conference in Bhurban of parliamentarians from each of the countries of South Asia in which it was agreed that the peace process should be made irreversible through institutional mechanisms in both government and civil society.

[31] For an elaboration of this concept see Akmal Hussain, "South Asia Health Foundation," Concept Note, SACEPS, Dhaka, November 8, 2004.

[32] The delivery efficiency of irrigation refers to the volumes (million acre feet) of water that reach the farm gate as a percentage of the volume of water taken from the river by the canal system. The application efficiency of irrigation refers to the volume of water that reaches the crops' root zone as a percentage of the volume of water received at the farm gate.

[33] For a detailed discussion on pro-poor growth, see Akmal Hussain, *A Policy for Pro-Poor Growth*, chapter, "Towards Pro-Poor Growth Policies in Pakistan," Proceedings of the Pro-poor Growth Policies Symposium, United Nations Development Programme–Pakistan Institute of Development Economics (UNDP-PIDE), Islamabad, March 17, 2003.

[34] Akmal Hussain, with inputs from A. R. Kemal, Agha Imran Hamid, Imran Ali, and Khawar Mumtaz, *Poverty, Growth and Governance*, UNDP, Pakistan National Human Development Report (Karachi: Oxford Univ. Press, 2003), chapter 5. For a more recent discussion on the subject, focused on the institutional basis of pro-poor growth, see Akmal Hussain, "Institutional Imperatives of Poverty Reduction," Paper contributed to the Institute of Public Policy, Beaconhouse National Univ., Lahore, May 2008.

SOUTH ASIAN REGIONALISM: A SRI LANKAN PERSPECTIVE

Saman Kelegama

How a small island economy sees regionalism in its neighborhood is an interesting topic of discussion from both a geopolitical and an economic development point of view. The issue becomes even more interesting when—as in South Asia—the neighborhood is dominated by a giant that accounts for 80 percent of the region's area, population, and gross domestic product (GDP). This chapter first provides some background to Sri Lanka's current perspective on India and South Asian regionalism. It then examines the Indo–Sri Lanka Bilateral Free Trade Agreement (ILBFTA), followed by the political economy of Sri Lanka's regional trading. The India–Sri Lanka Comprehensive Economic Partnership Agreement (ILCEPA) is then discussed, and finally some conclusions are drawn.

Background

The Sri Lankan perspective on South Asian regionalism is, to a great extent, shaped by country-specific factors such as Sri Lanka's (1) geographical position as an island in the shadow of a large neighbor; (2) status as the first nation in South Asia to liberalize its economy in the late 1970s; and (3) nearly thirty-year-long war with Tamil separatists, which as of 2010, is a painfully recent memory. In this chapter I argue that, influenced by these three factors, Sri Lanka's integration with South Asia depends on its economic integration with India—toward which goal the ILBFTA, signed in 1998, is an important first step.

After being a closed economy subject to import-substitution industrialization for nearly two decades, Sri Lanka liberalized its economy in 1977. The administration that came to office in that same year pursued pro-Western policies and was largely inclined toward the United States, a move that was not to India's liking. By 1981, under Indira Gandhi's leadership, the Indian establishment had become overtly hostile toward Sri Lanka.[1] Consequently, Sri Lanka looked to regionalism, both local and not: it convened the first meeting of the Council of Ministers of South Asia in 1981, the same year of its unsuccessful attempt to join the Association of Southeast Asian Nations (ASEAN).[2]

During its first six years of liberalization, Sri Lanka recorded impressive growth rates. These slowed down, however, after 1983 ethnic riots sparked civil war. As Sri Lanka's leaders faced international criticism of their handling of the problem, they renewed their search for more friends around the world, including in their own neighborhood. When the South Asian Association for Regional

Cooperation (SAARC) was born in 1985, Sri Lanka became an enthusiastic member. The island state realized that, given its small size and insignificant geopolitical status, it was a small player in global affairs and could gain much through the collective approach of SAARC.

The initial focus of SAARC was on confidence-building measures, such as reducing poverty throughout the region. Meanwhile, Sri Lanka's relations with India improved somewhat under Prime Minister Rajiv Gandhi but remained far from satisfactory. Since bilateral issues were left out of the SAARC process, Sri Lanka could do little within SAARC to improve its relations with India.

Indo–Sri Lanka relations reached their nadir in 1987, when India pressured Sri Lanka to sign the Indo–Sri Lanka Political Accord as a first step toward handling Tamil separatism. In exchange for a number of concessions, India agreed to stop assisting the separatists. That same year, the Indian Peace Keeping Force (IPKF) landed in Sri Lanka to neutralize the Liberation Tigers for Tamil Eelam (LTTE), who were fighting for a separate state in Sri Lanka's north and east. The presence of the IPKF only fueled anti-Indian sentiments. In March 1990, under new political leadership, Sri Lanka requested the IPKF to leave and embarked on its second wave of economic liberalization.

In 1991 India liberalized its economy, and later that year, Sri Lanka hosted the Sixth SAARC Summit. The president of Sri Lanka stressed that for SAARC to be meaningful, it should work for the common people. To best accomplish this, he pointed out that it was time for SAARC to embark on hard issues such as economic cooperation. At the summit, formulations for an Independent South Asian Commission on Poverty Alleviation (ISACPA) and a SAARC Preferential Trade Arrangement (SAPTA) were raised for debate.

When the SAPTA came into operation in 1995, it was evident from the start that it was an ineffectual framework for trade liberalization because it was limited to a "positive list" of tradable goods. Together with India and Bangladesh, Sri Lanka had experienced "positive list"–based regional liberalization in the Bangkok Agreement, with little success.[3] Sri Lanka's leaders recommended that, instead, the SAPTA be based on a sensitive (or negative) list of tradable goods, but expressed their willingness to sign on in order to build regional confidence in the measure.

Indo–Sri Lanka Bilateral Free Trade Agreement (ILBFTA)

By the next time the SAARC summit was held in Sri Lanka, in July 1998, the SAPTA had produced few visible results. Meanwhile, ASEAN was doing the preparatory work for an ASEAN Free Trade Agreement (AFTA), China was growing at a rapid pace, and the Asia-Pacific Economic Cooperation (APEC) organization was advocating for open regionalism. The Sri Lankan business community, after two decades of liberalization, was frustrated with the SAPTA and exerted pressure on the government to move forward on a bilateral free trade agreement (FTA) with India. Analysts supported the viability of such an agreement;[4] after all, Sri Lanka was already conducting 90 percent of its intra-SAARC trade with India.

Indo–Sri Lankan relations go back a long way: from the legend of the Ramayana, to the introduction of Buddhism by Emperor Asoka's son, to common colonial rule, to being joint pioneers of the Non-Aligned Movement, to the tension sparked by Tamil separatism and its support in the Indian state of Tamil Nadu.

The relationship between the two countries improved after 1991 for three reasons. First, the assassination of Rajiv Gandhi by an LTTE agent in 1991 changed India's attitude toward the LTTE dramatically. Second, the opening up of the Indian economy in 1991 improved trading with its neighbors, including Sri Lanka. Third, the "Gujral doctrine," which became operative in 1997, did not demand reciprocity from neighbors for Indian economic liberalization initiatives.

These factors revived the dormant proposal for an ILBFTA. After its 1998 nuclear test, India faced sanctions from a number of major markets (such as the United States); at the same time, India was exploring new markets to target its exports. The small size of the Sri Lankan market did not matter to India, and the interests of both countries converged in 1998. Both countries thus decided it was time to band together—at least for purposes of trade—and the ILBFTA was signed in December 1998.

But before it was implemented, local media played host to Sri Lankan fears of the FTA's implications for the existing deficit with India, the takeover of Sri Lankan industries by Indian corporate giants, and "big-brother bullying" in general. The agreement was, however, designed to accommodate the asymmetry of the two countries, with built-in rules favoring Sri Lanka (table 8.1). After much discussion over the sensitive list, rules of origin (ROO), and other agreement-related issues, the FTA came into effect in March 2000.

Table 8.1 ILBFTA: Special and Differential Treatment for Sri Lanka

• Larger sensitive list (Sri Lankan agriculture sector fully protected)
• Relaxed rules of origin: 35 percent (and 25 percent if Indian inputs used)
• Longer tariff phase-out period (eight years for Sri Lanka and three years for India)
• Sensitive list to be reduced based on Sri Lanka's comfort level
• Revenue compensation excluded, but Sri Lanka insisted that high-revenue import items would not be subject to tariff preferences (import duties = 2 percent gross domestic product [GDP] revenue)

Source: S. Kelegama and I. N. Mukherji, "India-Sri Lanka Bilateral Free Trade Agreement: Six Years of Progress and Beyond," RIS Discussion Paper No. 119, 2007, www.ris.org.in/dp119_pap.pdf; see also www.boi.lk.

By the time the South Asian Free Trade Area (SAFTA) became operative by superseding the SAPTA in July 2006, the ILBFTA had been effective for six years and had delivered far more visible results than the SAPTA. As table 8.2 shows, in those six years Sri Lankan exports to India had increased eightfold, overall trade turnover had grown by five times (crossing the $3 billion mark in 2007), and the trade deficit had been reduced—all in favor of Sri Lanka. Eighty-four percent of Sri Lankan exports to the Indian market were under the ILBFTA by 2005. The number of items exported to India had doubled and India had become the third-largest export destination for Sri Lanka after the United States and the European Union (EU). These results were impressive, since nearly 60 percent of Sri Lankan exports (namely, readymade garments, RMGs, and tea) were still subject to tariff rate quotas (TRQs) to protect Indian producers. Trade in services and investments also improved with the flow in trade in goods, but more gradually.[5]

Table 8.2 ILBFTA: Outcomes after Six Years, 1999–2005

• Sri Lankan exports to India: 1 percent in 1999 and 9 percent in 2005
• Sri Lankan imports from India: 8.5 percent in 1999 and 17 percent in 2005
• Import/export ratio for Sri Lanka: 10.5:1.0 in 1999 and 2.6:1.0 in 2005
• No. of products exported from Sri Lanka to India: 505 in 1999 and 1,062 in 2005
• India is third-largest destination of Sri Lankan exports
• Investment followed trade: India fourth-largest investor in Sri Lanka
• > 50 percent of Indian investment in SAARC is in Sri Lanka

Source: Kelegama and Mukherji, "India–Sri Lanka Bilateral Free Trade Agreement."

The Political Economy of Regional Trading

The results of the ILBFTA were far from perfect, but the positives outweighed the negatives.[6] Sri Lanka went on to strengthen its bilateral trade policy in the mid-2000s, as a consequence of the SAPTA's poor performance and the slow progress of negotiations with the World Trade Organization (WTO), especially after the collapse of the WTO Cancun Summit. Bilateral FTAs were explored with several countries, including the United States and Singapore. While several such attempts were fruitless, Sri Lanka did manage to establish a bilateral FTA with Pakistan by mid-2005.

It is important to note that the SAFTA came into operation at a time (mid-2006) when 93 percent of Sri Lankan exports had duty-free access to the Indian market under the ILBFTA. If the SAFTA had provided for trade liberalization to the same degree as the ILBFTA or the Pakistan–Sri Lanka Bilateral FTA (PSLFTA), Sri Lanka may have enthusiastically embraced it; instead, the

SAFTA's liberalization framework was much weaker than the others. A simple comparison of their sensitive lists (table 8.3) and ROOs (table 8.4) reveal this fact. With substantial sensitive lists, the SAFTA virtually prevented 53 percent of the intra-SAARC trade from preferential trading.[7]

Table 8.3 Comparative Sensitive Lists across FTAs in South Asia

	SAFTA	ILBFTA	PSFTA
Bangladesh	1,254[a]		
Bhutan	157		
India	884[b]	419	540
Maldives	671		
Nepal	1,310[c]		
Pakistan	1,183		
Sri Lanka	1,065	1,180	697

Sources: South Asia Free Trade Agreement, SAARC Secretariat (see www.saarc-sec. org); India–Sri Lanka Bilateral Free Trade Agreement (see www.boi.lk); and Pakistan–Sri Lanka Bilateral Free Trade Agreement (see www.boi.lk).
Note: [a] for LDCs 1,249 items; [b] for LDCs 763 items; [c] for LDCs 1,301 items.

Sri Lanka's pursuit of bilateral trade was also due to its weak economic performance, far below potential during the northeast war. The nation could not afford to wait indefinitely for the promise of regionalism to take effect. Sri Lanka, over the years, had seen the slow progress of SAARC and related frameworks such as the SAPTA. A proliferation of SAARC conventions, memorandums of understanding (MOUs), and other frameworks had proven ineffectual. The Group of Eminent Persons (GEP)[8] identified the SAARC institutions as a key area for reform, but no action was taken in this regard.[9] The Sri Lankan president, at the Ninth SAARC Summit in Malé, voiced concerns on the issue.[10]

While institutional reforms remained pending, the SAARC expanded its activities without consolidating existing structures. A prime example of this was accepting Afghanistan as a new member in 2007. While, geographically, Afghanistan's entry may have been meaningful, it increased the number of least-developed countries (LDCs) in the SAARC to five. With the LDCs in the majority, SAARC-related activities were going to be guided by the LDC agenda. In fact, the birth of the SAFTA, after the Fourteenth SAARC Summit in Islamabad, was delayed by more than two-and-a-half years due to a pending revenue compensation formula for the LDCs, among other factors. Article 7.2 of the SAFTA states that if members are willing to move faster in the liberalization of tariffs, they can proceed among themselves, leaving out the unwilling members.

Table 8.4 Comparative Rules of Origin across FTAs in South Asia

	SAFTA	ILBFTA	PSFTA
Single-country ROO			
DVA (% of FOB)			
• India and Pakistan	40	35	35
• Sri Lanka	35	35	35
• LDCs	30		
CTH	4-digit	4-digit	6-digit
Cumulative ROO			
Minimum aggregate content (%)	50	35	35
Input from exporting country (%)	20	25	25
Derogation from general rule (%)	DVA: 25, 30, 40, or 60%	Being negotiated under the CEPA	N/A
	CTH: at 4- or 6-digits		
	Process: PSR		

Sources: South Asia Free Trade Agreement, SAARC Secretariat (see www.saarc-sec. org); India–Sri Lanka Bilateral Free Trade Agreement (see www.boi.lk); and Pakistan–Sri Lanka Bilateral Free Trade Agreement (see www.boi.lk).
Notes: DVA = domestic value addition; CTH = change of tariff headings; ROO = rules of origin; FOB = free on board; PSR = product-specific rules of origin; CEPA = comprehensive economic partnership.

A fundamental objective of regional groupings is the formulation of a common position on international policy—an objective that SAARC has failed to meet. A case in point is the WTO: although a common SAARC position was formulated for the ministerial meetings in Seattle and Doha, it was soon sidetracked as SAARC member countries pursued their own agendas. The divergence of these agendas is understandable given that (1) India is emerging as a global player keen to liberalize services—in particular, the Mode 4 (Movement of Natural Persons); (2) member LDCs are pursuing their own agendas, with Bangladesh taking the lead; and (3) Sri Lanka is pursuing a separate agenda as a small and vulnerable economy (SVE).[11]

After the WTO-Doha Ministerial, it became clear that a common position on WTO ascension was difficult to formulate. SAARC member countries went their separate ways, sometimes joining with groups of common interest, such as the G-20 and G-33. At the WTO Ministerial in Hong Kong, Sri Lanka and Pakistan objected to the fact that LDCs would be given duty- and quota-free preference, thus eroding the competitiveness of their exports of RMGs, much to the annoyance of SAARC LDCs such as Bangladesh, Nepal, and others.

The Research and Information System for Non-Aligned and Other Developing Countries (RIS)[12] documents two occasions on which SAARC developed a common position on international fora, which happened to be on noncontroversial areas. With the Generalized System of Preference (GSP), for instance, Sri Lanka particularly found it difficult to fulfill the SAARC Cumulation ROO for RMG exports and, therefore, argued the case for the SAARC plus ASEAN Super Cumulation ROO. The argument was presented since Sri Lanka did not possess a domestic textile base and sought access to a wider textile market. But India, Pakistan, and Bangladesh opposed this position as they have strong textile industries that could benefit from the SAARC Cumulation ROO.

In fact, the SAARC agenda is overloaded with soft issues that hardly have an impact on the people in the region. Most often, new items put on the SAARC agenda are symbolic and valid only for political purposes. The existing SAARC institutions lack accountability and minimally contribute to the economic cooperation of the region.[13]

It has been observed that the SAARC's second-track activities hardly make a contribution to its official process. In early 2003 a leading second-track think tank—the South Asia Center for Policy Studies (SACEPS)—submitted a comprehensive report on the SAFTA,[14] highlighting lessons that the AFTA might be able to teach South Asian foreign ministries. However, when the SAFTA treaty was signed in 2004 and came into operation in 2006, there were no signs that the key recommendations of the SACEPS report had been considered. It is not surprising that SAARC has not ratified the 1998 GEP report—which articulated a vision and road map for SAARC—and SAARC still lacks the political will to do so.

Furthermore, it has become increasingly difficult to insulate the SAARC's economic agenda from regional politics.[15] The Eleventh SAARC Summit was postponed several times due to the Indo-Pakistan dispute over Kargil in Kashmir. Meanwhile, the SAPTA, with a fourth round of tariff exchanges, was postponed time and again until being finally ratified in late 2004. SAARC lacks political leadership—a key reason why the economic agenda is not moving forward as expected.[16]

It may also be highlighted that the SAFTA does not have a mechanism to supersede the existing bilateral FTAs in the region, such as the ILBFTA, PSLFTA, India-Nepal BFTA, and India-Bhutan BFTA. The SAFTA—like the proposed Free Trade Agreement of America (FTAA)—is facing the challenge of absorbing already-operating FTAs, a challenge that frameworks such as the AFTA never encountered.

Given these and other problems, Sri Lanka has increasingly become a reluctant partner in the regional body of SAARC, even though it was an enthusiastic member at the beginning.

Steps Toward a Comprehensive Indo–Sri Lanka Economic Partnership

When the Sri Lankan prime minister visited India in June 2002, a decision was made to explore the options of converting the ILBFTA into an Indo–Sri Lanka Comprehensive Economic Partnership Agreement (ILCEPA). Both countries appointed members of a joint study group (JSG) to examine the possibility in April 2003. The JSG submitted its report in October 2003 and both countries made a decision to move toward an ILCEPA by March 2004. However, elections in both countries in early 2004, and a subsequent change of government, delayed the process. The new governments needed more time to study the ILCEPA, and in February 2005, technical-level negotiation teams were appointed to formulate the framework for the ILCEPA. The year 2006 was set as the target for the ILCEPA to come into operation, but this was moved back due to the vanaspathi oil crisis under the ILBFTA.[17] Once the problem was solved in 2007, the ILCEPA was to be signed.[18]

Was it only frustration with the SAPTA and SAFTA that led to the making of the ILCEPA? No, since the ILBFTA has had many spillover benefits for the Sri Lankan economy. First, the economy benefited from cheap Indian imports not competing with domestic products—including vehicles, motorcycles, scooters, and machinery. These imports were a great source of strength at times when inflation went out of control due to domestic policy slippage. Second, the positive impact of the ILBFTA on trade in services and investment led to pressure from the private sector for further deregulation and new institutional frameworks to govern the flow of services and investment between the two countries. The idea behind the ILCEPA was to therefore broaden the ILBFTA to facilitate this flow.

With regard to services, Sri Lanka implemented a visa-at-arrival for Indian citizens in January 2002, which led to an increased tourist flow from India to Sri Lanka and more air connections between the two countries.[19] For instance, Sri Lankan Airlines routes flights to eleven destinations in India, while both Jet Airways and Sahara were given landing rights in Colombo in early 2004. In the early 2000s, most Indian foreign direct investment (FDI) flows were in services such as hospitals, restaurants, the retail sector, and oil.

Large Indian investors—such as the Indian Oil Corporation (IOC), CEAT, and Apollo—demanded more investment protection for further expansion. The ILCEPA's intention was to regularize these once they came into operation. Also, the ILCEPA has an economic cooperation window that is favorable to developing Sri Lanka's supply capacity with Indian assistance.[20]

For Sri Lanka, integration with South Asia meant integration with India, and this was manifested in the ILCEPA. Several relevant issues are subject to discussion at present:

- *The problems of Indo–Sri Lanka trade are not insurmountable.* Although the ILBFTA has contributed to enhancing Sri Lanka's exports, it is not without problems. At first it was assumed that the many Indian joint ventures in Sri Lanka with buyback arrangements would contribute to increasing exports from Sri Lanka to India. But more than 60 percent of the exports to India from Sri Lanka are in two products—vanaspathi and copper—both of which are unsustainable, based on tariff-jumping FDI from India. Tariff arbitrage facilitated these investments. Second, there has been the problem of TRQs, imposed by India on Sri Lankan vanaspathi and pepper exports, contrary to the spirit of the FTA. Third, a number of nontariff barriers (NTBs) and state-government-based taxes in India have discouraged Sri Lankan exports. Yet many in Sri Lanka believe that these issues could be rectified and the agreement fortified to ensure more gains and fewer losses.[21]

- *Trade imbalance is not an issue.* Sri Lanka had a $2.2 billion trade deficit with India in 2007, but following the ILBFTA, the ratio of exports to imports has moved in favor of Sri Lanka. Nonetheless, due to its experience in the open economy for three decades, Sri Lanka does not attach much importance to the trade deficit because it believes that with some global trade partners (for example, the United States and the EU there will be a trade surplus and with other global partners (for example, Japan and India), a trade deficit. Global trading and reducing the trade deficit is not a primary goal of Sri Lanka. Moreover, Sri Lanka sees the current deficit being somewhat offset by the surplus manifested in the capital account of Indian FDI to Sri Lanka.

- *Indian FDI is crucial.* It is well known that Japanese FDI and official development assistance (ODA) played a key role in ASEAN's economic integration. Sri Lanka believes that it is only India that can play a similar role in South Asia and that Indian investment can invigorate dormant complementaries in the region. It is here that the economies of scale, agglomeration, and inter-industry trade come into the picture (by way of Krugman's new trade theory). The RIS[22] has argued that efficiency-seeking industrial restructuring will play a key role in stimulating intraregional trade in South Asia; this argument is applicable at the bilateral level, too. For instance, CEAT-India produces tires in Sri Lanka as a joint-venture company and exports these to Indian motor-vehicle companies. Such inter-industry trade between Sri Lanka and India is slow in becoming reality due to the past security situation in Sri Lanka. Hameed[23] has argued that such efficiency-seeking industrial restructuring can take place in the expanding Indian IT sector with a "flying geese" impact on the rest of South Asia.[24] Sri Lanka is in a good position to benefit from this due to the ILCEPA framework.

- *Sri Lanka has little fear of corporate takeover.* Unlike some other South Asian countries, Sri Lanka has no great fears of its local corporations

177

being out-competed or absorbed by Indian entrepreneurs. Such bogeys were raised at the time the plantation sector was privatized in 1992 but proved unfounded.[25] The selling of 33 percent shares of the Ceylon Petroleum Corporation to the Indian Oil Corporation in 2003 also raised alarm, but nothing came of it. In fact, in 2008, the government of Sri Lanka made a decision to allocate land in Eastern Sri Lanka for a special economic zone (SEZ) for Indian investments. This move was made to encourage more investment flows from India.

Sri Lanka was long unsuccessful in attracting substantial FDI as its twenty-five-year northeast war created uncertainty in the investment climate. The country lost significant revenue by offering various tax concessions to FDI in order to offset the uncertainty-induced disincentives. The Sri Lankan government believes that foreign investors who shy away from Sri Lanka might think otherwise if Indian investment flows were strong.

Conclusion

Sri Lanka's vision for integration with South Asia is influenced more by economic than political factors. Sri Lanka does not see itself as a major mover of South Asian integration, given its small size and island geography. The two big powers—India and Pakistan—are seen as the key players. Most Sri Lankans hold the view that until the political differences between these two countries are settled, South Asian economic integration will move slowly.

In any case, with the forces of globalization, natural market integration is taking place. China's trade with India has increased to $30 billion—due not to preferential trading but to natural market integration. This will remain a strong force in South Asia, irrespective of how the SAFTA moves forward. While regional trade can be fast-forwarded by utilizing Article 7.2 of the SAFTA, given the politics of the region, this is unlikely to take place.

As stated, political leadership is lacking in SAARC, but existing bilateral trade relations—such as those of Sri Lanka and India—do have strong political leadership behind them. Sri Lanka will pursue bilateral trade with India, and takes the position that the increasing trade flows between the two countries will contribute to the overall integration of regional trade. Further, Sri Lanka sees India as an entry point for pan-Asian economic cooperation through initiatives such as the ASEAN-India FTA or the JACIK FTA (Japan, ASEAN, China, India, and Korea).

That India's economy will soon grow to be valued at $10 trillion GDP cannot be ruled out. If India's growth continues on its current trajectory, Sri Lanka hopes to exploit the advantages of being India's neighbor via the proposed ILCEPA. There is also the possibility that, as wages increase in Indian industries, multinational corporations will go to neighboring countries where wages are lower. A "flying geese" phenomenon could emerge, with spillover benefits for neighbors who have strong trade and investment connections to India.

Sri Lanka, while an integral part of the South Asian integration process, will not go out of its way to be an active player in the SAFTA. Its leaders realize that there is the political will to move forward with the ILCEPA, but not with the SAFTA. In sum, Sri Lanka no longer sees India as a threat, but as an opportune partner in its growth and development.

Notes

[1] Some Tamil separatist groups received training in southern India, and the Indian government did not take any action to prevent this.

[2] K. M. De Silva, "The European Community and ASEAN: Lessons for SAARC," *South Asian Survey* 6 (2) (1999): 271–82.

[3] Kelegama and others, 2001.

[4] V. R. Panchamukhi, Nagesh Kumas, and V.R. Rao, *Indo-Sri Lanka Economic Cooperation: An Operational Programme* (Helsinki: United Nations University–World Institute for Development Economics Research, UNU-WIDER, 1992); L. Jayawardena, Lakdasa Hulugalle, and Liaqut Ali, *Indo-Sri Lanka Economic Cooperation: Facilitating Trade Expansion through a Reciprocal Preference Scheme* (Helsinki: UNU-WIDER, 1993).

[5] S. Kelegama and I. N. Mukherji, "India-Sri Lanka Bilateral Free Trade Agreement: Six Years of Progress and Beyond," RIS Discussion Paper No. 119, 2007, www.ris.org.in/dp119_pap.pdf.

[6] Kelegama and Mukherji, "India–Sri Lanka Bilateral Free Trade Agreement."

[7] D. Weerakoon and J. Thennakoon, "SAFTA: Myth of Free Trade," *Economic and Political Weekly* XLI (37) (2006).

[8] GEP, *The Report of the SAARC Group of Eminent Persons* (Kathmandu: SAARC Secretariat, 1998).

[9] The SAARC is yet to officially accept the recommendations of the GEP Report. See also Dubey in this volume.

[10] SAARC, "Declaration of the Fourteenth SAARC Summit," 1997, www.saarc-sec.org.

[11] S. Kelegama, *South Asia in the WTO* (New Delhi: Sage, 2007).

12 RIS, *South Asia Development and Cooperation Report 2004* (New Delhi, India: RIS, 2004).

[13] M. Lama, "SAARC Programmes and Activities: Assessment, Monitoring, and Evaluation," in S. Ahmed, S. Kelegama, and E. Ghani, eds., *Economic Cooperation in South Asia: Beyond SAFTA* (New Delhi: Sage Publications, 2010).

[14] SACEPS, *SACEPS Task Force Report on SAFTA* (Dhaka, Bangladesh: SACEPS, 2002), http://www.saceps.org.

[15] D. Weerakoon and J. Wijayasiri, *Regional Economic Cooperation in South Asia: A Sri Lankan Perspective*, International Economic Series, No. 6 (Colombo: Institute of Policy Studies, 2001).

[16] S. Kelegama, "Towards Greater Connectivity in South Asia," *Economic and Political Weekly* XLII (39) (2007): 3911–15.

[17] Kelegama and Mukherji, "India–Sri Lanka Bilateral Free Trade Agreement."

[18] The ILCEPA was to be signed on the eve of the Fifteenth SAARC Summit in Colombo during early August 2008, but due to protest by an anti-Indian lobby group in Sri Lanka, the signing was postponed to 2009.

[19] In 2002 an Indo–Sri Lanka land bridge was also mooted from Thalaimannar to Rameswaran for better connectivity, but it never took off due to the civil war and the Sethusamudaram project proposed by India.

[20] ILCEPA can be viewed at www.ips.lk/publications/series/gov_reports/indo_srilanka_cepa/islcepa.pdf.

[21] Kelegama and Mukherji, "India–Sri Lanka Bilateral Free Trade Agreement."

[22] RIS, *South Asia Development and Cooperation Report 2008* (New Delhi, India: RIS, 2008).

[23] N. Hameed, "South Asia; Development Strategy for the Information Age," in the report of the South Asian Department of Economists Annual Conference, ADB, Manila, August 2006.

[24] See also Dossani, chapter 9, in this volume.

[25] Indian companies—namely, Harrisons Malayalam and Tata—showed an interest at the time of plantation companies' privatization in 1992. But Sri Lankans protested a possible takeover by the Indian corporate giants and, eventually, only Tata purchased the management contract of one company.

BUILDING THE SCAFFOLDING TO SUPPORT INSTITUTIONAL GROWTH

Supply-chain Fragmentation and Regionalism in South Asia

Rafiq Dossani

Regional trade and investment in postcolonial South Asia are at their lowest shares of total trade in the history of the subcontinent and are ranked last among regional trade groupings worldwide (see table 9.1). The leading causes for this are administrative barriers in the form of high tariffs and restrictions on the quantity, traffic, and transport of goods.[1] Other factors that have hampered economic integration in the region include the following:

1. Among the smaller countries, there is a fear that India, South Asia's largest country, would dominate an integrated market in finished goods and services and eventually monopolize the market for primary goods as well.
2. Further, there is a concern that such "economic colonialism" would lead to India's political and cultural domination of the region. Indian policymakers, for their part, are concerned about other deleterious forms of infiltration that integration might facilitate, including illegal immigration, terrorism, and trafficking in illegal goods such as narcotics.
3. In a certain sense, the economies of many South Asian countries are too similar to allow for any substantial complementary trade. For example, what can the textile-dominated economies (sometimes called *cottonomies*) of Bangladesh, Pakistan, and Sri Lanka collectively trade with each other?
4. Given the scale of the smaller countries' markets relative to the larger markets, and the opening of global trade that has followed from the establishment of the World Trade Organization (WTO), there is a strong trend in these countries toward multilateralism rather than regionalism. This is in part because each has proved it can survive in today's specialized markets. For example, as textiles respond to global competition, primarily from China, each of these countries has acquired a reputation for a different product: Bangladesh for knitted products, India for embroidered products, and Pakistan for denim.[2] Within this scenario, it is uncertain whether regional integration would be of any benefit.
5. Finally, given India's growth potential, its integration with China and the Association of Southeast Asian Nations (ASEAN) makes more sense than with the countries of South Asia.[3]

Table 9.1 Regional Groupings Worldwide: Regional versus Total Trade, 2002

Regional association	Regional trade as share of total trade (%)
ASEAN	26
COMESA	22
ECO	6
EU	67
GCC	8
NAFTA	62
SAARC	4

Source: K. Amin, *Promoting Greater Regional Cooperation in South Asia: Opportunities for and Role of the Private Sector in Pakistan* (Washington, D.C.: World Bank, 2004).
Note: ASEAN = Association of Southeast Asian Nations; COMESA = Common Market for Eastern and Southern Africa; ECO = Economic Cooperation Organization, Central Asia focused; EU = European Union; GCC = Gulf Cooperation Council; NAFTA = North American Free Trade Agreement; SAARC = South Asian Association for Regional Cooperation.

While policymakers worry, some private firms have flourished: trade in some areas has jumped when barriers have been even slightly reduced. Trade between India and Sri Lanka, bolstered by a limited free trade deal in 2000, rose from $600 million in 2000 to $2.7 billion in 2007.[4] Trade between India and Pakistan, which had been stagnant at around $250 million up to 2003, increased—due to slow but sure liberalization—to $1.7 billion in the financial year ending March 2007.[5] The few items that have been designated for bilateral trade between India and Pakistan include iron ore, engineered goods, industrial raw materials, dried fruits (some of it undoubtedly trade diverted from smugglers)[6] and, oddly, movies.[7]

This chapter discusses the threat of economic colonialism alongside the promise of what Athukorala[8] calls *fragmentation* or what is more commonly called *modularization*[9] of the supply chain. This implies the conversion of an integrated production process with one or more proprietary inputs, designs, or fulfilment techniques into component processes with standardized ones. Once a production process is modularized, the components become marketable as stand-alone products.

Fragmentation has been the driving force of East Asian manufacturing integration. Would integration in South Asia lead to a scenario of economic colonialism or one of fragmentation? If fragmentation emerged, would India produce the high-value-added components while the smaller countries of South Asia produced the low-value-added ones? While this is not necessarily economic colonialism, India remains the deciding factor in this scenario. Would it be possible to ensure that fragmentation benefits all regional players more or less equally?

To answer these questions, we can look at an industry over which India's domination is likely to continue—the software industry. Trade in software is difficult to regulate. A software developer in India can, almost without cost, create a virtual presence on the Internet and route payments via a third-party aggregator based in the United States. If this industry shows promise of regional fragmentation, it would support an argument for fragmentation of regional trade in South Asia across other goods and services.

Economic Colonialism versus Fragmentation

Economic colonialism theoretically develops in the following way: if two countries are at equal stages of development—roughly true for the economies of South Asia—the larger will produce goods and services more cheaply due to economies of scale, and the smaller country will specialize in those goods and services in which scale economies are less applicable, usually because of institutional arrangements (such as land-ownership arrangements in agricultural production). Eventually, the larger country will be the dominant player in the market.

As table 9.2 shows, regional trade in South Asia—limited as it is—conforms to the economic colonialism model. India is already the main regional trading partner of each of the South Asian countries, importing their primary goods while exporting finished goods to them. Interestingly, as the last row shows, India has the same relationship to China as the smaller South Asian countries have to India.

Table 9.2 Major Items of Regional Trade in South Asia, 2002

Country	Main export	Main import	Main trading partner
Bangladesh	Jute, seafood	PP&M	India
Bhutan	Timber, minerals	PP&M	India
India	PP&M, drugs	Industrial raw materials, edible oils	Pakistan
Nepal	Textiles, oilseeds	Chemicals, drugs	India
Pakistan	Cotton, dried fruit	PP&M	India
Sri Lanka	Tea, rubber, gems	PP&M	India
India's trade with China	Iron ore	Plant and machinery	2007–China

Source: Rows 1–6 based on K. Amin, *Promoting Greater Regional Cooperation in South Asia*. Author's compilation for row 7 based on A. Virmani, "India-China Economic Cooperation," Working Paper no.160, ICRIER, New Delhi, 2005, www.financialexpress.com/news/India-China-to-meet-trade-target-by-2010/288307/.
Note: PP&M = petrochemicals, plant, and machinery.

The East Asian experience has been different from South Asia's. Athukorala[10] defines East Asia as all the Asian countries to the east of South Asia: the developed nations (Japan and the newly industrializing economies [NIEs]—South Korea, Taiwan, Hong Kong, and Singapore) and the developing ones (China and the members of the ASEAN).

Athukorala[11] demonstrates that the result of tight regional integration in East Asia has been the fragmentation of the supply chain among these countries. China—which offers scale—has become the major final assembler of parts, components, and designs imported from the rest of East Asia. The countries of developing East Asia have specialized in middle-end component manufacturing, while high-end components and designs are produced in developed East Asia (see table 9.3, which also shows the stages of fragmentation of the software supply chain, for later reference).

Table 9.3 Stages of Fragmentation of the Supply Chain, East Asia, 2007

Exporter's role	Importer's role	Roles transferred to exporter	Country stage of development	Software services analogue to column 1
Assembly (L)	Design, input sourcing, QC	Production capacity	China	System integration (M)
OEM (M)	Design, QC	Input sourcing, QC	ASEAN	Programming (L)
ODM (H)	Purchase from exporter's catalogue	Product selection, QC	NIEs	Engineering services, R&D (H)
OBM (H)	None	Product innovation	Japan	Consulting (H)

Sources: Column 1–3 based on L. Wortzel and H. Wortzel, "Export Marketing Strategies for NIC and LDC-Based Firms," *Columbia Journal of World Business* 16, no. 1: 51–60; column 4 based on P. Athukorala, "Trade and Investment Patterns in Asia: Regionalization or Globalization," Working Paper, NCAER, 2008; and column 5 based on author's compilation.

Notes: OEM = original equipment manufacture; ODM = original design manufacture; OBM = original brand manufacture; L = low-value-added work; M = medium-value-added work; H = high-value-added work.

As China's share of global trade has grown, so has the share of the other developing countries in East Asia.[12] Overall, their share in global trade increased from 7.9 percent in 1979–1980 to 25.1 percent in 2005–2006; meanwhile, the share of the region's developed countries increased from 6.9 percent to 12.8 percent, and the share of the ASEAN countries increased from 3 percent to 6.3 percent. Even Indonesia, considered to be the weakest of the ASEAN countries, has seen its share increase from 0.5 percent to 0.9 percent.[13]

These figures show that early advantages such as better infrastructure and trading arrangements did not actually help the ASEAN countries (which earlier had been internally integrated, finished-goods manufacturers) to retain these integrated activities. However, they have continued to play a role in component manufacturing, which is a higher-value-added activity than assembly manufacturing.

One possible explanation for this value retention in the ASEAN countries could be that they are well ahead of China in higher education. Table 9.4 supports this hypothesis (data on South Asia are included for later reference). Relatively high levels of tertiary education have made it easier for the ASEAN countries to specialize in component manufacturing, which usually requires higher managerial and factory skills than assembly, even as they lost out to China in large-scale assembly manufacturing.[14] The fact that Indonesia, which falls behind China in higher education, also lost its advantage in both kinds of manufacturing also supports this argument. As for Japan and the NIEs, they had already begun to specialize in design and other business services in advance of China's entry into the world economy. After China's entry, this trend accelerated.

It is not clear whether disparities in education can explain the current pattern of South Asian trade; evidence to support this is weak. The differences between India and the rest of South Asia in education—at both the secondary and tertiary level—are minimal. This suggests that the current pattern of trade could change if barriers were lifted; that is, that Pakistan, Bangladesh, and Sri Lanka could export more finished goods to India if they were given the opportunity to do so.

The case of the Indo–Sri Lanka Bilateral Free Trade Agreement (ILBFTA) shows how liberalization can change trade patterns. The ILBFTA was signed in 2000, and to offset fears of economic colonialism, the agreement was designed to give preferential treatment to Sri Lanka. While Sri Lanka has exported more raw materials and commodities and fewer finished products (such as readymade garments, RMGs) than it had expected under the agreement, the primary benefit for Sri Lanka is in services rather than in the trade of tangible goods. By 2005 India had risen from being the fourteenth- to the sixth-largest investor in Sri Lanka.[15] Increased investment in services followed in the health-care and airline industries, and India has become the largest source of tourist traffic to Sri Lanka. India's successful experience with regulation has also triggered regulatory reform in Sri Lanka.[16] These were complementarities unforeseen at the time of the ILBFTA; Kelegama refers to them as "dormant complementarities."[17] They were perhaps triggered by the physical proximity between India and Sri Lanka, which has enabled investment in cross-border infrastructure.

Table 9.4 Primary Regional Exports versus Gross Enrollment Ratios in Secondary and Tertiary Education (%)

Region/Country	Tertiary 1997	Tertiary 2005	Primary regional export	Secondary 2002
East Asia				
China	6	19	Finished goods	70
Indonesia	11	17	Primary goods	61
Japan	41	52	High-end components, design, brands	100
Malaysia	12	29	Components	70
Philippines	29	28	Components	84
Singapore	39	46	High-end components, design	73
Thailand	22	40	Components	81
Vietnam	N/A	11	Primary goods	72
South Asia				
India	7	11 (2007: 13)	PP&M	53
Pakistan	3	4 (2007: 6)	Primary goods	23
Bangladesh	2	6 (2007: 7)	Primary goods	47
Sri Lanka	N/A	5 (2007: 5.5)	Primary goods	86

Sources: K. Guruz, "Higher Education in the Global Knowledge Economy," Working Paper, SUNY Binghamton, 2003; http://ddp-ext.worldbank.org/ext; http://www.ilo.org/public/english/region/asro/bangkok/skills-ap/skills; and news reports.
Note: Indonesia data in column 4 excludes oil exports; PP&M = petrochemicals, plant, and machinery.

Even in textiles—where access to cheap raw cotton in India and Pakistan gives the region an advantage and in which, as noted earlier, countries have successfully specialized—South Asia occupies the bottom of the value chain. The reason for this is that increased trade has not generated sufficient surplus to enable textile manufacturers to invest adequately in larger-scale operations, design, and marketing. Opening up the flow of trade among these countries and investing in specialization, design, and marketing will surely improve competitiveness through the "dormant complementarities" noted in the ILBFTA.

These complementarities will also emerge due to the proximity of these countries, low transport costs, and similarities in business practices.

The rest of this chapter examines the software-exporting sector in South Asia and focuses primarily on Bangladesh, India, Pakistan, and Sri Lanka. This case study shows why regional linkages may still matter in a sector where, theoretically, proximity provides no logistical advantage. The cost of sending a byte of information from Bangalore to anywhere in the world is nearly zero. (Of course, the cost of receiving that byte may vary according to bandwidth costs, which tend to be higher in some parts of South Asia—most notably in Bangladesh and Sri Lanka—owing to monopolistic telecommunications industries.) Also, as was previously noted, a software developer can easily and inexpensively create a virtual shop front via aggregators in the United States and other countries, thereby circumventing trade barriers.

The Software Services Industry in South Asia

As table 9.5 shows, the software-exporting industry—in which India was a global pioneer—has been a success story in many countries of South Asia, not just India.[18]

Table 9.5 Software Exports and Employment, 2007

Country	Exports ($ million)	Workforce	Revenue/employee
Bangladesh	27	1,200	22,500
India	29,300	865,000	33,900
Pakistan	1,000	40,000	25,000
Sri Lanka	50	3,000	17,000
Vietnam	300	15,000	20,000

Sources: Bangladesh data—*The Software and IT Service Industry in Bangladesh* (Dhaka: Bangladesh, 2006); India data—NASSCOM (National Association of Software and Services Companies), *Strategic Review* (New Delhi: NASSCOM, 2008), 50, 51; Pakistan data—www.pseb.org.pk/item/industry_overview, http://pashanews.org/wp-content/uploads/2008/05/psha_study_executive_summary.pdf, and www.pasha.org.pk/show_page.htm?input=page_131220070524; Sri Lanka data—www.softwaresrilanka.com/itinsrilanka/itinsrilanka.htm; Vietnam data—www.business-in-asia.com/software_industry_in_vietnam.htm.
Note: All data for financial year (FY) 2007–2008, except Bangladesh, which is for FY 2006–2007; Bangladesh and Sri Lanka data include IT-enabled services, such as business process outsourcing (BPO); India and Pakistan data exclude IT-enabled services.

The experiences of India, Pakistan, Bangladesh, and Sri Lanka are remarkably similar in the early stages, even though they started at different times (the Indian software industry began in 1974, a decade before the others). In all cases, the software industry came into being through the actions of a few entrepreneurial engineers, who returned to their home countries after an American education. Foreign capital and management and the diaspora in developed countries—important players in the development of the software industry in many other countries, such as Ireland and Israel—played an insignificant role. In the 1990s, reforms and fiscal and infrastructural support from the state bolstered the industry in all four countries.

As table 9.6 shows, by the late 1990s (over two decades after India's software industry began), the industry in all four countries had converged toward relatively low-value-added work, sending programmers overseas to clients' sites to work on software projects won by South Asian information technology (IT) firms. Subsequently, they diverged, largely due to different public policies on education, venture capital, and telecommunications; changes in technology; and changes in the global political environment. In India, domestic firms continue to lead the industry, but multinationals and returnees now play a key role in value-addition. In Pakistan, the diaspora and returnees have been critical to the industry's success. In Sri Lanka and Bangladesh, the role of returnees has increased, but is not yet a leading force.

The first four columns of table 9.6 summarize the main changes in the software services industry in the United States. The latter three columns list developments in the Indian and other South Asian (Bangladeshi, Pakistani, and Sri Lankan) software industries.

In its first decade, Indian independent software vendors (ISVs) focused on software maintenance, particularly of operating systems; other ISVs offered electronic data processing (EDP) services. In the 1970s, as work in the United States shifted to custom applications development (CAD), Indian programmers were imported to continue with system maintenance. In the 1980s, as technological change enabled CAD to shift overseas, the leading American ISVs shifted to systems integration (SI). Thus, India seemed to increasingly lag behind the United States in these areas. CAD was not to shift to India until 2001, nearly three decades after it started in the United States, and SI, not until 2004 (two decades after). However, in recent years, the shift to higher-end work has been rapid: managed services (MSs) started moving to India just five years after their introduction in the United States. Interestingly, the field of contract research and development (R&D) and engineering services (ESs) had always been the domain of small firms in the United States and never a major focus of American ISVs. It was only after in-house ESs were offshored to India by multinationals that firms (such as Wipro) began applying the same metrics-driven approach that had succeeded in CAD to contract R&D and ESs—in effect, India *invented* large-scale contract R&D and ESs.

Table 9.6 The U.S. Software Industry and the Evolution of South Asian Software Exports

	Market change	Technological change	U.S. ISV new work type	Indian ISV new work type	Indian primary ISV work type	Other SA primary ISV work type
1960–1970		Minicomputer	S/w maintenance, EDP	EDP	EDP	EDP, TNC s/w maintenance
1971–1980	IBM s/w and h/w separated		CAD	Programmers exported	Programmer export	Same as above
1981–1990	Complexity of IT systems	U-W standard	S/w SI	M, CAD	Same as above	Programmers exported
1991–2004		Internet, DBMS, PC-networks	Consultancy, MS	1998: MS, contract R&D/ES	Until 2001: Same 2001–2004: CAD 2005–2007: CAD, SI, MS, contract R&D/ES	Until 2001: Same 2001–2007: M, CAD (SL), M, CAD, MS (BD), CAD, MS, SI (P)

Sources: Author's compilation, based on D. Mowery, ed., *The International Computer Software Industry: A Comparative Study of Evolution and Structure* (Oxford: Oxford Univ. Press, 1996); www.siia.net/software/resources.asp#stats for columns 1 to 4; and author's interviews and analysis for columns 5–6.

Notes: Acronyms: CAD = custom applications development; DBMS = database management software; EDP = electronic data processing; ESs = engineering services; h/w = hardware; ISV = independent software vendor; M= website and system maintenance; MSs = managed services; R&D = research and development; s/w = software; SI = system integration; TNC = transnational corporation; U-W=Unix-Workstation; BD = Bangladesh; P = Pakistan; SL = Sri Lanka.

The other South Asian countries initially lagged behind India. The export of programmers from Bangladesh, Pakistan, and Sri Lanka to the United States began in the 1980s, a decade after India entered the industry. However, since such work continued to be the Indian industry's focus until 2001, all four countries were doing similar work as of 2001, and Y2K work prior to 2000.

Around 2001, all four countries began the shift to CAD. CAD is still the primary work type for Bangladesh, Pakistan, and Sri Lanka. Bangladesh, due to better bandwidth and multilateral agency support, also provides some MSs. Pakistan, driven by the improving quality of its engineering workforce, provides SI and MSs while Sri Lanka has remained focused on CAD and also does systems maintenance work.

As of 2010, India leads the way—it already accounts for 60 percent of non-U.S. software exports and 50 percent of global software outsourcing. India looks likely to grow in terms of scale, scope, innovation, and market share, and is central to large IT outsourcing projects anywhere in the world.

India's experience, particularly over the past decade, offers important lessons on how to move up the value chain. These lessons have been absorbed by India's neighbors (some more than others)—most notably Pakistan, which has progressed despite a very challenging external environment. Bangladesh's software sector, on the other hand, has struggled despite Indian aid and close business connections with India. For instance, Bangladeshi banks commonly implement Indian banking software; local firms support its maintenance thereafter. Still, Bangladesh lags behind its neighbor due to a weak regulatory environment in telecommunications and higher education. Likewise, Sri Lanka, despite its status as the most literate country in South Asia and its business connections with India, struggles due to a shortage of engineers. This shortage is due to resource constraints in the state-owned colleges and political resistance against the private provision of higher education.

In the software industry, which requires a highly skilled workforce, tertiary education is critical. As table 9.4 shows, enrollment rates at the tertiary education level in South Asia are generally low compared with the rest of Asia; the gap between the countries is usually not large enough for a fragmentation scenario to emerge, as in East Asia. However, if one considers the output of engineers, a significant gap is evident.

Linkages among India, Bangladesh, Sri Lanka, and Pakistan are, at present, limited. For example, Bangladesh uses Indian product software, and the business process outsourcing (BPO) operations of some Sri Lankan multinational firms are managed out of their Indian offices. Some venture capital managed by the Bangalore subsidiaries of U.S. firms has been invested in Pakistan. In other words, the overall scale of the associations among these countries is small, even as they demonstrate India's central role.

Table 9.7 Global Software Services Spending, 2007, and India's Share

	Global software services spending ($ bn)	India's global market share (%, 2003)	India's global market share (%, 2007)
Consulting	59.6	< 0.1	1.4
Applications development	25.2	16.4	39.3
System integration: Hardware and software deployment and support	119.3	< 0.1	1.3
System integration: Applications, tools, and operating system	84.9	< 0.1	0.8
IT education and training	23.3	0	1.3
Managed services	182.7	1.6	5.1
Contract R&D and engineering services	802	< 0.1	0.8
Total	1,297		

Source: Author's compilation from *The IT Industry in India, Strategic Review* (New Delhi: NASSCOM), 2008.

Table 9.8 Software Workforce Supply in South Asia, 2008

Country	Annual no. of graduates in IT-related fields*	Annual growth rate (%)	Share of private provision	Starting wage in IT services per year ($)
Bangladesh	5,500	20	25	3,500
India	350,000	25	80	7,500
Pakistan	20,000	30	30	7,500
Sri Lanka	3,500	16	0	2,000

Sources: Author's interviews for column 5 + India, NUEPA (National University of Education Planning and Administration), *Higher Education in India*, (New Delhi: NUEPA, 2007); Pakistan, www.hec.gov.pk/QualityAssurance/Statistics/Enrollment%20in%20 Higher%20Education%20Institutions.htm; Sri Lanka, www.icta.lk/DefaultEnglish.asp; Bangladesh: http://www.basis.org.bd/.
Note: * = computer science, computer engineering, electrical engineering, electronics engineering, communications, and IT.

Nevertheless, geographical proximity can be a powerful factor here. It makes sense for the supply chain to be clustered among the countries of South Asia due to similarities in business practices, languages, talent, and scale. If linkages develop, we see India as the supplier of higher-end services to the rest of South Asia. The services it will export would include software products for domestic markets, systems integration, venture finance, and software-aided design. Bangladesh would provide programming services and would therefore look more like China in the value chain, while India would look more like Taiwan. Sri Lanka's case is different; unlike Bangladesh and Pakistan, it lacks the population to achieve scale. If it does not reform its higher educational sector, it will be a limited participant in a linked South Asia; if it does, it may be able to join India in providing higher-end services. Pakistan's role in the cluster is the most difficult to predict. Its labor costs, rapid evolution of higher education, and telecommunications infrastructure make it look like India, although it is significantly below India in the value chain. This may be due to the absence of high-end projects since many multinationals consider Pakistan a high-risk environment for investment (as was the case with India after the nuclear tests of 1998). If cross-border linkages with Pakistan are established, Indian companies will probably be keen to hire the best-educated Pakistani engineers to do high-end work. These engineers would be equal in quality to the top Indian engineers, who are unavailable to work for Indian firms as they either migrate or join the Indian operations of multinational corporations, such as Google.

Table 9.9 Software Labor Distribution across Work Types, 2008, and the Likely Revenue Effects of Regional Integration

Software services value chain	U.S. wage rate ($/hour)	BD	I	P	SL
Software and Web site maintenance	12	40↑	5↓	5↓	50↑
Programming	20	50↑	25↓	50↑	40↑
Software systems integration	40	5↓	20↑	20↑	5↓
Managed services	80	5	20	15	1
R&D and engineering services	100	0↑	25	5↑	3↑
Consulting, product development, and venture finance	200	0	5↑	5↑	1

Source: Author's interviews.
Notes: BD = Bangladesh; I = India; P = Pakistan; SL= Sri Lanka; R&D = research and development.

The likely effect of the software industry's regional integration would be an increase in the share of programming work in Bangladesh, Pakistan, and Sri Lanka, while some higher-end work would decline in Bangladesh and Sri Lanka. This is because some high-end work, such as SI in Sri Lanka, is still integrated with low-end work for reasons of practicality and geographical proximity. Pakistan, because of its higher supply of engineers, would see absolute revenue increase across most categories. Regional integration would lead to a fragmentation of the supply chain, causing much of the high-end work to go to India. India would further profit by gaining low-end production capacity and shifting its engineers to higher-end work. Currently, Indian firms accept low-end work because it is still highly profitable, but with regional integration, they would shift such work to subsidiaries in the rest of South Asia.

The above analysis shows that India's role in South Asia promises to be different from China's in East Asia, primarily because of the superior tertiary educational infrastructure in India. Instead of being (like China) a large-scale manufacturer and assembler of components that are designed and manufactured in the rest of the region, India's role is likely to resemble that of the East Asian NIEs: it will occupy a position higher in the value chain, taking on software systems design or providing venture capital, while the other South Asian countries will offer programming and other lower-end work.

Conclusion

The objective of this chapter was to explore how an industry could be "shared" under regional integration. Using the software industry as a case study, we examined the likely supply chain in an integrated model. The software industry was chosen because it is already an important industry for India and Pakistan, and its global supply chain is already fragmented. We found that, unlike the current pattern of trade (for example, in petrochemicals and primary goods), fragmentation is a more likely outcome than economic colonialism.

In industries other than software, the disparity in educational standards at both secondary and tertiary levels among the South Asian countries is negligible. As a consequence, greater regional integration will lead to specialization at similar stages of the value chain, implying greater retention of value in the smaller South Asian countries.

Notes

[1] This is in addition to the normally high barriers to trade, traffic, and transport that characterize the economies of South Asia.

[2] H. Mashookullah, "Explaining Bangladesh's Textile Industry," Working Paper No. 8, Dubai Economic Forum, 2008.

[3] Saman Kelegama, "The Bilateral Track: The Case of the India–Sri Lanka Free Trade Agreement," *South Asian Survey* 13, no. 2 (2006): 295–301; R. Chadha and

G. Nataraj, "Trade in Services and Investment Flows in South Asia," Working Paper, National Council for Applied Economic Research (NCAER), 2008.

[4] Kelegama, "The Bilateral Track," www.colombopage.com/archive_07/December31142357JR.html.

[5] K. Amin, *Promoting Greater Regional Cooperation in South Asia: Opportunities for and Role of the Private Sector in Pakistan* (Washington, D.C.: World Bank, 2004); www.iht.com/articles/ap/2007/08/01/business/AS-FIN-India-Pakistan-Trade.php.

[6] The scale of unofficial trade across national borders in South Asia is estimated to be two to four times that of official trade. Pharmaceuticals are a typical smuggled item. India's disregard for patents, before signing on to the WTO rules in 2005, led to a flourishing generics drugs industry. (Flouting the rules appears to pay: India's leading generics firm, Ranbaxy, is being acquired by Japan's Daiichi Sankyo for up to $4.6 billion in a deal announced in June 2008.) As a result of India's lax interpretation of patent law, pharmaceuticals in India cost less than comparable pharmaceuticals in Bangladesh or Pakistan. As a result, Indian drugs regularly cross the border illegally.

It is fairly easy to cross the India-Pakistan border. In the mid-1980s, when the author of this paper worked for a nongovernmental organization (NGO) in India, he dealt regularly with the village head (*sarpanch*) of a northern Gujarat village. On one visit, the sarpanch casually announced that he had returned from Karachi the previous evening. It was revealed that the sarpanch was a smuggler and that he smuggled goat's meat (mutton) into Karachi from Gujarat several times a month. To get to Karachi, he simply rode a camel across the border overnight and traded his wares (often for cooking oil, which was heavily taxed in India in those days).

[7] The first movie ever allowed to cross the India-Pakistan border (officially) did so in 2007 when the 1960s Indian classic, *Mughal-e-Azam*, was released in Pakistani theaters, followed by the new Pakistani film, *Khuda Ke Liye*, which was released in 2008 to rave reviews in India. *Khuda Ke Liye* helped to dispel a long-held myth that Bollywood culture would swamp Lollywood (the Pakistani film industry, based in Lahore) if free trade were allowed, since Bollywood had long failed to shake off Kollywood (the Tamil film industry), the multiple Tollywoods (the West Bengal and Telugu film industries), and Mollywood (the Malayalam film industry).

[8] P. Athukorala, "Product Fragmentation and Trade Patterns in East Asia," *Asian Economic Papers* 4, no. 3 (2007): 1–207.

[9] C. Baldwin and K. Clark, "Managing in an Age of Modularity," *Harvard Business Review* (September–October 1997): 84–93.

[10] Athukorala, "Trade and Investment Patterns in Asia."

[11] Ibid.

[12] Ibid., 11.

[13] The electronics industry has played a significant role in this process. See M. Goh, "Issues Facing Asian SMEs and Their Supply Chains," Working Paper, National University of Singapore, 2001. Goh points out that the larger the scale and scope of the electronics industry in Southeast Asia, the greater the economies of scale and the more the opportunities for specialization in all the participating countries. In other words, without China, the countries of the ASEAN would have had less opportunity to specialize. Specialization has, in turn, made them highly competitive globally.

[14] The connection between secondary education and manufacturing in ASEAN is weaker, as seen in the final column of the table.

[15] Already, the largest investor in the Sri Lankan and Bangladesh textile sectors is not India or Pakistan, but East Asia, which accounts for 40 percent of investment in both countries. See M. Tewari, "Deepening Interregional Trade and Investment in South Asia: The Case of the Textiles and Clothing Industry," Working Paper No. 213, Indian Council for Research on International Economic Relations, 2008, 58; Kelegama, "The Bilateral Track."

[16] Kelegama, "The Bilateral Track," 6.

[17] Kelegama, "The Bilateral Track."

[18] Software offshoring, as an industry, began when American IT firms began to outsource software development to India (and to Ireland and Israel) in the 1970s, about a decade after offshoring IT hardware manufacturing. See S. Siwek and H. Furchtgott-Roth, *International Trade in Computer Software* (Westport, CT: Quorum Books, 1993), 93–94. These authors attribute this delay to the fact that software development, unlike manufacturing, is more closely linked to customer requirements and requires close coordination within a firm. The widespread knowledge of English and the relatively low cost of technical labor made the "three *Is*" very attractive as offshore sources. (Their small domestic markets and the lack of domain knowledge—less so for Israel—were the main disadvantages of using these countries.) Starting in the 1980s, many other countries began to export software, including Bangladesh, Pakistan, Sri Lanka, and the Philippines. By the 1990s, even more countries had joined the field, including China, the Czech Republic, Bulgaria, Hungary, Poland, Romania, Brazil, Mexico, Russia, and Vietnam.

DEMOCRATIZATION AS SCAFFOLDING FOR REGIONAL INTEGRATION

Ainslie T. Embree

This chapter discusses the forces underlying regional integration in South Asia and argues that democratization, which characterizes the political direction being taken by all the South Asian nations, is vital to this process. Political reasoning dictates that democratization—and the resulting improvements in trade, security, and cultural relations among nations—be a driving force for regional integration. At the same time, South Asia's recent history has been marked by internal militant uprisings, conflicting territorial claims, trade disputes, and wars, all of which have been embedded in nationalist movements and have worked against interstate collaboration. The word *scaffolding* in the chapter's title reflects the fact that, while there is evidence of democratic trends throughout South Asia, the commitment of political leaders and citizen majorities to the national unity and the use of natural resources necessary for a democratic polity is far from certain (except perhaps in India). The preliminary establishment of democratic procedures can, however, be the scaffold that will make regional integration possible.

This is not to say that regional integration cannot take place among authoritarian states, but it is difficult to imagine integration between such states and those committed to democratization. The integration of sovereign states, short of absorption or conquest, assumes mutual recognition of national interests, cultural differences, and bilateral relations with nations outside the area of integration. A scaffolding of democratic practices, institutions, and procedures—in particular in the legal and judicial arenas—promises to foster viable relations across national frontiers.

Does South Asia Exist?

The creation of such relations presupposes an affirmative answer to the question posed by the organizers of a June 2008 conference held at Stanford University: Does South Asia exist? The term *South Asia*—a recent addition to both geographic and political lexicons—was apparently introduced by the U.S. State Department as a convenient designation for a geographic region that had long been designated as "India" or "the Indian subcontinent." South Asia claimed a self-identity when seven countries of the region—Bangladesh, Bhutan, India, Nepal, Pakistan, Sri Lanka, and the Republic of Maldives (an island outlier)—united in 1985 to form the South Asian Association for Regional Cooperation (SAARC) in an effort to further regional integration; Afghanistan became a member in 2007. SAARC's origin and its history will be discussed later.

Several important cultural and historical factors provide a basis for regionalism in South Asia. Geographically, it forms a natural region, which for centuries has been host to trade, cultural exchange, and shifting political powers. Although all of South Asia has never been unified under one single political authority, it has borne witness to other important interregional connections. Throughout its recorded history, many major religions that originated in what is now India—including Buddhism, Hinduism, Jainism, and, in more recent years, Sikhism—have spread throughout the region. The influence of Indian art and architecture is also evident throughout the whole of Asia, most notably in the powerful grandeur of Angkor Wat and Borobodur, and in hundreds of smaller sites. The region also influenced cultures farther afield, via land and sea-trading routes that connect it with China, Central Asia, Southeast Asia, and the Mediterranean. Islamic culture and political power has also had an important influence since the first conquests by Muslim forces from Iraq early in the eighth century in what is now Pakistan, and then in the twelfth century when Turkic peoples from Central Asia entered the Indian heartland. These conquests culminated in the establishment of the powerful Mughal Empire dynasty early in the sixteenth century, which eventually controlled much of the Indian subcontinent. Of great significance for contemporary South Asia political and economic integration is that the subcontinent now has the largest Muslim population of any region in the world.

In emphasizing the importance of cultural factors for South Asian regional integration, one must be aware that Indian nationalists have at times claimed cultural and sometimes political hegemony over the whole of South Asia, a move resented by their neighbors. Prime Minister Jawaharlal Nehru came close to equating the identity of India with South Asia when he wrote to Chou En-Lai (during the dispute over the India-China border) that India's borders were where they have been for thousands of years, as defined by geography, custom, and tradition: from the encircling mountains that stretch from the northeast to the northwest and south to the ocean.[1] This includes territories to which China has laid historic claims, such as Tibet and adjacent lands, as well as areas that have asserted their political independence from either India or China, such as Nepal and Bhutan.

Nehru's nationalism recalled the glory of ancient Indian religion, art, and literature, but it was anchored firmly in two more recent legacies, those of the Mughal and British empires. When the British Indian empire was partitioned into India and Pakistan in 1947, the two new nations and surrounding territories were not just the residual legatees of two hundred years of British imperialism, but of at least six hundred years of rule by Turkic peoples from Central Asia, who brought with them their own Islamic culture and strong Persian influence. The movement for South Asian regional integration has thus echoed in many ways the attempts at unification of both the Mughal and the British empires, with varying degrees of success. Pakistan and Bangladesh are obvious inheritors of the Islamic legacy, reflecting the ideological allegiance made by the All-India Muslim League. In its Constitution, however, India declares itself to be a secular, democratic, socialist state to show that it did not favor any particular religion. Pakistan, in its Constituent Assembly, declared that it would establish "the principles of democracy, freedom, equality, tolerance, and social justice," but added a significant clause that these principles shall be fully observed, "as enunciated by Islam."[2] On the surface, there is no obvious reason why Pakistan could not have become a democracy in the fashion of India, but fierce arguments developed over how Islam was to be fully observed, weakening civil society and leading to a succession of military dictatorships in Pakistan.

The succession of East Pakistan, supported by India, from Pakistan led to a bitter civil war that has left searing memories that make regional integration problematic. But South Asia does exist—as a region of eight nations related by history, geography, and economic needs, with the strategic realities of their relations with one another, now dominated by the United States and China. In this complex situation the process of democratization, which has gone on along in a fitful fashion with state building and nation formation in different areas of the region for over a century, has to be traced. That process works both to hinder and to further regional cooperation.

"The building of the state comes first."

To say that the British Empire in India provided a coherent and organized framework in which democratization was later able to gain a foothold does not in any way imply that this was its intent. As Karl Marx pointed out, British rule "broke the cake of custom," allowing social change to take place. Even as Britain was "actuated only by the vilest of interests . . . she was the unconscious tool of history" in bringing about what Marx thought was the first social revolution in Asian history.[3] Though there was not as much social change as Marx assumed, there was the beginning of a powerful modern state, albeit not a politically independent one. The historical process at play illustrates the dictum of Carl Friedrich, the American political philosopher, who said that the "the building of the state comes first, and it is within the political framework of the state that the nation comes into being."[4] The imperial construct of the British Raj, with its political stability and modern structure of law, permitted the beginning, however unintended, of the process of democratization and, ultimately, of regional integration.

I will now trace, more or less chronologically, the processes of democratization, first in British India, then in the modern nation-state of India (where it has been most successful), and then, more briefly, in the other countries of South Asia. In Pakistan, Bangladesh, and Nepal, circumstances forced the political leaders to attempt state building, nation building, and democratization simultaneously, with little success. In all the South Asian countries, however, the process of democratization has certain commonalities that are the product of interactions between historical factors and present circumstances. It is necessary to be aware of these interactions to understand the process of democratization and to make progress toward regional integration in South Asia. As a result, this chapter is heavily weighted with historical references to the origins, successes, and failures of democratization and regional cooperation.

Self-Determination within National Movements

Struggles for independence took place against British imperialism as well as against the indigenous autocracies of Nepal, Bhutan, and Afghanistan. These movements for unity and independence were often complicated by the demands of ethnic, religious, and linguistic groups who wished to claim self-determination. Such groups were obstacles to the processes of both democratization and integration, which require that nations be united internally.

One such struggle by a group for some form of self-determination within a state took place in India, when the Indian National Congress claimed to speak for all India in a demand for independence and the creation of a democratic nation-state to succeed the existing British-controlled authoritarian government. This claim was vigorously opposed by the All-India Muslim League, which demanded recognition of a state based on the rights of groups, especially ones defined in terms of religious adherence, rather than a simple numerical majority of individuals electing legislative bodies and making laws without reference.

Democratization: Procedures

The process of democratization entails a movement away from authoritarian rule toward institutional arrangements that provide for legislative bodies to be elected by all adult citizens through free and fair elections. A realistic definition should also recognize that a functioning democracy must include procedures for constituting such governments: there must be (in the simplest terms) accepted rules for conducting elections, and, behind the procedures, a sense that the winners of elections will be guided by a desire to create a polity that will benefit the people. To put it another way, democracy in South Asia should make a promise of justice and stability and also ensure respect for individual rights, through legal processes accepted by the contending parties. In summarizing these characteristics of democratization, the contrasting experiences of India and Pakistan since 1947 come to mind.

Civil Society: Incubator of Democratization and Regional Integration

Civil society, like democracy and religion, is a term we all use, but one that can be interpreted in different ways. For our purposes, civil society is an autonomous arena in which various institutions exist free from state control, sometimes cooperating with the state but often in opposition to it. Both civil society and the state must recognize the legitimacy of the other, however, for the two to function effectively, and this must include the protection of the institutions of civil society by the state. A civil society—with its hallmark features of a free press, an independent judiciary, and the law-protected freedoms of political parties to organize and of individuals to speak out—becomes the ground in which democratization can take root. A state-supported system of both elementary and higher education is also a feature of such a society. Civil society of this kind existed to a considerable extent in India under British rule but, as in all authoritarian systems, it was prevented from challenging the governing authority's control in any way.

India: Democratization under Foreign Imperialism

The period that we will examine in India's democratization process runs from 1858—the year in which Britain defeated the last serious military uprisings against its rule—to the present day. Upon victory, the British Parliament immediately ended the East India Company's long involvement as ruler of the large territories it had influenced since 1765 by force and fraud. "India shall be governed," it was decreed, "by and in the name of Her Majesty." Democracy was not, of course, promised to India, but a proclamation was made in the Queen's name that has been called by Indian nationalist historians "the magna carta" of Indian civil society—a covenant between the British rulers and the people of India.[5] The Queen had instructed her ministers to prepare a document, "bearing in mind that it is a female Sovereign" who speaks to them "after a bloody civil war, giving them pledges which her future reign was to redeem." In the proclamation, the Queen declared it to "be our royal will and pleasure that none be in any wise favoured, none molested or disquieted, by reason of their religious faith or observances, but that all shall enjoy the equal protection of the law"; and (what was perhaps of equal interest to her educated, ambitious Indian subjects) it was also the royal will that her subjects "of whatever race or creed, be fully and impartially admitted to offices in our services, the duties of which they may be qualified, by their education, ability, and integrity, duly to discharge."[6]

It is not fanciful to date this as the beginning of democratization in India. In fact, in 1859, a group of citizens appealed—over the head of the viceroy and his council—to the House of Commons on the grounds that, within the government of India, "there is no representation of the voice of the people, their views, their wishes, or their wants"; they were especially critical of judges who were untrained and inefficient.[7] Surely this speaks of a self-conscious civil society, moving toward democratic procedures.

By the 1870s, the press (in English and in all the major Indian languages) was becoming a vehicle of opposition to British rule, leading British officials to argue for censorship of the press and Indians to call for freedom of the press, marking an important stage in the democratization process. In 1878 the Vernacular

Press Act was passed, giving local authorities wide powers to control the press. The censorship law, which applied only to Indian-language papers, infuriated educated Indians. It was seen as a racist measure, at a time when Indians were becoming increasingly sensitive to racial slurs, especially as their demands to participate on more levels of the imperial power structure were met by British declarations that Indians were inherently incapable of managing India.

While Indian judges made up the majority of magistrates, they were not allowed to have jurisdiction in cases involving Europeans, which further offended the Indian population. Indians also saw blatant racism in the reaction of the small European business class to what was known as the Ilbert Bill, which proposed to do away with this restricted jurisdiction, calling it "invidious and unnecessary." The English, both in Great Britain and India, protested furiously against the possibility that English men, and especially English women, might be tried by anyone but their peers. As protest memorials from English groups declared, it could not be contended that "the Natives of India . . . are the peers or equals of Englishmen."[8] The incident has an important place in the story of democratization, for Lord Ripon, the governor-general, was eventually forced to withdraw the Ilbert Bill, showing Indians how racism prevented even small increments of change.

The growing democratic concerns of educated, professional Indians— lawyers, medical doctors, journalists, college teachers, business men, and all those engaged in new forms of trading that had developed under the British— became clear with the founding of the Indian National Congress in 1885. This was not the first organization of its kind to seek a measure of Indian participation in the administration, but it proved to be the most influential in winning India's independence from Britain.

The demands of the Indian National Congress were far from revolutionary: essentially, it wanted Indians to be given a larger voice in the existing structures of British administration in India, especially in the Indian Civil Service and the officer corps in the army. Indians were deliberately excluded from these areas, even though they occupied the bulk of lesser government positions and the other ranks in the army were overwhelming Indian. The issue was power, as Lord Dufferin, the governor-general, expressed neatly in 1888: "We should be falling into great error if . . . we were to relax in the slightest degree our grasp of the Supreme administration."[9]

The founding of the All-India Muslim League in 1906 was a counter-response by Muslim leaders to what they saw as a threat to the Muslim community posed by the growing strength of the Indian National Congress, as well as the expressions of Hindu nationalism by powerful leaders such as B. G. Tilak, and a looming sense that Muslims were being given less of a share in Indian political and economic life. The League's central concern, according to its founding document, was "to protect and advance the political rights and interests of Mussalmans," and to ensure that "the principle of class [group] representation in the Legislative Councils is entirely in accord with the sentiments of the Mussalman community."[10] The League remained a fairly weak organization for nearly three decades, but it never wavered from its denial of democratic majoritarianism.

The Congress and the League were against British rule, but their leaders always stressed that they were not against the British people per se and their political form of government at home—constitutional democracy—but only against the repressive system they had established in India. The Congress leaders, especially Jawarharlal Nehru and Mohandas Gandhi, were popular in liberal political and religious circles in Great Britain, Europe, and the United States. In a curious way, while the Congress and the League denounced British imperialism, it was British liberal democratic ideas that gave these movements for independence a certain coherence.

A movement toward independence can be seen in the public rhetoric and formal resolutions of both the Congress and League. First, there was the demand for fuller participation by Indians in the administrative structures created by the British in India. Alongside this was demand for elected representation in the various legislative bodies. Next came an interest in attaining dominion status, with similar rights to those enjoyed by the colonies of settlement—Canada, Australia, and New Zealand. Finally, and surprisingly late, came the demand for full independence. Both organizations assumed, without much discussion, that when independence came, the government would be a democracy; the League insisted, however, on the assurance of guaranteed Muslim representation in the democratic franchise. There was also an assumption that the leaders of a democratic India would emerge, as a judge of the Calcutta High Court, Sir Rameshchandra Mitra, put it, consonant with the traditions of India, from the educated classes, based on "the natural order of things . . . that those who think must govern those that toil."[11] This acceptance of "natural leaders" in part explains both the success and the nature of democracy in India. Subhas Chandra Bose (1897–1945), a popular leader who admired the contemporary authoritarian models of Germany and Italy, argued that for an India that had long been in thrall to foreign powers and whose population was desperately poor and illiterate, full democracy would need to be postponed. M. N. Roy (1887–1854), the Communist intellectual, saw revolution on the Russian model as inevitable. But the democratization process had already begun, however tentatively, in the establishment of elected municipal councils in major towns and cities in the 1880s. These bodies did not have much power, but they provided their members, often affiliated with the Congress or the League, with the opportunity to take part in political discussion and to learn something of the working of elected bodies.

Democratization was still controlled and directed by the foreign rulers of India: the shifting administrations in Great Britain, which exercised final control over the government through the secretary of state for India (usually a member of the cabinet), a position for which there was no equivalent in any of Britain's other colonial possessions. This meant that party ideologies were always in play from 1858 to 1947, with the Conservatives generally opposing any extension of self-government to India. Lord Curzon, the former viceroy, spoke for them when he declared in 1907 that self-government would be a "ruin to India and treason to our trust."[12] The Liberals were, on the whole, more sympathetic to change; Gladstone, the hero of Indian nationalists, was convinced that he spoke for a strain of British liberalism that was dedicated to India's progress toward self-government.

By the beginning of the twentieth century, the demands from Indians for a share in power became so strong that the Liberal Party recognized the need for change. This led, in 1909, to the Morley-Minto Reforms, named for the secretary of state for India, John Morley, and the viceroy, Lord Minto. The reforms provided for a franchise, which passed on a property tax to elect a majority of the members of the various provincial assemblies, but which left the central legislature controlled by the administration. An important feature of the electoral provisions was the introduction of communal electorates, in which some seats in the legislatures were reserved for Muslims, and where only Muslims could vote. Few acts of British rule have been more condemned by Indian nationalists than the creation of this special provision for Muslim representation. The Congress leaders believed that this was a deliberate attempt by the British to create a division between Muslims and Hindus, while the League leaders saw the Congress reaction as preventing Muslims from getting a voice in the legislature.

Although Indian nationalists thought the Morley-Minto Reforms were too little too late, some of them saw the elected legislative bodies as a step toward democratization and the creation of a parliamentary government. This view was quickly rejected by Morley, even though he had said, in 1908, that the British ruled India in order "to implant—slowly, prudently, judiciously—the ideas of justice, law, humanity, which are the foundations of our own civilisation." Morley was explicit about the direction the reforms were not meant to take: "If it could be said that this chapter of reforms led directly or indirectly to the establishment of a parliamentary system in India, I, for one, would have nothing to do with it."[13]

Morley's rejection of parliamentary government for India was based on his belief, which he shared with many British officials, that the antagonism between Hindus and Muslims would prevent them from working together in a democratic structure. A century later, there are many who continue to argue that national identity based on religion is a principal barrier to regional integration and stability in South Asia. This argument fails to account for the fact that democracy has worked to a considerable extent in individual South Asian countries, despite their ethnic, religious, and linguistic pluralism, thus providing a basis for regional integration.

Democratization and independence made striking advances when in 1917 Edwin Montagu, the secretary of state for India, announced the British government's plan for the future of India:

The policy of His Majesty's Government, with which the Government of India are in complete accord, is that of the increasing association of Indians in every branch of the administration, and the gradual development of self-governing institutions with a view to the progressive realisation of responsible government in India as an integral part of the British Empire.[14]

The historical connection between this pronouncement and the formation of independent democratic nations in South Asia is clear. Many conservatives blamed this historic concession by the British government on Montagu and claimed that, because he was Jewish, he was unduly sympathetic to the "Orientals."

Indian nationalists, whether in the Congress or League, accepted this promise grudgingly. They were less satisfied, however, with the constitutional working out of the Montagu-Chelmsford Reforms in 1919, named after the secretary of state and the viceroy at the time. The franchise was greatly enlarged and established a system known as a dyarchy, so called because it divided authority between elected Indian legislators and British officials. The reforms gave a large measure of democracy to the provincial legislatures, which had a majority of elected members, but reserved final control for the governor, a British appointee, over such vital fields as taxation and the police. Some national leaders were willing to accept what they called a "half loaf" as better than none, but as Montagu and Lord Reading, the viceroy, saw it, events were depriving Britain of initiative in India. Lord Reading, like Montagu, was Jewish, had been a British ambassador to Washington, and admired American democracy. It was a common taunt among the Conservatives in England at the time that India was being lost by the Jews. That the system of dyarchy was moving toward both democratization and independence and could not be reversed had become the rallying cry of Indian politicians in both the Congress and League.

Three major factors determined the speed and direction of this process. One was the increasing tension between Hindus and Muslims caused by a number of events: cow slaughter by Muslims; fewer opportunities of employment for Muslims; the rise of the Indian National Congress, regarded as a Hindu organization by Muslims; and the increase in anti-Muslim sentiments by Hindu nationalists. Another was the reaction of the Congress to Muslim demands for separate electorates; and the third was the arrival of Mohandas Gandhi on the Indian political scene, the most powerful and enigmatic figure that either the British authorities or the Indian nationalist politicians were to encounter. The Muslim League leaders tended to see his emphasis on religion as equivalent to injecting Hinduism into politics.

At this time, the Balfour Declaration, which promised the Jews a homeland in Palestine, greatly complicated the situation in India. Montagu was in India preparing the reforms when the news reached him that the British Cabinet had approved the declaration. Montagu saw the effect this would have on Muslims in India as well as on the Arab people in Palestine. In India, Muslims were being told by two effective leaders, the Ali brothers (Maulana Mohammad Ali and Maulana Shaukat Ali, both active in the League) that Britain was carrying on a war, not just against the Ottomans, but also against the Muslims in Palestine and India. When he returned to England, Montagu had to plead in the House of Commons for the adoption of the Montagu-Chelmsford Reforms against Conservative opposition, while in India the Ali brothers declared that Jews and Christians were embarking on a new crusade against Islam. In the face of this outcry, Montagu was forced to make a concession to Indian Muslims by retaining separate electorates for them, which he had long decried. In a statement in the House of Commons, he stressed his disapproval of the Balfour Declaration, of Zionism, and electoral politics based on religion:

> Division by creeds and classes means the creation of political camps organized against each other, and teaches men to think of themselves as partisans and not as citizens; and it is difficult to see how change from this to national representation is ever to occur. The British government is often accused of dividing [Hindus and Muslims] in order to govern them. But if it unnecessarily divides them at the very moment when it proposes to start them on the road to governing themselves, it will be difficult to meet the charge of being hypocritical or shortsighted.[15]

That indeed was the charge made then and ever since by Indian nationalists who blame separate electorates for Muslims as one of the major causes for Partition.

The growing importance of Gandhi in Indian political affairs helped push forward the process of democratization, even though he rarely mentioned democracy per se. When Gandhi, soon to be called Mahatma ("great soul"), returned to India in 1914, after three years in England studying law and twenty years in South Africa fighting for the rights of Indian emigrants, he had come to the conclusion that violence was not the solution for India's problems. What was needed to fight poverty, illiteracy, and foreign rule must be drawn from India's own traditions. He proposed that the freedom of India would be won by the gospel of love, by pitting soul-force against brute-force, by relying on the strength that comes from one's inner "unity and truth." One of the most perceptive writers on Gandhi, Denis Dalton, outlines the concept of freedom, or swaraj, that Gandhi was to develop. Gandhi was insistent that freedom meant learning to rule our own selves. He strove to show the connection between his moral and religious ideas and the political freedom and democracy that the Indian National Congress wanted:

> We may petition the government, we may agitate in the Imperial Council for our rights; but for a real awakening of the people, the more important thing is activities directed inwards . . . one sometimes hears it said, 'Let the government of India be in our own hands; everything will be all right afterwards.' There could be no greater superstition than this.[16]

Montagu was in India during this crucial period and met all the great minds of the nationalist movement, including Gandhi and Muhammad Ali Jinnah, landowners and industrialists, Hindu nationalists, Muslims committed to an Islamic social order, and declared, "they are all seething with desire for some change."[17] It was at this point that Gandhi made a profound difference in Indian politics by making the Indian National Congress an umbrella for the many centers of power through his distinctive message grounded in Indian culture; but it became increasingly clear that while this had deepened political participation, it had sharpened the Hindu-Muslim divide. He brought together the centers of power in a loose federation that was willing to work under his leadership, although this, at times, was uneasily accepted. When Montagu had met "the renowned Gandhi," he was surprised, saying he was not a politician at all, but a "social reformer," only interested in improving the conditions of his fellowmen. This is not far from the truth, except that Gandhi believed that conditions could only be changed by the inward direction of the people, not by constitutional reform.

The Government of India Act of 1935, which brought about considerable advances in democratization, marked a movement away from centralization of power. While this undoubtedly meant a strengthening of democracy at the provincial level, it eventually worked against regional integration, as the political decisions that followed in the next ten years led to the bitter partition of British India into India and Pakistan, and then later, to the division of Pakistan and the secession of Bangladesh. Regional integration thus inherited a fraught legacy.

The provincial governments were given a large measure of autonomy, which provided a training ground for many of the politicians who came to power after independence in 1947. Elections in 1937 brought the India National Congress into power in seven of the provinces. But when Jinnah, as leader of the Muslim League, which had won only a few states, suggested a coalition of the parties to work against the British, Nehru and the Congress refused—they had won by a large majority of the votes, and democracy meant majority rule. The line to independence was direct, with Jinnah and the Muslim League arguing for autonomous provinces and a severely restricted central authority, which would have meant an India with at least three provinces with a Muslim majority—Bengal, Punjab, and the North-West Frontier Province (NWFP). What Muslims could not accept, Jinnah declared in 1940, was a strong central government based on a democratic system of a majority vote controlling the government because that meant a "Hindu raj."[18] The Congress stated its opposition in 1946, when it declared that it sought "the establishment of a united democratic Indian Federation with a Central authority which would command respect from the nations of the world."[19] Regional integration, therefore, would depend to a considerable extent on the strong commitment to override provincial interests within a country, as well as between countries.

The British Parliament's Indian Independence Act of July 18, 1947, declared that on August 15 of that year "two independent Dominions shall be set up in

India, to be known respectively as India and Pakistan." The moment of high drama came, however, when, "after the last stroke at midnight" on August 14, the members of the Constituent Assembly dedicated themselves "to the service of India and her people to the end that this ancient land shall attain her place in the world and make her full and willing contribution to the promotion of world peace and welfare of mankind."[20] It is telling that at the moment of freedom, India was looking outwards, concerned with her place in the world, not her place in the South Asian region.

India Since Independence: Democratization and Its Challenges

"We step out from the old to the new," was Nehru's message to India at the dawn of independence. He also said that "the soul of a nation, long suppressed, finds utterance . . . to build the noble mansion of free India where all her children may dwell." In the more prosaic language of a modern Indian social scientist, Partha Chatterjee, the daunting challenge confronting India was that of building a democratic civil society based "on equality, autonomy, freedom of entry and exit, contract, deliberative procedures of decision-making, recognized rights and duties of its members."[21] These qualities excellently summarize the lengthy constitution that was written over the next two years. The new government immediately set out to draft a constitution even as hundreds of thousands of people were being killed in the cities and villages by rampaging mobs, and millions were becoming refugees in India and Pakistan. This was an astonishing testament to the determination of the new Indian government. The fact that India and Pakistan were not at war, and that the governments of both countries were using their armies and police forces to try to restrain the violence, also helped save these two new nations.

The constitution was drafted by the Constituent Assembly, which was created in 1946 by the British Parliament and through which it had hoped to transfer its Indian territories. The commitment to democratization is inherent in the definition of India given in the Preamble to the Indian Constitution: "a sovereign, socialist, secular, democratic republic." The words *socialist* and *secular* were not in the original preamble but were added in an amendment to the constitution in 1976, and the words *unity and integrity of the nation* were substituted for *unity of the nation*. These additions accurately captured the intentions of the drafters of the original constitution, and they represent an implicit acknowledgement that these ideals had been fiercely contested in practice in the past and would continue to be in the future.

The implications of India's self-definition, in terms of sovereignty, unity, secularism, and democracy, must be taken very seriously in any discussion of South Asian regional integration, which depends on Indian support for success. Pakistan and Bangladesh's status as Islamic states—as well as their reputation as supporters of Islamic militant groups within India—prevents them from being true democracies in the eyes of many Indians.

The drafters of the constitution recognized that democratization called for procedures that would ensure free and fair elections for an electorate of a size unmatched anywhere else in the world. Electoral procedures were therefore spelled out in great detail in the constitution. To carry out these procedures an election commission and a chief election commissioner were appointed.

India and Regional Integration: Economic Development, Violence, and Foreign Policy

India in 1947 was a vibrant civil society with freely contested elections and a free press that encouraged lively intellectual debate over government policies. Remarkable economic development took place to such an extent that India, long synonymous with poverty and lack of progress, seemed headed for a leading place in the world economy. Industrialization and improvements in infrastructure, education, and technology reflected the changes taking place. No less important was the rise in the standard of living for millions of people as well as the attempts to remove age-old discriminatory practices, improve the social status of women and children, and increase literacy. All of these were related to the mechanisms that preserve democracy in civil society: a free press, freedom of speech and religion, and an independent judiciary.

It seemed unlikely in 1947, but in 2010 India seems positioned to initiate regional integration in South Asia. There are, however, a number of factors inherent in India's domestic affairs and in its relations with the other South Asian nations that militate against collaborative enterprises. Chief among these is India's relationship with Pakistan, rooted in the immense physical suffering caused to millions of both Indians and Pakistanis by Partition. Added to this has been the sense in India that Pakistan represents the destruction of a united India encompassing the entire subcontinent, the rightful inheritance of the Indian people. To Pakistan, this Indian attitude is a rejection of the legitimacy of Pakistan. The continuing violence in Kashmir is Partition's terrible legacy. The history of conflict between the two nations—three wars and others narrowly averted—makes regional integration extremely difficult, but it also indicates how desperately important integration is.

Unfortunately, relations between India and other South Asian states have also not fostered an environment conducive to regional integration. Bangladesh would not have attained independence when it did had it not been for India's armed intervention in 1971, but relations between the two countries have at times been acrimonious. Conflict over the illegal immigration of Bangladeshis into India and disputes over water rights following India's construction of the Farakka Barrage are ongoing. India has also accused Bangladesh of harboring Islamic terrorists. Meanwhile, Nepal's trade relations with India are particularly important since most of its exports and imports must pass through India, and at times India has tightened controls to prevent smuggling. Relations between Nepal and China have been of particular concern to India, and in 1989 relations were especially tense as India imposed a blockade on Nepal when it was reported that Nepal had bought antiaircraft guns from China.

India's support for regionalism has been further dimmed by militant insurgent movements in its border regions. These movements for self-determination are based on ethnic and religious struggles in Kashmir, the Punjab, and the NWFP. The insurgents have found sympathizers in India itself, and the leaders in these three areas argue that India, by rejecting their claims for autonomy, has left them no alternative but violence. When India has met violence with greater violence, some have charged that its armed forces violated human rights. India's position was especially ambiguous in the United Nations (UN) after the passing of the Declarations on Human Rights in 1960 and 1966, since both covenants, which India supported, were unequivocal on the subject of self-determination, emphasizing that groups of people within an existing state can claim the right of self-determination to attain their social and cultural goals. India argued that the Covenants on Human Rights could not be applied to minorities in a sovereign, independent state like India, as this would undermine its national integrity. Nehru's thinking was that India was created by a social contract with all the constituent groups participating, and that they were committed by this agreement to remain loyal to the central state in return for security and stability. Here, perhaps, is a suggestion that genuine regionalism can follow from a social contract among entities based on common economic interests, security, and shared cultural memories.

The greatest challenge to democracy—and to regional integration—came in 1975, not from insurgencies but from within the Indian government itself, when Prime Minister Indira Gandhi, with the consent of the president and a compliant cabinet, proclaimed a State of Emergency under Article 352 of the constitution, which entailed the suspension of most of the framework of democracy that had been built up over the previous thirty years. Ironically, however, the procedures of democracy were used to defeat the prime minister and her party, the Indian National Congress, through political organizations, the constitutional provisions for elections, and the courts.

That India considers itself primarily to be a part of the world economic and political system, and not a component of a regional system, is relevant to a discussion of India's role in any regional linkages. On the eve of independence, Nehru told the Constituent Assembly that the country must commit itself to "the ending of poverty and ignorance and disease and inequality of opportunity," a task to which India must dedicate her resources. India's decision to virtually exclude the importation of consumer goods and thereby to foster economic independence and gain control over essential industries—such as rail transport, fertilizer, and military supplies—demonstrated that this was not conventional political rhetoric. This policy of *autarky*, now so widely condemned by many economists, was a reaction to the deep-seated conviction of Indian nationalists that India had been impoverished by Britain pursuing the opposite policy in the nineteenth century. Moreover, the scope of this policy was not merely economic: it was also meant to address the age-old problems of social injustice in the context of a socialist democracy and produce a social order that would inform all the institutions of national life.

As of 2010, over sixty years after independence and its initial commitment to economic self-sufficiency, the Indian government welcomes foreign investment and cooperation between the private sectors in India and those of industrialized countries. This seismic economic shift from a planned economy was made without the dislocation that occurred, for example, in the Soviet Union, which underwent a somewhat similar shift. The Nobel prize–winning economist Amartya Sen argues convincingly that this is due to the long process of democratization that had already taken place in India. Despite "an untried government, an undigested partition and unclear political alignments, combined with widespread communal violence and social disorder," India, he argues, has been "held together by its working democracy."[22]

Nehru had what has been called a "grandiose vision" of an independent India with a dominant place in the world, contributing to its peace, security, and freedom. A year before independence he had articulated this vision when he declared, "whether one talked of the Middle East or Southeast Asia or China, all impinged on India and all depended on India economically and politically. They could not help looking and India could not help looking at them. In the modern world it was inevitable for India to be the centre of things in India."[23] After independence, he summed up this view of India and the world, reminding his people that "we are not some odd little nation . . . we are potentially a great nation and a big Power."[24] All of the nations of South Asia, one suspects, would have been assigned to his category of odd little nations, a designation felt as deeply by Bhutan as Pakistan.

India symbolically attained both her place in the world and the fruits of democratization on May 27, 1998, when Prime Minister Vajpayee declared that "India is now a nuclear state." It is noteworthy that he remembered the region, as few Indians leaders did, when he said that nuclear and economic achievements had increased India's "regional and global linkages," and that his government intended "to deepen and strengthen these ties."[25]

Pakistan: Democratization, the Military, and Islamization

Pakistan's large population, natural resources, reasonably efficient administrative framework, and large pool of well-educated citizens should have led to democratization and a civil society not unlike that of India, with which it shares so much history and culture. Instead, over sixty years after its founding, numerous writers have characterized Pakistan as a failing state, a refuge for Islamic terrorists, a nuclear threat to the world, and a state dominated by a fascistic and corrupt military and fanatic religious fundamentalism. Pakistan is not, however, a failed state; it is powerful and reasonably prosperous, with a well-educated elite. Perhaps a reasonable question to ask is not whether Pakistan is failing, but why its civil society has taken the direction it has. A partial answer would have to do with the nation's inability to establish productive relations with the other countries of South Asia, notably India, which would have made meaningful regional cooperation possible. Another factor here has been Pakistan's decision to be both an Islamic state and a democratic one. Finally, Pakistan has chosen to pursue a foreign policy simultaneously based on a close military alliance with the United States and hostility toward India. These and other political choices have increased the dominance of the military, which has hindered democratization and regional integration.

One should also be aware of the highly important differences that preceded Partition in 1947. The founding fathers of Pakistan had much less experience in local electoral politics than those that formed India. This meant that the new leaders had not been part of the civil society of the new state, as was the case in India. For example, neither Jinnah nor Liaquat Ali Khan (who succeeded him) was from territorial Pakistan—both were essentially the product of India's preindependence secular politics. Also, the Muslim League had its strength in the provinces that became India, not in those that became Pakistan, so the new state did not have a cadre of seasoned local politicians as India did.

Pakistan's civil society had also been divided by conflicting expectations in its commitment to the kind of state that was to be created. A majority of people, judging by election results after 1947, accepted the legal and electoral system that had been created in British India, assuming that it would work for a new state in which there would be a majority Muslim population in a democratizing society. How this vision of an Islamic society would be realized had not been worked out in detail. Two quotations set in sharp contrast two visions for Pakistan. The first is from Muhammad Ali Jinnah (1876–1948), who became governor-general of Pakistan in 1947, after a long struggle for the political rights of the Indian Muslim community. Jinnah's political career began by cooperating with the Indian National Congress in its efforts toward a free, united India; it is not clear when Jinnah became convinced of the need for a separate Pakistan. Until the mid-1940s, he seemed to have accepted the idea of autonomous provinces with Muslim-majority provinces in an India with a central government with limited powers. This meant that two of the most important provinces—Bengal and Punjab (which had bare Muslim majorities)—would not be integral parts of the independent India that the Indian National Congress had visualized, an idea which was seen by the Congress leaders as creating a weak, Balkanized India. Jinnah told the leaders of the new Pakistan to come to terms with history, and to forget the bitterness of the Hindu-Muslim divide:

> In course of time all these angularities of the majority and minority communities, the Hindu community and the Muslim community . . . will vanish . . . You may belong to any religion or caste or creed—that has nothing to do with the business of the State.[26]

Jinnah's vision of a democratic society for Pakistan was grounded in nineteenth-century British political thought. An utterly different vision was promoted by Syed Abul A'ala Maududi (1903–1979), the founder of the influential Islamic organization Jama'at-i-Islami. For Maududi, the civil secular society envisioned by Jinnah was a betrayal of Islam:

> We have all along been demanding a separate homeland for the purpose of translating into practice the ideals envisaged by Islam . . . If, now, after all these precious sacrifices, we fail to achieve the real and ultimate objective of making Islam a practical, constitutional reality which inspired us to fight for Pakistan, our entire struggle becomes futile and all our sacrifices meaningless.[27]

However attractive Jinnah's vision may seem to some in Pakistan, it is Maududi's vision that has captured a potent following. Even if its political followers did not win many electoral victories, there was wide acceptance of the basic premise that Pakistan was an Islamic state and its laws must be the congruent with the laws of Islam; it could not be a secular democracy, as Jinnah envisioned.

This fundamental clash over what constitutes a good society is one explanation for why Pakistan democratized differently than India. What one should see is not the failure of democracy, but the failure of the democratic politicians to engender trust in their capacity to govern. This lack of trust explains why there was no great outcry from the people when the military overthrew the civilian government at various times; it also accounts for the success of the Taliban, not just in Afghanistan but also in parts of Pakistan.

The Conflicted Path of Democracy in Pakistan, 1947–2010

The American historian Allen McGrath has written a careful study of the first seven years of Pakistan's political governance, titled *The Destruction of Pakistan's Democracy*. During this short period, the civilian democratic government yielded its authority to the bureaucracy and the judiciary, allowing the military to take over in 1958. According to McGrath's convincing analysis, Governor-General Ghulam Mohammad, the leader of the bureaucracy, disliked the idea of democracy and the constitution that the Constituent Assembly had produced. With the assistance of Mohammad Munir, the chief justice of the Supreme Court, he dissolved the Constituent Assembly in 1954.[28] He had already secured the approval of Gen. Ayub Khan, who had been commander-in-chief of the army since 1951. This paved the way for Pakistan to enter into what amounted to a military alliance with the United States in 1954. The Americans saw Pakistan as an ally in the Cold War against Communism; meanwhile, the Pakistani military hoped to strengthen itself against India. Their alliance, from the beginning, was fraught with dislike and mistrust on both sides—a phenomenon that continues to this day.

When General Khan took full control of the government in 1958, he argued that the people had completely lost confidence in the politicians and that only the army could save a Pakistan that had become a "spectacle of disunity and disintegration."[29] The military was to remain the real power in Pakistan, even during subsequent periods of civilian rule.

Civilian Rule and Questionable Democratization: Zulfikar Bhutto, 1971–1977

Civilian rule was restored in 1971 when, following the secession of East Pakistan, the military was discredited and Zulfikar Ali Bhutto (1928–1979) came to power as a populist leader with the slogan: "Islam is our Faith, Democracy is our polity, Socialism is our economy, all power to the people." Despite his education at Berkeley and Oxford, Bhutto had no more real interest in democratization than any of his predecessors or successors, but he apparently hoped to secure his power by setting forth the ideals of Islam and economic justice. Freedom of the press was restricted and the police were used to prevent political opponents from actively campaigning. Industries were nationalized, adding to the government's sources of control, but also allowing for widespread corruption and inefficiency. When elections were held in 1977, the results were so one-sided for Bhutto's party that they were widely discredited, and the opposition party, the Pakistan National Alliance, organized an effective protest that drew upon the dissatisfaction of many groups, including militant Islamic ones. The military was waiting in the wings.

Military Rule and Islamization: General Zia, 1977–1988

The outcome was a military coup in 1977 led by General Zia, the Chief of Staff of the Pakistan army. He ruled until 1988, with the commitment to make Pakistan a truly Islamic state, which he believed the previous Pakistan governments had failed to do. His was motivated by a religious zeal coupled with a military man's belief that an orderly society required all people to obey a common code of conduct. Legitimacy would be conferred to his rule from his giving the people of Pakistan a stable government, military security, and a just Islamic social order based on God's laws, and not from the will of an easily manipulated majority. "We, in our country should be united like a phalanx, more so in the matter of religion, so that outsiders should know that this country is so galvanized and united that no wedge can be driven, no cracks and fissures be created";[30] for Zia, there was no place in Pakistan for a party that subscribed to any ideology other than Islam, and no place for democratization. He made the nation's first real attempt to institute Shari'a, taking steps to align the economy, the educational system, the courts, and the media with a particular interpretation of Islamic law.

American military relations with Pakistan are part of the sorry record of democratization, since American administrations have usually been most cordial with Pakistan when it has been under military rule. During Zia's years in power, Pakistan became a front line in the American war against the Soviet Union in Afghanistan, with Pakistan serving as a conduit for American funds to the Afghan fighters—funds that bought the weapons that were used to bring the Taliban, America's later enemies, to power.

Return to Civilian Rule, 1988–1999

After Zia's death in an airplane crash in 1988, Pakistanis lived under civilian rule until 1999, but few look back at this period as a time of democratization, despite regular elections. As a British journalist reported with ample evidence, Pakistanis saw the post-Zia politicians, including the two that alternated as prime minister, Nawaz Sharif and Benazir Bhutto, as "self-seeking, corrupt, and unprincipled."[31] Pakistan also emerged as a nuclear power during this period; it was Prime Minister Sharif who announced that "our nuclear scientists and technicians too, by the grace of God, are endowed with divine capabilities" and that they had succeeded in testing nuclear weapons.[32] Now that both India and Pakistan were nuclear states, many feared an increase in the likelihood of war between them; others thought that the balance of terror would make it unlikely that either would dare start a war.

Military Rule under General Musharraf, 1999–2008, and Elections in 2008

The following year a military coup led by General Musharraf, the head of the army, overthrew Sharif and both he and his rival, Benazir Bhutto, went into exile. As with most coups in Pakistan, there was remarkably little opposition, as though the people had lost faith in a democratic process that had put in power leaders widely regarded as ineffective and corrupt. The American administration, however, was pleased since military rule promised stability in an area of great importance to its war on Islamic terrorism. Musharraf promised that the greedy politicians would be replaced through "a democratic, dynamic revolution" that would lay "the foundations of democracy."[33]

Musharraf wrote in his memoir, "Several times in the quiet of the night, sitting alone in my study, I have pondered over what has happened to Pakistan."[34] What has happened is simply that all Pakistan's leaders have tried to build a democratic nation-state, but one without the essential elements of a democracy—an independent judiciary, accountability of rulers to the people, and electoral procedures free from manipulation by the military.

At the end of 2007, Pakistan was in turmoil following Musharraf's dismissal of the chief justice of the Supreme Court and several other judges, who had declared some of his actions to be unconstitutional. In a startling display, thousands of lawyers took to the streets in protest; they recognized, as a Pakistani journalist put it, that "without a strong and independent judiciary, Pakistan, a nuclear armed-state, will forever be at the mercy of dictators and power-hungry politicians."[35] A long-promised election was about to take place, and Nawaz Sharif and Benazir Bhutto, the self-exiled political leaders, returned to lead their rival parties against Musharraf, with Benazir approved by the U.S. administration because she promised to work with Musharraf. However, at the start of her campaign she was assassinated, to the fury of her supporters. The resulting violence was contained, the election was held, and her party, the Pakistan's People Party, won under the leadership of her husband (who had been jailed for years). He and Nawaz Sharif (who had the next-largest number of votes) promised to cooperate in a coalition government.

While the newly elected politicians struggled to create a democratic government, they were confronted by a new phase in the American-led war on Islamic terrorism, as groups from the Taliban regime that had been overthrown in Afghanistan, along with others inspired by al-Qaeda, established bases in the Federally Administered Tribal Areas (FATA). The Pakistan government would not permit American forces to operate in the area, fearing that this would further anger many Pakistanis. This was the situation in the summer of 2008, when rumor spread of an imminent invasion of Pakistan by American forces that sought to destroy alleged terrorist bases, which greatly increased the already strong anti-American sentiment in Pakistan. A former Pakistani administrator from the NWFP, noting that the political leadership was too divided to take action, commented: "One wonders if there can be any other outcome than the de-establishment of Pakistan."[36]

Can Pakistan Be a Significant Actor in Regional Integration?

Forced by a divided leadership under great pressure from the American administration to act against Islamic extremism, the government is unlikely to give serious attention to plans for regional integration that would require significant concessions to India on Kashmir. The best hope for Pakistan and South Asia would be an elected government that has the confidence of the people, with no interference from the military, and that is not as financially dependent on the United States and, therefore, less susceptible to its demands. Reviewing Pakistan's history, it is hard to imagine that the generals would retreat—the army is too deeply entrenched to yield control to civilian ministers on such matters as Kashmir, nuclear weapons, and intelligence. What Pakistan surely needs to counteract this dark pessimism is a democratic statesman who could say, with authority, what Jinnah said to the Muslim League at Lucknow in 1916:

> With regard to our own affairs, we can depend upon nobody but ourselves . . . We should remove the root causes of and the evil effects of disintegration . . . We must show by our words and deeds that we sincerely and earnestly desire a healthy national unity.[37]

Bangladesh: Democratization and Regional Integration in a Secessionist State

According to its constitution, Bangladesh is a parliamentary democracy with Islam as its state religion. It is also a new nation, though with old cultural and linguistic ties to its neighbor, the Indian state of West Bengal. Bangladesh was part of the Bengal province of the Mughal empire and then of the British Raj until 1947, when Bengal was divided into East and West Bengal, with East Bengal, a Muslim majority area, becoming part of Pakistan, along with the Muslim majority areas of Punjab, Sind, and other contiguous Muslim areas. Pakistan thus became, in the terminology of the time, a state with "two wings," separated by a thousand miles of Indian territory. East Pakistan's history, language, and economy were quite different from those of West Pakistan, and these cultural differences were strengthened by what was increasingly felt in East Pakistan as discriminatory treatment by Pakistan's central government, housed in West Pakistan. In a way, East Bengalis had become colonized in their own country.

One issue of particular contention was the national language. The central Pakistani government decided to make Urdu the national language, despite the fact that it was allegedly spoken by only 1 percent of the people of East Pakistan. Bengali, the language of the people, was deliberately given second place by Jinnah's declaration in Dacca in 1948: "Let me make it clear to you that the state language of Pakistan is going to be Urdu and no other language. Anyone who tries to mislead you is merely the enemy of Pakistan."[38]

The Awami League was formed to channel the resentment of East Bengalis against the central government. When national elections were held in 1970, the leader of the Awami League, Sheikh Mujibur Rahman (1920–1975), known as Mujib, made a stirring emotional appeal for autonomy but not secession, although he did refer to East Pakistan as *Bangladesh*—"Bengali country." The parliament had 300 seats, and due to its larger population, East Pakistan would have 162 of them; Mujib won all but two of these, while in West Pakistan, his rival, Zulfiqar Bhutto, won only 81 seats. Mujib immediately claimed that he had won the right to be prime minister by this overwhelming democratic victory, which meant that he would be in charge of the new constitution that was to be written. He announced that if he became prime minister both "wings" would have autonomy. General Yahya Khan, the military administrator, and Bhutto, the leading civilian politician, refused to recognize Mujib's claim.

When Mujib burned the Pakistani flag and raised the new flag of Bangladesh, martial law was decreed, Mujib was arrested, and the Pakistani army began a brutal crackdown in Bangladesh. The Indian government denounced the Pakistani actions and moved its army into Bangladesh, defeating the Pakistani army. India's motivations were mixed and included an appeal to humanitarianism, a fear of instability from the flood of Hindu refugees crowding into India, and a long-standing hostility toward Pakistan. By the end of 1971, the worst of the war was over and Bangladesh was an independent nation.

Unfortunately, a democratic success story did not follow. Democratization was obstructed by instability in the government, and, in 1975, Mujib was assassinated by dissident army officers. General Rahman, who became president in 1978, was assassinated in 1981 and, following a brief period of civilian rule, the military took over again in 1982. Parliamentary government was restored, but the bitter relationship between both major parties—the Awami League and the Bangladesh Nationalist Party—had prevented the development of an institutional framework of democratic procedures that could be accepted by the parties and the military. Elections were the test of the success of democratization, and the signs from Bangladesh were not encouraging. In January 2007 the military installed a "caretaker government" when violence caused by the bitter election campaign between the Awami League and the Bangladesh Nationalist Party threatened civil society. Charges of nepotism and corruption led to the imprisonment of the parties' leaders, Sheikh Hasina and Khaleda Zia, with the military embedding itself deeply into the electoral process. When elections were held in December 2008, Sheikh Hasina and the Awami League won, and she was sworn in as prime minister in January 2009. Outside the electoral framework, radical Islamic movements have grown and there is some evidence that they derive ideological inspiration from al-Qaeda.[39] Indian officials suspected that the 2008 bombings that took place in India were the responsibility of groups from Bangladesh, which added to the tensions already existing between the two countries.

Bangladesh has a special place in the movement for South Asian regional integration because President Ziaur Rahman began discussing the idea of regional cooperation when he visited South Asian capitals in the late 1970s for Commonwealth meetings. Since the South Asian countries share common values rooted in cultural and historical traditions, he argued, cooperation was possible. He had economic cooperation in mind, but he was aware of the pitfalls in emphasizing it. As he explained, in South Asia, countries are at different stages of development so care must be taken that the "weak are not exploited and the strong do not dominate."[40] He was no doubt thinking of India's industrial and military strength, but he felt that regional cooperation could modify India's obvious superiority, smoothing some of the rough edges of bilateral relations, and increase bargaining capacity with India. "Peace, stability and security," President Rahman argued, "would be the fruit of regional cooperation." To the foreign affairs officials in Delhi this suggested that Rahman was being influenced by the United States and China, and Bangladesh had indeed developed good relations with China. To further allay India's suspicions, Bangladesh said that in making a suggestion for regional cooperation, it had no intention of forming a regional military bloc. Pakistan also feared that any regional accord would lead to India's economic and political domination, but they grudgingly supported Rahman's idea in the end, fearing isolation. Bangladesh said that it favored a step-by-step approach, agreeing that controversial political subjects would be avoided and that attention would be given to culture, science, and technology.

The first meeting of SAARC took place in Dhaka in 1985, with subsequent annual meetings in capitals across South Asia.

Sri Lanka: Militant Ethnic Separatism as a Threat to a Democratic State

Developments in Sri Lanka have followed a disheartening trajectory. The island state emerged from colonial control seemingly well prepared for independence— possessing a stable civil society, a working democratic system with universal suffrage since 1931, social welfare schemes, and a well-educated population with a higher standard of living than the rest of South Asia. Independence from Great Britain in 1948 had been peacefully accomplished without any of the turmoil that had marked the transfer of power in India, but then in the 1970s Sri Lanka became engulfed in savage internal strife fueled by ethnic tensions between the Sinhalese majority, who are Buddhists, and the Hindu Tamil minority. Ethnic and religious tensions were heightened by the decision to make Sinhalese the national language. The year 1955 was marked by the onset of ethnic and religious violence, centered on the Tamil majority area in the north and east of the island, but affecting much of the rest of the country. Thousands were killed, the economy was disrupted, and democracy was challenged by human rights abuses on a massive scale by both government and rebel forces. As a result, in 2004 the World Bank and the Asian Development Bank (ADB) considered Sri Lanka one of the world's most politically unstable countries. Despite this, the U.S. State Department classified it, in the midst of a long-running civil war, as "a stable democracy" in the following year. This designation was greeted with skepticism, but was testimony to the remarkable strength of Sri Lanka's democratic institutions, in particular its administrative legal system. In the midst of its internal strife, Sri Lanka continued to support SAARC, seeing a move toward regional integration as critical to its control of militant forces by isolating them from outside support, especially from Indian sympathizers.

Nepal: Toward Democracy through Regional Involvement and Marxist Rebellion?

Relations between India and Nepal illustrate how democratization may both help and hinder regional integration. Up to the 1950s, Nepal was deliberately self-isolated, with power concentrated in the hands of a privileged ruling class, the Ranas, who controlled the country with the kings subservient rois *fainéants*. Changes began, however, in 1950, when the Chinese asserted their authority over Tibet, which they had long claimed in a nominal fashion. This led Indian leaders to fear Chinese intrusion into Nepal. Believing that the Rana autocracy was vulnerable to Communist subversion, they concluded that it should be replaced by a "a more representative and modern system political system."[41] The Nepali Congress was formed with Indian assistance, leading to the Congress's participation in a coalition cabinet led by the king. Formal

221

arrangements were made for New Delhi to have a guiding hand in Nepal security concerns and economic policy. Pressure came from the Nepali Congress Party and other smaller groups for elections to a constituent assembly, but the king opposed this. Elections were held for a legislative body but were overruled by royal opposition; political parties were banned. Groups agitating for democratic elections, however, forced the king to lift the ban, and the Nepali Congress Party won the election in 1991. A succession of prime ministers faced many challenges, however, including charges of corruption and incompetence that prompted the king to reestablish monarchic rule in 2002.

The major threat confronting both Nepal's nascent democratic system and its king, however, is a Maoist insurgency that began as a guerrilla movement in the countryside in 1996. Insurgent leaders, drawn from the cadres of the Communist Party of Nepal, aim at overthrowing both the monarchy and the elected legislature. An uprising in Kathmandu in 2008 showed the extent of the rebels' support, leading to a ceasefire and a compromise between the Maoists and the government. What appears to have been a genuinely democratic election took place, with 60 percent of the electorate. When the Marxists won 30 percent of the vote, the Marxist leader, Pushpa Kamal Dalal, was elected prime minister. The new legislators forced the king's abdication and the Nepal army gave assurances that it would work under the elected government. In 2010, it seems quite possible that an era of democratic rule has begun in a state with a desperate need of regional integration.

Democratization and Regional Integration in Afghanistan, Bhutan, and the Maldives

Emphasis in this chapter has been heavy on the successes and failures of democratization in the three countries most intertwined—India, Pakistan, and Bangladesh. Less attention has been given to SAARC's less populous members. Afghanistan, Bhutan, and the Maldives will not receive the attention they deserve, integral as they are to the complex mosaic of the region. In all of them, the process of democratization has been uncertain and ambiguous. This is particularly true of Afghanistan, which has been involved in some fashion in all the great civilizations and empires based in Iran, China, Central Asia, and India, but whose fate is now intertwined with that of Pakistan and the United States—the latest major power to assert control in that crossroad of empires, trade routes, and religions. Afghanistan was accepted as a member of SAARC at the urging of India, but its democratization is so much a product of external powers and so nominal that it will not be discussed here. Nor will Bhutan and the Maldives (except very briefly), although they are members of SAARC, because neither have reached a point of political restructuring that suggests much advance in the democratization process.

Bhutan's government is hampered by a number of factors. One is the presence of a large and assertive Nepalese ethnic minority to which the government is unwilling to grant full citizenship. Another is government awareness of the acute need to maintain good relations with its giant neighbors, India and China, which are suspicious of each other's activity in Bhutan. Bhutanese officials welcome high-end tourism, but not "backpackers"—"we have been to Nepal," as one promoter of tourism remarked.

The government of Maldives also wants to be integrated into high-end tourism but keeps visitors segregated on island resorts, away from its people. The Maldives' political elites probably want neither democratization nor deep regional integration, and the system of government is very similar to that of British India, with control vested in district officers appointed by the president. Political parties have been permitted to operate only since 2005. While the government has signed the major UN covenants on human, civil, and political rights, human rights organizations such as Amnesty International criticize its treatment of political prisoners. Meanwhile, the government has apparently accepted the inevitability of Indian influence (a segment of its claims to a maritime economic zone coincide with those of India). When threatened by internal discontent, supported by Tamil mercenaries from Sri Lanka in 1988, the ruling elite called on military help from India to suppress the insurgents. As a member of SAARC, the government has promoted the formation of the South Asian Free Trade Area (SAFTA).

Conclusion: SAARC as a Symbol of Regional Integration and Democratization

When President Theodore Roosevelt declared that if British rule were withdrawn from India (what we have been calling South Asia), "the whole peninsula would become a chaos of bloodshed and violence—the only beneficiaries among the natives would be the lawless, the violent and the bloodthirsty," he was expressing what many in Europe and America believed at the time and still believed when Britain left at short notice in 1947.[42] Few in 1947 would have foreseen that over sixty years later, throughout South Asia would be credible signs of democratization and regional cooperation. Despite enormous natural disasters, armed uprisings, and military coups, there have been no "failed states" in South Asia; no brutal, tyrannical dictatorships; and no armed overthrow of other governments. This is so because of the complex transactions that have taken place between old traditions and new ways of structuring power—not without tension and conflict, but producing manageable democratic structures ready for regional cooperation.

India, the most powerful and democratic of South Asian countries, did not show much enthusiasm for South Asian regional cooperation when President Rahman of Bangladesh first suggested it. But regional cooperation was such a reasonable project that it could hardly be ignored, so India sought to make SAARC "compatible with essential aspects of its perceived interests in the region."[43] In 1981 the foreign secretary of India clarified what these interests were when he stated what the "ground rules" should be for SAARC: discussion of bilateral and contentious issues would be avoided, all decisions in regard to regional cooperation would be unanimous, and trade and cultural subjects were identified as of special interest to India. This last point aroused some unease in the other countries, since India's economic and industrial power is so overwhelming that the other countries fear domination. But there have been few real breakthroughs in trade, leaving South Asia the least integrated region in the world and one of the poorest. This underlines a journalist's comment, made after the 2007 SAARC Summit, that "it is time the South Asian countries unleashed the potential of the region to improve the lives of their people."[44] But as another journalist, from Pakistan, has pointed out, people have been too deeply indoctrinated in old disputes "to allow their governments to move to new paradigms of relations."[45] India, understandably, may not see the need to integrate with its smaller neighbors; meanwhile, there is widespread recognition that better political relations between India and Pakistan would be of advantage to all the countries of the region.

The members of SAARC have agreed that there are areas where cooperation would benefit them all, including rural development, health, science and technology, and transport. A new area was given prominence at a meeting of the regional ministers at Bangalore in 2008, when it was agreed that they should share data on weather patterns and their experiences with natural disasters, and act as one in international meetings on climate change and pollution. As so often in the past, however, one senses what one Indian scholar, Suman Sharma, sees as India's "compulsive pursuit of a global role" over concern with regional initiatives. Nevertheless, she concludes, the smaller countries must come to terms with India's dominance while India must recognize that taking "bold, positive and decisive steps to establish peace and harmony in South Asia" will require making concessions to the other countries, notably Pakistan, Bangladesh, and Nepal, with which India has long-standing disputes.[46]

Reports that have come out of recent SAARC meetings suggest both aspirations and hindrances to regional integration. The members regarded one major achievement as the setting up of a legal mechanism for mutual assistance in countering terrorism, but press reports pointed out that this had been done before, leading to dissension as to how it could be carried out.[47] One commentator, Mukul Kesavan, has insisted, as does this chapter, that only as they become pluralist democracies will it be possible for the South Asian countries to move with confidence toward regional integration. This is because democracies foster the civil society involvement necessary to gain consensus among competing interest groups, enabling regional integration in trade, security, environmental issues, and cultural relations. Such integration would be to the advantage not only of South Asia but of the entire international community.

Notes

[1] *Notes, Memoranda and Letters Exchanged between the Governments of India and China, September–November, 1959* (New Delhi: Ministry of External Affairs, 1959).

[2] "The Objectives Resolution," *Constituent Assembly of Pakistan Debates* 5, no. 1 (1952): 1–7 (Karachi: Government of Pakistan).

[3] Karl Marx and F. Engels, *The First Indian War of Independence, 1857–1859* (Moscow: Foreign Languages Publishing House, n.d.), 40, 56–57.

[4] Carl Friedrich, *Man and His Government* (New York: McGraw Hill, 1963), 547.

[5] R. C. Majumdar, H. C. Raychaudhuri, and Kalikinkar Datta, *An Advanced History of India* (London: Macmillan, 1960), 782.

[6] C. H. Philips, H. L. Singh, and B. N. Pandey, *The Evolution of India and Pakistan 1858 to 1947: Select Documents* (London: Oxford Univ. Press, 1962), 10–11.

[7] Ibid., 99–102.

[8] "Memorial of the Anglo-Indian Association, 1883," in Phillips, Singh, and Pandey, *The Evolution of India and Pakistan*, 122.

[9] Philips, Singh, and Pandey, *The Evolution of India and Pakistan*, 145.

[10] "Muslim Resolutions at Dacca, 30 December 1906," in Philips, Singh, and Pandey, *The Evolution of India and Pakistan*, 194.

[11] Quoted in S. N. Banerjea, *A Nation in Making* (Bombay: Oxford Univ. Press, 1963), 42–43.

[12] Lord Curzon, "The True Imperialism," in *The Nineteenth Century and After* (1908), LXIII.

[13] *Parliamentary Debates*, Fourth Series, House of Lords, December 17, 1908.

[14] "Report on Indian Constitutional Reforms," *Parliamentary Papers* 8 (1918): 60, Cmd. 9109.

[15] *Report on Indian Constitutional Reforms* (London: HMSO, 1918), sec. 132–151.

[16] Dennis Dalton, *Mahatma Gandhi, Non-Violent Power in Action* (New York: Columbia Univ. Press), 27.

[17] Edwin Montagu, *An Indian Diary*, ed., Venetia Montagu (London: Heinemann, 1930), 56–58.

[18] Jamil-ud-din Ahmad, ed., *Speeches and Writings of Mr. Jinnah*, (Lahore: M. Ashraf, 1946), 176–80.

[19] "Resolution of the Congress Working Committee, 25 June 1946," in Philips, Singh, and Pandey, *The Evolution of India and Pakistan*, 386.

[20] Jawaharlal Nehru, *Independence and After: 1946–49* (Delhi: Publications Division, Government of India, 1949), 3–4.

[21] Partha Chatterjee, "Post-Colonial Civil and Political Society," in *Civil Society: History and Possibilities*, ed., Sudipta Kaviraj and Sunil Khilnani (Cambridge: Cambridge Univ. Press, 2001), 174.

[22] Amartya Sen, *Development as Freedom* (New York: Knopf, 1990), 149–57.

[23] Suman Sharma, *India and SAARC* (New Delhi: Gyan Publishing, 2001), 32.

[24] Nehru, *Independence and After*, 203–5.

[25] Prime Minister A. B. Vajpayee, *Lok Sabha Debates, May 27* (New Delhi: Government of India, 1998).

[26] Mohammad Ali Jinnah, *Letters and Writings of Mr. Jinnah*, ed., Jamil-ud-din Ahmad, 2 vols (Lahore: Ashraf, 1946–47), 2: 399–404.

[27] Syed Abu'l-ala Maudoodi, *Islamic law and Constitution* (Lahore: Herald Press, 1954), 14.

[28] Allen McGrath, *The Destruction of Pakistan's Democracy* (Karachi: Oxford Univ. Press, 1996), especially chapters 5 and 8.

[29] Ayub Khan, *Friends, Not Masters: A Political Autobiography* (New York: Oxford Univ. Press, 1967), 194–201.

[30] Zia ul Haq, *Islam Stands for Unity and Brotherhood* (Islamabad: Government of Pakistan, 1983), 5–6.

[31] Owen Bennett Jones, *Pakistan: Eye of the Storm* (New Haven: Yale Univ. Press, 2002), 230.

[32] BBC News, home page, May 28, 1998.

[33] General Musharraf, *Development of Power and Responsibility* (Islamabad: Directorate of Films and Publications, March 23, 2000).

[34] Pervez Musharraf, *In the Line of Fire: A Memoir* (New York: Free Press, 2006), 275.

[35] Salman Ahmad, "A False Choice for Pakistan," *Washington Post*, November 19, 2008.

[36] Khalid Aziz, personal communication, July 21, 2008.

[37] M. Rafique Afzal, ed., *Selected Speeches and Statements of the Quaid-i-Azam Mohammad Ali Jinnah (1911–14 and 1947–48)* (Lahore: Research Society of Pakistan, 1966), 62–63.

[38] Anwar Dil and Afia Dil, *Bengali Language Movement in Bangladesh* (Lahore: Ferozsons, 2000), 82.

[39] Maneeza Hossain, *Broken Pendulum: Bangladesh's Swing to Radicalism* (Washington D.C.: Hudson Institute, 2007), 31.

[40] Quoted in B. F. Mohanan, *The Politics of Regionalism in South* Asia (New Delhi: Atlantic Publishers, 1992), 2.

[41] Leo E. Rose and John T. Scholz, *Nepal: Portrait of a Himalayan Kingdom* (Boulder, CO: Westview, 1980), 120–22

[42] H. W. Brands, *India and the United States: The Cold Peace* (Boston: Twayne, 1990), 3.

[43] S. D. Muni, "SAARC: Building Regionalism from Below," *Asian Survey* 30, no. 4 (April 1985): 396.

[44] "14th SAARC Summit: Will it Rise Above 'Just Another Meeting'?" *Businessline*, Chennai, April 4, 2007: 1.

[45] Khaled Ahmed, "South Asia's Unresolved Disputes," in *South Asia Journal* (January–March 2005), 6.

[46] Sharma, *India and SAARC*, 244–46.

[47] South Asian Perspectives, "SAARC Summit—An Exercise in Futility?" South Asia Program of the Carnegie Endowment for International Peace, no. 3 (August 2008), 7.

SECURITY IMPEDIMENTS TO REGIONALISM IN SOUTH ASIA

Feroz Hassan Khan

Regional integration efforts in South Asia remain stymied by interstate conflicts, internal challenges to domestic development, and global powers' security interests in the region. Key factors include India's asymmetric size and power, relative to the other South Asian states, and the capture of states' region-focused agendas—notably those of Bangladesh, India, and Pakistan—by territorial, religious, and ethnocentric interests.

Meanwhile, India's recent rise heralds both promise and danger for the future stability of this fragile region. On the one hand, India's leaders can use their position to help muster the collective will to make the difficult political decisions needed to stabilize the region. On the other hand, they may assert that their past decisions are immutable and that the rest of South Asia should adjust to India. Both stances are observed, leaving the region's future uncertain.[2] Pakistan and, to an extent, Bhutan and Nepal have sought to balance India's power by making alliances both interregional and external (as in the case of Pakistan's alliance with the United States and all-weather friendship with China).[3] India alleges that its smaller neighbors are also supporting cross-border ethnic tensions that further destabilize the region. India, in effect, serves as a hub of power to weaker nations, all of which have long-standing problems to resolve with it.

In this asymmetric environment, security concerns are the primary obstacle to integration. While some blame the region's fragmentation on Indian policy, few would dispute that, as of 2010, the security disputes between India and Pakistan are at the heart of the problem.

Accordingly, three main themes will be explored in this chapter, which focuses on the population centers of South Asia: Bangladesh, India, and Pakistan. First, India's economic rise has coincided somewhat accidentally with increasingly complex regional security issues such as violent extremism, water resource competition, increased migration, and nuclear weapons development. These and other issues challenge both India's political position and the region's prospects for integration. Second, some South Asian countries, notably Pakistan, fear a rising India based on India's past strategic behavior, but are so overwhelmed by their own internal security situations that they have little resources to expend toward regional security. The list of such countries has shortened with time, in part because most of the smaller countries have acquiesced to India playing a role in their security. It is, however, a variable list, with frequent entries and exits by countries such as Bhutan, Nepal, Bangladesh, and Sri Lanka. (As of 2010, the major responsibility for counterbalancing India seems to lie with Pakistan.) Third, international pressures, particularly the security interests of global powers, have thus far not provided individual countries with incentives to act in ways that might enhance regionalism and improve regional security.

In this chapter, I first assess the current state of security in the region, summarizing domestic and international crises, some of which continue to overwhelm the governments overseeing them. I then discuss India's rise in economic and political terms, and—based on the assumption that the success of South Asian regionalism primarily depends on India—I explore the strategic security choices that would promote regionalism. Also analyzed is the influence that major powers have on the development of South Asian security, using U.S. policy as an example. I conclude by making a case for the future of South Asian regionalism based on India's likely stance and its neighbors' likely responses.

The Current State of Regional Security in South Asia

South Asia has had a turbulent history of interstate rivalry and state consolidation. But, while India has stabilized with time, the woes of India's neighbors have only grown, with eruptions of internal strife and a lack of adequate mechanisms to contain it. In this chapter I argue that India's reluctance to promote regionalism is also responsible, in part, for the increase in its neighbors' security problems. To some of these countries, notably Pakistan, India's objective appears to be regional hegemony.[4] In the post–Cold War era, India has been both conciliatory and aggressive. The "Gujral doctrine," for example, prompted India's most conciliatory stance and notably improved relations with Sri Lanka, Bangladesh, and Pakistan.[5] The doctrine recommends engagement with India's smaller neighbors on the basis of non-reciprocity. It envisages "walking more than half the distance" in the pursuit of conflict resolution, envisioning India's rise on the wave of regional success.[6] In contrast, the "Gandhi doctrine" focuses on conserving India's energies by engaging the major global powers, and reconnection with the region and Indian Ocean littorals. This school of thought asks that India maintain a dominant posture and assertive policy toward its neighbors.

A key question here is whether India will act in its own interests—and pull the region along in its wake—or serve to facilitate greater regional integration. Outside factors undoubtedly play a role: globalizing trends, some Indian scholars believe, will "facilitate the integration of the region under Indian primacy."[7] The world's increasing economic interdependence could make traditional interstate security issues irrelevant. On the other hand, the challenges faced in South Asia are staggering and divisive, with terrorism and rising religious extremism being added to competing demand for energy, water, and food. As its economy has grown, India's attempts to walk alone—and ahead of its neighbors—have aggravated historic tensions, with Pakistan in particular. These are further compounded by intermittent terrorist attacks, for which India blames Pakistan, and the unresolved status of Kashmir.

Interstate Security Issues

Disputes over postcolonial state formation have evolved into seemingly irreconcilable divides. British imperial rule gathered the subcontinent into a common colonial system, but Britain's hasty retreat, instead of resolving the communal discords, created new cross-border issues that plague interstate relations even today.[8] Three issues overlaid differences between India and Pakistan over the ideology of the two-nation theory: Jammu and Kashmir; the distribution of assets at Partition; and the traumatic experience of the bloody migration of the people.[9] Similarly, the discord between Sri Lanka and India over the rights of Tamil nationals, including plantation workers, eventually resulted in a civil war that lasted nearly thirty years. The dispute between Bangladesh and India relates more to migration of East Bangladeshis, as well as water disputes. These are only three of the most outstanding examples. The bitterness generated between the ruling elites of the two major South Asian states—India and Pakistan—have gravely disrupted the cohesion forged in the nineteenth and early twentieth centuries. Indeed, the fact that Pakistan and Bangladesh are the severed limbs of what was once a united India under the British Raj speaks to the unique religious, ethnic, and linguistic complexities of the region.

Cross-border security issues not only remain largely unresolved but also became complicated over a period of time. Kashmir, for example, not only became a symbol of difference in ideology, but also of national identity.[10] And in some ways, the legacy of Partition's violent events still affect the policies of Pakistan and India.[11] Consequently, the two states have focused on both internal balancing (modernizing their armed forces and going nuclear) and external balancing (that is, forging alliances or "treaties of friendship" with great powers).[12] These moves have, in turn, contributed to the hardening of their respective stances on conflict resolution and the increasing frequency of cross-border crises. The nuclear capabilities of each only exacerbate the tensions inherent between the two countries, catalyzing yet more unilateral internal security-building measures. These capabilities have on the one hand contained crises and prevented major wars (deterrence optimism), but on the other, failed to prevent a series of military crises and dangerous confrontations (proliferation pessimism).[13] Meanwhile, violent extremism and terrorism imply that regional security issues are no longer the exclusive domain of any one state in the region.[14] Today, terrorist acts are not only affecting societies within South Asia; their ripple effects are felt around the globe. The stakes of conflict resolution now go far beyond the simple objective of regionalism.

India-Pakistan

Of course, the dominant interstate relationship in South Asia is that between India and Pakistan. The boundaries inherited by Pakistan and Bangladesh at Partition are unnatural and defenseless, and Pakistan's major cities and strategic arteries are perilously close to the Indian border. This lack of strategic depth leaves Pakistan perennially vulnerable to potential crisis or conventional war. Afghanistan disputes Pakistan's western borders and claims the entire Pashtu belt across the border in Pakistan. Pakistan's single port of Karachi would make a naval blockade easy. Bangladesh, a delta region of major rivers and tropical jungles, is exposed on all three sides. Inherited conflicts over disputed territories, cross-border movements, and distribution of resources has created a legacy of distrust among the South Asian Association for Regional Cooperation (SAARC) nations.

Jammu and Kashmir remain at the heart of the bitter rivalry and strategic competition between India and Pakistan. Kashmir became a seemingly irreconcilable issue after the region was split between India and Pakistan during a hurried Partition.[15] The conflict surrounding the area has since been interpreted in many ways: as the unfinished business of Partition, as a freedom struggle for the right of self-determination, as a territorial boundary dispute, a water-distribution dispute, a proxy war, and an excuse for cross-border terrorism.[16] Fundamentally, it remains the problem of a divided people, expressed in a military standoff along the Line of Control (LOC), now in its sixtieth year of eyeball-to-eyeball confrontation. No regional dispute in contemporary times has involved the investment of so much human and economic capital.[17] At another level, Kashmir now represents the diametrically opposed ideology between India and Pakistan. India claims Kashmir as the torchbearer of secularism even though the powerful influence of hardline Hindus remains effective in Indian polity. It therefore sees relinquishing the Muslim-dominated region as an anathema to its constitutional mandate.[18] Conversely, Pakistan, which was formed on the basis of protecting the rights of South Asian Muslims, sees the absorption of Kashmir as a national duty. These diametrically opposed schools of thought dominate Indo-Pak relations and do not bode well for regionalism.[19]

In addition to ideology, several practical issues are at stake. The seeds of the Siachen glacier controversy were sown when both sides mutually agreed not to demarcate the LOC beyond a point on the map called NJ 9842.[20] From that point, the distance to the Chinese border is 65 kilometers, an area not demarcated due to its inaccessibility.[21] Both India and Pakistan interpret the nondemarcation of this area in their own best interests.[22] India's position is that the de facto LOC extends along the high crests separating watersheds.[23] According to this interpretation, the delineation would be along the Saltoro ridgeline to the Chinese border in the vicinity of K-2.[24] The Pakistani argument is that the LOC extends beyond point NJ 9842 following its previous course, which places the Siachen glacier within Pakistani-controlled territory, terminating at the Karakoram pass.[25] From Pakistan's standpoint, Siachen is the eastern extremity of Baltistan, a subdivision of the Pakistani-controlled portion of the northern area that is clearly demarcated by the western boundary of the Nubra subdivision of Jammu and Kashmir's Laddakh district.[26] Pakistan further justifies its position by pointing out that major foreign mountaineering expeditions enter this area via Pakistan after getting formal permits.[27]

The Kashmiri uprising against India started in 1989, at a critical historical moment following the Soviet Union's withdrawal from Afghanistan and its subsequent collapse. The Kashmiri insurgency relied primarily on Pakistan, which, since 1994, had also been supporting the Taliban insurgency in Afghanistan, enabling demobilized warriors from Afghanistan to join the Kashmiri insurgents. This strategy of fueling a low-intensity war has tied down several hundred thousand Indian forces in Kashmir in a protracted counterinsurgency. Meanwhile, for the past several years, Pakistan is alleging India's complicity from Afghanistan in a rising insurgency in Pakistan's Baluchistan province. Additionally, well-endowed Islamic extremists have now begun operating across the arc of the entire region from Bangladesh to Afghanistan.[28]

India-Bangladesh

Since its division from India (1947) and then Pakistan (1971), Bangladesh has been a source of instability for the northeastern states of India. India's regional integration efforts and outward reach to Southeast Asia is stymied by conflicts with Bangladesh, including multiple insurgencies in India's northeast. In recent decades, despite ten years of democracy (1990–2001), rising Islamic militancy has deepened the crisis of governance in Bangladesh. Meanwhile, India alleges that terrorist attacks within its borders have connections to Bangladesh. Growing illegal immigration and cross-border movements into India have also raised tensions between the two SAARC neighbors. India has accused Bangladesh of conniving with Pakistan to destabilize India's northeast and also China of abetting insurgencies in northeastern India.[29] Porous borders facilitate illegal arms and narcotics trade, which in turn fund the separatist movements in India's northeast.[30] In opposition to Delhi's pressure on those issues, Dhaka has refused the transit of natural gas exports from the region.[31] Foreign direct investment (FDI) by Bangladesh in India has been heavily scrutinized and has greatly slowed down (and discouraged) cross-border economic dealings.[32]

India, Pakistan, and Afghanistan

Security dynamics in the borderlands of Afghanistan and Pakistan are no longer just regional issues but are now central to the global U.S.-led war on terrorism—with implications for the future of the region. The dispute goes back to 1893, when the British created a buffer between their imperial holdings and Czarist Russia. Now the border between Pakistan and Afghanistan, the

1,600-mile Durand line has been challenged by Afghans. The ethnic Pashtuns, who were divided as a result, never accepted it and treated it as if it were a "line drawn on water."[33] Kabul refused to recognize the newly independent Pakistan; in 1947 Afghanistan cast the sole vote against Pakistan's membership in the United Nations (UN) while laying claim to Baluchistan and the North-West Frontier Province (NWFP). Over the next decades, several clashes led to a severing of diplomatic relations between the two nations at various points in time. Then, in the 1980s, regional disputes become enmeshed in the Cold War as U.S.-supported Afghani insurgents battled their Marxist government and a Soviet invasion.[34]

Since, both India and Pakistan have competed for influence over Afghanistan.[35] India accuses Pakistan of using Afghan territory for training militants that wage jihad in Kashmir, denied by Pakistan; Afghanistan accuses Pakistan of continuing to support the Taliban, a charge also denied; and Pakistan, in turn, accuses India of conniving with Afghanistan to destabilize Pakistan and stoke irredentist claims, a charge denied by both Afghanistan and India.[36] The presence of the North Atlantic Treaty Organization (NATO) and U.S. forces in the region and the suspected presence of the al-Qaeda leadership in the area seem to have increased the region's volatility—something that was unexpected when U.S.-led forces invaded Afghanistan in 2001. As of 2010 the historical disputes, increasingly violent extremism, and abundance of terrorist havens around the tribal borderlands between Afghanistan and Pakistan have made it the front line of the war on terror.

Intrastate Security Issues

As might be expected, South Asian states, in their formative years, were more concerned with nation building than with developing external relations or state building.[37] The elite repeatedly overlooked the importance of developing the institutional capacity and legal accommodations necessary in the multiethnic, multireligious South Asian context.[38] Not surprisingly, most instances of armed conflict were intrastate rather than interstate, as is documented by several studies.[39] Intrastate conflict threatens each state with impending instability and is a security liability in the eyes of its neighbors.

India

After the various agitations and separatist movements of the 1950s subsided, a wave of organized insurgencies arose in the 1960s and 1970s. Generally, the violence can be categorized into two types: revolutionary and secessionist. Maoist organizations dedicated to the violent overthrow of the Indian government bloomed around the late 1960s, were largely suppressed during the 1970s, and have seen a steady increase in influence since the turn of the century. Naxalism, which typifies this movement, is still considered a serious threat to the central government's legitimacy and has significant influence throughout much of the country.[40] The Maoist movement, as it is called, focuses on tribal rights. Meanwhile, the Students Islamic Movement of India (SIMI), which emerged from a loosely organized group to command national attention as late as 2000, focuses on the rights of Muslim Indians.[41] While these movements pose a security threat, they do not challenge the borders of the Indian state.

Since the late 1980s secessionist violence has for the most part centered on the disputed territory of Kashmir, with grave implications for India-Pakistan relations. The Sikh insurgency, also secessionist, has been active from the 1970s. Although some argue that it still retains strong organizational capacity, its primary interest, the secession of Punjab, collapsed as a popular cause in the 1980s.[42]

Of all the insurgencies, little attention has been paid to the simmering low-intensity conflicts that plague India's northeastern states, also called the "seven sisters"; the most stubborn is in the second-largest "sister," Assam. Among other armed groups, the United Liberation Front of Assam (ULFA) has been active for twenty-nine years.[43] Problems that originated in arbitrary colonial boundaries have, through mismanagement, become regional security issues. Massive illegal immigration, much of it from Bangladesh, threatens Assamese identity and economic power.[44]

In sum, leftist, ethno-nationalist, and Islamist organizations have continued to survive amid India's economic liberalization and political decentralization. There is also strong anti-globalization sentiment in some parts of the country.[45] Rooted in decades of socialist, inward-looking policies, the country has cultivated a generational dependency on the welfare schemes of the central government. The vast numbers of the population who live below and just above the poverty line wield significant political power in the democracy. Even though stronger regional relationships would extend and broaden the economic gains of late, the risk posed by lower government protections against neighboring markets may be too much for the masses to accept.

Pakistan

Pakistan's state-formation issues are similarly complex. That nation building was prioritized over state building is evident, for example, in the push for Urdu as the national language. In 1954 the sacking of a top pro-Bengali politician by Pakistan's governor-general institutionalized authoritarian intervention in the name of nationalism.[46] Although Pakistan's two wings—East Pakistan (now Bangladesh) and West Pakistan (today's Pakistan)—were geographically divided, with India in between, there were centrifugal tendencies from its birth. Pakistan's two western provinces, the NWFP and Baluchistan, were initially wary of joining the new state, but they were coerced and persuaded into doing so (Pashtun and Baluch subnationalism is ongoing). The Federally Administered Tribal Areas (FATA) around the Afghanistan borderlands retain their autonomous stature to date, now legitimized in Pakistan's constitution. Added to this is the ongoing conflict with India over Kashmir.

Pakistan has focused most on the existential threat posed by India. This security imperative has forced Pakistan into external balancing, but even its long-standing alliance with the world's most powerful nations (United States and China) has not redressed Pakistani security concerns. Instead, Pakistan's reliance on U.S. support during its formative years—a counterbalance to the perceived threat of Indian hegemony—discouraged the development of state institutions in favor of the substantial and direct empowerment of the Pakistani military.[47] Triangulating statehood with religion (national identity) and ethnicity (subnationalism) was and remains a challenge of the first order. The result is a fundamental clash between the state and society—with no easy answer. Now, added to its history of weak state institutions and strained civil-military relations is the impact of 9/11—further dividing the interests of civil society from national security imperatives. This is unlikely to change in the near term. Ethnic crises in Sindh and Baluchistan continue to pose a problem in Pakistan, where threats of subnationalism do not subside.[48] Baluchistan's simmering state of low-level insurgency and unrest—ongoing for years—peaked as recently as 2006. The area is critical because of its strategic location as a corridor for energy pipelines and because its coastline has the potential to affect future trade in the region, alleviating or instigating new regional security concerns.

As the cases of India and Pakistan illustrate, even the stronger South Asian states suffer from serious intrastate issues. Some such problems—such as Kashmir's status—have interstate dimensions, further complicating the situation and making regional cooperation more unlikely.

India's Economic and Geopolitical Rise

India's economic and consequent geopolitical rise has occurred in a fairly short period of time. Apart from its responses to the dictates of a market economy—open to global influences since the economic reforms of the early 1990s—there are several political factors supporting its ascendance. First of these is India's robust democratic institutions, inherited from the British colonial system.[49] Jawaharlal Nehru, India's first prime minister, remained the leader of the country for seventeen years, which helped sustain India's democracy even though he followed a strong centralist policy designed to mitigate separatist trends. The second factor is India's relative geopolitical insularity. The Indian Ocean, the Himalayas, and the nations of Pakistan, Bangladesh, and Nepal act as buffers protecting it from direct outside threat. While Partition physically separated India from the Persian Gulf, Central Asia, and Southeast Asia on the one hand, on the other it allowed India to escape the consequences of the rough border dynamics of Afghanistan in Central Asia and the instabilities of the tropical jungles to India's east.[50] Except for a border problem with its strongest neighbor, China, which led to a brief war in 1962, the relatively powerful Indian military has found itself unmatched at borders with weaker nations' smaller militaries.

Third is the systemic change that India underwent when the Cold War ended, marking the end of its dependence on the Soviet Union. Post–Cold War India was seen as "a political West" outside Western countries: a multiethnic, multireligious country with the credentials of being a sustained democracy.[51] It has been able to leverage this identity to obtain the FDI and other support essential for its growth in a globalizing world economy. The fourth factor is India's soft power, manifest in a vibrant culture and a business-oriented society. The nation's economic turnaround post–Cold War is truly remarkable. After decades of autarky and sluggish performance, India's newly globalized economy successfully leveraged skills in information technology (IT) at the dawn of the information age. India's rise must also be seen in the context of its relations with Pakistan. In 1986–1987 the Indian army decided to challenge Pakistan in the famous military crisis known as Operation Brass Tacks, which followed India's surprise occupation of the Siachen Glacier, another significant crisis, just two years earlier. Both events brought the two countries to the brink of war, prompting quiet U.S. diplomacy to diffuse the tension. Soon after, rigged state elections in Jammu and Kashmir boiled over into an insurgency, which was exploited by Pakistan through military and financial support. This crisis, too, led both countries to the brink of war in 1990, an event which still overshadows Indo-Pak relations. These crises laid the foundations for two more: one in Kargil 1999 and another, compound crisis (Operation Parakaram), 2001–2002.

Meanwhile, India's rise confronted that of China. Concurrent with Operation Brass Tacks, India launched another exercise—code-named Chequer Board—in the Sumdurru Chu Valley that nearly erupted into a full-scale border clash with China. Several other incidents had already cast doubt on the future relations of the world's two most populous nations. The first was India's upgrading of the North-East Frontier Agency (NEFA) to the state of Arunachal Pradesh in December 1986. This implied that the disputed territory was absorbed into the Indian state. This incurred strong protest from Beijing, which charged that India had "seriously violated" China's territorial integrity and sovereignty. The second was the 1986–1987 border standoff in Sumdurru Chu in the eastern sector, where both sides deployed large number of troops and which almost escalated into an open conflict.[52]

India has, however, made progress in establishing itself as the key power on the Indian Ocean. This goes back to India's investments in naval power in the 1980s. In 1988 an attempted coup against President Gayoom of the Maldives prompted the Indian navy to send a task force to provide support. The amphibious intervention intended to restore the government. The Maldives, a state of multiple archipelagos, was insignificant from a security point of view; but the political success, including accolades from Washington, encouraged India's regional intervention and probably created the foundation for India's blue-water navy. Subsequently, South Asia has witnessed an emergence of Indian naval power and positive security roles in piracy, trafficking, and disaster relief.

By far the most muscular display of India's geopolitical power was its intervention in Sri Lanka, which was done in a manner that recalls America's enactment of the Monroe Doctrine. After years of abetting the Tamil insurgency in Sri Lanka, India decided to reverse its policy by introducing a peace accord between the Tamils and the incumbent Sinhalese regime and by cracking down on Tamil militancy. India signed the peace accord, which formalized India's commitment to end support to the Tamil insurgency by denying its own territory as a refuge and financing center for insurgents. Overall, the accord was humiliating to many Sri Lankans,[53] as it reflected what appeared to be India's hegemonic attitude toward the tiny island, blatantly undermining Sri Lankan sovereignty (as demonstrated in follow-up letters from Rajiv Gandhi to President J. R. Jayewardene).[54] The Indian peacekeeping intervention failed to subdue the Tamil insurgents, and India finally had to withdraw in the face of growing domestic insurgencies.

From the above analysis, it appears that India has, though somewhat tentatively, sought to leverage its growing economic strength to achieve regional political dominance. This is how a regional hegemony—undoubtedly a term laden with all sorts of undesirable implications—is defined. While still disputed, it should also be clear, as many chapters in this volume conclude,[55] that India's centrality is probably inevitable. Properly used, the power implied by India's position can be a strong and positive force for development. But this power has not always been so utilized; in the case of Pakistan, for example, India's attitude has almost invariably been counterproductive, while the opposite, as employed during the brief period of the Gujral doctrine, has been beneficial.[56]

Efforts to Resolve the India-Pakistan Conflict

Despite their contentious and rigid positions, India and Pakistan have made significant efforts to resolve cross-border issues whenever the moment seemed ripe to do so. At least four such moments can be cited: Tashkent in 1966, Simla in 1972, Lahore in 1999, and Islamabad in 2004.[57] Made after the 1971 war, the historic Simla Agreement of 1972 is still central to the commitment that binds both countries to seek a peaceful resolution. In particular, Article 4 obliges both sides to respect the LOC "without prejudice to the recognized position of either side."[58] Since 1997 India and Pakistan have been engaged in composite dialogue, which broke off after Kargil 1999 but was reiterated in a joint statement of President Musharraf and Prime Minister Vajpayee on January 6, 2004.[59]

In 2008 two developments occurred. First was the peaceful uprising in Kashmir in the late summer of 2008, which India suppressed by force. The second was the Mumbai terror attacks, which stalled all dialogue.[60] The dialogue resumed in February 25, 2010, but made no substantive progress. Earlier, on May 21, 2008, Pakistani foreign minister Shah Mahmood Qureshi and Indian external affairs minister Pranab Mukherjee had met to review the progress made in the fourth round of the composite dialogue. This ministerial-level meeting was preceded by a meeting between the foreign secretaries of both sides, Pakistan's Salman Bashir and India's Shivshankar Menon, on May 20, 2008. Before the Mumbai attacks the positions of both India and Pakistan were outlined on a number of issues, summarized below.

Kashmir

According a joint statement, both sides agreed to refrain from adopting hostile propaganda on the issue of terrorism and agreed that

> [T]o increase the frequency of Muzaffarabad Srinagar and Rawalkot-Poonch Bus service from a fortnightly to a weekly basis; to finalize modalities for intra-Kashmir trade and truck service as early as possible; to implement other measures to expand and facilitate travel a meeting of the Working Group on Cross-LOC CBMs would be convened within two months.[61]

An important dimension of the Kashmir problem pertains to river flows, as nearly all rivers flowing into Pakistan have their origin in Kashmir. In 1960 arbitration by the World Bank resulted in the Indus Water Basin Treaty. This treaty has survived several wars and military crises. But the construction of the Baglihar dam upstream in Indian Kashmir, which Pakistan believes to be in violation of the treaty 1960, has exacerbated the issue. The Baglihar dam controversy erupted when India dismissed Pakistani objections to the dam's design and Pakistan referred the issue to a World Bank tribunal. The World Bank's decision was that it would allow India to construct the dam, but partially accept Pakistan's objections as well. This dispute has added another layer of distrust to India-Pakistan relations, with direct implications for the prospects of regionalism as Pakistan strengthens its belief that India is unprepared to concede anything not to its advantage.

The Siachen Glacier

According to Shivshankar Menon, the former Indian foreign secretary and current national security adviser to the prime minister of India, considerable progress has been made by both the sides on the issues of Sir Creek and Siachen. The issue of Sir Creek is a dispute between India and Pakistan over their boundary along a creek that adjoins the delta region of the India and Pakistan border. The demarcation of the Sir Creek boundary would have eventually created a focal point from where the maritime boundaries between India and Pakistan could be delineated in the future. According to Menon: "In Siachen, we have to deal with environmental consequences and explore the possibilities of mountain climbing. Another proposal is to make it a mountain of peace and in the Sir Creek case, a lot of progress has been made. We have completed a joint survey and have a common map now."[62] According to a joint statement of May 21, 2008, "Both sides exchanged views on Siachen and reiterated their commitment to seeking an early amicable solution."

Baglihar and Other Dams

No settlements have been made since the composite dialogue started in 2004. After the fourth round of composite dialogue, although no reference was made to progress on the Wuller barrage and Baglihar dam, the Pakistani Indus water commissioner, Jamat Ali Shah, and his Indian counterpart, Oranga Nathan, stated in a joint press conference held on May 31, 2008, that both Pakistan and India have allowed each other to inspect the Baglihar dam and Neelum-Jhelum Hydropower Project. According to the Associated Press of Pakistan, "India has assured Pakistan that the Baglihar Dam is being built in line with the recommendations of the neutral expert's commission."[63] Furthermore, Jamat Ali Shah stated, "Pakistan had also pointed out that the Indian design for the dam was structurally unsafe. Pakistan had reservations over the storage capacity of the proposed dam, diversion of a river over which the dam was to be constructed and the de-silting process," adding that Pakistan also had reservations on the Indian formula of water storage.[64]

Meanwhile, India has expedited work on the Kishanganga water project, citing that Pakistan was also constructing a power project on its side of the same river (named River Neelum in Pakistan).[65] Moreover, the Indian union minister for power, Jairam Ramesh, was quoted as saying that the "National Hydroelectric Power Corporation (NHPC) will have to work faster on the Kishanganga power project in wake of Islamabad's efforts to complete the Neelam-Jhelum project on the other side of the LOC by 2015." However, he admitted that the stand-off between India and Pakistan over the two projects has geo-strategic implications.[66] Indian concern about the Pakistani project also stemmed from the fact that "over 2,000 Chinese engineers would be working very close to the LOC for the next eight years."[67]

An optimistic note may be struck from the above analyses. Despite the passage of time, there have been recurring talks during which both sides appeared to make progress. While in the Western press Pakistan appears to be on the wrong side of history as an Islamic nation, it continues to push for closer engagement with the United States even as it prioritizes the Kashmiri cause. As such, Pakistan hopes to raise awareness that the Kashmiri insurgency is not just "cross-border terrorism," even as India refuses to go beyond a bilateral approach. The attitude of President Obama's administration toward Kashmir is likely to be muted as it tackles what are, from the U.S. viewpoint, the more serious problems of the global economic downturn and the Taliban and al-Qaeda in Afghanistan. Meanwhile, Pakistan sees the prospects of Indian hegemony on the ascendant, a predicament summed up by Henry Sokolski as follows:

Pakistan now has to be concerned not just about maintaining good relations with Washington, but somehow fending off the encircling efforts of India. Most recently, these activities included formal military-to-military ties with Iran; the construction of a major naval port at Chahbahar near Pakistan's own new naval base at Gwador; the joint construction with Iran of roads to Afghanistan (and Indian aid efforts to Afghanistan); the stationing of Indian intelligence officers at Zahedan, Iran close to Baluchistan rebel activities in Pakistan; the creation of an Indian air base in Tajikistan; Indian energy investments and commerce with Iran and other Gulf countries; and continued Indian military, nuclear, and rocket enhancements. All of these developments have put Pakistan's military and political officials on edge.[68]

International Influence on India's Regional Policies

This section examines the role of the United States in South Asian regional security. China and the Soviet Union (and Russia to a lesser extent) do wield and have wielded their influence, too. Sometimes their policies were specifically to balance or counter those of the United States in Pakistan, India, or Afghanistan. Documenting all the strategic movements of the major powers goes beyond the scope of this chapter, which only strives to characterize how erratic and misguided major power involvements have adversely affected long-term regional security. Reviewing the U.S. policies in South Asia accomplishes this aim.

The Legacy of U.S. Intervention

U.S. policies have had a paradoxical impact on the South Asian region. The United States played a critical role, often underappreciated in the region, in bolstering Pakistan's survival as a nation, especially in the initial decades of its existence. U.S. military and economic support was central to Pakistani national confidence by the early 1960s.[69] Overall, however, the manner in which the United States pursued its own security interests inadvertently risked the regional integration process. This section will explain how the U.S. policy of balancing India and Pakistan caused security dilemmas within the region and affected the attitudes of regional players. The implication is that shortsighted policies impeded rather than promoted harmony and peace in the region.

U.S. foreign policy has generally shifted priorities based on perceived threats. South Asia specifically has been a marginal and strategic backwater for most of the second half of the twentieth century. The U.S. episodic focus on South Asia hardened the position of states and inadvertently compounded conflict resolution—thus obstructing regional integration.[70]

With two wings separated by a hostile India, a nascent Pakistan fought a war over Kashmir in the midst of the traumatic conditions unleashed by Partition. Pakistan faced enormous challenges early on, especially in defense of its territory. According to an American assessment, by the time a ceasefire along the LOC in Kashmir had been reached in 1949, the 137,000 Pakistani troops that were facing a 640,000-strong Indian army were "barely sufficient to meet the existing demands of [Pakistan's] internal security."[71] Pakistan was simultaneously confronted by another unfriendly neighbor: Afghanistan decided to renege on the border agreement of 1893 with the British through a parliamentary resolution, having earlier vetoed Pakistani membership to the United Nations on the same basis. This step essentially implied a reclaiming of the Pashtu belt of Pakistan's western provinces. This Pashtunistan movement, as it became known at the time, was abetted and encouraged by India. Jinnah, a great admirer of the United States, made desperate requests to the United States, which were repeatedly turned down[72] because Washington's focus was on India at the time; meanwhile, the Indian military received due attention from the U.S. State Department.[73]

Two events changed the U.S. focus: the Korean War and South Asian security developments. In 1951, amidst a military standoff with India; domestic political crises, including a threat of a communist coup (the Rawalpindi Conspiracy Case); and the assassination of Prime Minister Liaquat Ali Khan, Pakistan became important to Washington. Earlier, Pakistan's willingness to send troops to Korea—even as India proved unwilling—had left a positive impression on U.S. policymakers. Finally, in the 1950s, during President Eisenhower's administration, Pakistan became a formal member of the U.S.-led collective security arrangement involving a series of entangling alliances promoted by the United States to contain the spread of Communism. India was pursuing a nonaligned policy, but its inward-looking and leftist policies were more compatible with Communism, so it leaned toward the Soviet Union. For U.S. policymakers, Pakistan formed an essential part of the "northern tier of the Middle East."[74] Pakistan, on the other hand, saw the U.S. alliance as a means to balance its structural asymmetry with India. Regardless of their reasonings, Pakistan was not only standing on its own feet by the mid-1960s but was a model state boasting an average of 6 percent annual growth of its gross domestic product (GDP), despite unsettling political events within the country.[75] In the next four decades, wars, crises, and insurrections weakened the U.S. incentive to proactively involve itself in regional affairs, thereby dampening the potential for regional conflict resolution.

U.S. Roles: Objectives and Consequences

Armed with incoherent policies that did not reflect any cohesive strategy in the region, the United States failed to find a "regional supporter state in South Asia that would steward U.S. interests in the region."[76] These failed policies alone did not trigger regional problems, but Washington's approach to the region, even armed with the best of intentions, inadvertently hindered regional stability. The United States' commitment in the Cold War forced it to think of South Asia as a strategic backwater. Indian dominance was evident but there were large disputes leading to major regional crises. Propping up India as a regional hegemon would have required intense U.S. engagement in the region, which was further complicated by India's nonaligned independent position, as well its close alliance with the Soviet Union. These factors made any involvement a much more complicated exercise than Washington wanted. India, on the other hand, abhorred outside intervention and insisted on bilateral solutions to regional issues. This brought neither conflict resolution nor regional acceptance of India as a leader. An accepted hegemony required either absence of outside influence or acceptance of outside mediators when conflicting parties were unable to find a common denominator.[77] India's forays into regional hegemony have been unevenly supported by the United States, and its strategic behavior has not encouraged trust and support from its smaller neighbors.

In the 1980s, while Pakistan's importance as a front-line state was enhanced due to the Soviet Union's engagement in Afghanistan, the Reagan administration tacitly fed India's ambitions, hoping they would bolster U.S. strategic interests in the region. India was encouraged to assert itself with all its neighbors (Sri Lanka, for example), but this ended up having negative rather than positive consequences for regional security. India had no economic clout to offer its unequal neighbors, nor the political will to scale down its maximalist negotiating position. India's military exercises (Brass Tacks and Checker Board, for example, 1986–87) only exacerbated tensions, and thus the region suffers to date.

U.S. Encouragement of a Regional Approach

Twice the United States appointed a person to facilitate crises in the South Asian region, leading to possible conflict resolution and regional integration. First, in the 1960s, President Kennedy appointed Averell Harriman in the wake of the Sino-Indian crises; Harriman attempted to negotiate a Kashmir settlement. (The role of Ambassador Harriman ended with President Kennedy's death.) Then in 1998 President Clinton appointed Strobe Talbott, first to manage the crises following the nuclear tests and second to negotiate U.S. policy toward the region.

Strobe Talbot's engagement with India (and lack of it with Pakistan) was a turning point and laid the groundwork for an India-centric U.S. policy in the region.[78] The new U.S. regional policy of delinking India and Pakistan, based on the size and role of each country, made sense on one level; but nuclear weapons in the midst of a complex security situation and an intertwined geography "interlock the fate of the region."[79] The new U.S. regional policy hardened India's attitude toward its neighbors, reinforcing India's contention that they were failed states and that even equating India with them was an insult. India's regional ambition has since grown into a belief that it is now in the big leagues, with no incentive for magnanimity.

Since 9/11 Pakistan has become a front-line state in the war against terrorism. But unlike the Cold War era, when South Asia's importance was derivative to Soviet and American strategic behavior, the region now has direct relevance for international security. This has opened the door for major powers as well as the international community at large to reassess their South Asian policies in a new light. Instead of assisting or shunning individual countries in a bid to enhance their own interests, there exists an opportunity to break from traditional policies and engage in cooperative dialogues designed to enhance the prospects of long-term stability, sacrificing—at most—some short-term political gains.

Conclusion: The Future of South Asian Regionalism and Security

Interstate and intrastate issues, cross-border tensions, and the inconsistent interests of global powers in the region have shaped the architecture of regional security and obstructed regional integration. In this chapter I argue that India has been an unsteady proponent of South Asian regionalism, driven by its own varying assessments of its role in the region. This has meant that, on occasion, it has sought to exert its political will across borders. India's involvement has sometimes been accepted by its neighbors, either explicitly, such as in Nepal's treaties with India, or implicitly, such as in Sri Lanka's request for Indian help in the mid-1980s. At other times, and particularly in relation to India's unresolved issues with Pakistan, such behavior has been deemed unacceptable. At the same time, India's economic rise promises regional benefits if it exerts its political will with the idea of helping development. This will undoubtedly require sacrifices on all sides. Meanwhile, India-Pakistan tensions remain unabated, even as other countries in South Asia have accepted India's economic dominance and are keen to work with it to improve their own conditions. Properly shaped U.S., Russian, and Chinese policies can encourage South Asian countries to modify their strategic behavior toward their neighbors, thereby enhancing the region's global standing, strategic stability, and long-term security.

Notes

[1] The author is indebted to Lieutenant Commander Robert "Kelly," Federal U.S. Navy, M.A., National Security Affairs, Naval Postgraduate School, Monterey, CA; and Nick M. Masellis, M.S. Defense Analysis & Research Associate at the Center for Contemporary Conflict, Department of National Security Affairs, Naval Postgraduate School, for valuable research support and drafting. Thanks also due to Ms. Rabia Akhtar, PhD candidate, Quaid-e Azam University, Islamabad, for valuable research material from Islamabad.

[2] Former Indian foreign secretary Saran has stated, "Our neighbors should view us as an opportunity, not as a threat"; see also Saurabh Shukla, "Trouble in the Backyard; with Six of its Neighbours Ranking High on a Global Roster of Failed States, there is a Renewed Warning for India to Reassess its Policy Towards Them and Safeguard its Own Strategic Interests," *India Today*, May 2006, 68.

[3] Praful Bidwai, "India: World Influence Buys New Delhi Little in its Own Back Yard," *Global Information Network*, March 23, 2006, 1.

[4] Manjeet Singh Pardesi, "Deducing India's Grand Strategy of Regional Hegemony from Historical and Conceptual Perspectives," Draft Working Paper 76, Institute of

Defense and Strategic Studies, Singapore, April 2005, www.ntu.edu.sg/rsis/publications/workingpapers.asp?selYear=2005.

[5] See also Sohban, chapter 4, and Kelegama, chapter 8, in this volume.

[6] C. Raja Mohan, *Crossing the Rubicon: The Shaping of India's New Foreign Policy* (New Delhi: Viking, 2004), 156.

[7] Mohan, *Crossing the Rubicon*, 155–56.

[8] For a detailed account of the hurried departure of Britain, see Stanley Wolpert, *Shameful Flight* (New York: Oxford Univ. Press, 2006).

[9] The rational of the two-nation theory was that the Muslims in the subcontinent claimed entitlement to a separate nation-state because of the belief that their distinct culture, religious practices, and way of life would be fundamentally affected under a Hindu dominated system. They claimed nationhood based on geographic continuity of Muslim populations in the northwest, northeast, and south of India. In 1947 the British accepted the demand of the Muslim League, which became the basis of the Partition of India and Pakistan. The question of princely states remained undecided at the time of partition. One such state, Jammu and Kashmir, became the bone of contention between the two countries. For details see Victoria Schofield, *Kashmir and Conflict, India, Pakistan and the Unfinished War* (London: I. B. Tauris, 2000).

[10] For a comprehensive analysis, see Vali Nasr, "National Identities and the India-Pakistan," in *The India-Pakistan Conflict: An Enduring Rivalry*, ed. T. V. Paul (New York: Cambridge Univ. Press, 2005), 178–201.

[11] Rifaat Hussain, "The India-Pakistan Peace Process," *Defense & Security Analysis* 22, no. 4 (2006): 409.

[12] Stephen P. Cohen, *India: Emerging Power* (Washington, D.C.: Brookings Institution Press, 2001), 204, 209–11.

[13] Scott D. Sagan and Kenneth N. Waltz, *The Spread of Nuclear Weapons: A Debate Renewed* (New York: W. W. Norton & Company, Inc., 2003).

[14] Right-wing politics in both India and Pakistan generate religious hatred and extremist ideological positions. A ritual cleaning act was performed by Jamiat-i-Islami and Shiv Sena, respectively, after Prime Minister Vajpayee's visit to the Pakistan Monument in 1999 and President Musharraf's visit to the Gandhi Memorial in 2001. See Rizwan Zeb and Suba Chandran, "Indo-Pak Conflicts Ripe to Resolve," RCSS Policy Studies 34, Regional Center for Strategic Studies, Colombo, 2005, 23.

[15] See Wolpert, *Shameful Flight*.

[16] For themes in Kashmiri nationalism, see Maya Chadda, *Ethnicity, Security and Separatism in India*, (New York: Columbia Univ. Press, 1997), 49–76. Also see Stephen M. Saideman, "At the Heart of the Conflict: Irredentism in Kashmir," in *The India-Pakistan Conflict: An Enduring Rivalry*, ed. T. V. Paul, 202–24.

[17] For an analysis of the cost of India and Pakistan rivalry, see Maj. Gen. (Retd.) Mahmud Ali Durrani, *India and Pakistan: The Cost of Conflict, The Benefits of Peace* (Washington, D.C.: The Johns Hopkins Univ. Press, 2000). For a critique of Pakistan security policy, see Ahmad Faruqui, *Rethinking the National Security of Pakistan: The Price of Strategic Myopia* (Burlington, VA: Ashgate Publishing Limited, 2003).

[18] For a detailed account read Sumit Ganguly, *Conflict Unending: India-Pakistan Tensions since 1947* (Washington, D.C.: Woodrow Wilson Center Press, 2001). Also see Robert G. Wirsing, *Kashmir in the Shadow of War: Regional Rivalries in a Nuclear Age* (New York: M. E. Sharpe Inc., 2003), 137–81.

[19] See Robert G. Wirsing, *Kashmir in the Shadow of War: Regional Rivalries in a Nuclear Age* (New York: M. E. Sharpe Inc., 2003), 137–81.

[20] The demarcation is delineated as "From Delunang onwards the cease-fire line (CFL) will follow the general line (Point 15495), Ishmam, Manus, Gangam Gunderman (Point 13620), Junkar (Point 17628), Marmak, Natsara, Shungruti (Point 17531), Chorbat La (Point 16700), Chalunka (on the Shyok river), Khor, thence north to the glaciers."

[21] Robert G. Wirsing, "The Siachin Glacier Dispute: Can Diplomacy Untangle It," *Indian Defence Review* (July 1991): 95. Also see Zafar Iqbal Cheema, "The Strategic Context of the Kargil Conflict: A Pakistani Perspective," in *Asymmetric Warfare in South Asia: The Causes and Consequences of the Kargil Conflict*, ed. Peter R. Lavoy (New York: Cambridge Univ. Press, 2009), 48.

[22] Robert G. Wirsing, *Pakistan's Security under Zia, 1977–1988: The Policy Imperatives of Peripheral Asian State* (New York: St. Martin's Press, 1991), 156.

[23] Maj. Gen. (Retd.) Tariq Mahmood, "Siachin Dispute and Status of Northern Areas," *Defence Journal* 19, nos. 5–6 (1993): 21.

[24] According to the Indian argument, the Saltoro Range is northwest of the great Karakoram Range, which begins at Sia Kangri and terminates at Shyok and Nubra Valley. See, for example, Jasjit Singh, "Siachin Glacier: Facts and Fiction," *Strategic Studies* 12, no. 7 (1987): 667.

[25] Lt. Gen. (Retd.) M. I. Chibber, "Siachin: The Untold Story (A Personal Account)," *Indian Defence Review* (July 1989): 146.

[26] Raspal S. Khosa, "The Siachin Glacier Dispute; Imbroglio on the Roof of the World," *Contemporary South Asia* 8, no. 2 (July 1999): 194.

[27] Wirsing, *Pakistan's Security under Zia*, 154.

[28] After 9/11 Pakistan decided to eschew supporting insurgencies in the region. This change in policy resulted in a spate of suicide bombings that created unprecedented terror in the country. There were sixty-five suicide attacks in 2007 that primarily targeted the military and intelligence agencies.

[29] Sumit Ganguly, "The Rise of Islamist Militancy in Bangladesh," Special Report 171, United States Institute of Peace (USIP), Washington, D.C., August 2007.

[30] "Bangladesh: Eastward Policy Limited by India Influence," *OxResearch*, April 25, 2003, 1.

[31] Ibid.

[32] Puja Mehra, "Eagle Eye On FDI; Concerned about National Security, the Centre Plans a Law to Make Foreign Investment Terror-Proof," *India Today* (September 25, 2006): 58.

[33] Vartan Gregorian, "The Yearnings of the Pakhtoons," *New York Times* (November 15, 2001), 31, and earlier work by the same author, *The Emergence of Modern Afghanistan: Politics of Reform and Modernization, 1880–1946* (Stanford, CA: Stanford Univ. Press, 1969).

[34] For a comprehensive analysis of the war against Soviet occupation in Afghanistan, see Coll, Steve, *Ghost Wars* (New York: Penguin, 2004).

[35] The fourth regional player is Iran, with strategic interests in Afghanistan. Pakistan fears encirclement and strategic networking among the three countries.

[36] Henry D. Sokolski, ed., *Pakistan's Nuclear Future: Worries Beyond War* (Carlisle Barracks, PA: Army War College, January 2008), 3.

[37] Sumantra Bose, "Decolonization and State Building in South Asia," *Journal of International Affairs* 58, no. 1 (2004): 95–114.

[38] Intrastate conflict is defined as armed conflict between two groups, of which one is the state, and in which violence is used by either or both parties resulting in human and material casualties. Suba Chandran, "Intrastate Armed Conflicts in South Asia: Impact on Regional Security," in *Comprehensive Security in South Asia*, ed. Dev Raj Dahal and Nishchal Nath Pandey (New Delhi: Manohar Publishers, 2006), 159.

[39] Chandran, "Intrastate Armed Conflicts in South Asia," 159–75.

[40] As a testament to the scale of the problem, in April 2006, Prime Minister Manmohan Singh stated that the Naxalites were the "single biggest internal security challenge" ever faced by the country. See "India Politics: Naxalites Pose Internal Security Threat," *EIU ViewsWire*, New York, October 25, 2006.

[41] "Student's Islamic Movement of India (SIMI)," *South Asia Terrorism Portal*, www.satp.org/satporgtp/countries/india/terroristoutfits/simi.htm.

[42] Ibid.

[43] "In the first half of 2007 alone, Indian Ministry of Home Affairs reported 156 insurgency-related incidents took place in Assam between January 1, 2007, and March 31, 2007. ULFA was accused of carrying out 68 attacks in upper Assam between January 1, 2007, and June 10, 2007, killing 81 civilians, and 11 soldiers." *South Asian Terrorism Portal*, www.satp.org/satporgtp/countries/india/states/assam/timelines/index.html.

[44] Sumit Ganguly, "The Rise of Islamists Militancy in Bangladesh," USIP, August 2007.

[45] Sadanand Dhume, "Is India an Ally?" *Commentary* 125 (2008): 25–30; and Shoba S. Rajgopal, "Reclaiming Democracy? The Anti-Globalization Movement in South Asia," *Feminist Review* 70 (2002): 134–37.

[46] Bose, "Decolonization and State Building in South Asia," 95–114.

[47] Ibid.

[48] Subrata K. Mitra and R. Alison Lewis, eds., *Sub Nationalism in South Asia* (Boulder, CO: Westview Press, 1996), 43– 103.

[49] See also Embree, chapter 10 in this volume.

[50] India's northeastern states—Assam in particular—still face secessionist threats, while the areas around Burma and Bangladesh remain troubled.

[51] Raja Mohan, "India and Balance of Power," *Foreign Affairs* 85, no. 4 (July/August 2006): 18.

[52] For background and analysis, see Robert G. Sutter, *China-India Border Friction: Background Information and Possible Implications*, CRS Report for Congress 87-514F, June 19, 1987. See also Salamat Ali, "Tension on the Border," *FEER*, May 7, 1987, 33–35; David Bonavia, "Troubled Frontiers," *FEER*, September 4, 1986, 14–15; "Eye-Witness in Tibet," *FEER*, June 4, 1987, 46; Salamat Ali, "China Ups the Ante," *FEER*, May 21, 1987, 40. Also see Waheguru Pal Siddhu and Jing Dong Yuan, "Cooperative Monitoring for Confidence Building: A Case Study of Sino- India Border Areas," Occasional Paper 13, Sandia National Laboratories, Albuquerque, NM (August 1999), 15.

[53] An expression of this humiliation, a Sri Lankan sailor attacked Prime Minister Rajiv Gandhi when he was reviewing the parade at Colombo a day after signing the accord. For details on the attack, see Victoria Graham, "Honor Guardsman Strikes Indian Leader with Rifle," *Associated Press*, New Delhi, July 30, 1987; Dilip Ganguly, "Indian Prime Minister Hit by Guard," *Associated Press*, New Delhi, July 30, 1987; Anonymous, "Rajiv Gandhi's Assailant to Face Court Martial in Sri Lanka," *Xinhua News Service*, Colombo, August 3, 1987; Anonymous, "Mother Calls Son's Attack on Gandhi 'Regrettable Act'," *Associated Press*, Colombo, August 5, 1987; Sachi Sri

Kantha, "The Botched JVP Hit on Rajiv Gandhi Revisited," www.tamilnation.org/forum/sachisrikantha/060729rajiv_jvp.htm.

[54] India followed up with a letter signed by Prime Minster Gandhi to the President of Sri Lanka in which Indian concerns were spelled out: *I) Your Excellency and myself will reach an early understanding about the relevance and employment of foreign military and intelligence personnel with a view to ensuring that such presences will not prejudice Indo Sri Lanka relations. II) Trincomalee or any other ports in Sri Lanka will not be made available for military use by any country in a manner prejudicial to India's interests. III) The work of restoring and operating the Trincomalee Oil Tank will be undertaken as a joint operation between India and Sri Lanka. IV) Sri Lanka's agreement with foreign broadcasting organizations will be reviewed to ensure that any facilities set up by them in Sri Lanka are used solely as public broadcasting facilities and not for any military or intelligence purposes.* See text of the accord at www.tamilnation.org/conflictresolution/Tamileelam/87peaceaccord.html. Extract drawn from J. N. Dixit, *Assignment Colombo* (New Delhi: Konarak Publishers, 1998). Dixit was the Indian Ambassador to Sri Lanka (work cited in above link).

[55] See, for example, Sobhan, chapter 4, and Kelegama, chapter 8, in this volume.

[56] This observation is more true of India's dealing with Pakistan and is based on the author's personal experience of negotiating peace, security, and confidence-building measures (CBMs) and dialogue with India in 1998–2001, as well as the author's subsequent discussions with officials in the Pakistan foreign ministry and military.

[57] For analysis of the ripeness theory of conflict resolution, see Zeb and Chandran, "Indo-Pak Conflicts Ripe to Resolve."

[58] The text of the Simla Agreement is available at www.stimson.org/southasia/?SN=SA20020114291.

[59] The eight agenda items for the fourth round of the composite dialogue were: (1) peace and security including confidence-building measures (CBMs) (2) Jammu and Kashmir, (3) Siachen, (4) Sir Creek, (5) Wullar barrage, (6) terrorism and drug trafficking, (7) economic and commercial cooperation, and (8) promotion of friendly exchanges.

[60] Spokesman Briefings, Ministry of Foreign Affairs, Pakistan, May 15, 2008, www.mofa.gov.pk/Spokesperson/2008/May/Spokes_15_05_08.htm.

[61] Ibid.

[62] "Siachin, Sir Creek Issues Solvable: India," *Thaindian News,* May 20, 2008, www.thaindian.com/newsportal/uncategorized/siachen-sir-creek-issues-solvable-india_10050859.html.

[63] "Pak, India Allow Each Other for Hydel Power Projects Inspection," *Associated Press of Pakistan (APP),* May 31, 2008, www.app.com.pk/en_/index.php?option=com_content&task=view&id=39971&Itemid=2.

[64] "Indo-Pak Talks on Water Projects Inconclusive," *Daily Times,* June 2, 2008.

[65] "India to Speed Up Work on Kishanganga," *The DAWN,* June 8, 2008.

[66] "War Over Kashmir Water Heats Up," *The Economic Times,* June 8, 2008.

[67] Ibid.

[68] Sokolski, *Pakistan's Nuclear Future,* 3.

[69] U.S. support to Pakistan in the 1950s, '60s, '80s, and after 9/11 has repeatedly bailed the country out of economic crises. Meanwhile, the Kennedy administration supported India despite the emergence of the Cuban Missile Crisis during the same period.

[70] Katzenstein, *A World of Regions,* 236.

[71] Perviaz Iqbal Cheema, *Pakistan's Defense Policy, 1947–58* (New York: St. Martin's Press, 1990), 113.

[72] Ibid., 114–15.

[73] Ibid., 114.

[74] Ibid., 122.

[75] Feroz Hassan Khan, "Pakistan Nuclear Future," in *South Asia in 2020: Future Strategic Balances and Alliances*, ed. Michael Chambers (Carlisle Barracks, PA: U.S. Army War College, November 2002), 157.

[76] Katzenstein, *A World of Regions*, 237.

[77] See Ernst B. Haas, "International Integration: The European and Universal Process," in "Comparing Regional Institutions: An Introduction," in *Crafting Cooperation: Regional International Institutions in Comparative Perspective*, ed. Amitav Acharya and Alastair Iain Johnston (New York: Cambridge Univ. Press), 1–31.

[78] Strobe Talbott describes how Jaswant Singh took exception to India being hyphenated with Pakistan, which India resented as a false equation. This was the foundation of what became to be known as the dehyphenation of U.S. policy toward South Asia. See Strobe Talbott, *Engaging India: Diplomacy, Democracy, and the Bomb* (Washington, D.C.: Brookings Institution Press, 2004), 85.

[79] Talbott, *Engaging India*, 85.

GREAT POWER ATTITUDES TOWARD REGIONALISM

U.S. Attitudes toward South Asian Regionalism

Xenia Dormandy

On January 18, 2006, then–secretary of state Condoleezza Rice proposed a new vision of transformational diplomacy, to include relocating State Department personnel to regions of more importance to the United States, providing them with better training to be more actively engaged, not only among branches of the U.S. government but also with governments and citizens around the world.[1] Building on this, then–under-secretary of state for political affairs Nicholas Burns declared that the United States must reorient itself diplomatically toward Asia, a dynamic area that required increased attention. Staff were transferred from European embassies to embassies in Asia, and the bureaucracy changed internally to reflect this new focus, with portfolios moving between the State Department and the National Security Council (NSC) to create a South and Central Asia Bureau and Directorate, assimilating, for U.S. policymaking purposes, the Central Asian countries into South Asia.[2]

This reflects the changing challenges and opportunities that America faces around the world. Notwithstanding the Balkans, the situation in Europe is relatively peaceful today, and U.S. relations with both "old" and "new" Europe are stable and able to withstand differences of foreign policy opinion (regarding Iraq, for example). Increasingly, the challenges that America faces stem from the Middle East and Asia, and solutions must be implemented in concert with these nations and their governments. The broader global challenges—such as the environment, health, and energy security—must also be addressed in partnership with the Asian countries, in particular China and India.

Concurrent with the rising importance of Asia comes an increased dynamism in the region. Over the past five or so years, relations have been improving between India and its larger neighbors—China, in particular, and Pakistan (with ups and downs). There are fundamental political changes taking place in Nepal and Sri Lanka. Economic growth is transforming parts of India and China, and along with Japan, these countries are using their growth to develop more capable and active militaries. This dynamic could facilitate change in the region, creating opportunities to reconfigure the environment and making U.S. engagement with the nations in this region vital.

How the United States will meet these challenges and opportunities is not well defined. What is clear, though, is that in order to effect change, the United States must use all the collaborative tools available. There will be times when only one or two countries will be interested in cooperation and others when the legitimacy provided by an international organization will be necessary. The tools will vary with the task and may differ from one year to the next. For this reason, the United States will continue to implement its regional policy via multiple mechanisms, from bilateral engagement to regional and multilateral efforts to the occasional use of coalitions of the willing.

U.S. National Interests

In July 2000 a group of senior American policymakers and academics published a report that looked at America's national interests and ranked them as vital, extremely important, important, or secondary.[3] In brief, America's five most vital national interests were to:

- Prevent, deter, and reduce the threat of weapons of mass destruction (WMDs)
- Ensure allies' survival and cooperation
- Prevent the emergence of hostile major powers or failed states
- Ensure the viability and stability of major global systems
- Establish productive relations with China and Russia

Broadly speaking, U.S. vital national interests remain unchanged since this study (except that India today would fit into the second interest category and Pakistan into the third). However, the global war on terror (GWOT) and the wars in Iraq and Afghanistan have diverted American attention from other policy goals. The South Asian nations and perhaps Asia as a whole will play a critical role in helping address many of these issues. How this role will be manifested and whether the mechanism of action is best achieved on a bilateral, regional, or global basis—or perhaps all three—is still uncertain. In order to understand this, we must consider the issues at a more granular level.

There is much consensus regarding the greatest challenges facing the United States and, perhaps, the world today. These challenges largely fit within the broader interests outlined above and include such issues as: Iran, nonproliferation of WMDs, North Korea, Afghanistan and Pakistan, terrorism and narcotics, energy, the environment, economic growth, and water. Effectively addressing many of these, if not all, will require the participation of India and Pakistan, either on a bilateral basis or as part of a broader coalition.

Functional U.S. Interests in South Asia

These broad U.S. national interests can be applied to the South Asia region and its composite countries in a manner that demonstrates the importance of this area to the United States. These interests can be broken down into functional concerns (such as terrorism and nonproliferation) and country-specific interests (such as relations with Iran and China).

Terrorism and Extremism

During the Bush administration, the U.S. government's foreign policy focused, above all, on the GWOT. In numerous ways this objective trumped all others in America's bilateral relations.[4] Since September 11, 2001, the government has—as of 2009—spent over $600 billion (including the military spending on Iraq and Afghanistan)[5] to fight this war, whose stated goal is: "to stop terrorist attacks against the United States, its citizens, its interests, and our friends and allies around the world, and ultimately to create an international environment inhospitable to terrorists and all those who support them."[6] Judging both from anecdotes and from the 2008 State Department Country Report on Terrorism, it is apparent that the strategy has not been a success.

Despite the initial support from the North Atlantic Treaty Organization (NATO) in the form of the first-ever application of Article 5 of the North Atlantic Treaty after the September 11 attacks, many of America's friends and allies (not to mention its enemies) regard the GWOT not as a global war, but as an American one directed at threats principally targeted against the United States. In light of this, the Obama administration is having to (1) redefine the target of the war on terror (for instance, is more involved than just those groups that target the United States or its direct interests?); (2) identify terrorist safe havens; (3) regain the support of allies to fight this global scourge; (4) communicate America's objectives and intent more effectively;[7] and (5) reexamine America's policies and priorities to balance U.S. security with support for democratic growth.

South Asia is intimately caught up in the war against terrorism and extremism. As noted in the State Department report, India ranks as one of the world's most "terror-afflicted countries,"[8] and there are conflicts in the region, including, until relatively recently, in Sri Lanka and Nepal.[9] Pakistan and Afghanistan, apart from being terrorism's victims, are still seen as safe havens for terrorist groups—al-Qaeda, the Taliban, and many other groups continue to operate in the region—but in order to bring them down, the United States needs the active participation of these nations.

As has been U.S. policy for a number of years, the government is working to take its fight beyond the homeland. The 2006 National Security Strategy states: "The United States can no longer simply rely on deterrence to keep the terrorists at bay or defensive measures to thwart them at the last moment. The fight must be taken to the enemy, to keep them on the run."[10]

During the Bush administration, the public debate and in large part the debate within the government was focused on Iraq and the progress fighting al-Qaeda there.[11] However, Doug Bandow, a former special assistant to President Reagan, stated in 2007: "The epicenter of potential terrorism against the U.S. is Afghanistan and Pakistan. And that's where we should concentrate our military efforts."[12] According to the British chief of defense staff, the fight in Afghanistan is going to last for decades,[13] a position reinforced by President

Bush when he stated, in 2006, that the United States is fighting the "long war" against terrorism.[14]

As President Obama has made clear, his administration's principal foreign policy interests are both Pakistan and Afghanistan. Defense Secretary Robert Gates stated in his recent testimony to the Senate Armed Services Committee that Afghanistan is the top military overseas priority for the United States. The quick appointment of ambassador Richard Holbrooke, one of America's most able negotiators and diplomats, as special envoy for Afghanistan and Pakistan, emphasizes that this attention is not merely restricted to the Defense Department but also extends to State. In the first minute of his inaugural speech, President Obama noted the terrorism threat, warning that "For those who seek to advance their aims by inducing terror and slaughtering innocents, we say to you now that our spirit is stronger and cannot be broken; you cannot outlast us, and we will defeat you."[15] While the methods will be different, there is no question that the Obama administration is just as focused on terrorism as its predecessor.

Economic Development and Growth

The South Asian region has a population of 1.5 billion, almost a quarter of the global total; currently, 75 percent live in poverty.[16] India alone accounts for 1.1 billion people today and its population is expected to surpass China's by 2035.[17] Unlike its counterparts in the U.S. and Europe, South Asia's population is a young one—in the case of India, 54 percent of the population is under the age of twenty-five.[18]

This youth bulge supports the rapid South Asian economic expansion: 2007 gross domestic product (GDP) growth ranged from 2.5 percent in Nepal to 8.8 percent in Bhutan,[19] with a regional GDP growth of 8.6 percent.[20] Even in the severe global economic downturn underway since 2008, the region's positive growth trajectory is likely to continue. In India, this has translated, by some measures, to a new middle class of 200 million to 350 million (depending on the definition of middle class), perhaps larger than the entire American population.

This economic growth and population dividend is of great interest to American industry. Increasingly, South Asia is proving to be a robust market for U.S. goods: whether in biotech, infrastructure, energy, defense, or other commodities, it is one of the largest underpenetrated markets still remaining. Those nations in which English is still widely spoken and taught—namely India, Pakistan, Bangladesh, and Sri Lanka—are increasingly providing a pool of skilled white-collar workers (see also Dossani, chapter 9 in this volume).

Trade between the United States and the region has risen exponentially. The United States remains South Asia's biggest trading partner,[21] although China is quickly gaining ground. As was stated at the 2006 U.S.–India Trade Policy Forum, the United States and India were planning to double their bilateral trade over three years,[22] something that would no doubt be supported by the completion of a bilateral investment treaty (BIT) which, as of 2010 is still being discussed and, more importantly, a free trade agreement (FTA) (which will in all likelihood be long in coming). Indian exports to the United States rose by 75 percent between 2000 and 2007[23] and were valued at $24.024 billion in 2007;[24] U.S. exports to India were valued at $17.5 billion in 2007, an increase of 75 percent from the previous year.[25]

Led by India, South Asia is increasingly becoming an investment destination—one that still holds many risks, but where the rewards can be significant.[26] The value of U.S. direct investment in India tripled between 2000 and 2005, from $2.4 to $8.5 billion,[27] and the total foreign direct investment (FDI) in India for 2007–2008 was over $25 billion.[28] In addition to becoming a destination for investment, India in particular is also an ever-increasing source of international investment—with the acquisition of Corus Steel[29] and Jaguar,[30] India was the largest investor in the United Kingdom in 2007.[31]

Therefore, beyond the strong moral argument to support South Asian economic development in order to pull the local population out of poverty, U.S. commercial interests are much engaged in the region, particularly in India, and this form of engagement will only rise in the years to come; and as India has been less impacted by the economic downturn than many other countries, including the United States and Europe, it is likely that its role will only become more important.

Stability

India, Pakistan, and China are all nuclear weapons powers. Given the historical antagonism between China and India and between India and Pakistan, President Clinton, in March 2000, described South Asia as "the most dangerous place in the world."[32] To many, this region represents the world's greatest threat of nuclear war, a fact made more resonant by the three wars that India and Pakistan have fought since their independence and the Sino-Indian war in 1962—all of which were motivated in large part by border issues that remain unresolved.[33]

In addition to the threat of unconventional war, conventional war is also a concern—India spent more on defense acquisitions in 2005 than any other developing country.[34] While recognizing the futility of attempting to achieve parity, Pakistan currently spends 25 percent of its budget on defense[35] and tries to retain some low-level balance. Meanwhile, China's military buildup continues to be of great concern, not just to the United States but also to countries in South Asia and in Europe.

Compounding the military and nuclear upsurge in these nations[36] is the uncertainty that comes from instability elsewhere in the region. Following elections in 2008, the Maoists, led by Pushpa Kamal Dahal (a.k.a. Prachanda), took over leadership of Nepal's political establishment, stepping down shortly afterward when their efforts to remove senior military leaders were thwarted; the future stability of the country remains in doubt.[37] Sri Lanka's civil war has only recently ended, while Bangladesh, as of 2009, has reverted to democracy after two years of military-supported emergency rule (every indication is that the nation's leadership will be as messy, corrupt, and ineffective as before). While, from a realpolitik perspective, none of these countries is of vital national interest to the United States, the collapse of any of them could spread instability, resulting in a wider conflagration that would be significant for U.S. interests. This is particularly true of Bangladesh—a historically moderate Muslim nation that has seen a sharp increase in extremist violence in the past few years and from where, it is believed, two recent major terrorist attacks on India were launched.[38]

Finally, there are the issues that, while not currently causes of interstate conflict, will likely become so in the coming decade. The most notable of these is inadequate water supply—already an issue between India and Pakistan, its importance will only increase. India's water table is diminishing fast in many areas, and water could very easily become a domestic political issue in the coming years. Given the importance of the rural sector in these countries—60 percent of India's population is still rural, as is 66 percent of Pakistan's[39]—attention must be paid to ensuring sufficient water levels.

Narcotics

Afghanistan produces approximately 90 percent of the world's opium today,[40] and despite recent efforts by the British government (which took responsibility for destroying Afghanistan's narcotics industry in 2001), the amount of land devoted to poppy production has increased since the downfall of the Taliban.[41] Pakistan has made notable efforts to prevent the distribution of narcotics across its borders and by 2003 had largely ceased being a transit country,[42] but the increase in militant activity in the federally administered tribal areas (FATA) and the lack of government control over this area has reversed some of this progress. By 2009 it had once again become a common route out of Asia, along with the northern route through Central Asia.[43]

In addition to their intrinsic threat, Afghan poppies also create a more indirect threat to the region and beyond. There is evidence that the poppies provide a principal source of financing for Afghan warlords and support the ongoing militant operations of groups such as the Taliban and al-Qaeda.[44] If the threat of terrorism from this region is to be defeated, cutting off their financial flows needs to be part of the strategy. However, it should be noted that destroying poppy fields does have a major negative consequence: unless alternative livelihoods are provided that ensure sufficient economic benefits to the farmers, destroying their crops will only build support for the Taliban in these areas.

Weapons of Mass Destruction and Nonproliferation

As the aforementioned July 2000 report makes clear, preventing the spread of WMDs continues to be a principal U.S. foreign policy concern. The United States has long been a central supporter of the Nuclear Nonproliferation Treaty (NPT) and has exerted significant political influence to prevent the spread of WMDs.

Nonetheless, in 1998, despite pressure from the United States and others, both India and Pakistan tested nuclear weapons and became de facto nuclear powers. The United States subsequently imposed heavy sanctions on both nations.

U.S. interest in preventing the further spread of WMDs has not diminished. The two nations that provoke the most concern for America today are Iran and North Korea. Notwithstanding their cultural links and the strategic importance of Iran to both India and Pakistan, the United States would like to see these two nations support its efforts to keep Iran from acquiring nuclear weapons. If the United States is able to engage diplomatically with Iran, as the Obama administration has attempted to do, then both India and Pakistan could prove to be useful intermediaries.

In addition to preventing the creation of new nuclear weapons states, the United States is very concerned with the proliferation of WMDs, particularly nuclear weapons, to both state and nonstate actors. Pakistan's reputation in this area is dismal, with A. Q. Khan (the "father" of its nuclear program) leading the largest black market in nuclear materials, technology, and knowledge until 2004. While there has been a thorough investigation into his network, many remain concerned that parts of it still exist and that nuclear proliferation is most likely to originate in this region.[45] With that in mind, the United States has spent approximately $100 million since September 2001 to help secure Pakistan's nuclear weapons, but it is not clear whether this is enough.[46]

Any attempt to more broadly address proliferation and WMDs would be futile without the participation of India and Pakistan. In the case of Pakistan, after counterterrorism, nonproliferation is America's second-highest priority and will likely remain so. These are areas that the Obama adminstration has only now begun to focus on (vis-à-vis Iran, the START negotiations with Russia, and the recent nonproliferation conference in Washington), and they are supported by two strong appointments of senior nonproliferation experts from the Clinton administration—Robert Einhorn and Gary Samore, at State and the National Security Council (NSC), respectively. It is clear that nonproliferation is going to play a strong role in Obama foreign policy.

Energy

India is the world's fifth-largest consumer of energy today and is projected to surpass Japan and Russia by 2030;[47] it is also the world's second-fastest-growing energy market after China.[48] Although South Asia, as a whole, currently consumes only 4 percent of the world's energy,[49] in light of the region's rapidly growing energy consumption, the participation of India and China will become increasingly vital to developing solutions to an impending energy crisis.

New technologies, improving efficiency, and the use of alternative energy sources will need to be developed in response to the increasingly constrained energy market. The U.S.-India civilian nuclear deal—announced on July 18, 2005, and formally completed by the end of 2008, is part of this equation, at least for India. While nuclear power makes up only approximately 3 percent of India's electricity production,[50] it should account for a larger percentage in the future.

Like China, India is building relationships across the globe—from Africa to the Middle East to Latin America—and developing ties with energy-rich countries to ensure the continued flow of cheap hydrocarbons. Approximately 80 percent of India's oil imports come from the unstable Middle East.[51] While China receives most of America's criticism in this area, India, too, has pursued sourcing energy from nations with which the United States has antagonistic relationships (such as Sudan and Iran). Finding ways to integrate India's energy needs and America's broader foreign policy will be vital to the future of U.S.–Indian relations.

All these issues are also of import to other countries in the region, most notably Pakistan, which needs additional energy resources; Bangladesh is also negotiating with both India and China over transportation of its gas, as is Burma, which, because of the military junta's human rights abuses and suppression of democracy, is again contrary to U.S. foreign policy interests.

The Environment

Today, India is the world's fifth-largest producer of greenhouse gases.[52] It is anticipated that by 2030, India and China together will contribute 31 percent of the worldwide CO_2 emissions.[53] While per capita consumption of energy in India is approximately 4 percent of America's,[54] as this rises along with the growing population and much-needed economic development, India's impact on the environment will prove increasingly costly.

While there have been recent signs of flexibility, India's government, like China's, insists it will not limit its consumption patterns until per capita levels reach those of the West. Both argue that the developed world caused the ongoing climate disruption and thus needs to take action first. Despite such firm positions, an adequate response to this global scourge will only be possible with the engagement of the West, India, and China. While the Copenhagen negotiations in late 2009 lacked much concrete progress, action is vital; meanwhile, the impact of climate disruption is felt most keenly in South Asia.[55]

Democracy

As measured by elections, South Asia could represent the next wave of stable democracies.[56] In 2008 national elections occurred in Bhutan, Pakistan, Nepal, the Maldives, and Bangladesh. In 2009 elections were conducted in Sri Lanka, India, and Afghanistan. However, all of these democracies, except India's and Sri Lanka's, are unstable or unbalanced.

President Bush made support for democratization a principal part of his foreign policy.[57] Secretary Rice stated in June 2005 that the United States would no longer prioritize security above democracy, a position that President

Obama has supported in his earlier writings.[58] Democracy today holds a very important role in America's foreign policy, although it is not clear that Secretary Rice's sentiments have always been followed. While comparatively speaking the Obama administration has largely steered clear of strong statements toward democratization, America's long-standing support for democratic values will be maintained, both domestically (as was seen with the announcement of Guantanamo's closure) and in its foreign policy (regarding, for example, Afghanistan).

In the July 18, 2005, joint statement between President Bush and Prime Minister Singh, the two nations declared their intent to work together to strengthen democratic practices internationally.[59] While India is wary of pushing democracy on other countries, its government serves as a very powerful demonstration regionally and provides, when requested, its expertise and assets to help support other burgeoning democracies (such as Bhutan); these traits make India an important partner in spreading democracy across Asia and beyond.

Pakistan also is a very important player with regard to America's democracy agenda. While the nation has veered between democracy and authoritarian military rule since independence, following the February 2008 elections and the return of a legitimately elected government, albeit one that is rocked by allegations of corruption and inappropriate practices, it once again has the potential to become a more stable long-term democracy. While it is today perhaps an overly optimistic vision, it could perhaps exercise a powerful demonstrative effect for other majority Muslim countries.

Finally, the United States and NATO have pledged their support for Afghanistan as it builds, anew, its democracy. The success or failure of this endeavor will have major repercussions for the West, particularly for the reputation of the United States, a fact that has likely contributed to President Obama's focus on Afghanistan; it will also have significant influence on Afghanistan's potential for remaining a terrorist safe haven.

Given the uncertainty of the democracies (or quasi-democracies) of South Asia, stabilizing the legitimate governments and institutions of these composite nations would be a much-needed sign of success of America's broader policy objectives.

U.S. Regional Interests

China

U.S. policy toward China is divided between those (such as former deputy secretary of state Robert Zoellick) who see China as a "responsible stakeholder"[60] and those who believe China to be a threat to the United States and the West—a view supported by its military spending, engagement with countries such as Sudan and North Korea, and internal human rights abuses. India also is uncertain about China's direction: given its proximity, the Indian government, perhaps even more so than its American counterpart, is concerned with China's progress and is questioning whether China will develop into a military, economic, and diplomatic competitor or friend.

Notwithstanding this commonality of interest, India will not act as a counterweight to China for the benefit of the United States. However, even with this caveat, the United States and India have very similar interests with regard to influencing the direction of China's growth and improving their respective bilateral relations. Given this, there is great value in India and the United States collaborating with each other to urge China on a cooperative path of positive engagement. To that end, India is likely to play an influential role in the broader U.S.–China relationship.

Iran and Central Asia

Iran continues to be one of America's greatest foreign policy concerns and a priority for the Obama administration. Whether the United States decides to pursue a more cooperative policy with Iran or engage in more stringent sanctions, both Pakistan and India will play a role. Both of these nations have long-term cultural, strategic, and energy interests in Iran that mandate a continued relationship. India, for its part, has long proposed that it would act as a mediator between the United States and Iran if such a position was needed, in a capacity similar to China's with regard to North Korea. Additionally, with a 564-mile-long border between Pakistan and Iran, any sanctions regime would require Pakistan's participation.

Afghanistan, Pakistan, and India also have a role to play in the development of Central Asia—specifically the rebirth of the silk route. While the *arc of instability* is sometimes used to describe the region from the Middle East to Pakistan,[61] an arc of economic and democratic growth could in time be formed between Central Asia and Southeast Asia.[62] Given the uncertainty of the Central Asian democracies and their economic dependence on energy, India has a significant role in promoting a positive trajectory.

India

In addition to India's involvement and participation in helping to address all the functional issues discussed above, the United States also has a broader strategic interest regarding its relationship with India. This stems from America's historically strong leadership in Asia, a position that has swiftly declined given the diminished "soft power" of the United States and its distraction with Iraq and Afghanistan. The United States needs a reliable ally in Asia that will help it engage from afar and ensure broad positive trends.

America's historical allies in Asia have been Japan and South Korea. However, with the increased anti-Americanism in South Korea and the economic and political uncertainties in Japan, these two nations have been more wary of engaging as actively with the United States. They have been preoccupied with domestic issues and their own political troubles over international concerns. India, on the other hand, is following an opposite trend—expanding its international role actively. India has the potential to be a much stronger power globally given its population and its military and economic assets; therefore, the United States is engaging in a strategic relationship with India. The two nations rely on the commonality of their values and interests to presume that their broader objectives are similar, even if their tactics and priorities might at times be contrary.

Pakistan

In March 2006, President Bush announced that the United States wanted "a long-term strategic partnership" with Pakistan.[63] On taking office, with the appointment of Richard Holbrooke and the recent back and forth of senior U.S. and Pakistani officials, President Obama has also made clear the importance of holding to a strong relationship with Pakistan. However, given America's history with this country—one in which the United States engaged only when its own interests demanded, then pulled out—it is proving very difficult to persuade Pakistanis of the sincerity of U.S. objectives.[64]

If the United States is going to have a long-term engagement with Pakistan, it is likely to come about from a stronger relationship with its people as well as the elites. In order for this to occur, the United States needs to develop a long-term outlook on Pakistan, driven by a willingness to help build social services such as education, employment, and health care. The Biden-Lugar bill helps to do this (despite its bad press in Pakistan). As Vice President Biden's trip to Pakistan in the week prior to his inauguration makes clear, he remains very actively engaged toward this end. In order to engage with Pakistan in the vital areas mentioned above (including terrorism, nonproliferation, and democracy), it will be necessary to develop this long-term strategic relationship.

What Mechanisms of Action Are Available to the United States?

Multilateral

The United Nations (UN) has been stymied by disagreements among the Security Council Permanent Five[65] and by bureaucratic battles. Many have questioned its relevance in today's world given its antiquated structure reflecting the world post–World War II.[66] Given these trends, since the late 1990s there has been a drive for UN reform that would revitalize its ability to act and better represent a contemporary global organization.[67] Despite this reform agenda, progress has been and will continue to be slow given the resistance to change by many of the 192 member countries.[68] However, it is clear that President Obama intends to use the UN more given his appointment of Susan Rice and other positive engagements with the UN since taking office (including paying off U.S. arrears).

Other multilateral organizations, such as the World Bank and International Monetary Fund (IMF), are meeting resistance and are trying to establish new roles, relevancy, and processes to allow them to address the needs of today's underserved societies more effectively. As Kishore Mahbubani has argued, until the World Bank and IMF are not, automatically, led by either Americans or Europeans, the rest of the world is unlikely to perceive them as world bodies rather than Western organizations.[69] However, given the resources they bring to bear, in many cases they still remain important players in the region.

Intransigence in the World Trade Organization (WTO) stems from a different source—negotiations on the Doha Development Round have been ongoing since 2001. India—along with Brazil, China, and South Africa—has taken on a leadership role to advocate the developing world's position and is using this organization to try to effect change, particularly with regard to the agricultural sector. However, the developing world is coming directly up against the developed, with both groups trying to protect their farmers. While the WTO is an important potential lever of change with regard to developing-developed engagement, the implications of the failure of this round for U.S. relations with South Asia and for attitudes toward this region could be significant.

As bodies that reflect a broad swath of the world, multilateral organizations will inherently retain more legitimacy than smaller, less representative groups. However, it is also this wide membership that makes effecting change through these organizations so difficult and time-consuming; therefore, action through such parties will likely be limited to largely uncontroversial activities—such as the provision of development assistance or, on occasion, peacekeeping missions when requested by the country in question.

Regional

As the power and influence of multilateral organizations diminish in some areas, regional organizations are filling the vacuum. This is particularly true in Asia, which has shown much recent dynamism with regard to regional organizations. The Asia-Pacific Economic Cooperation group (APEC) has expanded to encompass issues far beyond the economic realm into security. However, with the decision in 1997 not to expand for a decade (which was extended in 2007), leaving India out of the group,[70] it is unclear whether this organization's historical influence will be maintained.

Meanwhile, similar organizations, such as the Association of South East Asian Nations (ASEAN), ASEAN+3 (including China, South Korea, and Japan), and the ASEAN Regional Forum (ARF), appear to be maintaining their relevance or even increasing it, and other nations (such as India) now want to join. The Shanghai Cooperation Organization (SCO), an organization that was primarily ideologically driven and anti–United States, is currently composed of Central Asian powers (including China and Russia) and is expanding its membership to include India, Pakistan, and Iran.[71]

The South Asian Association for Regional Cooperation (SAARC), an organization long held back by Indo-Pakistan antagonism, was somewhat revitalized in the late 2000s, as the relationship improved. Afghanistan was admitted in November 2005, and other nations—such as Iran, Russia, and China—are now observers.

Finally, and perhaps most notably, in 2005, Asia saw the creation of a new regional organization: the East Asia Summit (EAS). While its broader mission at birth was undefined, it was clearly intended by China and Malaysia to be an organization that excluded the United States and other powerful players. However, with the addition of India, Australia, and New Zealand, the organization has become more inclusive and more representative of the region. Though the mission remains uncertain, there would be few, if any, downsides to U.S. engagement with the EAS.

While the United States is a member of the APEC and ARF, it does not participate in any of the other Asian groups except as an observer—though many would suggest that this should be otherwise.[72] Even with the ARF, the level of engagement by the Bush administration has been low, a fact made clear by Secretary Rice's absence at the annual summit in 2005.[73] President Obama has made it clear that his administration will be much more multilateral and inclusive than the previous one.

Core Groups and Coalitions of the Willing

One of the most interesting phenomena in recent years has been the rise of coalitions of the willing, or core groups, as mechanisms of action.[74] Examples are as varied as the coalition of the willing in Iraq, the Proliferation Security Initiative (PSI), and the 2004 Asian Tsunami Core Group (which lasted only five days). The reasons behind the birth of such groups have varied: sometimes they have grown out of a lack of UN Security Council support for a mission or its inability to act quickly. While multilateral groups continue to be constrained by political differences and bureaucratic delays, in most cases such groups will address specific issues (such as proliferation), perhaps for limited time periods (for instance, the tsunami core group).

However, it should be noted that coalitions of the willing often lack legitimacy because they are composed only of nations on one side of the issue and often lack legal or defined rules of engagement (at least initially). In addition, the burdens that they are asked to bear often require the inclusion of large and resource-rich nations; perhaps, for this reason the United States has often been the instigator of such groups.

Bilateral Action

The final method of action, and perhaps the most popular, is bilateral. Given the inherent constraints of working in larger groups with diverging interests, it is often the fastest and most effective way to get things done. It is also often the most expedient politically, where small steps are more acceptable than larger regional ones.

How can the mechanisms listed above be best used to achieve U.S. objectives? Given the limitations and constraints of each, the national interests listed in the first half of this chapter may be addressed most effectively through multiple avenues: some lend themselves more readily to bilateral responses and others to regional or multilateral methods—there is no single universal approach. We should also consider whether, at times, the best solution might even be through a grouping that does not include the United States at all.

Where Would a Regional Focus Be Most Effective?

Some issues lend themselves to regional engagement, either with or without the participation of the United States. While in the current political environment,it is extremely hard for the United States to negotiate any regional economic deals[75] within the South Asian region, the South Asian Free Trade Area (SAFTA) exemplifies a useful path. Building an economic bridge regionally promotes economic development on all levels. While there continue to be some obstacles to the full implementation of the SAFTA, particularly between Pakistan and India, the SAFTA has already realized benefits.[76]

SAARC has also attempted to lead a regional effort against terrorism. Unfortunately, this has been stymied, as has a similar effort in the UN, by disagreement over the definition of terrorism. While norms-building efforts are difficult, using regional groups or coalitions of the willing to conduct activities can sometimes be more successful. As unilateral efforts against terrorism are limited by terrorists' refusal to recognize borders, it is vital that such groups do come together. Afghanistan's security problems cannot be addressed exclusively within the country; they also require the involvement of Pakistan and Iran—the tripartite group comprising the Afghani, Pakistani, and U.S. militaries is the embodiment of this. At the same time, bilateral efforts are sometimes appropriate—such as the Anti-Terrorism Mechanism between India and Pakistan[77] and the earlier Indo–Sri Lankan efforts to counter the Liberation Tigers of Tamil Eelam (LTTE).

In 2008 Iran, Afghanistan, and Pakistan announced the creation of a group to monitor and prevent the infiltration of narcotics across their national borders. The narcotics industry (production, refining, and distribution) is spread among these countries and a number of Central Asian nations; therefore, a regional response is likely to be most effective. At the same time, the scourge of narcotics, both in terms of fostering warlords and raising consumption levels, is increasingly affecting all these nations, ensuring that it is in the interests of each to work together with the others. While the United States may not play a direct role here, it is in U.S. interests that the affected nations of the region work together to address this global problem.

Energy security, as differentiated from energy consumption, is also an issue best addressed regionally, albeit with a different subset of nations, moving from India east. Over 50 percent of the world's oil goes through the Malacca Straits,[78] where piracy is rife. Beyond the direct interests of the Southeast Asian nations that currently monitor the straits (notably Indonesia, Malaysia, and Singapore), it is also in the best interests of India, China, the United States, and the rest of the world to ensure that the flow continues smoothly. To that end, it would be important to create a regional grouping responsible for ensuring that the channels stay open and that intelligence is shared.

As stated earlier, South Asia is composed largely of unstable democracies. India—which historically has been reticent to promote democracy actively—has the assets, capability, and experience to be a valuable partner to countries in the region that are attempting to stabilize their democratic institutions.[79] Given that the other South Asian nations hesitate to invite the powerful India to assist in this area alone, creating a broader regional organization to support nascent democracies—Afghanistan, Nepal, Pakistan, or one of several Southeast Asian nations—could be a more sensitive approach (see also Lama, chapter 6 in this volume). Meanwhile, an entity such as India could provide the convening power that would facilitate information and resource sharing.

It should be noted, however, that while the benefits could be significant, there are a number of factors that make a regional democracy grouping difficult. First and foremost, India has shown strong resistance to taking an active role in promoting democracy. It is also clear that regional groups have often found it hard to uphold democracy as a necessary characteristic of membership—as evidenced by the continued membership of Burma in the ASEAN[80] and Zimbabwe in the African Union.[81] Therefore, while there are inherent benefits to a regional pooling of democracy assets, it is hard to imagine such an objective being taken now or in the near term by SAARC or any other such group.

Regional groups also have the responsibility to ensure broader objectives— such as wider security and stability in the region, a goal that SAARC has attempted with little success so far. As Allan Gyngell argues, one of the elements necessary for a regional architecture is the promotion of regional security;[82] integrating local nations into a strong architecture can build bonds that inherently strengthen the relationships and become quite costly to break. However, the region currently lacks an organization with the capability or responsibility to do this, and given the history of the region—most notably between India and Pakistan—it is unlikely to establish one soon. It is possible that expanding such an organization to include the United States, China, and Russia might make it less effective (it would have the same problem as the UN Security Council has in coming to agreements) but more relevant (all the regional power brokers would be present).[83] Former Indian external affairs minister Mukherjee has suggested that India and China work together on such a new framework.[84]

Where Would a Global Focus Be Most Effective?

Some issues clearly require global efforts—climate disruption, for example, has no borders. This issue is already being addressed in international fora, such as in Copenhagen in December 2009. However, in order for these initiatives to be a success, it is vital that developing nations—particularly India and China—sign up to participate in conjunction with developed nations such as the United States.[85]

A number of other U.S. national interests are also addressed best through global mechanisms. Proliferation of WMDs, with its global repercussions, requires a worldwide strategy, currently exemplified by the NPT. While there is a place for regional nuclear-free zones, the norms created by the NPT and other such entities are global ones—and given India's and Pakistan's current nuclear status, a nuclear-free South Asia is unlikely anytime soon. The same is true for other nonproliferation treaties, such as the Chemical Weapons Convention (CWC) and Biological Weapons Convention (BWC).

Two other issues also require at least partial global solutions—energy and narcotics. As with WMDs, counternarcotics efforts can be addressed through norms-building, which is stronger in global initiatives than in regional ones. The response, however, can be undertaken on a regional or local basis (as described in the previous subsection). The energy market, by its very nature, demands a global response. Notwithstanding China's and to a lesser degree India's attempts to acquire ownership of energy resources around the world, the energy market is integrated globally, so that when China finds energy from one source its needs are diminished elsewhere. Therefore, managing energy consumption or price hikes is a global problem.

Specific Finite Problems Are Addressed Best through Core Groups

There can be overlap between issues that are handled most effectively through regional organizations and those addressed by core groups or coalitions of the willing. Terrorist networks can be regionally structured but also extraregional. Therefore, actions against specific groups will sometimes be most effective when applied regionally (for example, against the Nepalese Maoists or the LTTE) or sometimes when applied by core groups (for example, against al-Qaeda). However, agreement to act against any type of terrorism (for example, Sunni radical groups in the Middle East) will almost certainly be extraregional.

In the past few years, there have been a number of interesting core groups created: In December 2004, following the Asian tsunami, a response group was created that encompassed countries that could quickly bring assets to bear.[86] One of the most effective groups, the PSI, was created in 2003 to prevent proliferation of WMDs and delivery technologies around the world through the use of a nation's existing legal structure. Other nuclear-related groups include the six-party talks with North Korea or the five-plus-one talks with Iran, neither of which is regionally based. It is possible to cite many other examples where core groups would be the most effective solution to problems, whether security-related, humanitarian, or otherwise.

Core groups or coalitions of the willing are probably best utilized for issues that have a certain set of criteria and which address a specific, well-defined problem (such as narcotics flow or proliferation). In certain cases, the problems should also have a well-defined end-goal (such as the immediate response to a tsunami), and once that goal is achieved the group will be dismantled. The value of such groups comes from harnessing multiple sources of energy and resources together in order to address a problem with partners who think similarly and can often move quickly. As larger organizations become more flexible and swift, the need for such coalitions will likely diminish.

Sometimes Constraints Demand Only Bilateral Solutions

Finally, there are some issues for which only bilateral solutions are possible, or which need to be launched through bilateral initiatives that could expand later into regional or multilateral efforts. As mentioned earlier, given the political obstacles, the United States often needs to approach economic initiatives bilaterally—for instance, through a BIT or an FTA (though these are extremely hard to pass through Congress).

Equally, when progress is stymied in larger groups, regional or global, initial steps might be possible through bilateral efforts to which other countries can adhere later (such as efforts against terrorism or HIV/AIDS). Under these circumstances, a bilateral initiative may not be the best solution, but it might be the only one that is possible at the time.

Finally, for some issues that are particularly sensitive regarding a third party (China, for instance) or issue, the dialogue often must take place privately à deux, so as not to unnecessarily raise tensions.

Moving Forward: Recommendations for U.S. Policy

What may be inferred from the above analysis is that unconditional statements cannot be made regarding whether or not the United States should use bilateral, regional, or multilateral mechanisms to achieve its policy objectives in South Asia. Depending on the issue area, any one or more of these structures might be most effective.

The U.S. government will continue to engage bilaterally with South Asian nations in areas such as economic growth, terrorism, and democracy. At the same time, these issues might also be strategically promoted, regionally and globally, either with U.S. involvement or not. Some issues—such as nonproliferation and the environment—must be addressed at a global level, although specific bilateral or regional efforts in certain areas can be effective to back a global architecture. Increasingly, however, there is likely to be a proliferation of coalitions of the willing that may or may not be regionally focused, and that would address issues that cannot be encompassed on a larger scale or within a specific geographic area.

Like many nations, the United States is often wary of groups of which it is not a member, particularly in those areas in which it believes it has vital national interests at stake. On the other hand, there are clearly some issues for which a stronger South Asian architecture would have benefits, not just for the countries concerned but also, indirectly, for the United States. An example would include the SAFTA, where economic cooperation leads to growth that would benefit all parties regionally and globally, or even a stronger security-related SAARC. As then–deputy secretary of state John Negroponte said in 2008: "Closer economic relations among Pakistan, Afghanistan, and their neighbors are also essential to building a secure peace in South Asia."[87]

At the same time, the United States would be wary of South Asian groupings that include China but not the United States (the reverse also is true). If a regional security group is to be truly effective in the current Asian environment, both America's and China's participation will likely be necessary.

Conclusion

Since 1985, SAARC has served as South Asia's regional architecture. However, it has largely been ineffectual due to the intransigence between India and Pakistan. As the bilateral composite dialogue between these two nations continues, some progress has been made within SAARC on low-level security and economic (SAFTA) issues. However, SAARC will remain hostage to the relations between these two countries.

Whether through SAARC or another entity, there is a strong argument for building robust security, democratic, and economic bonds among the South Asian nations. Such a structure could swap lessons and assets—whether with regard to sharing intelligence and military knowledge or democracy training and trade—that would provide stability to all of the South Asian nations that are currently in turmoil.

In the future, a more robust SAARC could contribute meaningfully to addressing some important challenges in the region and more broadly. However, until SAARC members find a way to work together effectively and align themselves internally to act as one, the United States is unlikely to exert any of its own resources to bring them together. If, on the other hand, a new energetic SAARC was to be created by members, it is likely that it would find much support from the United States, both political and economic.

Given the burgeoning relationship between India and the United States, and what is perceived to be a similarity of interests and values, there is some confidence that any grouping including India would not be antagonistic to the United States. With this in mind, the United States would likely support any South Asian regional grouping, particularly one that was designed to address some of the concerns in the region, such as building security, intelligence links, and cooperation in narcotics and terrorism—issues that also impact the United States directly.

What is less clear, however, is whether the borders of this architecture are best formed around the South Asian nations or more broadly. India, Pakistan, and Afghanistan all have important roles in rebuilding the silk route linking Central Asia to Southeast Asia. Security in Asia is only truly addressed with the inclusion of China and, perhaps, Japan, Russia, and Australia. Given the nature of these issues, defining the right architecture is difficult.

However, an architecture of South Asian nations that is also inclusive of other nations could fall into the trap that larger organizations often do—it would be paralyzed by differences of interests. Nevertheless, such an organization could in time counter others of which the United States is less supportive (such as the SCO).

To conclude, while there would likely be U.S. support for a single and more robust South Asian regional organization capable of addressing some of the issues that lend themselves to regional solutions, there are many other issues for which alternative structures, including core groups, are more useful. Particularly for security, democracy, and even some economic issues, a broader coalition that goes beyond the South Asian nations would likely be more attractive to U.S. interests.

Notes

[1] Speech given at Georgetown University by Secretary Condoleezza Rice, "Transformational Diplomacy," on January 18, 2006, www.state.gov/secretary/rm/2006/59306.htm.

[2] As defined by the State Department, South Asia encompasses Afghanistan, Pakistan, India, Nepal, Sri Lanka, Bangladesh, the Maldives, and Bhutan.

[3] *America's National Interests*, Commission on America's National Interests, July 2000.

[4] Examples include U.S. policy toward Afghanistan, Pakistan, the Middle East, and Mexico, the immigration debate, and so on.

[5] It is anticipated that the cost of the GWOT could exceed $2 trillion over the next ten years. See Margaret Besheer, "US War on Terror Could Cost $2.4 trillion by 2017," Voice of America News, October 24, 2007.

[6] *National Strategy for Combatting Terrorism*, Office of the Press Secretary, the White House, Washington, D.C., February 2003, www.whitehouse.gov/news/releases/2003/02/counter_terrorism/counter_terrorism_strategy.pdf.

[7] For example, as P.W. Singer and Elina Noor make clear in their *New York Times* op-ed on June 2, 2008, using the word *jihadi* plays into the terrorists' definition of their role as fighting a legitimate war. See Elina Noor and P. W. Singer, "What Do You Call a Terror(Jihad)ist?" *New York Times*, June 2, 2008.

[8] *Country Reports on Terrorism*, Office of the Coordinator for Counterterrorism, U.S. Department of State, April 30, 2008, www.state.gov/s/ct/rls/crt/2007.

[9] It is unclear at this stage whether Nepal will fall back into militancy if the Maoists

do not find their interests sufficiently addressed, particularly with regard to the Maoist cadre currently in UN cantonment sites.

[10] "The National Security Strategy," National Security Council, Washington, D.C., March 2006, www.whitehouse.gov/nsc/nss/2006.

[11] As the U.S. election picks up speed, Iraq and, to a lesser extent, Afghanistan, remain the two principal topics of foreign policy debate.

[12] Doug Bandow, "Use Military in Pakistan, Not Iraq," *Los Angeles Times*, September 13, 2007. In January 2008, Patrick Basham, a South Asia expert at the Cato Institute, echoed this sentiment, arguing that "Pakistan is arguably the most dangerous country in the world. You have the epicenter of anti-U.S. terrorism combined with nuclear bombs." See Aida Akl, Jela de Franceschi, and Victor Morales, "What Lies Ahead for Pakistan?" Voice of America News, January 2, 2008. Back in 2003, Michael Evanoff, regional security officer in the U.S. Embassy in Islamabad, also noted Pakistan as the epicenter of terrorism. See Gretchen Peters, "The U.S. Embassy in Pakistan: Fortress Against Terror Threats," *Christian Science Monitor*, June 3, 2003. The Institute for Conflict Management maintains a comprehensive database of terrorist activities in Pakistan, which shows that the number of terrorism-related fatalities in the country has risen from 189 in 2003 to 3,599 in 2007. See "Pakistan Assessment 2008," South Asia Terrorism Portal, Institute for Conflict Management, http://satp.org/satporgtp/countries/pakistan/index.html.

[13] See Jane Merrick, "War with Taliban 'could last years' Warns Defence Chief," *Daily Mail*, October 26, 2007.

[14] In his 2006 State of the Union address, President Bush stated, "Our own generation is in a long war against a determined enemy—a war that will be fought by Presidents of both parties, who will need steady bipartisan support from the Congress." See "State of the Union Address by the President," Office of the Press Secretary, the White House, January 31, 2006, www.whitehouse.gov/stateoftheunion/2006/.

[15] President Obama's Inaugural Speech, January 20, 2009: "That we are in the midst of crisis is now well understood. Our nation is at war, against a far-reaching network of violence and hatred."

[16] Poverty is defined as surviving on less than $2 per day (PPP). See Mahbub ul Haq Human Development Center, *Human Development in South Asia 2006: Poverty in South Asia: Challenges and Responses* (Oxford: Oxford Univ. Press, 2006).

[17] Maseeh Rahman, "Population of India to Overtake China's within 30 years," *The Guardian*, July 12, 2004.

[18] David Rohde, "Young Workers Are Changing India's Politics and Society," *New York Times*, August 21, 2004.

[19] *CIA World Factbook,* updated May 15, 2008, https://www.cia.gov/library/publications/the-world-factbook.

[20] "South Asia: Review, Analysis, and Outlook," Global Development Finance–2007, World Bank, http://go.worldbank.org/Q2ER7NTX30.

[21] *CIA World Factbook* 2008, https://www.cia.gov/library/publications/the-world-factbook.

[22] "U.S.-India Joint Statement," Office of the Press Secretary, the White House, March 2, 2006, www.whitehouse.gov/news/releases/2006/03/20060302-5.html.

[23] Ibid.

[24] "India-U.S. Trade," Embassy of India, Washington, D.C. www.indianembassy.org/newsite/indoustrade.asp.

[25] "Doing Business in India," U.S. Commercial Service, 2008, www.buyusa.gov/india/en/motm.html.

[26] A number of U.S. investment banks opened up major funds in India in the 1990s, including Goldman Sachs, Morgan Stanley, JPMorgan Chase and Merrill Lynch. In recent years, these companies have expanded their holdings in India. See Tamal Bandyopadhyay, "Goldman Set to Flex India Muscles," Livemint.com, *Wall Street Journal*, March 6, 2008. The United States is the second-largest source of foreign direct investment in India (accounting for 13.4 percent of total inflow) and the second largest source in Pakistan (accounting for 13.9 percent of inflow). See "FDI in South Asia: Trends and Prospects," Asian Development Bank (ADB) Institute, 2005, www.adbi.org/discussion-paper/2006/11/28/2066.fdi.south.asia.policy.trends/fdi.in.south.asia.trends.and.prospects.

[27] "Expanding U.S., India Trade," Voice of America News, March 2, 2007, www.voanews.com/uspolicy/2007-03-05-voa1.cfm.

[28] "India Attracts $25 Billion FDI in 2007–08," *Hindustan Times*, May 20, 2008.

[29] "Corus Accepts £4.3bn Tata Offer," BBC News, October 20, 2006.

[30] "Britons Hail Tata's Takeover of Jaguar, Land Rover," *The Economic Times*, June 5, 2008.

[31] S. Majumder, "Mergers & Acquisitions: India Inc. on the Prowl," *The Hindu Business Line*, January 5, 2007.

[32] Jonathan Marcus, "Analysis: The World's Most Dangerous Place?" BBC News, March 23, 2000.

[33] See later in chapter for more on China.

[34] Ashling O'Connor, "Boeing Pitches in as India Offers Defence Contracts Worth $15bn," *Times Online*, December 4, 2006.

[35] Don Belt, "Struggle for the Soul of Pakistan," *National Geographic*, September 2007.

[36] Pakistan, India, and China have not committed to the Fissile Material Cut-Off Treaty (FMCT).

[37] Krittivas Mukherjee, "Nepal Maoists Not Ready to Renounce Violence, Yet," Reuters, April 24, 2008.

[38] Sreeram Chaulia, "Bangladeshi Immigrants Stoke Terror in India," *Asia Sentinel*, May 15, 2008. See Aminesh Roul, "Trail from Mumbai Blasts Leads to Multiple Terrorist Groups," *Terrorism Focus* 3, no. 29 (July 25, 2006).

[39] "Rural Poverty Portal," International Fund for Agricultural Development, March 7, 2007, www.ruralpovertyportal.org/english/regions/asia/.

[40] "Afghanistan's Poppy Conundrum," *Environment News Service,* March 15, 2007, www.ens-newswire.com/ens/mar2007/2007-03-15-03.asp.

[41] Ibid.

[42] "Annual Report Lauds Performance of Pakistan's Narcotics Courts," *Pakistan Times*, March 3, 2004.

[43] *International Narcotics Control Strategy Report 2008*, Bureau of International Narcotics and Law Enforcement Affairs, U.S. Department of State, March 2008, www.state.gov/p/inl/rls/nrcrpt/2008/vol1/html.

[44] Christopher M. Blanchard, *Afghanistan: Narcotics and U.S. Policy*, Congressional Research Service, updated December 6, 2007, www.fas.org/sgp/crs/row/RL32686.pdf.

[45] In early February 2009, A. Q. Khan was released from house arrest by the Pakistan government, much to the dismay of the U.S. government and other international actors.

[46] Given Pakistani reticence to allow U.S. officials to visit its nuclear sites, the U.S. government is having to rely largely on Pakistani assurances that the facilities are safe rather than on first-hand knowledge. This leaves many in the United States uncomfortable.

[47] Tanvi Madan, *Brookings Foreign Policy Studies Energy Security Series: India*, The Brookings Institution, November 2006, www.brookings.edu/reports/2006/11india.aspx.

[48] CSIS report, "India's Energy Dilemma," September 7, 2006.

[49] Energy Information Administration (EIA), "South Asia Overview," Country Analysis Briefs, March 2006. www.eia.doe.gov/emeu/cabs/South_Asia/Background.html.

[50] Andy Mukherjee, "The Cost of India's Nuclear U-turn," *International Herald Tribune*, October 16, 2007.

[51] Philip Bowring, "Oil-thirsty Asia Looks to Calm Gulf Waters," *International Herald Tribune*, February 9, 2006. India and Pakistan's relationship with Iran will strengthen if the proposed Iran-Pakistan-India (IPI) pipeline is actually implemented. As of 2010, talks continue and are unlikely to be completed anytime soon.

[52] "Climate Change: The Big Emitters," BBC News, July 4, 2005.

[53] In 1990 China and India produced a total of 13 percent of the world's CO_2 emissions, and in 2004, they produced 22 percent. See EIA, *International Energy Outlook 2007* (May 2007), www.eia.doe.gov/oiaf/ieo/emissions.html.

[54] International Atomic Energy Agency (IAEA), "Energy and Environment Data Reference Bank," 2006, www.iaea.org/inisnkm/nkm/aws/eedrb/data/IN-encc.html.

[55] One need only look at the impact of flooding in Bangladesh, earthquakes in China and Pakistan, and tornados in Burma to realize the importance of environmental change to this region.

[56] John Markoff, *Waves of Democracy: Social Movements and Political Change* (Thousand Oaks, CA: Pine Forge Press, 1996).

[57] President Bush stated in his second inaugural address that "it is the policy of the United States to seek and support the growth of democratic movements and institutions in every nation and culture, with the ultimate goal of ending tyranny in our world." See "President Sworn-In to Second Term," Office of the Press Secretary, the White House, January 20, 2005, www.whitehouse.gov/news/releases/2005/01/20050120-1.html.

[58] "Remarks at the American University in Cairo," U.S. Department of State, June 20, 2005, www.state.gov/secretary/rm/2005/48328.html.

[59] "Joint Statement Between President George W. Bush and Prime Minister Manmohan Singh," Office of the Press Secretary, the White House, July 18, 2005, www.whitehouse.gov/news/releases/2005/07/20050718-6.html.

[60] "From the Shanghai Communiqué to Global Stakeholders," Lecture by Robert B. Zoellick, National Committee on United States–China Relations, March 21, 2007, www.ncuscr.org/files/2007-B-O_lecture.pdf.

[61] While this term originated in the 1970s, it became common among members of the Bush administration. See "President Addresses American Legion, Discusses Global War on Terror," Office of the Press Secretary, the White House, February 24, 2006, www.whitehouse.gov/news/releases/2006/02/20060224.html.

[62] Deputy Secretary of State Negroponte stated this during a talk at the National Endowment for Democracy's Pakistan Forum on May 5, 2008, www.state.gov/s/d/2008/104366.htm.

[63] "Joint Statement on United States–Pakistan Strategic Partnership," Office of the Press Secretary, the White House, March 4, 2006, www.whitehouse.gov/news/releases/2006/03/20060304-1.html.

[64] The most notable case of this was following the Soviet pullout of Afghanistan; the United States soon after pulled away from its engagement with Pakistan.

[65] China, Russia, the United States, the United Kingdom, and France.

[66] Kishore Mahbubani, "The Case Against the West," *Foreign Affairs*, May/June 2008.

[67] "Secretary-General Discusses UN Reform in First Official Visit to Washington, D.C.," Press Release, Office of the Secretary-General, United Nations, January 23, 1997, www.un.org/News/Press/docs/1997/19970123.sgt2081.html.

[68] Resistance comes from multiple directions, whether with regard to veto rights that the Permanent Five are loath to give up or share, or with regard to new agencies, such as the Human Rights Council, which has garnered the antagonism of many countries where human rights abuses abound.

[69] Mahbubani, "The Case Against the West."

[70] "No Room for India as APEC Shuts Door on Hopefuls," Associated Foreign Press, September 5, 2007, http://afp.google.com/article/ALeqM5hwNnrKa6v_ylnfqt_BwWyoYyhSdg.

[71] India, Pakistan, and Iran have been observer states at the SCO since 2005. See Lionel Beehner and Preeti Bhattacharji, "The Shanghi Cooperation Organization," Council on Foreign Relations, April 8, 2008, www.cfr.org/publication/10883/shanghai_cooperation_organization.html.

[72] The United States attained observer status to SAARC in 2007. It also participates in the ASEAN Regional Forum but still does not hold observer status to ASEAN. See "US, EU, China, Japan to send observers to SAARC summit in India," Associated Foreign Press, www.eubusiness.com/news_live/1174561212.42. See also "About Us," ASEAN Regional Forum, 2005, www.aseanregionalforum.org/AboutUs/tabid/57/Default.aspx.

[73] "US's Rice 'to skip ASEAN meeting,'" BBC News, July 7, 2005, http://news.bbc.co.uk/2/hi/asia-pacific/4659441.stm.

[74] A notable early example was in the 1990 Gulf War when, unable to get UN cover, President H.W. Bush put together a coalition to drive Saddam Hussein out of Kuwait.

[75] One need only look at the current U.S. debate regarding NAFTA and the proposed FTA with Colombia to understand the constraints. See "Showdown on U.S.-Colombia Free-Trade Agreement," The Brookings Institution, April 9, 2008, www.brookings.edu/opinions/2008/0409_free_trade_agreement_blustein.aspx.

[76] In the year after SAFTA was negotiated (2004–2005), Pakistan's exports to India increased from $93.7 million to $288.3 million; likewise, India's exports to Pakistan increased from $382.4 million to $548.2 million. See Jamil Nasir, "Pakistan-India Trade from Porters to Trucks," *Dawn* 29 (October 2007).

[77] Shamsur Rabb Khan, "India, Pakistan for Joint Effort to Counter Terrorism," Institute of Peace and Conflict Studies, October 25, 2007, www.ipcs.org/Kashmir_articles2.jsp?action=showView&kValue=2418&issue=1012&status=article&mod=a&portal=pakistan.

[78] "Chilly Response to U.S. Plan to Deploy Forces in the Strait of Malacca," Institute for the Analysis of Global Security, May 24, 2004, www.iags.org/n0524042.html.

[79] It should be noted that many of these nations are nervous about India's influence, power, and size, and so there is some reticence (Bhutan aside) to taking assistance from India.

[80] See Hannah Beech, "ASEAN Turns Blind Eye to Burma Rights," *Time*, July 22, 2008.

[81] See Kennedy Abwao and Alan Cowell, "Undeterred by Criticism, Mugabe Joins Peers at African Union Meeting," *New York Times*, July 1, 2008.

[82] See Allan Gyngell, "Design Faults: The Asia Pacific's Regional Architecture," Lowy Institute for International Policy, July 2007, www.ciaonet.org/pbei/liip/0001108/0001108.pdf.

[83] In 2007 the Quadrilateral Initiative was formed by the United States, India, Australia, and Japan. The value of this organization remains unclear, while the cost in terms of Chinese antagonism is quite apparent. Such an organization does not promote security but diminishes it, and it indicates most clearly the importance of ensuring that any such organization has the right membership. If a similar grouping of the principal regional powers were to include China and Russia, however, it would be a valuable security stabilizer and venue to discuss issues of mutual concern.

[84] "Government Moots New Security Architecture with China," *The Economic Times*, June 6, 2008.

[85] Recent indications, however, suggest that both India and China are beginning to concede that they will have to take action soon, alongside actions by the developed world.

[86] The Core Group was made up of the United States, India, Australia, and Japan.

[87] Comments by Deputy Secretary of State Negroponte at a talk at the National Endowment for Democracy's Pakistan Forum on May 5, 2008, www.state.gov/s/d/2008/104366.htm.

THE "SOUTHERN VECTOR": RUSSIA'S STRATEGIC INTERESTS IN CENTRAL AND SOUTH ASIA

Igor Torbakov

After almost two decades of heated debates about Russia's direction following the collapse of the Soviet Union, a consensus appears to have emerged within the international analytic community: "Russia is back" as a key global player.[1] But another, no less intriguing, issue seems to continue to perplex pundits and policymakers around the world, and that is: What does Russia want?[2]

Indeed, what are the main drivers of the increasingly assertive Russian foreign policy? What are the principal strategic objectives of the present-day Kremlin rulers? And, more specifically, what is the place of Central and South Asia in the Russian strategic calculus? This chapter intends to address these questions. I begin by discussing how the sociopolitical system that has taken shape in Russia over the past decade affects the way the country behaves in the international arena; I then turn to an analysis of Russia's interests in Central Asia and of the policies that Moscow has been pursuing in the region; this is followed by a discussion of how South Asia—mainly India—figures in Russian strategic thinking.

The main points can be summed up as follows: Russia's foreign policy, in general, and its policies toward Central and South Asia, in particular, should be viewed within the dual context of Russia's post-Communist transformation and postimperial readjustment *and* Moscow's concept of a multipolar world as opposed to the perceived U.S. policy of unipolarity.

The specific importance of the "southern vector" of Russian foreign policy has been brought to the fore by three debacles that took place at the end of the twentieth century and in the beginning of the twenty-first century: (1) the Soviet-Afghan war, (2) the conflict in Chechnya, and (3) the developments following the September 11, 2001, attack on the United States.

Unlike the former Soviet Union, which was a true global superpower, Russia's principal strategic concern is the post-Soviet lands that Moscow considers the zone of its vital interests. Of particular importance is Russia's southern periphery—Central Asia—that presents both opportunities (due to the region's energy resources) and threats (stemming from the region's inherent instability). Moscow's most urgent concerns there are preserving the region's stability, strengthening control over its energy resources, and balancing the

275

major actors that are increasing their presence in Central Asia—the United States and China.

In Russia's strategic thinking, India—the key South Asian country—is regarded as a valuable ally. Historically, Moscow has always had good relations with New Delhi: both Russia and India are extremely wary of the rise of Islamic fundamentalism and terrorism; India shares Russia's concerns about unipolarity and staunchly supports the idea of a multipolar world. As the geopolitical competition among the great powers in Eurasia intensifies, Moscow's strategic planners contemplate engaging India in Central Asia with a view toward creating a potential counterweight to a rising China.

However, while Russia appears to perceive India as the least problematic big power in the region, India's new closeness with the United States does not sit well with the Moscow security community.

Russia's goal to maintain strategic preeminence in Central Asia, underpinned by Moscow's significantly increased economic and political clout, may ultimately not be realized. India will likely remain Russia's main partner in South Asia, but India's own increasingly multivector diplomacy leaves Russia as just one of several important strategic partners.

Russia as an Independent Great Power

Most "Russia watchers" seem to agree that, since the 1998 financial meltdown, Moscow has managed to reverse the process of its strategic decline and, mainly due to the massive energy windfall, succeed in regaining its geopolitical posture as the Eurasian great power. However, at the same time, Russia's relations with the West have significantly deteriorated, leaving quite a few observers puzzled. Why is it, some might ask, that "the more capitalist and Westernized Russia becomes, the more anti-Western its policies seem"?[3] At the same time, Moscow appears keen to intensively develop trade ties and political cooperation with the major non-Western powers—particularly the Asian giants such as China and India—giving rise to speculation in some quarters that the Kremlin is about to turn its back on the West and embrace the "rising East."[4] The key to understanding Russia's international behavior, in my view, lies in grasping the nature of the regime that emerged from under the rubble of the Soviet Communist empire and matured on President Putin's watch.

A detailed analysis of the Russian sociopolitical system is beyond the scope of this chapter. Several crucial things, though, must be pointed out: After the Soviet Union's disintegration and Communism's collapse, Russia's new leaders embraced democratic rhetoric and set out—so they claimed—to build a political system based on rule of law and liberal market democracy, similar to that of the West. At the time, as there seemed to be no other viable ideology at hand except Western-style democracy, the Russian elite's decision seemed only natural, and the West was very enthusiastic about and supportive of Russia's initial post-Communist transformation. However, due to its historical legacy, Russia (and most other ex-Soviet nations) could not build a Western-style polity and economy; neither the country's elite nor the public was prepared culturally, intellectually, or psychologically to pull off such a feat. Instead, a different kind of system emerged in Russia, distinct from both the old Soviet Communism and Western liberal democracy. Quite aptly, some political scientists call this system a "patrimonial authoritarianism," noting that it is based, both in its political and economic spheres, not so much on formal rules and institutions as on informal patronage networks.[5] While substantially different from the liberal Western model, the Russian authoritarian system continues to make use of democratic rhetoric and quasi-democratic procedures to legitimize its rule.

This deeply dichotomous nature of the current Russian regime—with its central contradiction between authoritarian ways and pseudo-democratic phraseology—is clearly reflected in Moscow's international behavior, which also appears to be contradictory and inconsistent. While its seeming adherence to democratic values would call for an ever-closer alliance between Russia and the West, the undemocratic nature of the country's sociopolitical system forces the elite to make sure that the Western impact on Russia's domestic order and the way it does business is minimal. Furthermore, seeking to preserve the strategic environment that would be most conducive for the perpetuation of the political and economic well-being of Russia's powers-that-be, Moscow strives to counter what it perceives as Western attempts at undermining the kindred authoritarian regimes in post-Soviet lands. Supporting same-type systems, in what Russia's policy elite believes is its geopolitical sphere of influence, appears to be viewed as a sine qua non for its ultimate long-term survival. It is precisely the belated realization that the persistence of the current Russian political and economic system makes its integration with Western institutions unfeasible, along with its inability to find a mutually acceptable modus operandi, that badly sours the relationship between Moscow and the West.

The Russians seem to have recognized the incompatibility of patrimonial authoritarianism and liberal democracy sooner than their Western counterparts did. As integration with the West proved impractical, the Russian policy elite advanced an updated vision of the global order encapsulated in Moscow's pet concept of multipolarity. In the twenty-first century, the concept holds, the U.S. unipolar moment has ended—mainly due to America's drastically reduced influence as a result of the Iraq debacle, the rise of China and India, and the rebirth of Russian power. In the new multipolar global system, Russia is destined to be one of the principal poles acting as a major independent player in the international arena.

The idea of Russia's strategic independence is additionally upheld in the auxiliary concept of "sovereign democracy," which does not pertain, as some commentators believe, only to the sphere of Russian domestic politics. Rather, the notion of sovereign democracy neatly describes the nature of Russia's international identity by claiming that national sovereignty has an absolute priority over any other foreign policy notions. Some Kremlin theorists basically equate sovereignty with a country's competitiveness in international affairs and, therefore, implicitly put Russia on par with America. As they view it: in the contemporary world there is only one true sovereign democracy—the United States—and the other main global poles are either not democratic enough (for example, China) or sovereign enough (the European Union, EU).[6]

The vision of a global order based on the concepts of multipolarity and sovereign democracy leads the Russian political class to formulate the country's main foreign policy objectives, which appear to be: (1) continuing the process of turning Russia into Eurasia's leading great power; (2) engaging the United States and the EU while preventing the West from undermining political regimes of Russia and its allies in post-Soviet Eurasia; (3) developing close economic and political ties with other important Eurasian nations, including Iran, and, in particular, Asia's rising great powers—China and India.

Russia in Central Asia: Reclaiming Leadership in the Volatile Southern Periphery

The fact that, historically, Russia—both Tsarist Russia and the Soviet Union—has been an empire (and a continental empire at that) cannot be emphasized enough. For a huge land-based empire, the necessity to protect its extremely long and often porous borders is a security issue of paramount importance. In fact, constantly expanding its outer periphery, absorbing new lands, and creating buffer zones is a set of policies a land-based empire usually resorts to in order to make its vulnerable frontiers secure.[7] This strategy has been a key factor behind the continental empires' territorial growth—the same pattern that brought Russia into Central Asia in the middle of the nineteenth century and has kept it there ever since. It is true that following the collapse of the Soviet Union, Russia has been involved in the painful process of "post-imperial disengagement from the former provinces and simultaneous re-engagement with its new neighbors on a new set of principles."[8] But what should these new principles be? Most contemporary Russian strategists appear to be convinced that Russia must respond to security challenges along its southern frontier by revisiting, in the words of one recent policy paper, "the Russian traditional idea of maintaining security of its borders—either by expanding these borders or, at a minimum, by expanding the zone of stability around Russia."[9] So, it is probably worthwhile to keep in mind that Russia's postimperial readjustment is, in effect, an open-ended affair.

Although, unlike the Soviet Union, Russia is not an empire and, as one foreign policy expert put it, "Russia's business is Russia itself," the former continental empire finds it difficult to disengage from its former colonies (far more so than a maritime empire would). For one, the interpenetration of an imperial metropol and a colonial periphery is more intimate and intensive. Once an empire ends, territorial contiguity demands that former colonies be seen not only as phenomena exclusively pertaining to the sphere of foreign policy but also as factors directly affecting the domestic situation of the former imperial center. Despite imperial nostalgia and the ongoing heated debate among the Russian intellectuals as to whether the postimperial Russia is able to reinvent itself as a "normal" nation-state, the bulk of the Kremlin policy elite do not want a reestablishment of the Eurasian empire. But while formally recognizing the independence of the ex-Soviet Central Asian republics, Moscow clearly continues to view the region as a zone of vital security and economic interest. There are several reasons why the "southern vector" of Russia's foreign policy has become exceptionally important.

First, remarkably, in the 1970s–1980s and then from the 1990s on, the USSR and Russia have been involved in military conflicts exclusively along their southern frontiers. The ill-starred Soviet war in Afghanistan, the two wars against the Chechen separatists, the instability in Russia's North Caucasus provinces and the interethnic conflicts across the Great Caucasus range, the civil war in Tajikistan, and the U.S.-led invasion of Afghanistan following the terrorist attacks against America in 2001, all have underscored the potential vulnerability of what the nineteenth-century Russian military strategists used to call Russia's "soft underbelly."

Second, following the disintegration of the Soviet Union, Russia was immediately faced with grave security problems in the newly independent Central Asian states along what had been purely administrative borders at the time of the Soviet Union. Suffice it to mention that Russia's border with Kazakhstan, stretching for about 7,500 kilometers, is the longest interstate border in the world. It is along these new borders with post-Soviet Central Asia that Russia is being challenged by a host of threats: ethnic conflicts, Islamist fundamentalism and international terrorism, illegal migration, and drug and arms trafficking. Furthermore, a number of Russian strategists note that Central Asia and the Caspian region directly above the Greater Middle East have—particularly after 9/11—acquired a special significance in global geopolitics.[10]

Third, while it is surprising that all five Central Asian nations managed to survive and retain their sovereignty despite the internal and external challenges they have faced following the Soviet Union's demise, their current political regimes are inherently unstable due to institutional weaknesses and the clannish nature of the power there. Therefore, the general sociopolitical situation in Central Asia remains precarious, and Russian analysts and policymakers are fully aware that any crisis in the region will have direct implications for Russia's own security.

Finally, Central Asia is strategically important because of its abundance of mineral resources—particularly oil and gas. Participating in the development of the region's hydrocarbon resources and exercising control over its transportation to world markets is seen as key to Russia's dominance as a geopolitical actor in Eurasia. The growing competition over these resources among Russia, the United States, China, and the EU, as well as the increasing tendency of Central Asian nations to maneuver among these great powers, playing them off against one another, compels Russia to keep a watchful eye on regional developments and to come up with counterstrategies.

The complex mixture of challenges and opportunities that Russia faces in Central Asia shapes Moscow's main strategic interests in the region. Russia's principal concern remains the preservation of Central Asia's internal stability. Any local turmoil—whether caused by a botched succession crisis, by political confrontations gone out of control, by the resurgent Islamists challenging the region's secular regimes, or by interethnic clashes—will be viewed by Moscow as a direct threat to Russia's stability and security.

Along with this paramount interest in keeping Central Asia stable at all costs, Russia is keen on retaining as much control as possible over the extraction, transit, and access to the world markets of Central Asian oil and gas.

Moscow also appears determined to keep its military presence in the region, with the view of turning the Russian-dominated Collective Security Treaty Organization (CSTO) into the foundation of a regional system of security. The Russian strategists proceed from the assumption that no other great power but Russia is ready to take on the responsibility of providing security for Central Asian nations. Therefore, some Russian experts assert that Moscow needs to strive to transform the CSTO's rapid reaction task force into a viable instrument capable of coping with the potential crisis situations in Central Asia.[11]

Regulating the massive migration inflows of Central Asians coming to Russia as guest workers, often illegally, seems to have become an increasingly growing concern of Russian authorities. As one commentary notes, it would appear that Central Asia is now "moving into Russia" as millions of Uzbeks, Tajiks, and representatives of the region's other ethnic groups seek to settle in the Russian Federation, either permanently or at least temporarily.[12]

Finally, it is Russia's key strategic interest to find accommodation in Central Asia with its two main geopolitical competitors in the region—the United States and China. To be sure, the majority of Russian experts readily admit that in a rapidly globalizing world, the Kremlin's geopolitical monopoly in Central Asia is a completely unrealistic proposition. Russia, however, will likely continue to seek ways to limit U.S. influence in the region while also trying to check China's Central Asian ambitions.[13]

Although the Russian political class appears to be aware of Moscow's core interests in Central Asia, the outcomes of Russia's actual policies in the region are mixed. Most Russian analysts agree that throughout the entire period following the disintegration of the Soviet Union, the Kremlin failed to elaborate and pursue a coherent Central Asia policy.[14] Some experts argue that Russian policies in relation to Central Asia can in fact be described as a sequence of distinct evolutionary phases, such as: the "leave and forget" policy, the "outposts as placeholders" policy, and the "reconquista" policy, none of which were particularly successful.[15]

Giving top priority to stability, Russian policymakers are intent on keeping the local regimes afloat by trying to contain the advance of Islamic fundamentalism and to prop up the region's secular authorities. But these two sets of policies appear to run at cross-purposes as Moscow supports those regimes that actually are secular dictatorships, pure and simple: clannish, corrupt, repressive, and utterly averse to any kind of democratic reform. With their political base remaining narrow and claims to legitimacy flimsy, the Central Asian regimes are potentially brittle with an ever-more alienated and impoverished populace—particularly in Uzbekistan and Tajikistan—becoming increasingly religious and radicalized.[16] Analysts predict that at least several Central Asian countries may well become religious states soon. "I think you're going to get another Islamic state down the road," Martha Brill Olcott, a Central Asia expert at the Carnegie Endowment for International Peace, has recently said of Uzbekistan; "The question is whether it's going to be tolerant or intolerant."[17]

Yet Russia, although fixated on the struggle against "terrorists," appears to be completely unprepared to deal with any kind of large-scale political turmoil caused by the rise of Islamic fundamentalism in the region. Arguably, the Kremlin finds itself in a trap of its own making: for Russia, the only way to make the region truly stable is to be able to act as an agent of change, as a force for genuine modernization, nudging the local authoritarian regimes to transform, democratize, and broaden their sociopolitical base—but the nature of Russia's own political regime effectively acts as a brake on this progressive kind of policy. As a result, Moscow is instead compelled to act as a conservative force that seeks, through various "counterrevolutionary" measures, to stem the tide of what has come to be known as "color revolutions"—political upheavals in the post-Soviet lands that Russia perceives as Western-inspired revolts aimed at undermining those regimes that are geopolitically loyal to the Kremlin. If there is no change in Moscow's policy toward the region, Russia's appeal for Central Asians will likely continue to diminish.

Likewise, in the crucial energy sphere, Moscow's Central Asia policy seems to be shaped and constrained by the specific characteristics of Russia's current political and economic system. Of all the resources that the Central Asian countries possess, Russia is most interested in gas as key to Moscow's lucrative energy relationship with Europe. The scheme is simple: taking advantage of its monopolistic control of the Central Asian gas market, Russia buys fuel on the cheap from Central Asian producers, and then either uses it for subsidized domestic consumption or sells it at escalating world prices to EU countries while enjoying a huge price differential; yet, all the while, its monopoly is being eroded by China's growing appetite for Central Asian energy. Beijing is prepared to pay a better price than Russia—though, still not a world-market price—for the region's gas. The Russo-Chinese competition over Central Asian resources is bound to intensify and is already producing a threefold result: First, the region's energy-rich nations, like Turkmenistan and Kazakhstan, are increasingly emboldened and ready to break Russia's stranglehold on their gas exports (with help from the Chinese). Second, the emergence of an alternate non-Russian export route encourages local gas producers to band together to increase their collective leverage with Russia (and also China), potentially leading to a formation of a more or less institutionalized regional consortium of energy producers. Finally, the regional countries' unified stance in relation to Russia gives them more clout to renegotiate gas prices and make Moscow pay a "real" (that is, an almost world-market) price for the region's fuel.[18]

For Russia, there appears to be two ways to respond to this situation. The first is to modernize its gas-guzzling industries, drastically revamp wasteful domestic consumption, and dramatically increase investment in the exploration of the new gas fields in Eastern Siberia and the Arctic; together, these measures would likely reduce Russia's current overdependence on Central Asian energy. The second way is to continue the struggle for a dominant position in the Central Asian gas market and to shift the burden of the price-hike further afield—making the Eastern European countries, like Ukraine, and customers in the EU pay more for Russian gas supplies. Remarkably, in today's Russia, those who control the Kremlin also control Gazprom, the country's giant energy monopoly. As the top leaders personifying the opaque nexus of political power and energy business in Russia seem more interested in "rent-seeking" than in long-term investment and reform, the Kremlin energy policy in Central Asia will likely be more of the same; such a policy clearly lacks vision. But again, as one astute commentator points out: "Russian political and business leaders have always been influenced by the thought that they might not be here tomorrow; they consequently have a very short-term mentality."[19] Yet Russia's stubborn desire to retain control over the Central Asian market of hydrocarbons is unlikely to be fulfilled, especially in the long run—mainly due to the steady rise of the Chinese influence in Central Asia.

Another crucial factor of Russia's Central Asia policy is Moscow's interaction in the region with other outside great powers. The interrelations within the triangle of Russia, China, and the United States—as these three heavyweights pursue their interests in Central Asia—appear to be extremely complex and contradictory. This complexity stems from the fact that the agendas that Moscow, Beijing, and Washington pursue in the region are all different and not necessarily always compatible.

Russia, the former imperial overlord for almost two hundred years, seeks to reestablish the regional leadership that was thrown into doubt by the country's almost-decade-long strategic retreat following the Soviet Union's 1991 unraveling. For its part, China, which was mainly absent from Central Asia for the past two centuries, is reemerging to reclaim what historians argue has always been its traditionally exceptional place in the region.[20] While Russia and China are Central Asia's direct neighbors, America is geographically far removed from the region. The U.S. economic interests there are relatively limited, being largely concentrated on developing and marketing the abundant energy resources in Kazakhstan's sector of the Caspian. It would appear that Washington's true stake in Central Asia is mainly geopolitical. Being the only true global power, the United States seeks to prevent the emergence of a peer competitor—a reestablishment of a "Eurasian empire" either under a Russian or Chinese aegis. To forestall the realization of such a scenario, the United States strives to preserve the "geopolitical pluralism" in Central Asia. Politically, that means supporting the independence and sovereignty of the regional states; economically, it means advancing the principle of "multiple pipelines" for Caspian energy resources. Additionally, in the aftermath of 9/11, America was keen to set up and maintain military outposts in the region, meant to serve a twofold strategic purpose: provide logistical support for the U.S.-led war in Afghanistan and, in the long run, help contain China.[21]

Both Moscow and Beijing are wary of the U.S. military presence in the lands they regard as their geopolitical backyard. While all three outside great powers hold that the stability of Central Asia is of paramount importance, Russia and China oppose the specific American strategy aimed at securing regional stability—meaning the set of policies known under the rubric of "democracy promotion." By contrast, China and Russia strongly believe that the only way to keep Central Asia calm and stable is to support the local authoritarian regimes, that any careless push for reform at this stage will lead not to democracy and greater stability but to chaos and warfare among various regional clans.[22] Russia and China's shared suspicion of American designs in the region brings the two countries closer together in their mutual desire to balance the global hegemon. The Shanghai Cooperation Organization (SCO), a grouping of regional countries set up in 2001 and dominated by Beijing and Moscow, is one of the key instruments for this balancing.[23] It would be farfetched, however, to conclude that what is being witnessed is the emergence of a kind of strategic Sino-Russian axis. Instead, we can talk about a Russo-Chinese "axis of convenience," to use the expression suggested by the London-based analyst Bobo Lo—a relationship based on a set of certain selected common interests rather than shared values.[24] But interests, as everyone knows, can and do change and, when this happens, the interest-based relationship might find itself under severe strain.

In fact, as a number of experts point out, the Russia-China relationship is already being tested. For Moscow, one of the major irritants is China's aggressive economic penetration of Central Asia—particularly in the spheres of energy and trade.[25] Beijing appears to be extremely skillful in making good use of the SCO to advance its economic interests; under the cover of regionalism, the Chinese are making ever bolder inroads into what Moscow still believes is mainly its turf.[26] The Russians jealously eye China as it robustly builds bilateral ties with its Central Asian partners, often surpassing Russia both in the volume and efficiency of its investments in the local economies. The policymakers in Moscow seem to have legitimate grounds for being apprehensive. The main question that is troubling for them is: for how long will China, given its phenomenal growth rate and the scale of its economy, be prepared to accommodate Russia's interests within the framework of the SCO? So far, the Russians still are the largest outside stakeholders in the region but, as one observer notes, the pushy Chinese "are eager to buy in despite an obvious Russian reluctance to sell."[27]

The Russian experts have long been aware of the true goals of the Chinese game within the SCO. "China is seeking to quickly transform the SCO into the single integrated economic space," professor Vilya Gelbras, one of Russia's leading sinologists, argued in a 2005 interview; "For China, the SCO is one of the [efficient] tools it is using to economically reclaim those territories that China believes had belonged to it in the past."[28] The Russian political analyst Dmitry Trenin puts it even more succinctly: the SCO "actually stands for China in Central Asia."[29] No wonder some Moscow strategists suggest that for Russia, the need to check China's Central Asian ambitions may soon become a far more urgent concern than American penetration of the region.[30] In a recent essay tellingly titled "Russia between China and the West," Fyodor Lukyanov, the editor-in-chief of the influential journal *Russia in Global Affairs*, forcefully argues: "Russia must maintain maximally good relations with China"; however, he adds, "Moscow should make no mistake as to what extent its long-term trajectory may coincide with China's." Russia's new president, Lukyanov predicts, will soon "face a tough question—how to keep political parity with the People's Republic of China?"[31]

The issue of Russian-Indian cooperation in Central Asia is being discussed by the Moscow policy elite within the context of these complex geopolitical equations.

The Strategic Environment in Eurasia and the Russia-India Partnership

As Russia's anxieties about China's growing geopolitical stature and assertiveness in Central Asia become more acute, the Kremlin appears to be aiming at creating a greater strategic diversity in Eurasia. One way to achieve this goal, analysts note, is to form a triad with China and Japan: it was suggested that "such strategic triangularism has been only a peripheral factor in the steady improvement of Russia-India relations under Putin." The argument has been that "the Kremlin does not view India as a strategic counterweight to China, but rather values good ties with New Delhi for their own sake—as a key market for Russian weapons and nuclear energy."[32]

There are signs, however, of a subtle shift in Russia's strategic outlook as experts argue for a more robust Russia-India partnership, considering it beneficial in itself and also as a useful instrument to balance China. A recently released report by the Institute of National Strategy, a Moscow-based independent think tank, has assessed the foreign policy legacy of the Putin administration and concluded that in the ongoing competition between Russia and China over the leadership position in Central Asia, Beijing's prospects, so far, look much better. To offset the China factor, Russia, the authors of the report suggest, should forge a "strategic alliance" with India. The report adds that this pact should specifically contain a clause of mutual military assistance in case of aggression.[33] Most Russian experts view India's participation in Central Asia's geopolitical equation as particularly desirable: "Introducing India to the region as a security factor would have the effect, from Russia's perspective, of limiting China's ambitions," one policy paper contends.[34]

Two recent developments appear to have influenced Russian strategic thinking about India. The first is the spectacular rise of India's international stature—Moscow is just one of the world capitals that has realized India is on the cusp of achieving a great power status. Second, India itself has become more assertive in its foreign policy, seeking to "reclaim its standing in the 'near abroad,'" of which Central Asia is considered to be an important part.[35] As the Indian prime minister Manmohan Singh stated at the 2006 Combined Commanders' Conference, "We have traditionally conceived our security in extending circles of engagement. Today, whether it is West Africa, the Gulf, Central Asia, or the Indian Ocean region, there is increasing demand for our political, economic, and defense engagement."[36]

In Central Asia, India seeks strategic depth, viewing the region (like China and Russia) as part of its extended strategic neighborhood. Being alarmed by the resurgence of the Taliban, India is keen to preserve stability and security in the autocratic yet secular regimes of Central Asia. New Delhi is obviously in favor of a cautious and gradual reform of the regional sociopolitical systems while being extremely wary of what one Indian analyst called the "promotion of any aggressive democratic practices," clearly referring to the perceived U.S. policy in Eurasia.[37] With the Indian economy growing rapidly and the demand for energy imports steeply rising, New Delhi hungrily eyes the Central Asian and Russian energy resources. Significantly, holding an observer status in the SCO, India is constantly stressing the importance of including energy cooperation in the bloc's key objectives, pointing out that the SCO is composed of energy producers and consumers. And, like the SCO's leading members, Russia and China, India fully shares the grouping's other principal goals: the struggle against terrorism, extremism, and separatism, as well as the curtailment of drug trafficking in the region.[38]

From Russia's perspective, India is indeed an extremely valuable partner in this volatile strategic part of the world. There are two crucial factors that bring Moscow and New Delhi closer together and make their vital interests compatible at the regional revel—Central and South Asia. Historically, India and Russia (in its previous incarnation of the Soviet Union) enjoyed cordial relations undisturbed by any major geopolitical disagreements. "India is a natural friend of Russia," asserts one of Moscow's leading India experts.[39] Both countries share a similar geopolitical outlook: rejection of the vision of a unipolar world and support for multipolarity, respect for national sovereignty and the principle of autonomy in foreign policymaking, and a negative attitude toward the doctrines of intervention and regime change.[40]

For Russian strategists, India's current geopolitical profile appears to be just right for it to be Moscow's useful ally. For one, it has already become strong enough to play the role of an important balancer in relation to China—it was India's increased clout that made the Russians treat it with due respect as an emerging great power in the first place. On the other hand, India still remains a second-tier player in Eurasia—which is also a plus from the Russian standpoint, as this prevents New Delhi, at least for now, from becoming Moscow's serious competitor on par with Beijing. At a recent roundtable discussion on Russian-Indian relations at the Moscow-based Institute of World Economy and International Relations, it was suggested that Moscow should be interested in the rise of India's influence in Eurasia since it is the only country whose growing weight in Central Asia "will not pose a threat to Russian national interests."[41]

For its part, New Delhi appears to appreciate Moscow's eagerness to recognize India's preeminence in South Asia. Russia's major focus of interest in this region is India, and it has never tried to take advantage of the many differences and rivalries between New Delhi and its neighbors. In general, Russia never concerned itself with strategic balance in South Asia—a fact eagerly acknowledged by Indian analysts. Furthermore, Russia's consistent refraining from selling arms to Pakistan has undoubtedly added to Indian-Russian strategic understanding.[42]

Remarkably, as Russia would not like to see India weakened, a weak Russia is not in India's interest. "India is probably the only big country that would genuinely welcome a resurgence of Russian power, not in the context of a renewed Cold War or East-West conflict, but for a better international equilibrium," argues Kanwal Sibal, India's senior diplomat.[43] The prominent Indian foreign policy commentator S. Nihal Singh concurs: "A resurgent Russia is in India's and the world's interest because it makes the emergence of a unipolar world that much more unlikely and gives greater scope to the concept of a multi-polar era."[44] It would appear, though, that America, the current global hegemon, is not New Delhi's only or even principal concern—it is China that is largely on the minds of India's strategic planners. Sibal spells it out very clearly: "Russia's rise would be desirable for India and for others as it would be a counterweight to Chinese ambitions."[45]

So, on the face of it, the Russian-Indian "strategic partnership" seems to be solid, with the two countries' geo-strategic outlooks converging in a traditionally friendly relationship underpinned by massive military-technical cooperation. New Delhi has long been the largest client of Russia's military-industrial complex—around 70 percent of the military hardware and equipment used by India's armed forces are of Russian origin. The broad strategic understanding between the two countries appear to have culminated in Russia's support for India's desire to acquire a military base in Central Asia. Having received Moscow's green light, India has maintained a presence at the Ayni air base near Dushanbe (the Tajik capital) since 2002, and spent over $1.5 million on renovating the facility. In 2005 Russia, India, and Tajikistan agreed to share command and control over Ayni; Moscow and New Delhi also pledged to jointly maintain the base.[46]

However, the strategic environment in Eurasia is in a state of flux, and the power configurations of Russia, India, China, the United States, and the Central Asian nations keep changing—sometimes in dramatic ways. From the Russian perspective, the crucial factor currently affecting the Russian-Indian strategic partnership is the spectacular warming-up of U.S.–Indian relations. To be sure, Moscow has been aware of the rapprochement between New Delhi and Washington over the past several years, but it appears to have fully realized the implications of the new flowering of Indo–U.S. ties only following the unveiling of the nuclear deal between the two countries.

The new relationship between India and America is likely driven to a large extent by Washington's desire to use India as a counterweight to a growing China. Moscow, of course, has similar concerns about the rising Middle Kingdom and also shares the vision of India as a capable balancer; but this is hardly a case of a U.S.–Russia meeting of the minds. Most Russian analysts suspect that America's move to forge closer ties with New Delhi seeks to thoroughly revamp the system of international relations in Eurasia while "folding India into the American [strategic] worldview."[47] The very notion of a "Greater Central Asia"—the vision of Central and South Asia as one geo-strategic entity—while being actively advanced by the United States is seen as inimical to Russia's vital interests. The Kremlin is wary of Washington's plans to connect ex-Soviet Central Asia with South Asian nations in a web of common programs and initiatives that would help maintain security, expand trade and energy cooperation, develop transportation links, and promote democratic reform. America's grand strategy—in which India is, of course, destined to play a key role—seeks, according to a commentary published in the Russian Army newspaper, to turn this vast region "into a single military-strategic and geopolitical space" and "wean [Central Asia] away from Russia's and China's influence."[48] The United States' generous offer of nuclear technologies and military hardware to India only adds to Russia's anxieties. The Kremlin appears to be especially annoyed by the fact that it is America and not Russia who is emerging as a kind of viable successor to the Soviet Union, which had been a protector of India's strategic interests during the Cold War era. One can get a good sense of how seriously the Russian policy elite is alarmed by the U.S.–India rapprochement from a commentary by Andrei Volodin, an Indian expert at the Institute of World Economy and International Relations: "If Indo-American 'Entente' achieves its full potential, while the scope of the relations between Moscow and New Delhi remains as it has been for the last twenty years, Russia will end up being the biggest loser—both in the East and in the West."[49]

Indeed, Russia's perception of the bilateral relationship appears to be lagging behind the pace of India's transformation. The economic reforms that India carried out allowed the country to bring its relations with the West, including the United States, to a qualitatively new level. At the same time, Russia's inability to provide capital and new technologies has made the traditional partnership less intensive. The level of bilateral trade, at a meager $4 billion, remains inauspiciously low. According to Russian and Indian experts, the core of the bilateral relationship still is, as it has been over the past decades, in the defense supplies sector. But in this sphere, too, problems have been cropping up. The Indians have been complaining that product support for Russian military hardware (maintenance of support facilities, supply of spare parts, etc.) does not meet India's expectations. Furthermore, the present-day mercantilist Kremlin is keen to shift from the Soviet-time "friendship prices" to "commercial prices"; but this new pricing policy often makes Russian equipment as expensive as the military hardware made by other producers. Remarkably, over the next few years India is expected to spend around $40 billion on new weapons systems. The competition for the Indian defense market promises to be cutthroat and the Russians are anxious that New Delhi, Moscow's longest-served customer, might now turn to the United States and other Western arms makers. Additionally, the Kremlin realizes that it will now have to compete with Washington, too, also on the Indian nuclear market.

It appears that Moscow, uneasy about India's new closeness to the United States and unhappy about the prospect of losing at least some part of India's lucrative defense market to Western competitors, has decided to send New Delhi a warning signal via Central Asia. According to media reports, India's great power dreams in Central Asia—the long-planned deployment of its MiG fighter bombers at the Ayni base in Tajikistan—were dashed, at least for now. Not only did the Tajik authorities refuse India permission to deploy the aircraft, apparently pressured by the Russians, they appear intent on denying New Delhi access to the base.[50] Russia's message seemed to be clear: if India wants to keep a beachhead in strategic Central Asia, it must be more attentive to Russian interests and maintain a distance from the Americans.

Conclusion

The Ayni base issue demonstrates how contradictory Russia's India policy is. Moscow's reluctance to let New Delhi develop its Central Asian outpost—the only military base India would have beyond its national borders—because of the new Indo-U.S. friendship clearly runs contrary to the idea of engaging India in Central Asia to help create an additional counterweight to China. But the incident also betrays a larger problem: Russia's diminishing ability to realize its main strategic objective in Eurasia. The Kremlin does not make a secret of its desire to have a controlling influence over the region's political and economic affairs. But it seems to possess a limited number of tools to pursue this goal: making use of corrupt power networks in the neighboring countries, resorting to various kinds of pressure, or using outright coercion. Such international behavior, as Moscow analysts themselves readily admit, creates a bad image problem for Russia—the leaders of other ex-Soviet states tend to think of the

Kremlin as a bully and not as a genuine friend. The task seems more challenging for Russia when we consider the fact that the former Soviet lands, ever more diverse, are becoming an area of intense competition, where Moscow's strategic interests clash with those of Beijing, Washington, and Brussels. As the Central Asian states develop economic and political relations with a broad range of partners, embodying what has come to be known as multivector diplomacy, they are feeling more emboldened to take independent diplomatic action. Symptomatically, Central Asian analysts and policymakers increasingly point out that while they understand Russia's concerns about the presence in the region of other outside powers, it's time for the Kremlin to understand that the Central Asians may have their own views on the foreign presence in their neighborhood—views that are not identical to Russia's.[51]

One of the major problems preventing Russia from playing a leadership role in Eurasia is the nature of its political regime. So far, Moscow does retain the status of the largest outside stakeholder in the region. But with the Kremlin ruling elite being reluctant to turn Russia into the principal force for modernization in the post-Soviet lands—mainly due to their group interest in rent-seeking and personal aggrandizement, which necessitates the preservation of "socially akin" power networks in neighboring countries—the growing geopolitical competition in Eurasia will inevitably lead to the erosion of Russian influence.

Remarkably, the character of Russia's sociopolitical system seems to be negatively affecting the development of Indo-Russian relations as well. A number of Russian India experts warn about the increasing divergent trajectories the two countries are moving along: India, they note, is a country with a genuine vibrant democracy and robust civil society institutions; by contrast, in Russia, political democracy is basically an imitation, civil society barely visible, and political institutions (barring an omnipotent executive) do not play a significant role. Therefore, India and Russia "are in fact headed in opposite directions," argues Viktor Krasil'shchikov, a leading India specialist at the Institute of World Economy and International Relations; given this fact, he continues, "It is difficult to talk about any serious prospects for strategic cooperation" between the two countries.[52] Significantly, some Russian and Indian analysts note that commonality of values is one of the important factors bringing India and America closer together. True, the Indian nuclear market appears to be a powerful magnet, but besides common interests there are also shared values: "India's attraction for America is that it is a democracy," argues S. Nihal Singh.[53]

To be sure, there is an influential school of thought with representatives in both countries that still views Russia as a "partner of choice" for India due to its historically friendly relations with New Delhi, its defense industrial base, and its vast energy reserves.[54] However, India, not unlike ex-Soviet Central Asian nations, is well aware that it will be better off if it manages to strike a balance between the numerous aspirants to the role of its "principal" strategic partner.

India will likely continue pursuing its own multivector diplomacy, seeking to get as much as possible on the best possible terms.

Notes

[1] Richard Sakwa, "'New Cold War' or Twenty Years' Crisis? Russia and International Politics," *International Affairs* 84 (2008): 2; Sergei Karaganov, "Novaia epokha protivostoianiia," *Rossiia v global'noi politike* 4 (2007).

[2] See, for example, Ivan Krastev, "What Russia Wants," *Foreign Policy*, May–June, 2008.

[3] Ibid.

[4] For example, in her commentary on Medvedev's China visit, Masha Lipman, a Russia expert at the Carnegie Moscow Center, asserted, "He [Medvedev] is going east, not west, thereby sending a signal that the East is more important than the West for Russia." See Chloe Arnold, "Russia: Medvedev Looks East, Not West, on First Foreign Visit," *RFE/RL*, May 21, 2008.

[5] Dmitry Furman, "Politicheskaia sistema sovremennoi Rossii," in *Rossiia mezhdu Zapadom i Vostokom: Mosty v budushchee* (Moscow: Mezhdunarodnye otnosheniia, 2003); Celeste A. Wallander, "Russian Transimperialism and Its Implications," *Washington Quarterly* 30 (2007): 2.

[6] See Dmitry Trenin, "Vneshniaia politika Rossii: samoutverzhdenie ili modernizatsionnyi resurs," Polit.ru, May 13, 2008, www.polit.ru/institutes/2008/05/13/vneshpol_print.html.

[7] Alfred J. Rieber, "How Persistent Are Persistent Factors," in *Russian Foreign Policy in the Twenty-first Century and the Shadow of the Past*, ed. Robert Legvold. (New York: Columbia Univ. Press, 2007); idem, "Persistent Factors in Russian Foreign Policy: An Interpretive Essay," in *Imperial Russian Foreign Policy*, ed. Hugh Ragsdale (Cambridge: Woodrow Wilson Center and Cambridge Univ. Press, 1993).

[8] Dmitry Trenin, "Russia and Central Asia: Interests, Policies, and Prospects," in *Central Asia: Views from Washington, Moscow, and Beijing* (Armonk, NY: M. E. Sharpe, 2007), 80.

[9] Aleksandr Knyazev, "Rossiia vozvrashchaetsia v Tsentral'nuiu Aziiu," *Tsentral'naia Aziia i Kavkaz* 5 (2007), 36.

[10] See Mikhail Margelov, "Rossiia na Bol'shom Blizhnem Vostoke," *Rossiiskaia gazeta*, May 6, 2008.

[11] Dmitry Trenin, "Yuzhnyi vektor," *Mezhdunarodnaia zhizn'* 5 (2005): 102–103.

[12] Knyazev, "Rossiia vozvrashchaetsia," 42.

[13] Mikhail Troitskiy, "Institutionalizing U.S.-Russian Cooperation in Central Eurasia," *Kennan Institute Occasional Paper* no. 293 (Washington, D.C., 2006).

[14] Andrei Grozin, "Postsovetskaia Tsentral'naia Aziia: Novye geopoliticheskie tendentsii i rossiiskie interesy," *Tsentral'naia Aziia i Kavkaz* 5 (2007): 62.

[15] Trenin, "Russia," 118–123.

[16] Some political scientists, though, argue that the jury is still out on whether ruthless autocratic regimes are inherently less stable and therefore more vulnerable to political, religious, or terrorist outbreaks than democratically governed states. Such an assumption, they say, "may well be true in the long run but it may not be true for the

short term . . . Nor are those regimes for the most part visibly unstable—they have been quite the contrary, if anything excessively stable, with very little political change since their advent. The argument that appearances of stability are superficial and conducive to elite self-deception should perhaps be given greater credence, but it is empirically difficult to measure an invisible sub-surface threat." See Lowell Dittmer, "Central Asia and the Regional Powers," *China and Eurasia Quarterly 5*, no. 4 (2007): 21.

[17] Sabrina Tavernise, "West Treads Softly on Uzbekistan," *International Herald Tribune*, May 29, 2008.

[18] See Elena Mazneva, "Aziia trebuet doplatit," *Vedomosti*, March 12, 2008; Aleksei Grivach and Arkady Dubnov, "Sredneaziatskii front," *Vremia Novostei*, March 12, 2008; Stephen Blank, "Russia and Central Asian Gas: Recent Trends and Their Implications," *CACI Analyst*, March 19, 2008, www.cacianalyst.org/?q=node/4817.

[19] Bobo Lo, "Russia-China: Axis of Convenience," openDemocracy, May 20, 2008, www.opendemocracy.net/russia/article/Russian-fears-of-China-not-based-in-reality.

[20] As one scholarly comment has aptly put it, "China was a presence in Central Asian oases and caravan nodes ever since the Silk Road first connected the Middle Kingdom to the Roman Empire. Among the world's other 'wheels of commerce'—the Mediterranean, the Middle East, India—China was by far the greatest." See Georgi Derluguian, "Shifting Forces Along the Silk Road," *Moscow Times*, August 5, 2005. For a more detailed analysis of China's interests and policies in Central Asia, see Huasheng Zhao, "Central Asia in China's Diplomacy," in *Central Asia: Views from Washington, Moscow, and Beijing* (Armonk, NY: M. E. Sharpe, 2007); Shi Yinhong, "Great Power Politics in Central Asia Today: A Chinese Assessment," in *Islam, Oil, and Geopolitics: Central Asia After September 11*, ed. Elizabeth Van Wie Davis and Rouben Azizian (Lanham, MD: Rowman & Littlefield Publishers, 2007).

[21] For a broader discussion of American interests in Central Asia, see Stephen Blank, "U.S. Interests in Central Asia and Their Challenges," *Demokratizatsiya 3* (2007); Olga Oliker and David A. Shlapak, *U.S. Interests in Central Asia: Policy Priorities and Military Roles* (Santa Monica, CA: RAND Corp., 2005).

[22] The divergent views on the process of democratization in Central Asia are apparent in the reminiscences of the former U.S. ambassador in Tajikistan, Richard E. Hoagland: "[I]n November 2001, I instituted the first-ever U.S.-Russian consultations on Central Asia and the Caucasus. To the surprise of both sides, at the upper working level, we found much common ground—except on one absolute fundamental. Whereas I advocated for my government the necessity for political and economic reform in Central Asia, the Russian side advocated status quo—telling me that the United States was too naïve to understand the clan complexities of Central Asia." See Troitskiy, "Institutionalizing U.S.-Russian Cooperation," 6.

[23] See Gene Germanovich, "The Shanghai Cooperation Organization: A Threat to American Interests in Central Asia?" *China and Eurasia Quarterly 6*, no. 1 (2008); Aleksandr Lukin, "Shankhaiskaia organizatsiia sotrudnichestva: chto dal'she?" *Rossiia v global'noi politike 3* (2007); Ivan Safranchuk, "Konkurentsiia za bezopasnost' Tsentral'noi Azii," *Rossiia v global'noi politike 6* (2007); Adil Kaukenov, "Politika Kitaia v Shankhaiskoi organizatsii sotrudnichestva," *Tsentral'naia Aziia i Kavkaz 3* (2007). The United States was turned down when it applied for an observer status in the SCO.

[24] Lo, "Russia-China."

[25] Bruce Pannier, "Central Asia: Beijing Flexes Economic Muscle Across Region," *RFE/RL*, May 29, 2008.

[26] Russia and China have clearly divergent views on what should be the SCO's main dimension. Beijing puts a special emphasis on economic cooperation and promotes free trade between Central Asia and China, while Moscow tends to focus on security issues.

[27] Dittmer, "Central Asia," 21.

[28] *Novaya Gazeta*, July 11, 2005.

[29] Trenin, "Yuzhnyi vektor," 105.

[30] Troitskiy, "Institutionalizing U.S.-Russian Cooperation," 3.

[31] Fyodor Lukyanov, "Rossiia mezhdu Kitaem i Zapadom," *New Times*, June 2, 2008.

[32] Bobo Lo, "A Fine Balance—The Strange Case of Sino-Russian Relations," *Russie. Cei.Visions* 1 (2005): 5.

[33] "Itogi s Vladimirom Putinym: vneshniaia politika Kremlia i raspad Rossiisskoi imperii," APN.ru, May 2, 2008, www.apn.ru/publications/print19830.htm.

[34] Trenin, "Russia," 95.

[35] C. Raja Mohan, "India and the Balance of Power," *Foreign Affairs* 85, no. 4 (2006): 17.

[36] Vinod Anand, "Politico-military Developments in Central Asia and Emerging Strategic Equations," *China and Eurasia Quarterly* 4, no. 4 (2006): 173.

[37] Ibid., 172.

[38] See Scott Moore, "Peril and Promise: A Survey of India's Strategic Relationship with Central Asia," *Central Asian Survey* 26, no. 2 (2007).

[39] Sergey Lounev, "Russian-Indian Relations in Central Asia," in *Islam, Oil, and Geopolitics: Central Asia After September 11*, 173. The other specialist, F. N. Yurlov of the Institute of Oriental Studies, argues that India-Russia relations should be characterized not just as a strategic partnership but as a *natural* strategic partnership. See "Rossiia-Indiia: Sostoianie i perspektivy sotrudnichestva na sovremennom etape," *Mirovaia ekonomika i mezhdunarodnye otnosheniia* 10 (2004): 54.

[40] See Kanwal Sibal, "India-Russia Relations: An Analysis," *Indian Foreign Affairs Journal* 3, no. 2 (2008); Sergey Lounev, "Indiiskii marsh," *Rossiia v global'noi politike* 4 (2007).

[41] "Rossiia-Indiia," *Mirovaia ekonomika i mezhdunarodnye otnosheniia* 11 (2004): 42.

[42] See Martin Malek, "Russian Policy toward South Asia: An Update," *Asian Survey* 44, no. 3 (2004).

[43] Sibal, "India-Russia Relations," 31.

[44] S. Nihal Singh, "Emerging Frontiers of India's Foreign Policy," *Indian Foreign Affairs Journal* 3, no. 1 (2008): 35.

[45] Sibal, "India-Russia Relations," 31.

[46] Vladimir Ivanov and Igor Plugatarev, "Triplet po-moskovski: Kreml' stremitsia prevratit' ShOS iz ekonomicheskogo v voenno-politicheskii soiuz," *Nezavisimaya gazeta*, December 7, 2005.

[47] Nihal Singh, "Emerging Frontiers," 30.

[48] Vladimir Kozin, "Evraziiskii perekrestok: Soedinennye Shtaty stremiat'sia stat' ego 'regulirovshchikom,'" *Krasnaia Zvezda*, June 3, 2008.

[49] Andrei Volodin, "Novaia indiisko-amerikanskaia 'Antanta': Moskve est' nad chem zadumat'sia," Rustrana.ru, October 11, 2007, www.rustrana.ru/print. php?nid=11178.

[50] See Stephen Blank, "Russian-Indian Row over Tajik Base Suggests Moscow Caught

in Diplomatic Vicious Cycle," *EurasiaNet*, January 11, 2008; Sudha Ramachandran, "Russian Turbulence for Indian Airbase," *Asia Times*, February 1, 2008.

[51] See, for example, Farhad Tolipov, "Rossiia tsentral'noaziatskaia: ukhod, uderzhanie ili vozvrashchenie?" *Tsentral'naia Aziia i Kavkaz* 5 (2007).

[52] "Rossiia-Indiia," *Mirovaia ekonomika i mezhdunarodnye otnosheniia* 10 (2004), 56.

[53] Nihal Singh, "Emerging Frontiers," 32.

[54] Anand, "Politico-military Developments in Central Asia," 177.

CHINA AND SOUTH ASIAN REGIONALISM: SAARC AND BEYOND

Guihong Zhang

S outh Asian regionalism has gained new momentum with the revival of the South Asian Association of Regional Cooperation (SAARC) in recent years. The South Asian countries are trying to follow in the steps of the phenomenal regional integration developing in their neighboring areas: East Asia, Southeast Asia, and Central Asia. Yet many existing issues and obstacles—economic imbalance and disparity, social diversity and inequality, political competition and rivalry, security conflicts and confrontations, strategic dissonance and incompatibilities—need to be overcome before substantial progress toward integration can be achieved in this region.

China is leaning toward regional cooperation because it is advantageous to China's foreign policy. In China's own neighborhood, the benefits of regionalism have included economic integration and an ongoing security dialogue over the past decade. China's joining SAARC as an observer in 2005 gave it a further chance to achieve its regional goals through a multilateral institution rather than its traditional bilateral means. The joint efforts of China and SAARC member states on regional cooperation promise benefits for both sides.

This chapter aims to (1) explain the role of South Asia in China's regional strategy, including China's interests and goals in this region; (2) analyze the background and significance of China's joining SAARC as an observer; and (3) summarize the challenges that China and SAARC must address in the future, as well as ways their cooperation can be strengthened.

The Position of South Asia in China's Regional Strategy

South Asia is located at the southern rim of the Asian continent and surrounded, clockwise from west to east, by West Asia, Central Asia, East Asia, and Southeast Asia; it also straddles the vital sea lane of the Indian Ocean, thus enjoying a position of strategic importance in the world. Not only is South Asia one of the world's fastest-growing regions—with more than roughly 7.5 percent gross domestic product (GDP) growth over the past decade—it is also home to a third of humanity, with a burgeoning middle class.

There are various ways to define South Asia, though most people, including the Chinese, accept six countries—Bangladesh, Bhutan, India, the Maldives, Nepal, Pakistan, and Sri Lanka—as South Asian. Afghanistan, however, is now often considered South Asian by many scholars, from a political and security perspective. The United Nations has a unique definition of South Asia that includes Iran,[1] but the most controversial definition may come from Richard Lynn, who has defined South Asia as the area "from Bangladesh in the east through India, Pakistan, Iraq, Iran, the Gulf states, the Near East, and Turkey."[2]

At the least, the earliest contacts between China and South Asia date back to the time of the world-famous Silk Road, a trade channel that connected ancient China with the outside world via South and Central Asia. When Western colonial countries came to the subcontinent in the mid-eighteenth century and to China in the mid-nineteenth century, the nature of relations between China and South Asia changed, leaving behind a legacy of boundary disputes—not only among the South Asian countries but also between India and China, which won their independence in 1947 and 1949, respectively, after the defeat and withdrawal of the Western colonists. Moreover, the rivalry between the East and West during the Cold War era divided the South Asian countries, impacting their relations with China.

After a dozen years of enjoying a relatively friendly relationship, a border conflict broke out between China and India, resulting in India's military failure and political distrust of China. Since, China and India have been adversaries, not only because of bilateral divergence but also because of a switch in external rivals: China became a friend to Pakistan (India's enemy) and an enemy of the Soviet Union (India's friend), and vice versa. Fortunately, due to China's reforms and opening-up policies and India's rapprochement with China in the late 1970s and early 1980s, the relationship between Beijing and New Delhi has stabilized to a degree. The end of the Cold War gave further impetus for an even better relationship between the two rising Asian powers. However, the Pokaran II nuclear tests (1998), along with an unresolved boundary dispute with Tibet, brought up old tensions once again. Thanks to the efforts of political leaders, the bilateral relationship between China and India has improved. Moreover, both China and India maintain good relations with the small South Asian countries, with the important exception of the ongoing India-Pakistan discord. As two emerging economies and rising regional powers, China and India have increasing confidence in dealing with bilateral and regional issues from a rational and reasonable perspective: both sides see that their peaceful coexistence is not only necessary but also feasible, and are finding more ways to converge than not.

The South Asian region is very important to China for several reasons: First, from a geographical point of view, China is South Asia's largest neighboring country, sharing more than five thousand kilometers of its border with five South Asian countries—Pakistan, India, Nepal, Bhutan, and Afghanistan—which account for one-third of China's fourteen land neighbors. In other words, South Asia is the region in which China has the most neighbors, more than in Northeast Asia (Russia, Mongolia, and North Korea), Central Asia (Kazakhstan, Kyrgyzstan, and Tajikistan), or Southeast Asia (Vietnam, Laos, and Myanmar). Second, from a political and security point of view, all the developing South Asian countries are located near China's southwestern border region and thus have an immediate and direct impact on its security and stability. Third, from an economic point of view, South Asia serves as a guarantor of energy security, a market for Chinese goods, and a potential partner in the development of China's western region. Fourth, the importance of both major South Asian countries—India and Pakistan—to Chinese foreign policy cannot be underestimated. While Pakistan is China's bridge to the Islamic world—with importance to South Asia's strategic balance—it in turn needs China to help mediate its territory disputes with India, the major country of South Asia and a rising power in the world. Thus, Pakistan must be carefully accommodated by China. The India-Pakistan rivalry is one of the most unstable and challenging factors in China's security environment. This is particularly so now that India and Pakistan are de facto nuclear states that along with China constitute the only nuclear triangle in the world.

On the one hand, the characteristics of the South Asian geopolitical reality require China to formulate a balancing strategy in South Asia—that is, balancing security and economic relations, traditional and nontraditional security issues, India and Pakistan, and the interests of the larger versus the smaller countries in the region. Such a balancing strategy may be expressed in both bilateral and multilateral relations. Meanwhile, with dynamic regional integration ongoing in East, Central, and South Asia, China has found itself able to utilize multilateral institutions to facilitate its rise.

China and the South Asian countries, however different, complement each other. Unfortunately, China–South Asian relations have lagged considerably in comparison to China's embrace of essentially all of distant Africa (the China-Africa Summit) and seven Pacific Island countries (the China–Pacific Island Countries Economic Development and Cooperation Forum), not to mention China's robust engagement with the Association of Southeast Asian Nations (ASEAN), its leading role in the Shanghai Cooperation Organization (SCO), and its position as host of the six-party talks.

China and the South Asian countries share many common interests, including: (1) an enlargement of trade and investment in the area; (2) participation in South Asian regional cooperation; (3) more balanced and stable relations between India and Pakistan; (4) the avoidance of territorial conflicts, in particular among any of the three regional powers (India, Pakistan, China); (5) cooperation in nontraditional security fields, including water resource management and countering terrorism; and (6) nuclear nonproliferation and disarmament.

Accordingly, China's main goals in South Asia include gaining access to markets and raw materials in the region, preventing instability in South Asia from spilling over its borders, and preventing the region from emerging as a source of anti-China activities.

The realization of China's goals and interests in South Asia will be based on several factors: (1) Pakistani political stability, economic development, and social progress; (2) Indian policy regarding China's influence in South Asia; (3)

the India-Pakistan peace process and possible rapprochement; (4) the mutual coordination and accommodation of the dual rise of China and India in Asia; and (5) the positive role of the United States in South Asia.

To achieve these goals in South Asia, China needs to take the following steps: (1) develop comprehensive relations with South Asian countries and focus more attention on South Asia's smaller countries; (2) develop deeper economic and cultural ties to the region; (3) consolidate its friendly relations with Pakistan while at the same time developing more comprehensive relations with India (better China-India relations need not come at the cost of damaging China-Pakistan relations, and good China-Pakistan relations need not be an obstacle to the improvement of China-India ties); (4) make suitable adjustments to China-Pakistan relations, adapting them to new situations; (5) maintain strategic stability and avoid a serious imbalance in South Asia; and (6) avoid embroilment in the India-Pakistan conflict but persuade these countries to resolve their disputes through peaceful dialogue.

China as Observer to SAARC

China was accepted by SAARC as an observer in 2005, approved in 2006, and for the first time, invited to attend a SAARC summit in New Delhi in 2007. China sent a large delegation to attend the Fifteenth SAARC Summit in Sri Lanka in 2008. This event, along with other developments, shows, on the one hand, that China–South Asian relations are entering a new phase and, on the other, that China has a new multilateral, institutional approach to South Asia.

Background

Multilateral and institutional cooperation has been a prominent phenomenon in Asia over the past decade. Regional arrangements such as the ASEAN, ASEAN Regional Forum (ARF), East Asian Summit (EAS), and SCO play a unique role in the stability and prosperity of the region. China has actively participated in the increasingly multilateral integration process in greater Asia but as of yet has not engaged South Asia as a region.

There are five factors that promote China's new multilateral approach to South Asia: First is the revival of SAARC as a regional cooperation organization, even as South Asia's degree of regional integration lags behind that of the rest of Asia. The Twelfth and Thirteenth SAARC summits marked an important milestone in the organization's twenty-five-year history. Covering a wide range of issues in need of regional cooperation, from alleviating poverty and combating terrorism to environmental protection and collaboration in information and communication technology, the Islamabad Declaration of 2004 signaled a substantial step toward South Asian regionalism.[3] At the opening ceremony of the Twelfth SAARC Summit, Indian prime minister Vajpayee stated: "[W]e need to move from the realm of ideas to plans of action. Our statements of good intentions have to be translated into a program for implementation."[4] The Dhaka Declaration of the Thirteenth SAARC Summit stated the intent to set up a South Asian Free Trade Area (SAFTA) from 2006 and accepted Afghanistan as the organization's eighth member state.[5] SAARC's decision to open its door to extraregional bodies—the United States, European Union (EU), South Korea, China, and Japan—to observe the fourteenth summit indicated that SAARC had thoroughly changed its introverted policy of the previous twenty years.

The second factor at play is Pakistan's regional status. China and Pakistan have experienced the ups and downs of an all-weather partnership for more than half a century. This time-tested relationship has been given new momentum in the twenty-first century. China contributed much to Pakistan's observer status in the SCO. Accordingly, Pakistan welcomed China's engagement in South Asia on a multilateral platform. This engagement, on the one hand, will contribute to the strategic dynamic of this area and, on the other, may refresh Beijing and Islamabad's relationship.

Third is India's policy of accommodation. India does not favor China's increasing influence in the subcontinent, which New Delhi considers as its "sphere of influence." However, alongside the trend of increasing transregional connections, the gradual improvement of India's relations with both Beijing and Islamabad, and the benefits India gains from its participation in Central and Southeast Asian economic integration, New Delhi's policymakers have come to recognize that there is enough space in Asia to accommodate the rise of China and India both. They have also realized that a Chinese role in South Asia is not unacceptable, particularly if other Asian powers (such as Japan and South Korea) take part in this process, too.

Fourth, China has the full support of South Asia's smaller countries. Nepal, Bhutan, Bangladesh, the Maldives, and Sri Lanka expressed their full and strong support for China's participation in SAARC. It is reported that during the Thirteenth SAARC Summit Nepal joined Pakistan to insist that Afghanistan become a new member state and that China participate as an observer of SAARC; Nepal stated that it would like to provide a "transportation bridge" for China and India, the two world markets. Sri Lanka, Bhutan, and the Maldives are also willing to see China play a role in South Asia, in spite of India's negative attitude in this regard.

Fifth is China's role and rising influence in Asia. It is in the context of the geographical, historical, and political nexus between China and the subcontinent that China constitutes an inalienable part of South Asia's strategic environment (for India in particular), and vice versa. Given the fact that China has, more or less, adjusted its policy toward South Asia and considerably improved its relations with all the South Asian countries, Indian analysts have recognized that China "has gradually moved away from its initial politico-strategic concerns and now towards a pragmatic approach to economic engagement."[6] China's constructive role and increasing influence in Central and Southeast Asia set a good example for is potential place in South Asia.

Significance

To reiterate, over the past two decades, China has successfully carried out multilateral diplomacy in Southeast, Northeast, and Central Asia: by hosting six-party talks, participating in the ASEAN and ARF, and establishing the SCO, it has played a constructive role in the stability and prosperity of the area.

The observer status that SAARC has given to China opens a window to cooperation with South Asia: this is the first time that China has regarded all seven (or eight, if Afghanistan is included) South Asian countries as a whole. An ongoing dialogue within the SAARC framework, significant for China–South Asian relations, will provide a basis for interaction between China and the South Asian countries.

This implies a breakthrough for China's multilateral diplomacy in South Asia. A spokesperson for China's Foreign Ministry remarked that through the entry of China into the SAARC movement, "a new chapter is unfolding in relations between China and the South Asian nations."[7] The fundamental objectives of China's policy toward South Asia are stability, development, and good neighborly relations. China had long hoped to expand cooperation with the South Asian countries, but the lack of a multilateral mechanism had been an obstacle to close ties. Therefore, SAARC promises to be an important high-level platform where China can promote relations, sit with the South Asian countries, and discuss how they can grow together. Among the five SAARC observers, China is the only one that is a neighbor to the South Asian countries: this will undoubtedly ease China–SAARC cooperation.

It will also provide a new momentum for the promotion of the Sino-Indian strategic and cooperative partnership. Given the size of India's and China's territory and population, their level of economic prowess and potential, and the position of India's de facto and China's recognized nuclear weapons positions, the relationship of the two Asian giants cannot be trivial. Both leaderships hold that the Sino-Indian relationship has gone far beyond a bilateral level and "is of global and strategic significance"; in 2005, when Chinese prime minister Wen Jiabao visited India, the two countries culminated their "strategic partnership."

In the political sphere, both China and India have moved beyond their 1962 border conflict and are learning to accommodate each other. Alongside the accelerated growth of their two large economies, Sino-Indian two-way trade is rapidly expanding and mutual investment is no longer a new phenomenon.[8] In the nuclear and security realm, the two countries have basically walked out from under the shadow cast by India's nuclear weapon testing, when India cited China's threat as a reason for its tests. China has joined the Nuclear Suppliers Group (NSG), which, more or less, relieves India's concern over the China-Pakistan nexus of sensitive technology transfer; the two sides also have agreed to promote cooperation in the field of nuclear energy, consistent with their respective international commitment.

During most of the Cold War era, Beijing and New Delhi belonged to different camps and their mostly bilateral relationship was indifferent, even hostile at times. Along with the rapprochement of the two countries following the Cold War, both China and India took part in the "ASEAN plus one" (10+1) summit and the ARF framework in Southeast Asia. India's observer status in the SCO places it in a position to discuss energy issues with China (and Russia) in Central Asia. SAARC promises to provide those countries with yet another multilateral platform on which to cooperate and communicate.

In doing so, SAARC also promises to contribute to transregional cooperation and integration in Asia. China is surrounded by the Northeast, Southeast, South, and Central Asian countries, and thanks to this unique geographic location, has a special role to play for each. In Northeast Asia, China has hosted six rounds of six-party talks; in Southeast Asia, China, since 1991, has taken part in the ASEAN plus one (10+1) and the ASEAN plus three (10+3) cooperation frameworks, and joined the ARF in 1994; in Central Asia, China, along with Russia and the Central Asian Republics (CARs), established the SCO in 2001; and now in South Asia, China has entered into SAARC as an observer.

The ASEAN, SCO, and SAARC reflect the process of economic integration in their respective regions. Despite their different positions in the three organizations, both China and India have, more or less, participated in this integration. China and India initiated the process of establishing a free trade area with the ASEAN in 2002 and 2007—hopefully to be completed in 2010 and 2011, respectively. In Central Asia, the collaboration in energy and combating terrorism is no longer a new phenomenon. China and India also have formally launched talks to study the feasibility of signing a bilateral free trade agreement (FTA), as well as a comprehensive Economic Cooperation Agreement (ECCA), to cement their booming economies. China has enough reasons and interest to take part in the process of the SAFTA. If China and India—the world's two largest countries, whose economies are experiencing the fastest growth—can work out a road map of transregional integration, the vast East, Central, and South Asian markets would receive a significant boost, while Asian economic integration would be facilitated.

Predicting the Future of China–SAARC Relations

SAARC, however, is more a platform for dialogue than a vehicle for action. Despite the recent and inspiring revival of SAARC,[9] it still has a long way to go when compared with the other regional international organizations, such as the SCO and ASEAN.

Challenges

Considering the relative low level of development and cooperation among the South Asian countries, plus the as-yet-to-be-improved relationship between

Beijing and New Delhi, there are a number of challenges facing both China and SAARC.

First, how to reduce distrust—and increase mutual trust—between China and India, and among SAARC member states? To some extent, India's will is key to the future of SAARC. For a long time, China and India, as neighboring regional powers, have been perceived as "natural competitors" economically, geopolitically, and strategically.[10] It is widely acknowledged that three schools exist among Indian analysts responding to the rise of China: "pragmatists, hyperrealists, and appeasers"—or the "mainstream, China-is-not-threat, and China-is-threat factions."[11] While most Western experts increasingly tend to see the future of India-China relations as a rivalry,[12] many Indian scholars describe it more in terms of a challenge.[13] India's negative perceptions focus on its concerns about China's military buildup and defense relations with the rest of the South Asian countries.[14]

Similarly, India's emergence as a major power has attracted growing attention from Chinese analysts and officials, who evaluate the implications and adjust policy accordingly.[15] Beijing is now paying increasing attention to India's drive for global-power status and specifically to India's diplomatic initiatives and military buildup.

According to Chinese experts, India's rise has both negative and positive implications for China. An emerging India will constitute a challenge on the one hand—implying strategic contravention, economic competition, military pressure, and diplomatic trouble—and a potential partner on the other, as it shares economic cooperation potential and common diplomatic and security concerns.[16]

As a recognized leader in South Asia, India has the duty and responsibility to be an active advocate of SAARC's development and a strong promoter of regional cooperation. To do this, it must find a way to gain the trust of the other South Asian nations—a great challenge for India.

Another question is how to enlarge and deepen cooperation between China and SAARC. Despite the significance of recent developments, it is still a distance from Beijing to the Indian Ocean. SAARC is not yet sufficiently mature to be a dialogue platform for China and the South Asian countries, and has yet to become an entity able to send a uniform message to the world outside Asia. Therefore, SAARC will not be a key consideration in China's South Asia policy, and the traditional bilateral approach will remain the mainstay of China–South Asia interaction.

As one of the key member states of SAARC, India would not welcome a stronger Chinese influence within the SAARC framework. Moreover, based on their respective national interests, some external countries—such as the United States and Japan—are alert to the enhancement of the China–SAARC relationship.

In sum, given SAARC's inherent limitations, how to deepen multilateral cooperation with SAARC while not offending countries sensitive to its involvement within and beyond the region poses a great challenge for China.

Yet another question is how to handle bilateral issues through a multilateral mechanism. According to the SAARC charter: "[B]ilateral and contentious issues shall be excluded from the deliberations."[17] This indicates that SAARC's focus is on economic cooperation, while it hopes to steer clear of politically sensitive issues. This focus may have been appropriate in the early stages of SAARC's evolution, but from a long-term perspective, bilateral relations and security issues must be properly handled or managed in order to pave the way for deeper economic cooperation.

SAARC, when compared with the neighboring ASEAN and SCO, has yet to become an efficient and highly integrated regional organization, despite its more than twenty-year history. As I have stated, the ASEAN was established mainly to address political and security considerations, yet later paid more attention to economic and social affairs, and now is regarded as a successful medium of regional economic and security cooperation. Meanwhile, the SCO's initial focus on economic cooperation has expanded to encompass security issues.

SAARC has much to learn from the ASEAN and SCO. It is high time for SAARC to review its charter and reconsider its vision for South Asian regional cooperation.

Ways Forward

On April 3, 2007, then–Chinese foreign minister Li Zhaoxing announced five proposals—covering poverty alleviation, disaster relief, human resource development, infrastructure, and the energy sector—and workshops and seminars that focused on cooperation between China and SAARC. While these proposals cover many areas of economic, social, and personnel cooperation, several more important approaches and steps, based on a long-term and strategic perspective, need to be explored.

- *First, the exchange of development experiences and lessons.* SAARC member states share an interest in prioritizing development. Development will stay at the top of China's agenda, too, for the foreseeable future.

  South Asia is one of the poorest regions in today's world, with four countries listed by the UN as least-developed nations; if this situation is not addressed soon, it will be impossible to correct in the near future. Meanwhile, China has made world-acknowledged progress in the past three decades through reform and opening policies, from which the South Asian countries may learn.

  Undoubtedly, China does have lessons to learn with regard to its development model. This is why the author proposes the ideas of scientific development, a harmonious society, anticorruption, and so on.

  China's achievement over the past three decades keeps it a step ahead of—and thus a useful model for—the South Asian countries. China's lessons and problems today are akin to what SAARC member states may meet and need to resolve tomorrow.

- *Second, the enlargement of trade and investment.* International trade and foreign investment have proven to be good ways of promoting development. China is willing to share its development lessons with the South Asian countries on the one hand, and to enlarge its trade and investment on the other.

  China's comparative advantages complement those of its South Asian neighbors. One example is China's position as a "world factory" while India is a "world office." Or, as China's former premier Zhu Rongji described it in the late 1990s, the world depends on "China's hardware and India's software."

- *Third, a dialogue on "low politics" and nontraditional security issues.* "Low politics" denote issues of development, assistance, trade, and investment, as opposed to "high politics," which relate to territory, sovereignty, military, and the like. Nontraditional security issues include energy security, information security, and financial security. Considering SAARC's aspirations in the unique context of South Asia, it is advisable to set "low politics" and nontraditional security issues as priorities for China–SAARC cooperation.

Just as former Chinese foreign minister Li Zhaoxing stated at the opening ceremony of the Fourteenth SAARC Summit, China is ready to discuss the possibility of establishing cooperation mechanisms for poverty alleviation, disaster relief and mitigation, infrastructure construction, human resources training, personnel contacts, and academic exchanges[18]—all of which belong to the field of "low politics." Meanwhile, nontraditional security issues such as global and regional warming, water resources management, environmental protection, and antiterrorism, among others, are increasingly causes of concern for the political leaders and ordinary people of both China and SAARC member countries.

Conclusion

For some time, China's South Asia policy focused on achieving security through bilateral means. Within the SAARC framework, China is now able to develop comprehensive relations with all the South Asian countries through a multilateral approach. There is great scope for cooperation on economic and nontraditional security issues. It is also very important for China to pay more attention to the smaller South Asian countries and to assist in their national construction.

Considering that India is the largest state in the region—in economic, political, military, and international terms—its political will is key to the success of SAARC. At the same time, India's concerns about China's presence and influence in South Asia put future cooperation between China and SAARC in an uncertain light. The success of China's increasingly multilateral approach to South Asia depends on India's understanding and Pakistan's support, in addition to China's own efforts.

As the two largest countries in South Asia, India and Pakistan share primary responsibility for mitigating conflict and poverty in the region. As their neighboring giant, China has an opportunity to cooperate with them and to thus contribute to security and development in South Asia and the world at large.

Notes

[1] See http://millenniumindicators.un.org/unsd/methods/m49/m49regin.htm#asia.

[2] Richard Lynn, *Race Differences in Intelligence: An Evolutionary Analysis* (Washington Summit Publishers, 2006), 79.

[3] *Islamabad Declaration*, Twelfth SAARC Summit, Islamabad, January 4–6, 2004, www.saarc-sec.org/data/summit12/summit12declaration.pdf.

[4] Vajpayee's statement at the Twelfth SAARC Summit in Islamabad, on January 4, 2004, http://meaindia.nic.in/cgi-bin/db2www/meaxpsite/coverpage.d2w/coverpg?sec=s s&filename=speech/2004/01/04ss01.htm.

[5] *Dhaka Declaration*, Thirteen SAARC Summit, Dhaka, November 13, 2005, www. saarc-sec.org/main.php?id=159&t=7.1.

[6] Swaran Singh, *China–South Asia: Issues, Equations, Policies* (New Delhi: Lancer's Books, 2003), 12.

[7] *China Daily*, April 3, 2007.

[8] The volume of bilateral trade reached $38.6 billion in 2006, and is to be raised to $60 billion by 2010.

[9] For example, the elaboration of the SAARC Development Goals (SDGs) for poverty alleviation, the establishing of South Asian University (in India), the initiation of the SAARC Development Fund (SDF) (with initial capital of $300 million), the preparation of the SAARC Food Bank, the organizing of the first ever South Asia Energy Dialogue (in March 2007, in Delhi), the ratification of the SAFTA Agreement, the launching of 2007 as the "Year of Green South Asia," the plan of the South Asian Customs Union and a South Asian Economic Union, the implementation of the existing SAARC Conventions to combat terrorism and transnational crime, and the inclusion of China, Japan, Korea, the European Union, and the United States as observers to SAARC. For details, see *Declaration of the Fourteenth SAARC Summit*, www.saarc-sec.org/data/summit14/ ss14declaration.htm.

[10] See, for example, John W. Garver, *Protracted Contest: Sino-Indian Rivalry in the Twentieth Century* (London: Oxford Univ. Press, 2001), 5 and 110–111; Sujit Dutta, "China's Emerging Power and Military Role: Implications for South Asia," in *In China's Shadow: Regional Perspectives on Chinese Foreign Policy and Military Developmen*, ed. Jonathan D. Pollack and Richard H. Yang (Santa Monica, CA: RAND, 1998), 94; Ma Jiali, *Guanzhu Yindu: jueqi zhong de daguo* [Focus on India: emerging power] (Tianjing: Tianjing Renming Chubanshe, 2002), 14.

[11] Mohan Malik, "Eyeing the Dragon: India's China Debate," in *Asia's China Debate*, ed. Satu P. Lymaye (Honolulu, HI: Asia-Pacific Centre for Security Studies, December 2003), www.apcss.org/Publications/SAS/ChinaDebate/ChinaDebate-Malik.pdf; Steven A. Hoffmann, "Perceptions and China Policy in India," in *The India-China Relationship:*

What the United States Needs to Know, ed. Francine R. Frankel and Harry Harding (New York: Columbia Univ. Press, 2004), 39–49; Subramanian Swamy, *India's China Perspective* (New Delhi: Konark, 2001); Swaran Singh, *China-India Confidence Building: Indian Perspectives*, paper presented to the international conference on "Living with China: Dynamic Interactions between Regional States and China," organized by the S. Rajaratnam School of International Studies (RSIS), Singapore, March 8–9, 2007; Zhang Guihong, "The Rise of China: India's Perceptions and Responses," *South Asian Survey* (New Delhi) 13, no. 1 (2006): 93–102.

[12] See, for instance, Ashley Tellis, "China and India in Asia," in Frankel and Harding, *The India-China Relationship* (New York: Columbia Univ. Press, 2004), 143–177; Sumit Ganguly, "Assessing India's Responses to the Rise of China: Fears and Misgivings," in *The Rise of China in Asia: Security Implications*, ed. Carolyn W. Pumphrey (Carlisle Barracks: The Strategic Studies Institute, 2002), http://carlisle-www.army.mil/suassi/welcome.htm.

[13] Bharat Karnad, *Nuclear Weapons and Indian Security* (New Delhi: Macmillan, 2002), 540–544; K. Subrahmanyam, "Partnership in a Balance of Power System," *Strategic Analysis* (New Delhi) 29, no. 4 (2005): 559; Brahma Chellaney, "India, China Mend Fences," *Washington Times*, April 7, 2005.

[14] Zhang Guihong, "The Rise of China: India's Perceptions and Responses," *South Asian Survey* (New Delhi) 13, no.1 (2006): 98–99.

[15] Ma Jiali, *Guanzhu yindu: jueqi zhong de daguo* (Tianjing: Tianjing remin chubanshe, 2002); Zheng Ruixiang and Rong Ying, eds., *Yindu de jueqi yu zhongyin guanxi* (Beijing: Dangdai shijie chubanshe, 2006), 363; Hu Zhiyong, *Wenming de liliang: yindu jueqi* (Beijing: Xinhua chubanshe, 2006); Zuo Xuejin, Pan Guang, and Wang Dehua, *Long xiang gong wu: dui zhongguo he yindu liangge fuxing daguo de bijiao yanjiu* (Shanghai: Shanghai shehui kexue yuan chubanshe, 2007).

[16] Ma, *Guanzhu yindu*, 14–16.

[17] *Charter of the South Asian Association for Regional Cooperation*, Article X, www.saarc-sec.org/main.php?id=10&t=4.

[18] Remarks by Foreign Minister Li Zhaoxing at the opening ceremony of the Fourteenth SAARC Summit, New Delhi, April 3, 2007, www.chinaembassy.org.in/eng/sgxw/t308596.htm.

INDEX

offshoring, 195n18
regional integration, 192, 192t
and supply-train fragmentation,
182–84, 184t
workforce supply and education,
190, 191t
Sokolski, Henry, 236–37
South American regional
organizations, 66
South Asia. *See also* regional
integration; SAARC; SAFTA *and*
specific nations
China's relations with: balance of
trade, 140; goals and policies,
294–302
defined, 293–94
democratization in, 200
diversity of cultures and national
interests, 22, 47, 156–57, 198,
226
economic development: growth
rates, 51–52, 98, 98t, 99t;
interregional trade, 53–54;
potential benefits from, 60,
97, 151–52, 160–61; regional
trade levels, 194n6; role in
global marketplace, 149–50;
tourism industry, 140–42;
trade disparities, 186; and
trade liberalization, 100–101;
trade liberalization, 100t, 181;
trade with other regions, 106t;
unilateral initiatives, 15; U.S.
promotion of, 252–53
educational levels, 190
electronics industry, 194n13
energy cooperation, 127
geography, 16–17, 27, 51, 83
historical context, 22, 47, 51, 73
main regional exports and
imports, 183t
new regionalism in, 116–17
and nuclear weapons
development, 149, 151–52
regional identity, 13, 109n3, 197–98
U.S. relations with, 259–61,
264–65
South Asia Center for Policy Studies

(SACEPS), 173–74
South Asia Education Foundation
(SAEF), 161
South Asian Commission on Poverty
Alleviation (ISACPA), 119t
South Asian Development Bank, 66
South Asian Development Fund
(SADF), 63–64, 71, 120
South Asian economic union, 62
South Asian Free Media Association
(SAFMA), 165n30
South Asian Growth Quadrangle
(SAGQ), 85
South Asian Preferential Trade
Arrangement (SAPTA), 17, 30,
54–55, 168
Southeast Asia, 13, 43–45
Southern African Power Pool
(SAPP), 128
South Korea, 42–43
sovereignty, national
in India, 20, 208–11
in Nepal, 26–27, 114, 123, 220
as obstacle to regional integration,
23–24, 28, 42–43, 108–9
in Pakistan, 216
Russian concept of "sovereign
democracy," 275–76
species extinction, 150–51
Sri Lanka. *See also* ILBFTA (Indo–
Sri Lanka Bilateral Free Trade
Agreement)
economic development: bilateral
agreements, 18–19, 101, 170;
capital account convertibility,
53; main exports and imports,
183t, GDP growth rates,
99t, 102t, 169t; intraregional
trade, 52–54, 167; monetary
cooperation, 72; poverty and
well-being in, 98, 164n11;
privatization of plantations, 176,
178n25
geography, 167
governance, 219
hydropower resources, 116t
regional integration: factors
promoting, 19, 24t, 25; obstacles

U

V

ABOUT THE CONTRIBUTORS

Ummu Salma Bava is chairperson and professor of European Studies at the Centre for European Studies, School of International Studies, Jawaharlal Nehru University (New Delhi). She also serves as guest faculty at the Foreign Service Institute, Ministry of External Affairs (New Delhi); and associate fellow of the Asia Society (New York). She is one of the leading experts in India on contemporary Indian and European foreign and security policy. Her other areas of research are European and South Asian politics, regional integration and organization, international politics, globalization, and norms and conflict resolution. Her latest research articles are published in *Partnerships for Effective Multilateralism: EU Relations with Brazil, China, India, and Russia* (Chaillot Paper No. 109, Paris, May 2008) and *Europe-Asia Relations: Building Multilateralisms* (London: Palgrave, 2008). She is fluent in English, Hindi, and German.

Rafiq Dossani is a senior research scholar at Shorenstein APARC, responsible for developing and directing the South Asia Initiative. His research interests include South Asian security and financial, technology, and energy-sector reform in India. He is currently involved in projects on regional integration, innovation in outsourcing, engineering education, access to capital, and entrepreneurship in information technology on the South Asian subcontinent. His most recent books are *India Arriving* (2007 in the United States, 2008 in India, and 2009 in China), *Prospects for Peace in South Asia* (coedited with Henry S. Rowen, 2005), and *Telecommunications Reform in India* (2002).

Dossani earlier worked for the Robert Fleming Investment Banking group, first as CEO of its India operations and later as head of its San Francisco operations. He has also been the chairman and CEO of a stockbroking firm on the OTCEI exchange in India, the deputy editor of *Business India Weekly*, and a professor of finance at Pennsylvania State University. He holds a BA in economics from St. Stephen's College, New Delhi; an MBA from the Indian Institute of Management, Calcutta; and a PhD in finance from Northwestern University.

Xenia Dormandy is the executive director of the PeaceNexus Foundation, based just outside Geneva. Prior to this she was at Harvard Kennedy School's Belfer Center, where she was the director of the Project on India and the Subcontinent and the executive director for research at the Belfer Center, as well as being a member of the center's board.

Dormandy served with the U.S. Government from 2001 to 2005, culminating in a role as director for South Asia at the National Security Council (NSC). Prior to her NSC post, she served in the State Department in the Bureau of South Asia, the Bureau of Nonproliferation, and in the Homeland Security Group. Shortly after September 11, 2001, she was detailed from the Department of

State to the Office of the Vice President (OVP) to help launch the Office of Homeland Security Affairs.

Dormandy is the author of numerous articles and op-eds in publications such as the *Washington Quarterly*, the *Washington Post*, the *Boston Globe*, the *Christian Science Monitor*, and the *International Herald Tribune*. She has been interviewed in broadcast media for such programs as BBC World TV, NPR, CSPAN, Fox News, Al Jazeera, and the News Hour with Jim Lehrer. Prior to her government service, Dormandy worked in the nonprofit and private sectors in California, Israel and the West Bank, and the United Kingdom, and for UNICEF in New York. She is a graduate of the Kennedy School of Government, where she completed her master's in public policy. She earned her BA degree from Oxford University.

Muchkund Dubey is currently the president of the Council for Social Development, New Delhi, and the chairman of the Asian Development Research Institute, Patna, Bihar. As a member of the Indian Foreign Service, he served as India's High Commissioner in Bangladesh and the Permanent Representative of India to the United Nations, Geneva. He also worked in the UN (Department of Economic and Social Affairs) and UNDP headquarters in New York. After retiring as the foreign secretary to the Government of India, he served as a professor at Jawaharlal Nehru University for seven years. His more recent assignments include: Indian member on the executive board of UNESCO; chairperson of the Common School System Commission, Bihar; and deputy chairman of the Planning Commission of Sikkim.

Dubey has written many articles, papers, and chapters of books on regional integration, development strategy, international development cooperation, and international security and disarmament issues. He is the author of the book *Unequal Treaty: World Trading Order after GATT*, and has edited and coedited seven additional books, including *The South Asian Growth Quadrangle*, *South Asia and Its Eastern Neighbours*, and *Social Development in Independent India*.

Dubey holds a master's degree in economics from Patna University and has studied economics at Oxford University and New York University.

Ainslie T. Embree, professor emeritus of history at Columbia University, was chairman of the history department and associate dean of the School of International and Public Affairs. He was president of the American Institute of Indian Studies and of the Association of Asian Studies. From 1978 to 1980, he was Counselor for Cultural Affairs at the American Embassy in Delhi and served as special consultant there to the American ambassador from 1994 to 1995. His books include: *India's Search for National Identity*; *Imagining India: Essays on Indian History*; *Utopias in Conflict: Religion and Nationalism in India*; and *Pakistan's Western Borderlands*. He was editor-in-chief of the *Encyclopedia of Asian History* (4 vols.) and *Sources of Indian Tradition* (2 vols.).

Akmal Hussain is currently distinguished professor at Beaconhouse National University in Lahore, Pakistan, and senior fellow at the Pakistan Institute of Development Economics. He has advised the present federal government of Pakistan on economic policy as chairman of the Working Group on Institutions for Development, Panel of Economists, and as chairman of the Working Group on Poverty Reduction for Pakistan's Tenth Five-year Plan. Hussain is also conducting policy research and advocacy on South Asian economic cooperation under the auspices of the South Asia Centre for Policy Studies, Kathmandu.

Hussain has helped to build organizations for overcoming poverty at the village, district, provincial, and national levels in Pakistan. These include the Pakistan Poverty Alleviation Fund (PPAF) at the national level and the Punjab Rural Support Programme (PRSP) at the provincial level.

In addition to many papers and reports, Hussain has authored three books on development policy and has coauthored fifteen other books on issues of poverty, peace, and development, which have been internationally published.

Saman Kelegama is the executive director of the Institute of Policy Studies of Sri Lanka (IPS). He is a fellow of the National Academy of Sciences of Sri Lanka, and was the president of the Sri Lanka Economic Association (SLEA) from 1999 to 2003.

He has published extensively on Sri Lankan and regional economic issues in both local and international journals. His latest books are *Trade in Services in South Asia: Opportunities and Risks of Liberalization* (2009), *South Asia in the WTO* (2007), *Development under Stress: Sri Lankan Economy in Transition* (2006), *Contemporary Economic Issues: Sri Lanka in the Global Context* (2006), *South Asia After the Quota System: The Impact of the MFA Phase-Out* (2005), *Economic Policy in Sri Lanka: Issues and Debates* (2004), and *Ready-Made Garment Industry in Sri Lanka: Facing the Global Challenge* (2004). He is the coeditor of the *South Asia Economic Journal* and serves as a referee for a number of international journals.

He serves and has served on a number of government and private-sector boards as an independent member. He is a member of the National Economic Council under the president of Sri Lanka, and the presidential Taxation Commission of Sri Lanka.

Kelegama earned his D.Phil and M.Sc in economics from the University of Oxford. He also has an M.Sc in Mathematics from IIT-Kanpur (India).

Brigadier General (retired) **Feroz Hassan Khan** is currently on the faculty in the Department of National Security Affairs at the U.S. Naval Postgraduate School, Monterey, California. He previously served with the Pakistani Army for 32 years. His final Army position was that of director of Arms Control and Disarmament Affairs within the Strategic Plans Division, Joint Services Headquarters, which is the secretariat of Pakistan's Nuclear Command Authority.

Khan's military career was overlaid with numerous diplomatic and scholarly assignments. He has experienced combat action and command on active fronts on the line of control in the Siachin Glacier and in Kashmir. He has also served domestically and abroad in the United States, Europe, and South Asia, and assisted in particular with Pakistan's nuclear diplomacy.

Among his academic degrees, Khan holds an MA from the Paul Nitze School of Advanced International Studies, Johns Hopkins University, Washington, D.C. He has held a series of visiting fellowships at Stanford University, the Woodrow Wilson International Center for Scholars, the Brookings Institution, the Center for Non-Proliferation Studies at the Monterey Institute of International Studies, and the Cooperative Monitoring Center, Sandia National Laboratory.

Since the mid-1990s, Khan has made key contributions in formulating and advocating Pakistan's security policy, especially on nuclear and conventional arms control and strategic stability in South Asia. He has produced recommendations for the Ministry of Foreign Affairs and represented Pakistan in several multilateral and bilateral arms control negotiations. He has participated in several security-related national and international conferences and seminars. He also teaches as a visiting faculty member in the Department of the Defense and Strategic Studies, Quaid-e-Azam University, Islamabad.

Khan is currently writing a book on the history of Pakistan's nuclear weapons, *Eating Grass: Pakistan and the Bomb* (forthcoming).

Rajiv Kumar is currently the director and chief executive of the Indian Council for Research on International Economic Relations (ICRIER), one of India's leading independent think tanks. He is a nonexecutive member of the Central Board of Directors of the State Bank of India, and a member of the Board of India Brand Equity Foundation. He was a member of the National Security Advisory Board for two years (until October 2008) and a part-time member of the Telecom Regulatory Authority of India for three years (until January 2010). Kumar was a professor at the Indian Institute of Foreign Trade (1987–89); worked with the Government of India (1989–95), first in the Bureau of Industrial Costs and Projects, Ministry of Industry (1989–91), and then as an economic adviser in the Department of Economic Affairs, Ministry of Finance (1991–95). He worked at the Asian Development Bank, Manila, for more than ten years (1995–2005) and was the chief economist at the Confederation of Indian Industries, New Delhi, from 2004 to 2006. He is an active columnist. Kumar holds a D.Phil in economics from Oxford University, a PhD from Lucknow University, and has several books and publications to his credit.

Daniel C. Sneider is the associate director for research at the Walter H. Shorenstein Asia-Pacific Research Center at Stanford University. He currently directs the Center's project on nationalism and regionalism and the Divided Memories and Reconciliation project, a three-year comparative study of the formation of historical memory in East Asia. His own research is focused on current U.S. foreign and national security policy in Asia, including work on a diplomatic history of the building of the United States' Cold War alliances in Northeast Asia.

Sneider was a longtime foreign correspondent and most recently the foreign affairs columnist of the *San Jose Mercury News*. His twice-weekly column looking at international issues and national security from a West Coast perspective was syndicated nationally on the Knight Ridder Tribune wire service. Previously, Sneider served as national/foreign editor of the *San Jose Mercury News*. From 1990 to 1994, he was the Moscow Bureau chief of the *Christian Science Monitor*, covering the end of Soviet Communism and the collapse of the Soviet Union. From 1985 to1990, he was Tokyo correspondent for the *Monitor*, covering Japan and Korea. Prior to that he was a correspondent in India, covering South and Southeast Asia. He also wrote widely on defense issues, including as a contributor and correspondent for *Defense News*, the national defense weekly.

Sneider's writings have appeared in many publications, including the *Washington Post*, the *New York Times*, the *New Republic*, *National Review*, the *Far Eastern Economic Review*, the *Oriental Economist*, *Newsweek*, *Time*, the *International Herald Tribune*, the *Financial Times*, and *Yale Global*. He is the coeditor of both *Cross Currents: Regionalism and Nationalism in Northeast Asia* (2007) and *First Drafts of Korea: The U.S. Media and Perceptions of the Last Cold War Frontier* (2009). He has also contributed to other volumes, including "Strategic Abandonment: Alliance Relations in Northeast Asia in the Post-Iraq Era" in *Towards Sustainable Economic and Security Relations in East Asia: U.S. and ROK Policy Options* (2008).

Sneider has a BA from Columbia University in East Asian history and an MPA from the John F. Kennedy School of Government at Harvard University.

Rehman Sobhan has served as a professor of economics at Dhaka University; member of the Bangladesh Planning Commission; director-general of the Bangladesh Institute of Development Studies; visiting fellow at Queen Elizabeth House, Oxford; member of the Advisory Council of the President of Bangladesh; founder and executive chairman of the Centre for Policy Dialogue (CPD); executive director of the South Asia Centre for Policy Studies (SACEPS); visiting scholar at the Initiative for Policy Dialogue, Columbia University; and senior research fellow at the Ash Institute of Democratic Governance, Harvard University. He is currently chairman of CPD.

Sobhan has held a number of important professional positions, which include that of president of the Bangladesh Economic Association; member of the UN Committee for Development Planning; member of the Governing Council of the UN University, Tokyo; member of the board of the United Nations Research Institute for Social Development, Geneva; member of the executive committee of the International Economic Association; member of the Group of Eminent Persons appointed by the SAARC Heads of State to review the future of SAARC;

and chairman of the board of Grameen Bank. He is currently a member of the board of SACEPS and chairman of the Pratichi Trust (Bangladesh), set up by Nobel Laureate Amartya Sen.

Sobhan has published a large number of books, research monographs, and articles in professional journals, relating to the political economy of development, public enterprise and privatization, foreign aid, petropolitics, agrarian reform, regional cooperation in South Asia, democracy, and governance. His latest work, *Challenging the Injustice of Poverty: Agendas for Inclusive Development in South Asia*, is forthcoming from Sage Publications.

Vikram Sood is vice president of the Centre for International Affairs at the Observer Research Foundation, a New Delhi–based independent think tank that specializes in public policy. He earlier headed the Research and Analysis Wing of India's external intelligence unit, and regularly contributes articles to leading newspapers, journals, and magazines on international security and foreign policy.

Igor Torbakov is senior researcher at the Finnish Institute of International Affairs in Helsinki. A trained historian, he specializes in Russian and Eurasian history and politics. He has served as a research scholar at the Institute of Russian History, Russian Academy of Sciences (Moscow); a visiting scholar at the Kennan Institute, Woodrow Wilson International Center for Scholars, Washington, D.C.; a Fulbright Scholar at Columbia University, New York; a visiting fellow at Harvard University; and a fellow at the Swedish Collegium for Advanced Study in Uppsala, Sweden.

Torbakov holds an MA in History from Moscow State University and a PhD from the Ukrainian Academy of Sciences.

Guihong Zhang is professor of international relations at Fudan University in Shanghai. He is executive director of the University's Center for UN Studies and associate dean of the Institute of International Studies. Prior to joining Fudan in 2006, Zhang was deputy director of the Institute of International Politics at Zhejiang University.

Zhang is a council member of China's Association for South Asian Studies, the China-India Friendship Association, the United Nations Association of China, and vice president of the Association of Asian Scholars (AAS), as well as the convener of AAS in China. He has been a visiting scholar at the Henry L. Stimson Center (2002–2003), at the Monterey Institute of International Studies, and at the University of Georgia (2008). In 2003 Zhang participated in the International Visitor Leadership Program, sponsored by the U.S. Department of State. From 2004 to 2005, he served as ASIA Fellow at Jawaharlal Nehru University and at the Institute for Defence Studies and Analyses, India. His major areas of research are Sino-U.S.-Indian relations, international organizations, and Asia-Pacific security.

RECENT PUBLICATIONS OF THE
WALTER H. SHORENSTEIN
ASIA-PACIFIC RESEARCH CENTER

Books (distributed by the Brookings Institution Press)

Jean C. Oi, Scott Rozelle, and Xueguang Zhou. *Growing Pains: Tensions and Opportunity in China's Transition.* Stanford, CA: Walter H. Shorenstein Asia-Pacific Research Center, 2010.

Karen Eggleston, ed. *Prescribing Cultures and Pharmaceutical Policy in the Asia-Pacific.* Stanford, CA: Walter H. Shorenstein Asia-Pacific Research Center, 2009.

Donald A. L. Macintyre, Daniel C. Sneider, and Gi-Wook Shin, eds. *First Drafts of Korea: The U.S. Media and Perceptions of the Last Cold War Frontier.* Stanford, CA: Walter H. Shorenstein Asia-Pacific Research Center, 2009.

Steven Reed, Kenneth Mori McElwain, and Kay Shimizu, eds. *Political Change in Japan: Electoral Behavior, Party Realignment, and the Koizumi Reforms.* Stanford, CA: Walter H. Shorenstein Asia-Pacific Research Center, 2009.

Donald K. Emmerson. *Hard Choices: Security, Democracy, and Regionalism in Southeast Asia.* Stanford, CA: Walter H. Shorenstein Asia-Pacific Research Center, 2008.

Henry S. Rowen, Marguerite Gong Hancock, and William F. Miller, eds. *Greater China's Quest for Innovation.* Stanford, CA: Walter H. Shorenstein Asia-Pacific Research Center, 2008.

Gi-Wook Shin and Daniel C. Sneider, eds. *Cross Currents: Regionalism and Nationalism in Northeast Asia.* Stanford, CA: Walter H. Shorenstein Asia-Pacific Research Center, 2007.

Stella R. Quah, ed. *Crisis Preparedness: Asia and the Global Governance of Epidemics.* Stanford, CA: Walter H. Shorenstein Asia-Pacific Research Center, 2007.

Philip W. Yun and Gi-Wook Shin, eds. *North Korea: 2005 and Beyond.* Stanford, CA: Walter H. Shorenstein Asia-Pacific Research Center, 2006.

Jongryn Mo and Daniel I. Okimoto, eds. *From Crisis to Opportunity: Financial Globalization and East Asian Capitalism*. Stanford, CA: Walter H. Shorenstein Asia-Pacific Research Center, 2006.

Michael H. Armacost and Daniel I. Okimoto, eds. *The Future of America's Alliances in Northeast Asia*. Stanford, CA: Walter H. Shorenstein Asia-Pacific Research Center, 2004.

Henry S. Rowen and Sangmok Suh, eds. *To the Brink of Peace: New Challenges in Inter-Korean Economic Cooperation and Integration*. Stanford, CA: Walter H. Shorenstein Asia-Pacific Research Center, 2001.

Studies of the Walter H. Shorenstein Asia-Pacific Research Center
(published with Stanford University Press)

Gi-Wook Shin. *One Alliance, Two Lenses: U.S.-Korea Relations in a New Era*. Stanford, CA: Stanford University Press, 2010.

Jean Oi and Nara Dillon, eds. *At the Crossroads of Empires: Middlemen, Social Networks, and State-building in Republican Shanghai*. Stanford, CA: Stanford University Press, 2007.

Henry S. Rowen, Marguerite Gong Hancock, and William F. Miller, eds. *Making IT: The Rise of Asia in High Tech*. Stanford, CA: Stanford University Press, 2006.

Gi-Wook Shin. *Ethnic Nationalism in Korea: Genealogy, Politics, and Legacy*. Stanford, CA: Stanford University Press, 2006.

Andrew Walder, Joseph Esherick, and Paul Pickowicz, eds. *The Chinese Cultural Revolution as History*. Stanford, CA: Stanford University Press, 2006.

Rafiq Dossani and Henry S. Rowen, eds. *Prospects for Peace in South Asia*. Stanford, CA: Stanford University Press, 2005.

The authorized representative in the EU for product safety and compliance is:
Mare Nostrum Group
B.V Doelen 72
4831 GR Breda
The Netherlands

www.ingramcontent.com/pod-product-compliance
Lightning Source LLC
Chambersburg PA
CBHW020335270326
41926CB00007B/194

* 9 7 8 1 9 3 1 3 6 8 1 7 9 *